ARCHAEOSEISMOLOGY

Edited by

S. Stiros & R. E. Jones

A joint publication by

I.G.M.E. — INSTITUTE OF GEOLOGY & MINERAL EXPLORATION
70, Mesoghion Street, 115 27 Athens, Greece

&

THE BRITISH SCHOOL AT ATHENS
52, Souedias Street, 106 76 Athens, Greece

FITCH LABORATORY OCCASIONAL PAPER 7
1996

ISBN 0 904887 26 X

Front cover: Fallen colums of the 5th century BC Temple of Zeus at Olympia (W. Peloponnese) with a characteristic domino-style arrangement of its drums. The temple was destroyed by an earthquake, probably in the Byzantine period. See article by S. Stiros. (Photo: I. K. Whitbread)

Back cover: The site of Susita (Lake of Galilee) is situated close to the surface trace of the Dead Sea Transform. Granite columns from a Roman palace complex have fallen parallel to each other and testify to an earthquake, probably that of AD 363, which caused destruction in the wider area. The direction in which the columns are lying is believed to indicate the direction of the strong seismic motion. See article by A. Nur and H. Ron. (Photo: A. Nur)

Printed in Great Britain
at The Short Run Press
Exeter

ARCHAEOSEISMOLOGY

Series Editor:

I. K. Whitbread
Fitch Laboratory, British School at Athens

Layout and typesetting:

M. Papaconstantinou
Fitch Laboratory, British School at Athens

Contents

SCIENTIFIC APPROACHES

APPENDIX

INDEXES

List of Reviewers

The papers submitted to this volume were each reviewed by two of the following referees and the editors:

N. AMBRASEYS, Imperial College, London
S. ASCHENBRENNER, University of Minessota, Duluth
J. COULTON, Ashmolean Museum, Oxford
A. DEMAKOPOULOU, Archaeological Museum, Athens
N. FLEMMING, Institute of Oceanographic Sciences, Godalming
E. R. GEBHARD, University of Illinois at Chicago
S. GOGOS, University of Vienna
J. JACKSON, University of Cambridge
N. KALOGERAS, National Technical University of Athens
M. KORRES, Acropolis Restoration Project, Athens
J. MACGILLIVRAY, Columbia University, New York
K. MAKROPOULOS, University of Athens
P. MARINOS, National Technical University of Athens
S. MILLER, University of California at Berkeley
A. NUR, Stanford University
G. PAPADOPOULOS, Antiseismic Protection Organization, Athens
D. PAPANIKOLAOU, University of Athens
J. PAPAPOSTOLOU, Ioannina University
K. PERISSORATIS, IGME, Athens
P. PIRAZZOLI, CNRS, Meudon
G. RAPP, Jr., University of Minessota, Duluth
H. RON, Institute of Petroleum Research and Geophysics, Holon (Israel)
J. RUTTER, Dartmouth College, Hanover, USA
G. SANDERS, British School at Athens
A. SINOPOLI, University of Venice
A. SNODGRASS, University of Cambridge
G. VALENSISE, Instituto Nazionale di Geofizica, Rome
H. WILLIAMS, University of British Columbia, Vancouver

Introduction

Ancient earthquakes are the professional interest of some seismologists; they also impinge on the work of archaeologists working in certain parts of the world, and to the general public they can be a source of fascination. The appearance of scholarly articles in popular journals has helped project this fascination, for instance the graphic and brilliantly illustrated accounts given by Sorren (1988) and Sakellarakis & Sapouna-Sakellaraki (1981) respectively on the devastating destruction of Kourion on Cyprus in around AD 365 and the terrible events in a Minoan shrine near Knossos on Crete in the 17th century BC.

In the interpretation of the archaeological record either through excavation or study of ancient monuments in certain regions, notably the Mediterranean, earthquake damage has been a convenient and often logical explanation of, say, a destruction layer, damaged building or displaced column. But over the years such an explanation has on occasions proved too tempting, for instance Laciani (1918) writing on the 'Signs of earthquakes on the buildings of Ancient Rome'; in other cases the fertile imagination has invoked earthquakes almost like a *deus ex machina* to explain abrupt changes in the settlement history of a site. Yet just as this issue has in the past been rather uncritically assessed by archaeologists, whether in the course of excavating or studying standing monuments, so the same can be said of seismologists who have been intent on enlarging their catalogues of seismic events with information other than that provided by modern scientific methods and by the fragmentary and often poor historic records (Ambraseys, 1971).

During the last decade a significant change has been taking place. Emerging out of palaeoseismology — the identification of past earthquakes using geological techniques (Crone & Omdahl, 1987) and the study of their effect on the natural environment — is the subdiscipline of **Archaeoseismology**. Here, superimposed on the broad palaeoseismological record, interest focuses on individual seismic events occurring at precise moments over relatively recent time (the last few millennia), whose action affected precise locations — human constructions and their environment — which in turn can be studied in detail through the archaeological record. In essence, then, it is the opportunity to regard human construction as a potential source of palaeoseismic information that is an essential feature of Archaeoseismology. Thus earth scientists have involved themselves in archaeological excavations, in particular examining critically the evidence for supposed earthquakes at individual sites, a notable case being Troy (Rapp 1982), or on a broader geographical scale (for instance, Israel (Karcz & Kafri, 1978)). They have also sought evidence of seismic faulting through offset ancient constructions (Trifonov, 1978; Zang *et al.*, 1986; Stiros, 1988a, b).

We believe the potential of Archaeoseismology has now been realised and its foundations can be said to have been laid (Nikonov, 1988; Stiros, 1988b; Rapp, 1986; Guidoboni, 1989). Whatever the validity of this view, Archaeoseismology presents a classic example of a field that draws on the skills of many diverse disciplines including, besides archaeology and seismology, branches of geology, engineering, architecture and history. Each of these disciplines having its own terminology, approach and method poses particular questions directed at the other member disciplines. In the case of archaeology the first question is likely to be: what are the criteria for identifying earthquake destruction at a given site? The future progress of Archaeoseismology depends crucially on facilitating communication between its component disciplines and creating an interdisciplinary approach. With this in mind a meeting was organised in Athens in June 1991 by the Institute of Geology and Mineral Exploration and the British School of Archaeology at Athens. It brought together around a hundred specialists from several countries, in many cases for the first time, to exchange ideas and discuss the problems of identification and study of ancient earthquakes from the complementary standpoints of their social, cultural, historical and physical effects.

The meeting was held in the fine, newly restored Weiler Building at the foot of the Acropolis, which itself has proved to be a remarkable archaeoseismic laboratory (see Korres, this volume). Following two days of lectures, discussion and a visit to the Acropolis, a field trip was made to sites in the N Peloponnese to examine at first hand the evidence for seismic events. We believe the meeting achieved many of its objectives; moreover, there was a consensus among the participants that its value would be enhanced by taking the final step, that of publishing its proceedings. In this way the member disciplines, but especially archaeology and seismology, would have the opportunity of examining the full spectrum of activities and approaches, reflecting the current state of the field in the Aegean and neighbouring regions. The present volume thus includes case studies, providing, on the one hand, unequivocal evidence of seismic destruction and, on the other, more problematic, even ambiguous evidence. All papers submitted were reviewed; revision of individual papers was made in the light of comments by an archaeologist, earth scientist, as well as the editors. We are confident this process was beneficial, and we warmly thank the contributors for their efforts, while regretting our long delay in finalising the publication.

The layout of the volume follows that of the meeting. Following the introductory papers, the first section presents the case studies at individual archaeological sites and monuments. The second section covers those papers that highlight individual methods and approaches, while a paper considering the perception of the earthquake in Greek antiquity appears in the Appendix. Those readers unfamiliar with seismological terminology may consult pp. 32f and 131f.

The organisation of the meeting and publication of this volume would not have been possible without the grant made available by the Council of Europe's Centre for the Prevention and Forecasting of Earthquakes. The Ministry of Culture and the Archaeological Service's Ephoreia at the Athenian Acropolis are thanked for their support. We also gratefully acknowledge the financial contribution from the British School at Athens. Finally, the preparation of the volume owes much to the patient efforts of Dr Ian Whitbread and Miss Maria Papaconstantinou in the Fitch Laboratory, British School at Athens.

This volume is dedicated to the memory of Klaus Kilian, a prehistorian with, as those who attended the meeting will recall, a lively interest in the archaeoseismology of the Aegean.

S. Stiros (IGME, Athens, Greece)

R. E. Jones (Department of Archaeology, Glasgow University, UK)

January 1995

References

Ambraseys, N. (1971). Value of historical records of earthquakes. *Nature* **232**, 375–379.

Crone, A. & Omdahl, E. (Eds) (1987). *Proc. XXXIX Conference of USGS: Directions in Palaeoseismology*. Denver, Colorado, USGS Open File Report, 87–673.

Guidoboni, E. (Ed.) (1989). *I terremoti prima del Mille in Italia e nell'area Mediterranea: storia, archeologia, sismologia*. Bologna; SGA — Istituto Nazionale di Geofisica.

Karcz, I. & Kafri, U. (1978). Evaluation of supposed archaeoseismic damage in Israel. *J. Archaeological Science* **5**, 237–253.

Lanciani, R. (1918). Segni di Terremoti negli edifizi di Roma Antica. *Bull. della Comm. Arch. Communale Roma*, 1–30.

Michetti, L, Serva, E. & Vittori, E. (Eds) (1990). Proc. 1st National Workshop on Palaeoseismology. *Rend. Soc. Geol. Italy* **13**, 3–84.

Nikonov, A. (1988). On the methodology of archaeoseismic research into historical monuments. In (G. Marinos & G. Koukis, Eds) *Engineering Geology of Ancient Works, Monuments & Historical Sites*, 1325–1320. Balkema; Rotterdam.

Rapp, G. (1982). Earthquakes in the Troad. In (G. Rapp & J. A. Gifford, Eds) *Troy: The Archaeological Geology*, 43–58. Princeton.

Rapp, G. (1986). Assessing archaeological evidence for seismic catastrophes. *Geoarchaeology* **1**, 365–379.

Sakellarakis, Y. & Sapouna-Sakellaraki, E. (1981). Drama of death in a Minoan Temple. *National Geographic* **159**, 204–222.

Sorren, D. (1988). The day the world ended at Kourion: reconstructing an ancient earthquake. *National Geographic* **174**, 30–53.

Stiros, S. (1988a). Earthquake effects on Ancient Constructions. In (R. E. Jones & H. W. Catling, Eds) *New Aspects of Archaeological Science in Greece*. British School at Athens, Fitch Laboratory Occasional Paper 3, 1–6.

Stiros, S. (1988b). Archaeology, a tool to study active tectonics — the Aegean as a case study. *Eos, Trans. Am. Geophys. Union* **13**, 1636, 1639.

Trifonov, V. (1978). Late Quaternary tectonic movements of western and central Asia. *Geol. Soc. Am. Bull.* **89**, 1059–1072.

Zang, B, Liao, Y, Guo, S, Wallace, R, Buckham R. & Hanks, T. (1986). Fault scarps related to the 1739 earthquake and seismicity of the Yinchuan graben, Ningxia Huizu Zizhiqu, China. *Bull. Seismol. Soc. America* **76**, 1253–1287.

INTRODUCTORY PAPERS

Archaeology and Historical Seismology: the Need for Collaboration in the Mediterranean Area

Emanuela Guidoboni

SGA, Storia Geofisica Ambiente,
via Bellombra 24/2, 40136 Bologna, Italy

Archaeological sites may or may not occur in areas of seismic activity — that is obvious — but only rarely is the scientific information and the many possibilities of obtaining it taken into consideration by the archaeologist. The lack of communication between different fields of research has often led to the archaeologist assuming the role of the seismologist or, at best, consulting some list of earthquake zones. As for the seismologist, the possibility of contact with the world of archaeology is frequently remote, as a result of the starting point and aims of an excavation, which tend to exclude problems lying outside the objectives of the excavator.

Sometimes archaeologists call upon the seismic expert as a *deus ex machina,* forgetting that it is not possible to offer a constructive contribution without having earlier been involved in the excavation; put another way, the seismic expert must have knowledge of the situation preceding and accompanying the actual fieldwork, from the identification of the effects to the establishing of their dates.

It is difficult to obtain intelligent and precise answers when the different disciplines are only called in at the later stages of a problem. This is why it is only very rarely that the archaeological identification of traces of earthquakes has gone beyond conjecture, even on those occasions where admittedly a geophysicist has been called in.

Thus, it has not been possible up to now to evaluate the methodological correctness with which hypotheses about seismic effects and their importance have been reached in the course of an excavation. If the procedures followed are not scientifically transparent and correct, the results cannot be used in a scientific context. The problems are legion: unlike volcanic eruptions and floods, identifiable from an examination of the composition of the soil, the traces of strong earthquakes left in buildings and soil are hard to interpret.

Although there have been significant attempts by archaeologists to incorporate a recognition of seismic effects, it has become evident that their seismic certitudes have a worrying lack of basic data regarding the seismic characteristics of the area in which they are excavating. There is a big difference between considering an earthquake as only one of many possible occurrences in the modification of a site, a structure or the soil, and knowing that it is in a seismic area, what are the characteristics of the local seismic activity — seen as a permanent element in the inhabited environment over a long period — and what kind of effects may be expected from an earthquake characteristic of that particular region.

Archaeologists have generally restricted their 'curiosity' to the seismic history of the site and to historical evidence more or less contemporary with the level of the excavation with which they are concerned. Until now, they seem to have been chiefly attracted to the idea of 'discovering' the effects of a famous seismic event, recorded in written sources. Although this may well be a fascinating line of investigation, it should not be forgotten that it is quite unusual to make such discoveries and that this type of investigation only touches on the wealth of interesting problems concerning earthquakes in the field of archaeology. There exists no real relationship between the seismic activity mentioned in old sources and real seismicity, in the sense that the written sources only represent casual fragments of a world that has largely disappeared. Even if we had been able to preserve a more consistent body of old sources, they would still refer only to a very small number of actual earthquakes. It is for this reason that the sources referring to earthquakes in a little documented context often offer little of significance in an area of an archaeological excavation. What we need to concentrate on, therefore, is not so much the written evidence about any one particular earthquake as the possible history of earthquakes in the area up to the present day.

Long-term seismic history takes on a fundamental role because it introduces precise empirical data into the archaeological analyses, thus favouring a general reading of the elements to be analysed. The question remains of what instruments to use to encourage this coming together of different points of view. Only very cautious use should be made of the various maps of historical epicentres. If, in fact, we transfer the dots representing historical epicentres to a sub-regional scale (1:500,000 or 1:100,000) the scarcity of information becomes evident. We clearly know nothing about the territorial effects of the earthquakes, nor about their propagation, because they are marked on these maps with no more than a dot or a circle that almost always indicates the parameters arbitrarily deduced with mathematical formulae (depth, magnitude etc.).

The different scale, in the absence of other elements, can also lead to inaccuracies. The mere localisation of historical epicentres cannot establish if and how the earthquake might influence in a significant way a network of constructions. Since the effects of strong earthquakes can be felt over hundreds or thousands of square kilometres, it is not possible to deduce the extent and characteristics of a seismic area merely from the values of maximum intensity. Such an area can be affected by an earthquake whose epicentre may be several kilometres away. The characteristics of the propagation of earthquakes can vary considerably from area to area and can be empirically deduced from observed effects. They provide us with an essential key to the interpretation of local seismicity.

Recent studies in this field have tended to avoid the traditional and approximate representations of the effects (such as, for example, isoseismal lines drawn up on the basis of geological models or based simply on a knowledge of a few estimated points of intensity), developing instead a basis of data regarding seismic effects observed in wide geographical areas, involving whole networks of installations or else concentrating their attention on very detailed urban seismic scenarios. There are obviously cases where, because of the distance in time or where there is a lack of written sources, even one piece of evidence of seismic effects becomes very valuable. For all that, in all these cases, the useful evaluations are based on 'organic' historical research, carried out according to critical and disciplinary criteria. Since the sites of earthquakes can be known and their characteristics noted and differentiated, the deliberate generalising of seismic effects has little meaning. The representation of the values of intensity is usable both where the traditional macroseismic scales are used and, in the case where there is an insufficient number of elements, when simplified classifications of effects are created. In both cases, a good seismic cartography on historical lines will assist an understanding of seismic effects at archaeological sites.

There are also, however, cases in which the seismic effects are due to earthquakes with very long intervals between activity, or where the information has been lost in the course of time. In these situations the specific contribution of the archaeological sources is doubly interesting since it enables us to see traces of seismic activity in areas believed to be 'non-seismic'.

The different data in the various situations can provide information of differing levels of importance:
1. generic localization of seismic effects in a determined area;
2. precise localization of seismic effects and their archaeological dating (chronological span);
3. localization, dating and evaluation of the seismic effects in one or more regional sites.

Generic localization of seismic effects

Even if this first level may seem limited, it is of great importance for historical seismology. If seismic effects are localised everywhere, it will make it possible to improve the estimations of seismic danger in an area for which, in the best cases, there is documentation covering ten centuries of written history. In these cases the archaeologists can open a wider temporal window on the seismic history of an area.

Precise localization and dating of seismic effects

This second level adds a piece of data which is of great interest: the chronological indication. This makes it possible to increase our understanding of the time of recurrence of an earthquake. This is a very important piece of information and one which, in my opinion, should be provided by archaeologists, always and only according to the instruments for dating appropriate to their discipline — that is as an indication of a chronological period. It is of little value to historical seismology for an archaeologist to indicate a single year, often under the mesmerising influence of a particular historical source. I would maintain that this is to switch methodologies, which often results in glaring errors. In this way it is possible to create false earthquakes or 'universal' earthquakes simply as a result of a piece of information that seems to be reliably attested in the sources of a particular period. To use simply that which is reasonable and appropriate to the peculiar procedures of archaeology makes it possible to discuss various different hypotheses: whether various seismic events happened within one period of time or whether a seismic event was of particular importance.

Localization, dating and evaluation of seismic events

This, the third level, is the most ambitious contribution that seismic archaeology can offer to the science of earthquakes. Here, besides determining the place and the date of the earthquake, it is possible to assess the 'quality' of the local seismic reaction on given structures. Thus it is possible to some extent to correlate the physical extent of the earthquake with the effects. An exact correlation, registered numerically, is not as yet possible because there are too many interrelated aspects to be explored. In this area it is better to have a few accurate pieces of information than many more imaginative ones. The relationship between qualitative data (the description of effects) and quantitative data (magnitude, depth) is still approximate. If it becomes increasingly possible to process 'imprecise' collections of information, perhaps these qualitative data will take on a greater importance in statistical evaluations.

The interaction between historical and physical data is not immediate. Historical data belong to a particular category of empirical data that can in part escape the control of the user. In practice, it is as if a researcher in the field were obliged to use data collected by someone else, with different and sometimes unknown criteria and with other aims, quite extraneous to his particular research. Historical evidence on earthquakes indeed reflects quite different mental attitudes and aims from those of the researcher who studies this evidence today.

It is obvious that such data — heterogeneous and the product of different historical and cultural situations — require particular understanding in order to be used and applied in the field of science. It is not traditionally very common, either among historians or among archaeologists, to face such problems, because very rarely do the results of historical or archaeological research find applications in other disciplinary fields. Generally, the people who carry out this type of research coincide with those who ask the questions and use the results. The data that concern the seismic effects are different in nature if they come from voluntary sources, such as written sources, or from involuntary sources, such as archaeology.

In the first case, the evidence is conditioned by numerous cultural and social contingencies and by the cognitive filters of the various historical epochs. It is necessary to understand the historical, cultural, social and economic context. This understanding will, of course, determine the quality of the research. If the historical data come from archaeological sources, it is possible to show particular situations or local structures that are never to be found in the written sources alone. For this reason seismic archaeology today can make an important contribution, not least to the techniques of the restoration of monuments or the conservation of whole archaeological sites in areas of seismic activity.

The recognition of seismic indications by archaeological methods: the way forward

By seismic archaeology, then, we mean the understanding of the effects of seismic activity on historic buildings, ancient cities or archaeological sites by the use of archaeological methods. In our present state of knowledge there is no official classification (atlases, systematic lists, etc.) of the effects of earthquakes on old buildings, and even less so in the case of archaeological stratification. The most advanced forms of the archaeological approach look at the stratifications of the ground and of buildings suitable for analysis by the same means — the stratigraphical method. The problem is how to place within a general framework of knowledge the results of the anthropogenic and natural actions within a diachronic stratigraphic reading of a site or a building.

Some interesting results, hitherto little applied, have emerged from excavations carried out in the last decade in Mediterranean areas of seismic activity. Still important and relevant are the basic definitions formulated by Karcz & Kafri (1978; 1981). They bring the following elements to our attention:

- type and quality of the construction of the buildings and structures damaged (masonry, stone, adobe, etc.; type of mortar, reinforcements and foundations);
- type of damage (landslides, directional or inclined collapse, breaches, subsidence, fissures and dislocation);
- extent and distribution of the damage throughout the site (number of damaged elements, differences in the amount and intensity of damage, direction of the typical damage and every possible alignment of the fallen items, etc.);
- evidence of similar damage in other sites of the same period;
- differences between the aspects of damage observed and the same characteristics of damage caused by man;
- geomorphologic arrangement of the site (elevations, distance from rocky areas or slopes, characteristics of slopes, distances between river beds and banks, etc.);
- type and composition of the land (rock, alluvial detritus, clay, depth in relation to bedrock, etc.);
- characteristics of recent signs of land instability (landslides, rock falls, cracking from drought, gorges, eroding streams, karst phenomena);
- structural placing of the site (distance from geological faults and their orientation, examples of junctions — joins in stratification — and their orientation, the inclination and structural position of the strata).

It is necessary to make one general observation: the damage encountered in any particular structure should only be attributed to an earthquake when all other possible causes have been excluded, or where the action of such causes has been limited in time. Taking this point of view, I would accept the classification of possible causes offered by Nikonov (1989):

- actions brought about by man: wars, fires, building over older structures, partial or complete demolition, restructuring, reconstruction, repair;
- slow-acting natural destructive actions: deterioration, erosion, fissures and other surface effects, landslips, subsidence, deformation resulting from gravitational forces, contraction or expansion of the ground and other deformations in the rock supporting the structure, leaching, slow tectonic movements;
- fast-acting natural processes of destruction: landslides and falling rocks, avalanches, rushing water, mud flows, floods, tsunami, storms, hurricanes, whirlwinds, gales.

We should also bear in mind periods of economic prosperity (intense building activity, trading and cultural development); stagnation (decline in productive activity, emigration, contraction of inhabited areas, etc.); periods and incidents of war (occupations, widespread fires, destruction of buildings in single areas and/or an entire region, the construction (or reconstruction) of fortifications, religious buildings or other important buildings); periods of political change (migration of populations, ethnic changes, reconstruction of religious or productive buildings).

It should be added that it is not enough to 'think' about war as a general cause of destruction. The technology of war specific to any one period of time and in a given area should, in my opinion, be made clear, since different technologies can leave damage of different kinds: collapses due to military advances, or explosions, that could easily be mistaken for collapses brought about by seismic shocks.

As well as an understanding of seismic effects, I believe that there are two other aspects that should not be neglected: an overall knowledge of the history of the constructions of the whole area under examination and the boundaries of possible seismic activity in the area under examination. This latter aspect ought to fit in geographically with identified local effects (which often give rise to a degree of suspect identification of seismic effects deriving from a single occurrence in different and disparate regional areas).

According to Stiros (1988a; 1988b) and Stiros & Dakoronia (1989), the identification of an earthquake in an archaeological site is dependent on meeting situations sufficiently favourable to enable a firm conclusion to be reached, such as to allow an affirmative response to the following questions:

- from the geological-geophysical point of view, is an earthquake, in the form of a shock or macroseismic effect, such as subsidence, a reasonable possibility?
- can human factors or other natural phenomena such as landslips be excluded as the cause of the destruction observed?
- has a good stratigraphical check been carried out (*terminus ante quem* and *post quem*) so that one can be sure that the deformations observed are not due to later seismic events?
- does the hypothesis of an earthquake accord with archaeological and historical evidence?
- is the destruction widespread and can it be correlated with other similar situations over a wider area?

These are precise questions and ones that an archaeologist should always ask himself before acting on a seismic hypothesis. We are unlikely, according to Stiros, to find an answer to all these questions, consequently the approach to the problem has to be based on certain assumptions. I believe that this is a wise decision and methodologically sound.

In our present state of knowledge, there are only very few cases where an archaeological excavation has demonstrated beyond doubt the destructive effects of an earthquake. In these cases the evidence has been rich: collapses with the presence *in loco* of victims where histological examination has revealed without doubt the cause of death. Such analyses are important because the mere finding of an unburied skeleton can be explained in many ways, from deliberate concealment to accidental death or death in battle.

It has been possible to find victims within the area of seismic collapse of a building where the earthquake appears to have coincided with a period of significant economic decline. The damaged site has been abandoned, leaving the victims behind. As for small seismic effects, traces of which may be preserved both in abandoned buildings and in those that continued to be used, it is important to remember that such evidence can all too easily be destroyed during the excavation or restoration of a site, or as a result of post-excavation deterioration. It should be said, however, that smaller seismic effects, comparable in typology and degree with those produced by seismic effects of the VIII degree MCS of intensity (occasional total collapse of buildings, generally already in a bad state; partial collapse of roofs, supports and walls; cracks, etc.), cannot usually be distinguished from those produced by the normal wear and tear of time in centres inhabited over several centuries. We cannot arrive at this 'understanding' without involving seismology, seismic engineering and geotechnics.

Can we avoid the destructiveness of archaeological investigation? Excavation as hypertext
I have attempted to define the term 'seismic archaeology' — a genuine neologism — not as a specialist branch of archaeology but as a specific multi-disciplinary field. In addition to our plea for a greater dialogue between the representatives of the different disciplines (seismologists, historians, geologists and engineers), we can now ask ourselves in what way the traditional work of the archaeologist could be modified. A problem in this area is that current archaeological methods are destructive. This fact tends to limit the contribution that could be

made by the different disciplines in analysing, from other non-archaeological viewpoints, the results from an excavation. By this I mean both the possible information about seismic effects that at present are almost always totally lost, and information on the seismic response of archaeological sites in relation to local seismic characteristics.

Taken as a whole, these questions could have two levels of answer, depending on whether the scholar was involved in the collection of archaeological data or only in its interpretation. In the case of the former, the collection of data, the problem could perhaps be tackled if certain aspects of the present methods of excavation were modified. The excavation as a whole could, for example, be treated as a kind of hypertext, available for a variety of uses. This would introduce the necessity of recording in complete images the stratigraphy of the excavation. It would require the elements present in the various strata to be collected in a way that was neutral (in relation to the questions asked) and total (with respect to the quantity of data).

The recorded monitoring of the excavation would make it possible *a posteriori* to identify and extract specific elements; these would take on meaning if we could consider at the same time several aspects of the different excavation levels. Earthquakes are not kind, and they do not care for researchers. Their traces can travel through the strata and upset methods of dating in unexpected ways. This is one reason why so many important pieces of archaeological evidence are lost for seismology.

References

The bibliography useful to seismic archaeology is becoming ever longer. The works listed below include just some of the many excellent bibliographies.

Adam, J-P. (1983). *Dégradation et restauration de l'architecture pompéienne*. Paris.

Brogiolo, G. P. (1988). *Archeologia dell'edilizia storica*. Como.

Francovich, R. & Parenti, R. (Eds) (1988). *Archeologia e restauro dei monumenti*. Florence.

Funiciello, R., Boschi, E., Di Bona, M., Malmagnini, L., Marra, F., Rovelli A. & Salvi S. (1992). Local seismic amplification in the city of Rome inferred from observations of damage in monuments of imperial age: ground motion estimates based on subsurface geology data. In *ESG. The effects of surface geology on seismic motion,* Odawara (Japan), March 25–27 1992, 341–346.

Guidoboni, E. (Ed.) (1989). *I terremoti prima del Mille in Italia e nell' area mediterranea. Storia, Archeologia, Sismologia*. Bologna; SGA — Istituto Nazionale di Geofisica.

Karcz, I. & Kafri, U. (1978). Evaluation of supposed archaeoseismic damage in Israel. *J. Arch. Science* **5**, 237–253.

Karcz, I. & Kafri, U. (1981). Studies in archaeoseismicity of Israel: Hisham's Palace, Jericho. *Israel J. Earth Sciences* **30**, 12–23.

Magri, G. (1989). Dislocazioni sismiche e valutazioni di intensità. In (E. Guidoboni, Ed.) *op. cit.* 413–418.

Nikonov, A. A. (1989). Orientamenti dell'archeosismologia in Unione Sovietica. In (E. Guidoboni, Ed.) *op. cit.* 418–422.

Parenti, R. (1985). La lettura stratigrafica delle murature in contesti archeologici e di restauro architettonico. *Restauro e città* **2**, 55–68.

Rapp, G. (1982). Earthquakes in the Troad. In (G. Rapp & J. A. Gifford, Eds) *Troy. The Archaeological Geology*, 43–58. Princeton; Princeton University Press.

Rapp, G. (1989). Tracce sismiche in geoarcheologia. In (E. Guidoboni, Ed.) *op. cit.* 398–405.

Soren, D. & Lane, E. (1981). New ideas about the destruction of Paphos. *Report of the Department of Antiquities of Cyprus*, 285–293.

Stiros, S. (1988a). Earthquake effects on ancient constructions. In (R. E. Jones & H. W. Catling, Eds) *New Aspects of Archaeological Science in Greece*. British School at Athens, Occasional Paper 3 of the Fitch Laboratory, 1–6.

Stiros, S. (1988b). Archaeology, a tool to study active tectonics — The Aegean as a case study. *Eos, Transactions of the American Geophysical Union* 13 December 1988, 1633, 1639.

Stiros, S. C. & Dakoronia P. (1989). Ruolo storico e identificazione di antichi terremoti nei siti della Grecia. In (E. Guidoboni Ed.) 1989, *op. cit.* 422–439.

Palaeoseismology: a branch of Neotectonics linking Geological, Seismological and Archaeological data — an Introduction

Spyros B. Pavlides

Department of Geology, Aristotle University,
540 06 Thessaloniki, Greece

Introduction

In the current bibliography there are many terms to describe recent movements and deformation of the earth's crust. Such terms in common use are Neotectonics, Active Tectonics, Seismotectonics, Palaeoseismology, and rarely Palaeogeodynamics, Palaeogeophysics, Earthquake Geology etc. All these are widely overlapping and are often used more or less as synonyms. Neotectonics seems to dominate in recent terminology and denotes all kind of recent movements, while Palaeoseismology is a rapidly developing new branch. But how does one identify these 'recent' or 'active' geological structures and processes? Where does one draw a 'line' between the 'old' and 'young' deformation, and how? Is such a distinction necessary? Do the terms Neotectonics and Palaeoseismology describe well enough the subject?

The terms 'Neotectonics' and 'Palaeoseismology' are now in current use. They are also new scientific branches and have been used quite differently by many geologists and seismologists who are not familiar with this subject. Thus, there are reasons for discussing the definition of the terms and the subjects they describe.

What is Neotectonics?

The study of young tectonic processes began at the end of the 19th century, but their systematic study only started after the decade of 1940 when the term 'Neotectonics' was employed for the first time by the Russian geologists and geomorphologists, Schulz, Obruchev, Mescherikov and others (see Pavlides, 1989). Neotectonics is derived from the Greek words Νέο- (new) and Τεκτονική (Tectonics) meaning to a first approximation geologically young, recent or living (active) crustal structures and processes. From the point of view of the geological time-scale, it includes middle Miocene (10–5 Ma) to active earth movements of local to plate scale, while the main subject of Neotectonics is the study of crust discontinuities (faults), mainly young ones, as well as geologically older ones and their recent reactivations (instrumentally, historically, archaeologically or geologically recorded).

Alternative definitions of Neotectonics include the following view points:

a. Those which accept an age limitation for the neotectonic period, and emphasize the geological methods, such as ' . . . the young and recent tectonic movements which encompasses the end of Tertiary and the first half of Quaternary', or 'to Neogene and recent brittle and ductile deformation . . .' (Obruchev, Manzoni, Bloom, C. Vita-Finzi and others; see Pavlides, 1989).

b. Those which do not accept any fixed time limitation for the neotectonic period, because the study field of Neotectonics extends from the present as far back into the past as is necessary to understand present or active tectonic process (Mercier, Angelier, Pavlides, Fourniguet; for references see Pavlides, 1989; Vittori *et al.*, 1991; REGINE Group, 1991). It is worth referring to Fourniguet's (1987) definition: 'Neotectonics corresponds to all recent deformation affecting the earth's crust. It includes understanding of the starting mechanisms and the progress of such deformation. No time limit is fixed, and the field of investigation extends from the present as far back into the past as is necessary to understand present or active deformation.'

c.   Those emphasizing the future extrapolation of neotectonic results. The Neotectonics Commission of INQUA (International Union of Quaternary Research) has accepted the definition of N. Mörner as 'Neotectonics is defined as any earth movement or deformation of the geodetic reference level, their mechanisms, their geological origin, their implication for various practical purposes and their future extrapolation'. (See *Bull. INQUA*, 'Neotectonics Commission', inside cover).

d. The definitions which focus the neotectonic studies on the active deformation only (late Quaternary - Present), such as ' . . . the study of contemporary stress field . . . ' (Hancock & Williams, 1986). That is, Neotectonics is synonymous with active tectonics.

In a pragmatic sense, Neotectonics in Greece and the Mediterranean in general is usually understood to comprise all deformation that postdates the last Alpine compression (post- middle Miocene). Thus Neotectonics is the study of young tectonic events, which have occurred or are still occurring in a given region after its final orogeny (at least for recent orogenies) or more precisely after its last significant tectonic reorganization (Pavlides & Mountrakis, 1986).

Definition of Palaeoseismology

The importance of pre-instrumental earthquakes is prominent. In tectonically active areas, the recurrence of major earthquakes and the estimation of their magnitudes are of extreme value in understanding past seismic history. Historical records, which are useful in some places, incomplete and of minimal value elsewhere, could provide an estimation of the occurrence rate and the magnitude of some pre-instrumental events. But a real history of the behaviour and character of seismically active regions comes from the study of active faults; the geological information arising from this study is of great importance. Thus, the study of the history of active faults, the generators of earthquakes, is the major subject of Neotectonics, Seismotectonics, and also Palaeoseismology studied in a number of different ways.

Seismicity is a quantity describing the seismic potential of a region, which is defined mainly in the instrumentally recorded earthquakes **(Instrumental Seismicity)**. That is, data arising from seismographs and other modern instruments expand over a time scale of 10 to 100 years. But pre-instrumental seismicity can be divided into:

a. **Historical seismicity**, which is based mainly on descriptions of destructive earthquakes, in historical documents, generally covering a time scale of 100 to 1,000 years. In some regions, such as the Mediterranean, the Middle East, Japan and China it extends to 2,000 years or more, while the best historical data for earthquakes belong to the 19th century. **Archaeological Seismicity** supplements the historical data. There is a clear overlap between archaeological and other kinds of dating when applied to geology. The archaeological literature is full of reports of ancient buildings whose destruction is likely to be associated with seismic or volcanic effects, permitting an estimation of major shock recurrence intervals. Of great importance are destructions of ancient constructions caused by vertical and horizontal offsets; the latter may reflect seismic faulting and can therefore describe tectonic processes (for the Mediterranean region, see Guidoboni, 1989). Seismological and historical records alone are usually too short in time to estimate seismicity, so geological (palaeoseismological) data appear as the only way to expand seismicity research further into the past.

b. **Geological seismicity,** which draws information from neotectonic and active faults, as well as from palaeoseismological studies, is used for a more complete description of the seismic regime of an area. It is estimated from geological records and can often be interpreted to obtain fault slip rates or regional strain rates, where it is possible to detect seismic events of the past expressing their location, size and age. Geological seismicity estimates the occurrence rates of earthquakes over a time interval of a thousand to a million years, or more. Palaeoseismology, because of the up-to-date available methods and techniques, specifies its subject mainly in the near geological past (Holocene ~ 10,000 years or at least late Pleistocene) and attempts to identify 'fossil' earthquakes.

c. **'Palaeoseismology'** can be defined as the 'identification and study of Prehistoric earthquakes', that is, the study of the geological record of earthquake occurrence in late Quaternary sediments (Sieh, 1978; Wallace, 1981). Generally, Palaeoseismology is the science and art of reconstructing the nature, timing and locating of past earthquakes that today are recorded (or traceable) by bedrock structures (faults and fractures), geomorphological features (shorelines, moraines, stream offsets, scarp degradation etc.), sedimentological (seismites) and stratigraphic criteria, because the majority earthquakes are documented in the geologic record only.

Palaeoseismological studies in fact are not new; they began more than a century ago, when some ideas on earthquake geology, such as 'fossil earthquakes' and 'the importance of palaeoseismic events' were developed. G. Gilbert (1884, from Wallace 1987), for example, defines 'fault scarps' emphasising the 'cohesion and sliding' motion along them, as well as the 'little by little mountain rise' in association with earthquake catastrophes. Also, the 1891 Nobi earthquake in Japan gave a great impulse to the study of the geological effects of earthquakes. But the first use of the term 'palaeoseismology' appears in a paper by the Russian, Kuchay, while in the English literature Engelder used the term first (see Wallace, 1987). The 1970's and 1980's were a new era for Palaeoseismology, which developed mainly in the USA, Japan, China, the former Soviet Union, as well Italy and recently in many other countries where earthquakes are common (Wallace, 1977; 1981; 1987; Bucknam & Anderson, 1979; Bonilla *et al.*, 1984; and many others). For these references and a more complete bibliography are available the proceedings of the first conference on Palaeoseismology (Crone & Omdahl, 1987), as well as *Active Tectonics* (Geophysics Research Forum, 1985), Nikonov (1988); 1st National (Italian) Workshop on Palaeoseismology (1989) and Vittori *et al.* (1991).

The techniques of palaeoseismology are primarily geological, including quantitative analysis of microstratigraphic relations along faults, fault-scarp and fault-trace geomorphology (degradation), regional tectonic relations, seismically induced sedimentary structures (seismites) and river and marine terraces related to uplift and faulting. Dating techniques for Quaternary geology serve to determine the timing and rates of occurrence of prehistoric seismic events. Quaternary (and especially Holocene) geology has a critical role in palaeoseismology because most of the evidence of major prehistoric earthquakes is preserved in Quaternary deposits or interpreted from recent geomorphic features. Excavations along active faults (trenching) are of crucial importance in understanding their seismic history in the geological past. Geodetic, geophysical, geomorphic and quaternary dating techniques supplement the geological data.

Palaeoseismology occupies a key position in earthquake-hazard forecasting in that it can greatly extend the known earthquake history for many fault zones, individual faults or fault segments. It can also provide recurrence information for faults not associated with known historic earthquakes — a crucial point in palaeoseismological research. Palaeoseismic data can be also used in construction design of nuclear plants, dams etc. There is now an eruption of neotectonic-palaeoseismological activities and an increasing interest in them, both for their scientific and their social relevance.

Examples of neotectonic research in Greek territory, which has been expanded to specific palaeoseismological studies by the group of Neotectonic Research of the Geology Department of the University of Thessaloniki, cover the following areas: Mygdonia (Volvi and Langada) basin in Macedonia, which is the area of the 1906 ($M_s = 6.6$), 1978 ($M_s = 6.5$) and many historical earthquakes (Mountrakis *et al.*, 1989; Pavlides & Soulakellis, 1990; Chatzipetros & Pavlides, 1993); Epirus (Souli strike-slip fault), where a complete palaeoseismological research is in progress (Pavlides *et al.*, 1992); Thessaly plain faults (Caputo & Pavlides, 1993); and Stratoni-Ierissos seismic fault (Pavlides & Tranos, 1991).

Conclusion

The study of seismic events that predate the instrumental seismology records, and are not covered or presented by historical information, depends entirely on geological and archaeological investigations. Geological research focuses mainly on Neotectonic and more specifically on Palaeoseismological studies. Palaeoseismic methods and techniques are rather limited at present, but they are likely to advance in the near future. The recent boom in the use of these techniques reflects the need to answer such questions as the recurrence intervals of strong and moderate earthquakes and the level of seismic hazard in a certain area.

References

Bonilla, M., Mark, R. & Lienkaemper, J. (1984). Statistical relations among earthquake magnitude, surface rupture length and surface fault displacement. *Bull. Seismol. Soc. Am.* **74**, 2379–2410.

Bucknam, R. C. & Anderson, R. E. (1979). Estimation of fault-scarp ages from a scarp-height-slope-angle relationship. *Geology* **7**, 11–14.

Caputo, R. & Pavlides, S. (1993). Late Cenozoic geodynamic evolution of Thessaly and surroundings, central northern Greece. *Tectonophysics* **223**, 339–362.

Crone, A. J. & Omdahl, E. M., Eds (1987). *Proc. Conference XXXIX, Directions in Paleoseismology*. USGS Open File Report, 87–673.

Chatzipetros, A. & Pavlides, S. (1993). Fault scarp height-angle relationship from the active basin of Mygdonia, Northern Greece, EUG VII (Congress of the European Union of Geosciences) Strasbourg. (Abstract).

Engelder, J. (1974). Microscopic wear grooves on slickensides — Indicators of Palaeoseismology. *Journal of Geophys. Res.* **79**, 4387–4392.

Fourniguet, J. (1987). Néotectonique. In (Miskovksy Ed.) *Géologie de la Préhistoire* GEOPRE, 281–292.

Geophysics Research Forum (U.S.) Geophysics Study Committee, Ed. (1985). *Active Tectonics*. Washington DC: National Academy Press.

Guidoboni, E., Ed. (1989). *I Terremoti Prima del mille in Italia e nell' area Mediterranea*. Bologna; SGA — Istituto Nazionale di Geofisica.

Hancock, P. & Williams, G. (1986). Neotectonics, *J. Geol. Soc. London* **143**, 325–326.

Mountrakis *et al.* (1989). Neotectonic map of Greece: Langada and Thessaloniki sheets 1:100,000 scale (unpublished).

National Workshop on Paleoseismology. (1989). *Rend. Soc. Geol. Ital.* **13**.

Nikonov, A. A. (1988). Reconstruction of the main parameters of old large earthquakes in Soviet Central Asia using the paleoseismological method. *Tectonophysics* **147**, 297–312.

Pavlides, S. B. (1989). Looking for a definition of Neotectonics. *Terra Nova* **1**, 233–235.

Pavlides, S. & Mountrakis, D. (1986). *Neotectonics: an introduction to recent geological structures*. Thessaloniki: University Studio Press.

Pavlides, S. & Soulakellis, N. (1990). Multifractured seismogenic area of the Thessaloniki 1978 Earthquake (N. Greece). In (Savascin & Eronat, Eds) *Proc. IESCA-90 (International Earth Sciences Colloquium on Aegean Region)* **VII**, 64–74.

Pavlides, S. & Tranos, M. (1991). Structural characteristics of two strong earthquakes in the North Aegean: Ierissos (1932) and Agios Efstratios (1968). *J. Struct. Geol.* **13**:2, 205–214.

Pavlides, S., Caputo, R. Zouros, N., Mountrakis, D. & Boccaletti, M. (1992). Palaeoseismological history of the Souli Active strike-slip fault (Epirus, NW Greece) (Abstract). *Neotectonics*, Quat. Res. Ass. **56**.

REGINE GROUP (1991). Proposal for classification of fault activity in an intraplate collision setting: definitions and examples. *Tectonophysics* **194**, 279–293.

Sieh, K. E. (1978). Prehistoric large earthquakes produced by slip on the San Andreas fault at Pallet Creek, California. *J. Geophys. Res.* **83**, 3907–3939.

Vittori, E., Labini, S. S. & Serva, L. (1991). Palaeoseismology: review of the state-of-the-art. *Tectonophysics* **193**, 9–32.

Wallace, R. E. (1977). Profiles and ages of young fault scarps north-central Nevada. *Geological Society of America Bulletin* **88**, 1267–1281.

Wallace, R. E. (1981). Active faults, paleoseismology, and earthquake hazards in the Western United States. In (D. W. Simpson & P. G. Richards, Eds) *Earthquake prediction — an international review*, 209–216. Washington DC; American Geophysical Union.

Wallace, R. E. (1987). A perspective of Paleoseismology. In (A. J. Crone & E. M. Omdahl, Eds) *Directions in Paleoseismology*. U.S. Geol. Survey. Open-File Report **87-673**, 7–16.

ARCHAEOLOGICAL AND HISTORICAL EVIDENCE OF PALAEOSEISMIC EVENTS, AND THEIR SOCIAL AND CULTURAL IMPACTS

Material for the Investigation
of the
Seismicity of Central Greece

Nicholas N. Ambraseys

Department of Civil Engineering,
Imperial College of Science & Technology, London SW7 2BU, UK

Introduction

The historical seismicity of Central Greece is imperfectly known; its coverage is discontinuous and its record is grossly deficient. The period from 1800 onwards is relatively well-documented. However, further back in time it becomes increasingly difficult to find data, and the minimum size of the earthquake for which there is guaranteed detection increases.

Our studies show that the total number of important earthquakes in Central Greece identified for the period between the 5th century BC and the 18th century AD amounts to just over eighty (Fig. 1). Seen by historical periods, we may identify a comparatively acceptable level of reported activity during the 5th century BC, literary sources providing information for twelve earthquakes. While it is certain that many small earthquakes must be missing from the record, we can reasonably assume that most of those of which details survived were relatively important events. It is also reasonable to assume that any major or damaging earthquakes in the vicinity of the larger urban centres of the time should be mentioned.

After the 5th century BC, however, the number of earthquakes identified gives way to a generally very low level in the Greco-Roman, Byzantine and Venetian periods. This decline has to be seen in terms of inferior reporting of events in sources lacking material of local origin rather than due to lack of seismic activity. After the 14th century the situation gradually improves, but our dependence on information from Venetian and Turkish sources gives the distribution of earthquakes a bias in favour of coastal areas, while data from places further inland continue to be almost totally lacking.

It is only after the 17th century that documents, such as consular correspondence, Turkish unpublished material, the diaries of European travellers and press reports, begin to preserve data that would otherwise have escaped notice in more general works and provide information about seismic activity. For this and earlier periods local, Greek sources are almost totally lacking. Fig. 2 shows the time distribution of the number of earthquakes per century in the region shown in Fig. 1.

A typical example of the incomplete earthquake record of Greece is that for the city of Athens.

Earthquakes in Athens

The historical record of Athens appears to have been almost free of destructive earthquakes. There is little in literary sources and no epigraphic material referring to earthquakes in the city (Robert, 1978). Earthquake damage known to have occurred in the Athens area during its twenty-five century long history has been very infrequent, small, and chiefly due to relatively large earthquakes originating either on land or off shore at some considerable distance from the city.

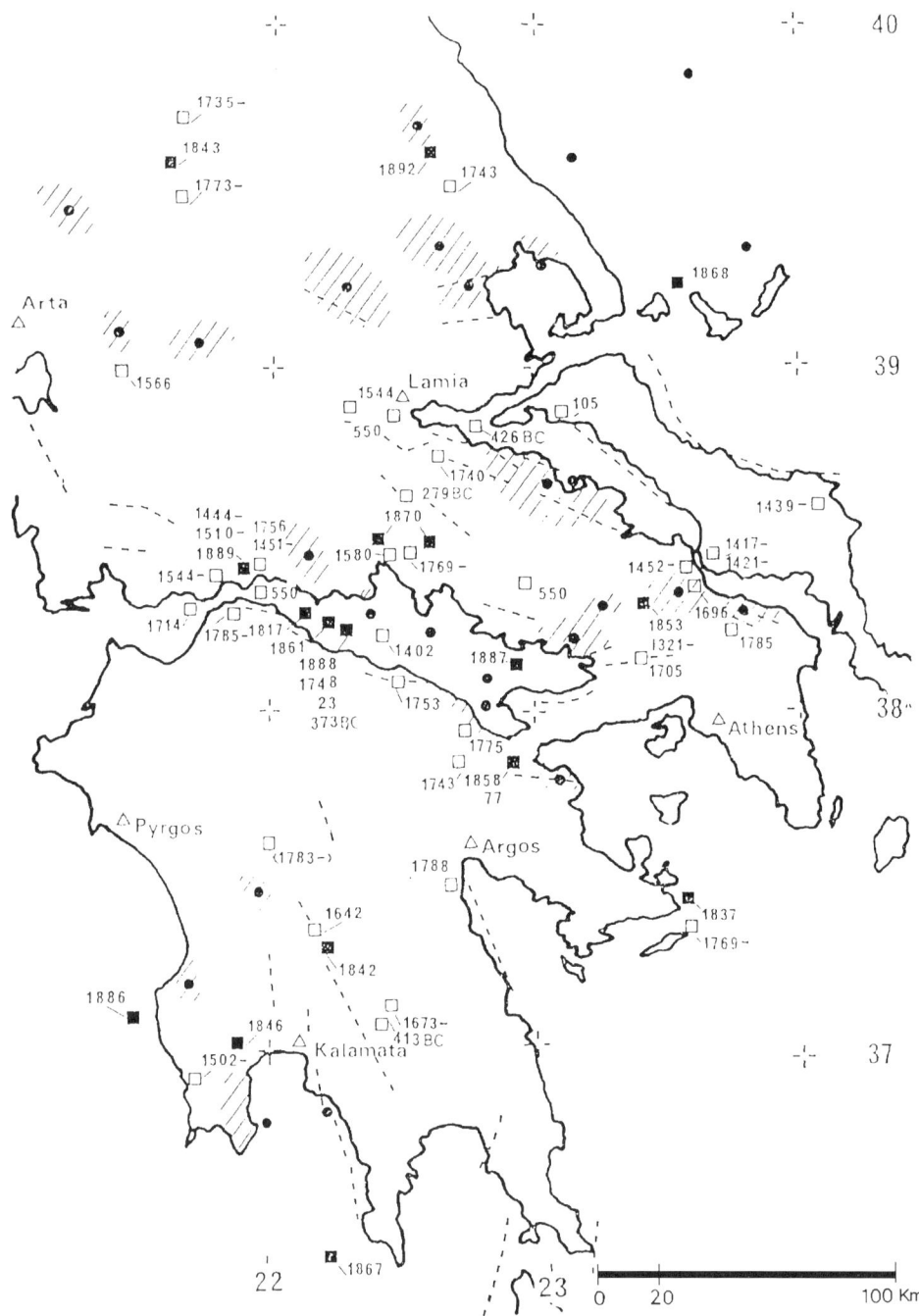

Figure 1. Distribution of earthquakes of $M_s > 6.0$ in Central Greece. Solid circles are for events after 1890, and their epicentral regions are shaded. Solid squares are approximate epicentres of events of the 19th century. Open squares are locations of events before 1800. Pre-1890 events are labelled with the year of their occurrence: those that may have been smaller than $M_s = 6.0$ are labeled with a bar. Dashed lines show major tectonic structures, see Figure 3; updated from Ambraseys & Jackson (1990).

427 BC

The earliest known earthquake to have caused some concern in Athens occurred in the winter of 427 BC. During that period there were repeated shocks in Athens, but also in Evia and Boeotia, particularly at Orchomenos. The passage in Thucidides (iii.87) that refers to these events clearly implies that these shocks originated some distance away from Athens, perhaps from the region just south of Atalanti, about 90 km from the city, where they caused no damage.

426 BC

Archaeological evidence suggests that an earthquake in 426 BC was responsible for the dislocation of the N-E corner of the Parthenon, and for the displacement of about one third of the E facade of the temple by about 2.5 cm (Korres 1985, 97).

The shock of 427 BC was apparently a precursor of the large magnitude earthquake that followed in the summer of 426 BC in the region between Atalanti and Scarpheia. However, Athens, at an epicentral distance

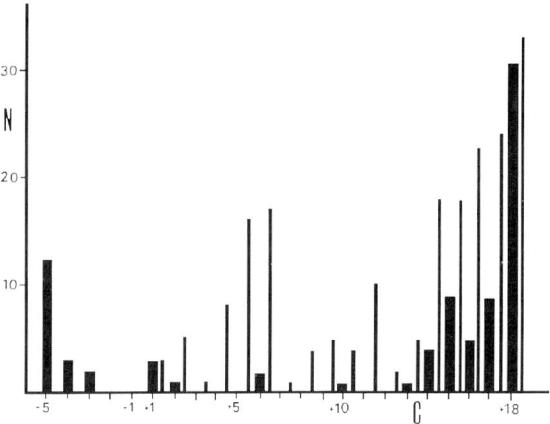

Figure 2. Time distribution of earthquakes in Greece for the period prior to 1750. N is the number of earthquakes per century identified. Thin bars show, for comparison, distribution of damaging earthquakes in the Marmara Sea region (Ambraseys & Finkel, 1991).

of about 140 km, is not mentioned by Thucidides (iii.89), nor by later writers such as Demetrius of Callatis in Strabo (i.3.20) and Diodorus (xii.59), who describe the destructive effects of this event (see also Bousquet & Pechoux (1981)). An earthquake of this magnitude would certainly have been felt in Athens, but at such a large epicentral distance its effects should not have been serious. The silence of historical sources about damage to the Acropolis and to the city of Athens, as well as to other towns as far as Opous, contrasts strangely with the interpretation and dating of the damage of the Parthenon observed by Korres & Bouras (1983). An earthquake sufficiently strong to cause damage to the solidly built structure of the Parthenon should have been more damaging or even destructive in the city of Athens, probably with casualties, and for this we have no evidence. It is possible that the Parthenon was damaged much later, possibly in the explosion of 1687, or alternatively, that its ruins were dislodged by earthquakes after the 18th century. Destructive earthquake effects in Athens clearly stretch the size of the 426 BC earthquake beyond the limits of the possible (see Appendix).

420 BC

The second and last earthquake of the Classical period in Athens occurred in the summer of 420 BC (Thucidides: v. 45). The shock is described as slight by Plutarch (Nic. 271), presumably originating at some considerable distance from the city.

c. AD 32

An earthquake in Athens is alluded to by Dionysius (7) c. AD 32. This was probably the result of a large earthquake in the Sea of Marmara, or more likely, a 'supernatural' event associated with the Crucifixion.

For the following sixteen centuries we could find no information relating to earthquakes in Athens. During this period the city gradually ceased to be a centre of importance; it became remote and ultimately well removed from the great centres of literature and culture.

1705, September 3

Evidence for earthquake damage in Athens about the turn of the eighteenth century is found in a four-page manuscript history of Athens, the so-called Anargyrian Fragments, published by Pittakis (1853). This, most probably 18th-century manuscript, whose authenticity was in doubt, is made up of fragments of a history of Athens and contains two garbled passages about earthquake damage to the town. Unfortunately, events in this chronicle are not dated and they are hopelessly confused; later events are given first and a series of earlier events, running consecutively, is given later. Attempts to date the fragments in this chronicle and identify conclusively their sequence, have been so far unsuccessful.

The first page of the manuscript contains the following passage:

(a) ' ... and the citizens [of Athens] restored the S wall of the Fort, which the earthquakes had destroyed two years age ... '.

The second page ends with the following passage:

(b) 'During this year there was a great earthquake, and all the houses were shaken, and the church of St. Dionysius was rent in two, and the upper story of the residence of the Metropolitan was destroyed by the fall of a boulder from the Rock above. This happened in the evening of St. Chariton's day; and many dwellings belonging to the monastery of Sotiros Nikodimou were overthrown, and the Vasiliki Ekklisia was cracked, and on the third day, in the cathedral (metropolis), Demetrios was struck dead by a thunderbolt ... ' (Pittakis, 1853).

The year in which this happened is not given, but the context in which these events are recorded suggests that they must have taken place after the return of the Athenians to the town from their voluntary exile, about three years after the departure of the Venetians in 1688.

Recent writers, using some poetic licence in the interpretation of the very few elements in the Anargyrian Fragments, have deduced a variety of dates for this event. In fact, the only real evidence in these Fragments for an earthquake suggests that the event must have occurred sometime between 1687 and 1751. This we may surmise from the fact that the residence of the Metropolite was intact in 1676, when seen by Spon (1678), and also probably during the Venetian occupation of Athens, while in 1751 only the ruins of this building and the remains of the church of St. Dionysius could be seen (Stuart & Revett, 1789). It is quite clear that to fix the year of this earthquake requires information additional to that in the Anargyrian Fragments.

Such additional information is now provided by a series of unpublished Turkish documents that fix unambiguously the year of the earthquake, confirming at the same time that the passages referring to such an event in the Fragments are not a fabrication (Ambraseys & Finkel, 1992).

One of these documents, dated 7 Ramadan 1117 A.H./23 December 1705 states that the castle of Athens was damaged in an earthquake in 1117 A.H., as reported by the cadi of Athens on 16 Rajab 1117 A.H./3 November 1705: 'Athens castle ... was this year damaged and ruined in an earthquake ...'; the earthquake may thus be dated to between 25 April (which fell on the first day of 1117 A.H.) and 3 November 1705. An estimate of the extent of the damage, 6,264 cubits, and the amount which it would cost to repair, 6,369 gurus, of which the Porte agreed to provide 4,000 gurus from central funds, was recorded in the registers of the central treasury on 4 Sha'ban 1119 A.H./31 October 1707: 'For the repair of some places and the cistern and the armoury inside the castle of Athens in the liva of Egriboz (Chalkis), which was earlier ruined and damaged by an earthquake ...'; it is further noted that the earthquake had ruined all but 5 or 6 of the 24 cisterns within the castle, and that because of continual pirate raids in the vicinity, the repair of all the earthquake damage was deemed of the utmost urgency. By 7 Rabi-II 1120 A.H./26 June 1708, repairs were complete, according to strict specifications as to the local sources from which should be drawn materials and labour.

The shock caused considerable damage to various structures in the Acropolis as well as in Athens, to buildings already weakened by the siege of 1687 and subsequently abandoned. Of the buildings affected by the earthquake in Athens, the church of St. Dionysius and the nearby residence of the Metropolitan, neither of which is extant, were located at the N foot of the rock of Areopagus. The cells of the monastery of Nikodimou must have been located in the vicinity of the modern Russian church. The location of the Vasiliki Ekklisia is not certain: perhaps it was located near the Stadium. There is no evidence that the earthquake caused any loss of life among the inhabitants and garrison of the Acropolis or serious damage in the town itself: the extract from the Fragments shows, for example, that the Cathedral of Athens must have survived the shock intact, since three days later it was safe enough to be used for congregation. The occurrence of an earthquake is not mentioned in the history of Athens written by the Ottoman cadi at the time. Nor is any damage mentioned by the French traveller Lucas (1712) who was in Athens a year after the earthquake, between 27 June and 9 August 1706, and who found the town sparsely inhabited but prosperous; the ruins which he noticed, he attributed to the recent wars: this confirms our impression that its effects were not serious for had there been serious damage due to an earthquake a year earlier, it is unlikely that it could have escaped him, and he would have recorded it, as he did for other places on his travels.

There is no reason to suppose, however, that other towns were not affected in this earthquake. It is possible that some of the damage reported in Turkish unpublished documents from Negreponte (Chalkis) at about the same time, dated Sha'ban 1117 A.H., could have been the result of the same earthquake. However, damage in Negreponte cannot have been too serious, and was probably quickly repaired, as the same traveller, Lucas, who was passing through Negreponte a year after the event, did not remark on it.

Although some doubt must remain as to the actual date of the event, 3 September, the year of the earthquake which is not mentioned in the Anargyrian Fragments can now be fixed in 1705, and the epicentre of the event located somewhere between Oropos and Plataeae, a location about 30 km distant from both Athens and Negreponte. Unfortunately, Venetian sources for this region become scarce after the Carlowitz treaty in 1699, and no information about this event so far has been found therein. A shock reported from Zante in 1705 (Schmidt 1867, 5) may well be a different event, belonging to the aftershock sequence of the earthquake of November 1704 in the Ionian islands. However, the fact that as yet we have found no mention of an earthquake in 1705 in Central Greece in the consular and Jesuit correspondence from towns in the Peloponnese and neighbouring regions (Aigina, Corinth, Nauplion, Patra, Smyrna, Constantinople), as well as no mention in the European press of the time, implies that perhaps the shock that affected Athens in 1705 was not felt very far and did not cause any great concern in nearby towns — in other words, that the 1705 earthquake was not a large magnitude event.

1785, June 13

Another earthquake was felt in Athens on 13 June 1785 (OS) (Burnias, 1892), but it is very unlikely that it caused any damage; a number of travellers who passed through Athens shortly after that date do not mention any noticeable effects. However, we know that this earthquake originated from the region of Oropos, 35 km N of Athens, where it caused considerable damage that extended to the fortress of Egriboz (Chalkis), to Oropos and to farms in the region of the Darbent of Sulesi.

With the advent of the 19th century, there is an obvious improvement in the volume and quality of data, which becomes more complete as we approach the 20th century. This is largely due to the availability of additional published sources of information. Archival material nevertheless continues to provide much useful data. Thus, the number of earthquakes identified in Greece for the 19th century amounts to over 1500. However, only very few caused concern in Athens, chiefly relatively large, distant earthquakes, the more important of which are:

1805, September 17

On the night of 17 September a shock was felt in Athens as a result of which 'some blocks of the western tympanum (of the Parthenon) were thrown down' (Dodwell 1819, 329, 474). The context in which the event is recorded suggests the 17th, either of September or of November 1805. The shock caused no damage in Athens and it is not mentioned in other sources. Sieberg (1932) says that this earthquake was responsible for great damage in the town and this inaccurate information is repeated by later writers. This was a small, probably local shock that triggered the fall of pieces of marble from the Parthenon, loosened by the dismantling operations of 1801–1803.

1837, March 18
An earthquake in the southern part of the Saronic Gulf near Hydra, of a probable magnitude 6.4, caused great panic and some damage in Athens, 58 km away. In the Agora, blocks of marble from the gable-end of the tetrakionion were thrown down to the W (Schmidt, 1879).

1853, August 18
This earthquake, having an estimated magnitude of 6.0, affected the region of Thiva (Thebes), about 53 km from Athens. The shock caused considerable panic in the city but no damage. We could find no evidence for damage to historical monuments in Athens.

1874, January 17
In the morning there was an earthquake in Athens (pop. 65,000). According to Schmidt (1879, 325), the shock caused the collapse of a part of the wall of the Acropolis built by Odysseus Androutsos in 1822. However, the press in Athens (*Aeon, Ethnophylax, Alitheia, Eph. Syzitiseon*) does not confirm Schmidt's information, and the effects of this event on the Acropolis are in need of authentication. Otherwise, the shock was not felt by the majority of the inhabitants of the city and it was not reported from other places. Galanopoulos (1956, 467) says that this was a damaging shock, which is clearly an exaggeration. Apparently this was a small local earthquake and the collapse of the wall could have been due to its high vulnerability rather than the severity of shaking.

1889, January 22
At 6h 15m an earthquake caused some damage to the monastery of Daphni, causing vertical cracks to open in the dome and walls of the church and in some of the cells (Galanopoulos 1953, 190). We could find no original source for this event.

1894, April 20
The earthquake of 20 April, had a magnitude 6.4, and originated in the region of Martino. In Athens (pop. 140,000), at an epicentral distance of 90 km, a few old houses were thrown down and several buildings were fissured. A block of marble fell from Hadrian's Gate and the capital of an old column in the Agora was thrown down.

1894, April 27
A few days later, a larger earthquake of magnitude 6.9, occurred at Atalandi, 100 km NW of Athens. In the city the shock caused great panic and some minor damage, but no casualties. In the Acropolis a few existing cracks in the eastern pediment of the Parthenon were enlarged by the shock and small blocks of marble fell of the epistyle.

After 1900, the availability of documentary information continues to improve, supplemented by instrumental data. During this century few earthquakes pass unrecorded, generally only so far as minor events are concerned, only very few of them being of any consequence in Athens. Of the many hundreds of shocks felt in the city during this century, the following caused some concern or damage to historical monuments.

1914, October 17

This earthquake occurred between Thiva (Thebes) and Chalkis and had a magnitude 6.2. In Athens, at an epicentral distance of 47 km, the shock caused panic; a small number of dilapidated houses collapsed and a few buildings suffered minor damage. So far as we can tell, there was no damage to the monuments on the Acropolis.

1928, April 22

This was a magnitude 6.3 earthquake near Corinth. In Athens, at an epicentral distance of 77 km, the shock caused some alarm and minor damage to a small number of old houses. There is no evidence that it caused any concern to those involved at the time with the restoration of Acropolis monuments.

1930, April 17

This 5.9 magnitude shock occurred on the SW coast of the Saronic Gulf, 59 km from Athens. In the city, 4 old houses collapsed, and few were cracked. There is no indication that the shock caused any damage to historical monuments in the city.

1938, July 20

The earthquake in Oropos, 37 km N of Athens, had a magnitude 6.1. It was strongly felt in the city where it caused little panic, and insignificant damage. We could find no information about damage to historical monuments in Athens.

1965, July 6

This earthquake had a magnitude 6.4 and an offshore epicentre in the Gulf of Corinth, 122 km from Athens. It was generally felt in the city where it caused absolutely no damage.

1981, February 24

The main shock of the earthquake sequence in the eastern Gulf of Corinth had a magnitude 6.7. In Athens (pop. 3,000,000) at an epicentral distance of 77 km, the main shock and its strong aftershocks ruined about 500 houses and caused widespread but minor damage to a number of public buildings. In archaeological museums a number of exhibits were broken and the Parthenon sustained minor damage; the S-E, but chiefly the N-E corners of the monument were displaced by a few centimetres and some of the joints were caused to open up (Zambas 1985, 134).

Five hours later, there was a strong aftershock of magnitude 6.4, originating from an epicentral distance of 60 km. This shock caused no further displacements and had no effect on the opening of the joints (Korres & Bouras 1983, 328–343).

Discussion

The general conclusion is that the long-term historical seismicity of Central Greece for the period before the 18th century is very imperfectly known. The main factors seen to influence the completeness of data are the quality of the contemporary literary record, the prevailing historical circumstances, the geographical location of events and their magnitude. For this period, local sources seem to be the only fund of macroseismic information for the region, and in the absence of such sources our data is clearly incomplete.

Consequently, the apparent low earthquake hazard of a number of regions shown on modern seismic maps of Central Greece, such as the Gulf of Argos, the Evrotas-Taygetos graben, northern Evia (Euboea) and Parnassos, may not be genuine, and it may reflect partly the lack of long-term observations. The only conclusion that we can draw from this re-evaluation is that there is no historical or instrumental evidence, so far, that any of the earthquakes identified on land have exceeded magnitude $M_s = 7.0$ in size.

The question now arises whether an insight into the likely maximum earthquake in Central Greece may be gained from seismotectonic considerations. The Aegean Sea, and its surrounding coastal regions, are one of the most rapidly extending areas on the continents today, with a N-S rate of extension across the whole province, i.e. between Crete and Bulgaria, of about 50 mm/yr (Jackson & McKenzie, 1988a). The general pattern of faulting throughout Central Greece is chiefly normal (extensional) (Billiris et al., 1991) and the overall style of deformation is roughly N-S extension, balanced by crustal thinning. Calculations show that for the period 1890 to 1988 displacements correspond to N-S velocities of about 6 mm/yr, with little or no aseismic creep component (Ambraseys & Jackson, 1990).

Fig. 3 shows faulting associated with major tectonic structures on land and in coastal regions of Central Greece, excluding the Ionian Islands. The tectonic activity in Greece is expressed in the topography, geomorphology and movement of the coastline relative to sea level. The structure of the region is dominated by large grabens that have been active since at least lower Pliocene, are bounded by faults that affect Quaternary or Recent formations, and strongly influence the present-day pattern of drainage and sedimentation. Fig. 3 shows only major active faults and is not complete; it is certain that some have been omitted, particularly from offshore regions and in remote areas N of the Gulf of Corinth and in the Pindos. On several of these faults slip is known to have occurred at the surface during recent historic earthquakes, and fault-breaks associated with known earthquakes are also shown in Fig. 3.

An important characteristic of active normal faulting on the continents is that individual fault segments are rarely continuous along strike for more than about 20 km (Jackson & White, 1989). Instead, long valleys, or grabens, like those in Central Greece, are typically bounded by fault segments that step *en echelon* or change the polarity of their dip along strike. This has the effect of limiting the extent of fault rupture in earthquakes, and thus limiting the maximum earthquake size or magnitude.

Fig. 1 shows the seismic activity in the region, that is, the distribution of chiefly shallow earthquakes of surface-wave magnitude M_s equal to or greater than 6.0. Solid circles are the epicentres of the period 1890 to 1988, and their epicentral regions or regions of heavy damage, are shaded. Solid squares are the approximate epicentres of 19th century earthquakes. Open squares are approximate epicentres of events before 1800. The pre-1890 events are labelled with the year of their occurrence: those that may have been smaller than $M_s = 6.0$ are labelled with a bar. Dashed lines show the faults identified in Fig. 3. It is of interest that the largest earthquake of the last 300 years in Fig. 1 did not exceed an estimated magnitude $M_s = 6.9$.

On a worldwide basis, the larger an earthquake is, the more likely it is to be associated with a surface fault. But from Fig. 1, no truly large earthquakes have been recorded historically or instrumentally in Central Greece. This is not surprising, since there are no major through-going faults. Earthquakes larger than about $M_s = 7.0$ require normal faults of 40 km or longer, and as Fig. 3 shows, there are no such faults in Central Greece. Although some of the major topographic features, such as the north Gulf of Evia and Gulf of Corinth, are longer than 100 km, the normal faults that bound them are segmented, with individual fault segments being no longer than about 15 km: a length sufficient only for earthquakes of $M_s = 6.0$ to 6.5. Although normal faulting earthquakes larger than $M_s = 7.0$ are known elsewhere, they are generally multiple events, with sub-events apparently not larger than equivalent to less than $M_s = 7.0$, a maximum likely magnitude for Central Greece. This has obvious implications, not only for the assessment of seismic hazard, but also for the survival of historical information. Note, however, that strike-slip events larger than $M_s = 7.0$ are known offshore in and around the North Aegean Trough, and that the far-field effects from such events may add to the hazard of Central Greece (Jackson & McKenzie, 1988b).

Conclusions

Our studies bring out a number of points that should be taken into consideration when historical events are used in earthquake hazard assessment.

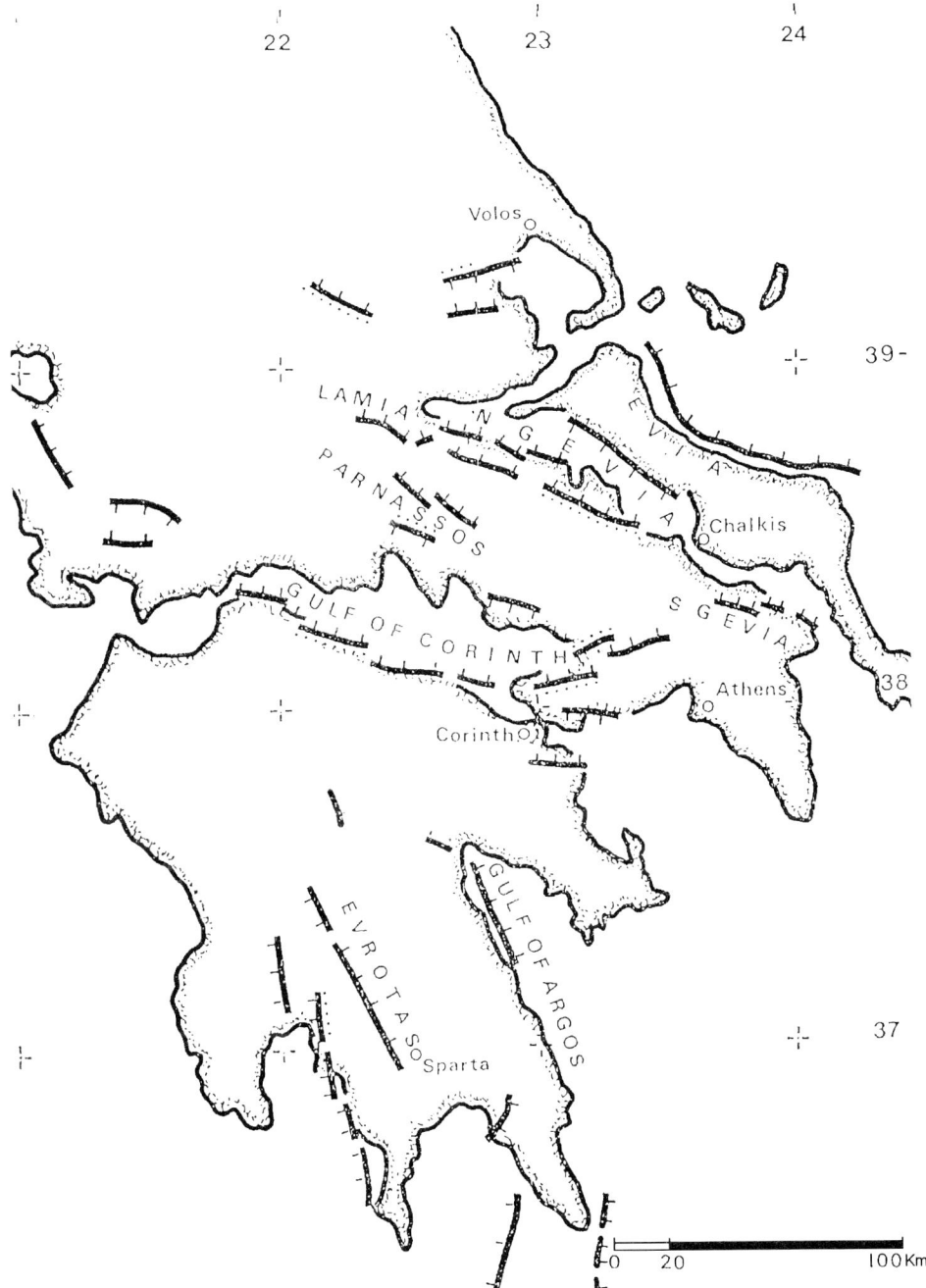

Figure 3. Faulting associated with major tectonic structures on land and in the coastal regions of Central Greece, summarised from Lyon-Caen *et al.* (1988), Roberts & Jackson (1990) and unpublished work. Dotted traces show fault breaks associated with historical and recent earthquakes. This map shows only major active faults and is not complete: it is certain that many active faults have been omitted, particularly from offshore regions; modified from Ambraseys & Jackson (1990).

The vulnerability of modern man-made structures differs in many respects from that of old ones. Historical monuments are sensitive to differential settlements and their lateral stability is almost exclusively dependent on frictional resistance. To judge the destructiveness of an historical earthquake from 20th century case histories can be seriously misleading.

We should not, as we consistently have done, presume that the orderly or disorderly distribution of masonry pieces always implies earthquake effects and presume that an earthquake, many tens or hundreds of miles from the site, however well attested in the sources, necessarily caused the damage.

Great care must be taken to establish the simultaneity of the destructive effects of early earthquakes at places located large distances apart. Quite often the amalgamation of the effects of two or more different historical events stretches the size of the earthquake beyond the limits of the possible, and leads to speculation and to the development of 'catastrophe' theories.

The long-term seismicity of Central Greece is clearly different from that of neighbouring Anatolia in that either (a) no earthquakes of magnitude greater than 7.0 occur, or (b) 500 years is not long enough to reveal such events in Central Greece, whereas 100 years is more than adequate in Anatolia and in other parts of the Middle East.

Earthquakes in Central Greece are numerous, of medium size, preceded and followed by damaging shocks, causing localised destruction and relatively small loss of life. Occasionally, earthquakes must have triggered the premature decline of the local economy of a city-state or caused a crisis in local human affairs. However, their lasting effects would not seem to have been very significant.

Appendix

This appendix provides useful but rather specialised details in certain aspects of engineering seismology that may be of interest to the historian and archaeologist.

Magnitude of earthquakes is a measure of their size in terms of the energy released by the fault rupture.
Intensity is a measure of ground shaking at a particular place assessed from the damage done to structures and from other felt effects.
Isoseismals are contour lines drawn to separate one level of seismic intensity from another.
Epicentre is the point on the Earth's surface directly above the focus of the earthquakes.
Focus is the point in the earth at which fault rupture commences.
Fault is a pre-existing fracture or zone of fractures in rock along which the two sides have been displaced relative to each other. For other definitions see Bolt (1978).

We may define **earthquake hazard** as the aggregate of probabilities of occurrence of seismic ground motion at a given site and during a given period of time. The earthquake hazard is, therefore, a function of the regional and local tectonics, and also of the activity of these geologic elements.

A historical site or monument may be vulnerable to earthquake ground motion, but it will be at no risk unless there is a finite probability of such motion occurring at the site during the lifetime of the monument. We may define **earthquake risk**, therefore, by equation 1 (Fournier d'Albe, 1982). This equation expresses Risk as a function of the Seismic Hazard, that is of the probability of occurrence of ground motion due to an earthquake during the lifetime of the structure, of the Losses due to the hazard, and of the Vulnerability of the structure to damage or destruction by earthquake ground motion, i.e.

$$[\text{Earthquake Risk}] = [\text{Seismic Hazard}] * [\text{Vulnerability}] \times (\text{Loss}) \tag{1}$$

Seismic hazard is obviously beyond human control, but an accurate knowledge of it from seismicity studies over a long period of time is possible. The vulnerability of buildings and structures to earthquake forces is the subject-matter of engineering; it is determined by the physical characteristics of structures and it can be assessed, controlled and reduced by appropriate action, though sometimes at a cost which must be justified by a diminished probability of loss.

One of the most important parameters in the assessment of the damaging potential of an earthquake is its **magnitude**, which is a measure of the energy released during faulting. We may estimate the magnitude of an earthquake from the dimensions of the causative fault-rupture. For Eastern Mediterranean crustal earthquakes we may use the following expression:

$$M_s = 4.63 + 1.43\log(L) \tag{2}$$

where **L** is the observed length of fault-break in km and M_s is the surface-wave magnitude of the associated earthquake (Ambraseys 1988b, 309). A better estimate of M_s from the dimensions of rupture and dislocation, can be made from:

$$M_s = 1.10 + 0.40\log(L^{1.58}R^2) \tag{3}$$

where **L** and **R** are the length of the fault-break and slip respectively, in centimetres (Ambraseys, 1988a). Thus, for the Atalandi earthquake of 27 April 1894, which was associated with a rupture length of about 25 km, extending from Martino to Atalanti, and an average observed slip of 150 cm, equations 2 and 3 predict a magnitude M_s between 6.6 and 6.9.

The size M_s of an historical shallow earthquake can also be assessed in terms of the mean radius R_i of the isoseismal of intensity I_i expressed in the Medvedev-Sponheuer-Karnik (MSK) scale. The attenuation law derived for the S. Balkans, including Greece, is given by:

$$M_s = -0.902 + 0.578(I_i) + 1.1 \times 10^{-3}(R_i) + 2.11\log(R_i) \tag{4}$$

where R_i is in km. For the Atalanti earthquake of 1894, the fact that the shock was felt with an intensity of about III (MSK) (on the Medvedev-Sponheuer-Karnik scale) in S. Bulgaria, Edirne, Gelibolu, Cos and Iraklion, i.e. at an average distance from the epicentre of $R_3 = 410$ km, implies that from equation 4, the magnitude of the event was $M_s = 6.8$, a value consistent with that derived from other considerations.

Alternatively, equation 4 may be used to assess the intensity of shaking I_i at a distance R_i from the source of an earthquake of magnitude M_s. For example, in the Atalanti earthquake of 1894, which had a magnitude $M_s = 6.9$, Athens, at an epicentral distance $R_i = 100$ km, should have experienced the shock very strongly. From equation 4 we find that the intensity in Athens should have been about $I = VI+$ (MSK scale).

Another measure of hazard is the maximum ground acceleration generated at a distance **d** from an earthquake of magnitude M_s and focal depth **h**, where **h** and **d** are in km. For shallow earthquakes in the European area the peak horizontal acceleration **a** (in g), may be estimated from the attenuation equation:

$$\log(a) = -0.87 + 0.217(M_s) - \log(r) - 0.00117(r) \tag{5}$$

where $r = (d^2 + h^2)^{0.5}$. The vertical maximum acceleration may be taken to be 0.5 of the horizontal (Ambraseys & Bommer, 1991).

Thus, a relatively large magnitude earthquake of say, $M_s = 7.0$, nucleating at a focal depth of $h = 7$ km, will produce, very close to where it happens ($d = 0$), a maximum ground acceleration of $a = 56\%$g, that is, an equivalent lateral force equal to more than half of the weight of a structure. At a distance of $d = 50$ km, however, the peak ground acceleration will be only $a = 7\%$g, and this will cause little or no damage to well-built dwellings.

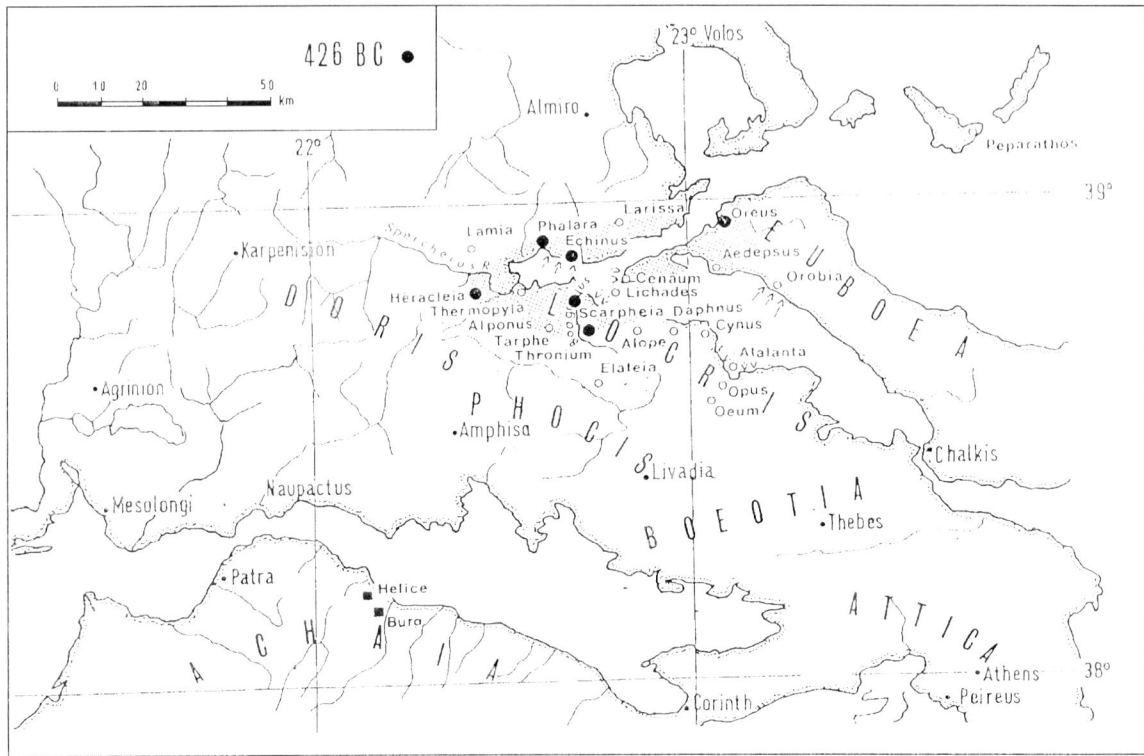

Figure 4. Area affected and estimated epicentral region of the earthquake of 426 BC (shaded) which extends from near
  Herackeia to Oreus and from Phalara to Scarpheia: an equivalent radius of 20 km. Large full circles show sites for which
  there is evidence of destruction; open circles show other sites affected. Arrows show sites affected by the associated
  seismic sea-wave.

From the foregoing it is obvious that the intensity of shaking produced by the 426 BC earthquake in Athens
should have been far below damage level, even for vulnerable structures. Fig. 4 shows the area affected and
the epicentral region of the earthquake (shaded) which extends from near Heracleia to Oreus and from Phalara
to Scarpheia, of an equivalent radius of 20 km. For an intensity $I_9 = 20$ km, equation 4 gives a magnitude M_s
of just over 7.0. We obtain the same value from equation 2 assuming that the length of faulting was 3/4 of the
linear dimension of the epicentral area, i.e. 45 km. Athens was 120 km from the source of this earthquake,
and from equation 5 we have that the peak acceleration in Athens should have been about 3% g, or from equation
4, the intensity should have been about V (MSK). On the Acropolis, because of the topography, these values
were perhaps larger but well below damage level. These values cannot substantiate damage in Athens.

References

Ambraseys, N. (1988a). Engineering seismology. *J. Earthq. Eng. & Struct. Dynam.* **17**, 1–105.
Ambraseys, N. (1988b). Magnitude-fault length relationships for earthquakes in the Middle East. In (W. Lee,
    Ed.) *Proc. Hist. Seism. & Earthq.* London; Academic Press.
Ambraseys, N. & Jackson, J. (1990). Seismicity and associated strain of central Greece between 1890 and
    1988. *Geophys. J. Intern.* **101**, 663–708.

Ambraseys, N., & Finkel, C. (1991). Long-term seismicity of Istanbul and of the Marmara Sea region. *Terra Nova* **3**, 527–529.

Ambraseys, N. & Finkel, C. (1992). The seismicity of the Eastern Mediterranean during the turn of the 18th century. *Istanb. Mitteil. Deuts. Arch. Institut* **42**, 323–343.

Ambraseys, N. & Bommer, J. (1991). The attenuation of ground accelerations in Europe. *J. Earthq. Eng. & Struct. Dyn.* **20**, 1179–1202.

Billiris, H. et al. (1991). Geodetic determination of tectonic deformations in central Greece from 1900 to 1988. *Nature* **350**, 124–129.

Bolt, B. (1978). *Earthquakes*. San Francisco; W. Freeman.

Bousquet, B. & Pechoux, P-Y. (1981). Séismes et espaces séismiques. *Annal. Univ. de Toulouse* 17, nouv. ser. fasc.3, 53. Toulouse.

Burnias, G. (1892). Chronikon tou 18ou aionos. In (D. Kambouroglou, Ed.) *Mnimia Istorias ton Athinon*, 240. Athens. (In Greek).

Diodorus Siculus (C. Oldfather *et al*, Eds) Loeb, 1933–1967.

Dionysius Areopagites (M. Kugener, Ed.) *Oriens Christianus* 7. (Rome, 1907).

Dodwell, E. (1819). *A Classical and Topographical Tour through Greece* 1. London; Rodwell.

Fournier d'Albe, M. (1982). An approach to earthquake risk management. *Eng. Struct.* **4**, 147–152.

Galanopoulos, A. (1953). Katalog der Erdbeben in Griechenland für die Zeit von 1879 bis 1892. *Annales Geol. Pays Helléniques*, 5, 114–229.

Galanopoulos, A. (1956). I seismiki epikindynotis ton Athinon. *Praktika Akadem. Athenon* **31**, 464–472. (In Greek).

Jackson, J. & McKenzie, D. (1988a). Rates of active deformation in the Aegean and surrounding regions. *Basin Research* **1**, 121–128.

Jackson, J. & McKenzie, D. (1988b). The relationship between plate motions and seismic moment tensors and the rate of active deformation in the Mediterranean and Middle East. *Geophys. Journal* **93**, 45–73.

Jackson, J. & White, N. (1989). Normal faulting in the upper continental crust. *J. Struct. Geol.* **11**, 15–36.

Korres, M. & Bouras, Ch. (1983). *Meleti apokatastaseos tou Parthenonos*. Athens: Ministry of Culture & Science. (In Greek).

Korres, M. (1985). Twelve programs for the restoration of the Parthenon. *Proc. 2nd Intern. Meeting Restor. Acropolis Monuments*. Athens; Ministry of Culture & Science.

Lucas, P. (1712). *Voyage du sieur Paul Lucas dans la Grèce, l'Asie Mineur, La Macédoine et l' Afrique* 2 vols. Paris; N. Simart.

Lyon-Caen, H., Armijo, R., Drakopoulos, J., Baskoutas, J., Delibassis, N., Gaulon, R., Kouskouna, V., Latoussakis, J., Makropoulos, K., Papadimitriou, P., Papanastassiou, D. & Pedotti, G. (1988). The 1986 Kalamata (South Peloponnesus) earthquake: Detailed study of a normal fault, evidence for E-W extension in the Hellenic Arc. *J. Geophys. Res.* **93**, 14967–15000.

Pittakis, K. (1853). Apospasma ek tou cheirographou tis historias ton Athinon. *Archaeologiki Ephimeris* 942–945. (In Greek).

Plutarch (K. Ziegler, Ed.) Teubner, 1914–1935.

Robert, L. (1978). Documents d'Asie Mineur; stèle funéraires. *Bull Corresp. Hellénique* **107**, 395–408.

Roberts, S. C. & Jackson, J. A. (1990). Active normal faulting in central Greece: an overview. In (A. M. Roberts, G. Yielding & B. Freeman, Eds). *The Geometry of Normal Faulting*. London: Spec. Publ. Geological Society 56, 125–142.

Schmidt, J. F. (1867). *Pragmatia peri tou genomenou to 1867 seismou tis Kephalinias*. Athens; Ethniko Typographio. (In Greek).

Schmidt, J. F. (1879). *Studien über Erdbeben*. Leipzig: A. Georgi.

Sieberg, A. (1932). Die Erdbeben. In (B. Gutenberg) *Handbuch der Geophysik* **4**, 77. Berlin: Borntraeger.

Spon, J. (1678). *Voyage d'Italie, de Dalmatie, de Grèce, et du Levant, fait aux années 1675 et 1676*. 2 vols. Lyon.

Strabo (H. Jones, Ed.) Loeb, 1917–1933.

Stuart, J. & Revett, N. (1789). *The Antiquities of Athens and other Monuments of Greece*. London.

Thucidides (C. Hude, Ed.) Teubner, 1913–1925.

Zambas, C. (1985). The problems of the Parthenon's earthquake resistance. *Proc. 2nd Internat. Meeting Restor. Acropolis Monuments*. Athens; Ministry of Culture & Science.

Signs of an Earthquake at Midea?

Paul Åström[a] & Katie Demakopoulou[b]

[a]Göteborg University, V. Hamngatan 3,
411 18 Göteborg, Sweden
[b]National Archaeological Museum,
Tositsa 1, Athens 106 82, Greece

Abstract

The end of the Late Helladic IIIB2 period (*c.* 1190 BC) at Midea in the Peloponnese in southern Greece is marked by a major destruction, with a general conflagration followed by the collapse of walls, buildings and gates. An earthquake is the most likely cause of this destruction which is roughly contemporary with those at the nearby sites of Mycenae and Tiryns, where there is also evidence of earthquakes.

Introduction

The Citadel of Midea, on a hill not far from Mycenae in the Peloponnese, was recognized as early as the 1890's by the Swedish professor, Sam Wide, as a site of potential archaeological interest. A small excavation was opened at this site by the German Archaeological Institute in 1907 (Meyer, 1932), while A. Persson, assisted by Torgny Säve-Söderbergh, dug several trenches inside the Citadel wall in 1939 (Persson 1942, 3ff). This excavation brought to light Mycenaean and Middle Helladic layers, as well as an ash layer (Persson 1942, n.3, 13, fig. 10, cf. 4, fig. 1) which was the subject of a later excavation by N. Verdelis and P. Åström in 1963. From the pottery they found in a trench near the East Gate the ash layer was dated to LH IIIB2. In this layer animal bones, which had been extremely well utilized were found, but no fish bones, suggesting that the Citadel had been besieged and thereafter conquered by enemies (Åström, 1964; 1968; 1983).

Since 1983, however, excavations in the Acropolis of Midea by the Greek-Swedish expedition, directed by K. Demakopoulou in association with P. Åström and covering a much wider area (Åström & Demakopoulou, 1986; Åström *et al.*, 1988; 1990; 1992; Demakopoulou *et al.*, 1994), have come up with an alternative interpretation. It now seems likely that the Citadel was struck by a catastrophic earthquake like that at Tiryns (Kilian 1980, 177, 185; this volume) and possibly Mycenae, where the earthquake happened at an earlier date (Mylonas-Shear 1987, 154–155; Mylonas 1975, 158–161; Taylour 1981, 9; Iakovidis 1986, 259; French, this volume). It is possible that the inhabitants of Midea left the site, perhaps in panic, and fled to Tiryns, where the population increased after 1190 BC. Apart from Midea, several other sites in the Argolid were also deserted, and it seems that the population concentrated in a few major sites, a kind of *synoikismos* (Kilian 1988, 134).

The new excavations

Since 1983, the Swedish team of the joint Greek-Swedish expedition has cleared the East Gate and uncovered an inner gate inside the East Gate. Excavations have also been carried out on the higher terraces and also on the lower terraces, where for the first time remains of the LH IIIC period have been found showing a

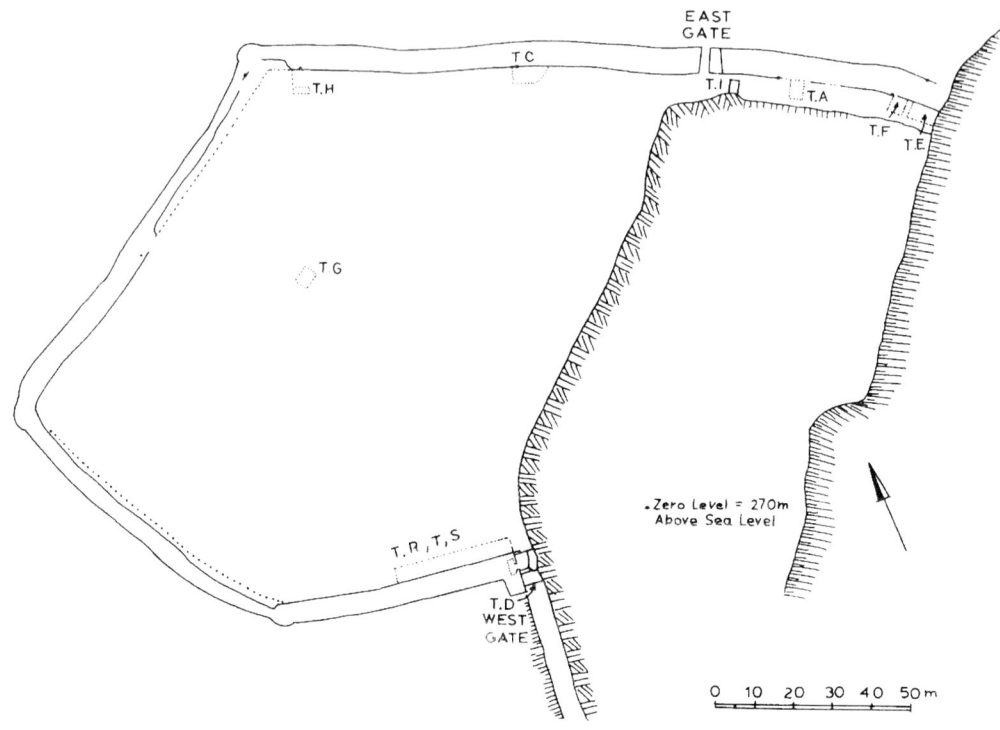

Figure 1. Plan of the Acropolis of Midea.

reoccupation of the site on the lower parts of the Citadel after the destruction. Undisturbed layers of the Middle Helladic period have also been uncovered for the first time near the top of the Acropolis (Fig. 1).

The Greek team investigated the West Gate of the Acropolis. The West Gate is defined by a bulky retaining wall which had been built to cover the cliff face of the rock to the S-E, and by the W termination of the fortification wall which at this point was extended to form an imposing bastion, measuring 5.50 x 5 m, to protect the Gate (Figs 1–2). An intact room was excavated inside the bastion. The excavation showed that a great catastrophe had befallen the West Gate, which was found literally buried under its own remains. Underneath this debris was a thick and very pronounced destruction layer due to fire. A large amount of LH IIIB2 pottery was found in this layer, which dates the destruction to the end of the 13th century BC.

Inside the Acropolis to the left of the West Gate an area running along the inner face of the fortification wall was excavated. Remains of Mycenaean buildings constructed next to the Citadel wall were found in that area. In most cases only the floors and/or the foundation walls are preserved. The excavation of this area showed that most of the buildings were destroyed by a large conflagration which happened at the end of the LH IIIB2 period, at the same time as the destruction of the West Gate. The traces of fire were especially prominent on the inner face of the fortification wall and the adjoining area. The debris covering the buildings contained piles of stones fallen from the walls of the rooms and the fortification wall and a very large number of broken terracotta tiles and vases.

The cause of the destruction

The collapse of the West Gate and the buildings inside the Acropolis cannot have been the result of war. Instead it is likely that Midea suffered from a devastating earthquake (Åström *et al.*, 1990), which may well have been the cause of a great fire. Signs of a possible earthquake are seen everywhere inside the Citadel of Midea in collapsed, distorted, curved and tilting walls and in the ash layers which have been found in most trenches. Several stones and more or less complete pieces of mudbrick from the walls and the superstructure of the Citadel wall had fallen

Figure 2. The West Gate of the Midea Acropolis from the S-W.

down, mostly S of the walls which may suggest that the seismic thrust was in a southward direction. It would seem that Midea and Tiryns suffered more from a possible seismic destruction *c*. 1200 BC than Mycenae, where the traces of the earthquake are less obvious (French, this volume).

Appendix

The 1994 excavation in Midea supplied more evidence for an earthquake destruction in the end of LH IIIB2. In one of the rooms in the East Gate area the skeleton of a young girl was found, whose skull and backbone were smashed under fallen stones; it seems to belong to an earthquake victim. The skeleton was found in a LH IIIB2 context.

References

Åström, P. (1964). Excavations in the Citadel of Midea. *Archaeologikon Deltion* **19**, B1, 134.

Åström, P. (1968). The destruction of Midea. In: *Atti e Memorie del 1o Congresso Internationale di Micenologia* (Roma, 1967). *Incunabula Graeca* **25**, 54–57. Roma: CNR, Edizioni dell'Ateneo.

Åström, P. (1983). *The Cuirass tomb and other finds at Dendra. 2: Excavations in the cemeteries, the lower town and the citadel*. Studies in Mediterranean Archaeology IV:2. Göteborg.

Åström, P. & Demakopoulou, K. (1986). New excavations in the citadel of Midea 1983–1984. *Opuscula Atheniensia* **16**, 19–25.

Åström, P., Demakopoulou, K. & Walberg, G. (1988). Excavations in Midea 1985. *Opuscula Atheniensia* **17**, 7–11.

Åström, P., Demakopoulou, K., Divari-Valakou, N., Fisher, P. & Walberg, G. (1990). Excavations in Midea 1987. *Opuscula Atheniensia* **18**, 9–22.

Åström, P., Demakopoulou, K., Divari-Valakou, N. & Fisher, P. (1992). Excavations in Midea 1989–1990. *Opuscula Atheniensia* **19**, 11–22.

Demakopoulou, K., Divari-Valakou, N. & Walberg, G. (1994). Excavations and Restoration work in Midea 1990–1992. *Opuscula Atheniensia* **20**, 19–41.

Demakopoulou, K. & Åström, P. (1983). Greek-Swedish excavation in the Midea Acropolis. *Archaeologikon Deltion* **38**, B1, 76–78. (In Greek).

French, E. B. (this volume). Evidence for an Earthquake at Mycenae.

Iakovidis, S. E. (1986). Destruction horizons at Late Bronze Age Mycenae. *Filia Epi eis G. E. Mylona* A, 233–260. Athens. (In Greek).

Kilian, K. (1980). Zum Ende der mykenischen Epoche in der Argolis. *Jahrbuch des Römisch-Germanischen Zentralmuseums Mainz* **27**, 166–195.

Kilian, K. (1988). Mycenaeans up to date, trends and changes in recent research. In (E. B. French & K. A. Wardle, Eds) *Problems in Greek Prehistory*, 115–152. Bristol Classical Press.

Meyer, E. (1932). Mideia, In: *Pauly's Real Encyclopaedie* **XV**:2 (columns), 1540–1543. Stuttgart.

Mylonas, G. (1975). Excavations at Mycenae. *Praktika Archaeologikis Etaireias*, 158–161. (In Greek).

Mylonas-Shear, I. (1987). *The Panagia Houses at Mycenae*. Philadelphia.

Persson, A. (1942). *New Tombs at Dendra near Midea*. Lund.

Taylour, W. D. (1981). *Well-built Mycenae. The Helleno-British Excavations within the Citadel at Mycenae 1959–1969. Fascicule 1, The Excavations*. (W. D. Taylour, E. B. French & K. A. Wardle, Eds). Warminster.

Earthquakes of the Late Helladic III Period
(12th century BC) at Kynos
(Livanates, Central Greece)

Phanouria Dakoronia

14th Ephoreia of Prehistoric and Classical Antiquities
Lamia Castle, Lamia 351 00, Greece

Abstract
Recent excavations on the hill of Pyrgos, at Livanates, near the 50 km long Locris 1894 fault, have brought to light storerooms of a LH IIIC settlement, identified with the Homeric town of Kynos. These storerooms suffered at least two destructions. The earlier one was identified by mudbrick walls which had detached from their dry stone foundations and had fallen into clay bins, while the remains of the following building phase are capped by what are likely to be tsunami deposits.

Introduction
The Homeric town of Kynos, harbour of Opous, capital of East Locris, has been identified with the small hill of Pyrgos, on the coast at Livanates (Homer, *Iliad* B 5318; Oldfather, 1924; Philippson 1950, 348, 30; Pritchett 1985, 179ff; see also Fossey, 1990). The hill was partly formed by the superposition of remains of various buildings, dating from at least as early as Middle Helladic to a Hellenistic fortification still preserved on its top. Recent excavations by the 14th Ephoreia of Antiquities, still in progress, have brought to light storerooms of a complex belonging to the Late Helladic (LH) IIIC period. These storerooms suffered at least two destructions which may have been caused by earthquakes, probably related to the reactivation of the nearby Locris or Atalandi fault (Fig. 1).

The Earlier Phase of Destruction
The walls of the earlier phase of the excavated storerooms were made of mudbricks, while their foundations were of dry stone masonry; on the floor lay large clay bins made of impure, unbaked clay (Dakoronia, 1985; 1986; Fig. 2). This building phase ended in a destruction that can be recognized by a lateral shift of the walls relative to their foundations (Fig. 3a), by dislocation of certain mudbricks (Fig. 2) and by mudbricks that fell into the clay bins (Figs 3b, 4). Sherds found around the bins (Fig. 5) indicate that this destruction took place in a period during which the pottery style of early LH IIIC dominated, probably at the end of this period (*c.* middle of 12th century BC).

The data available make unlikely a deliberate destruction or a failure of foundations, while the offset of the walls testifies to a high acceleration event, probably an earthquake. This event was not fatal to the building: after the destruction, the floor was levelled, the walls were repaired and the building was used as a storehouse again, this time with baked pithoi (Fig. 2).

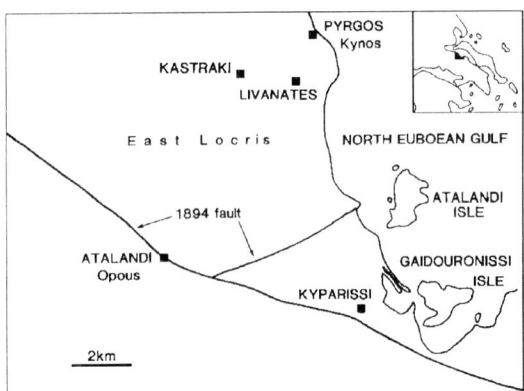

Figure 1. Location map. Upper case letters indicate modern names, lower case ancient names, according to unpublished data. The 1894, 50 km long fault is after Skuphos (1894). Atalandi and Gaidouronissi islets were formed because of seismic subsidence of coastal areas during the 426/425 BC and 1894 earthquakes. The ancient Opous is identified with Atalandi or Kyparissi.

Figure 2. General view of the excavated storerooms (trench A, 1986, view from N); (1) earlier wall; (2) base of a clay bin destroyed and filled by fallen mudbricks (3); (4) base of a pithos on the floor, just above the destruction layer of the previous building phase; (5) layer containing burials, just above the postulated tsunami deposits that cap the destruction layer of the second period discussed here. Rod divisions 5 and 50 cm.

Judging from the pottery style (Fig. 5), this destruction correlates with a destruction of the first building phase of the LH IIIC period at Lefkandi (Popham & Sackett 1968, 5), as well as with a destruction of the same period at Tiryns (Kilian 1981, 192–193). In both cases, the destructions were not fatal for the history of the sites, for damaged buildings were soon repaired and reused.

The Second Phase of Destruction

At Kynos, another destruction, which occurred less than 100 years later and was accompanied by fire, seems to have been more decisive for the site. But whether this destruction was also due to an earthquake is difficult to ascertain, since certain deformations in the walls may be attributed to various causes.

An argument that supports the hypothesis of an earthquake is the fact that in the layers of this phase, advanced LH IIIC to Late LH IIIC, numerous pebbles and rounded marine fossils (rounded fragments of *Spondyle*, *Cerithium*, *Arca*, *Murex* and *Patella* have been recognized in a sample) and pottery fragments were found. This material was spread all over the excavated site, and had no functional relationship with the building: pebbles and sherds had not been used for pavements, filling or other building material, nor was any local industry at this time making use of the marine fossils, including *Murex*. They had been rounded by wave action either in the water or on the beach, and may have been swept in by a tsunami following an earthquake.

Two arguments can support this hypothesis. First, tsunamis are not unusual in the area (Ambraseys, 1962). Second, the building is only about 16 m above present-day sea level and 100 m away from the shore, and these figures were not much different in ancient times (Stiros & Papageorgiou, 1989). Even after this destruction, the building was not abandoned but was no longer used as a storehouse. Yet the repaired buildings in the subsequent Latest Helladic IIIC to Sub-Mycenaean period show a poorer construction, their floors being the layer of fallen mudbricks of older walls; these floors contain baby burials in pits or cists (Fig. 2).

a.

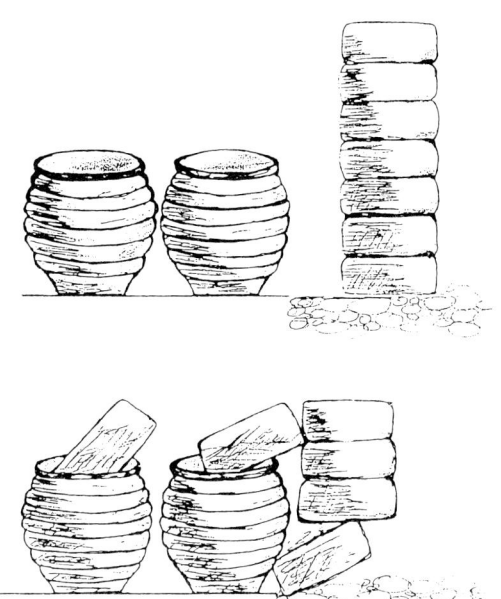

Figure 4. Model for the destruction of the first phase.

b.

Figure 3. Details from the first phase of destruction: The wall of mudbricks was in several parts detached and shifted *en bloc* relative to its foundations made of dry masonry (a), or destroyed, with mudbricks failing into the clay bins, shown in sections as darker parts (b). Rod divisions 5 and 50 cm.

Figure 5. Representative pottery found among the remains of the first period of destruction discussed above. Based on such evidence this destruction is dated to the end of the early LH IIIC period (cf. Mountjoy 1986, 143, fig. 178).

The Role of Earthquakes

The excavation data from East Locris reveal that earthquakes, though they frequently hit the area and caused much destruction, as ancient writers report (for example Thucydides III, 89; Diodoros XII, 59; Strabo I, 60; Orosius 7, 12, 5, Aur. Vict. Epit. 13, 12), were not critical events for its settlement history from Mycenaean times onwards (Stiros & Dakoronia, 1989). For example, the ancient site at nearby Kastraki, which has been identified by some scholars as the Homeric Opous (see Oldfather, 1924), was not abandoned until the Byzantine period, despite the earthquakes that hit the area. This is also the case with Atalandi (probably the real Opous) which, in the light of recent excavation (Dakoronia, 1990), has been continually occupied from Late Helladic IIIA until today. For East Locris, therefore, there is no indication that earthquakes played a major role in the occupation history of ancient settlements.

Acknowledgements

Marine fossils were identified by J. Laborel and F. Laborel-Deguen.

References

Ambraseys, N. (1962). Data for the investigation of the seismic sea-waves in the Eastern Mediterranean. *Bull. Seism. Soc. America* **52**, 895–913.

Dakoronia, Ph. (1985). Kynos. *Archaeologikon Deltion, Chronika* **40**, 173. (In Greek).

Dakoronia, Ph. (1986). Kynos. *Archaeologikon Deltion, Chronika* **41**, 68–69. (In Greek).

Dakoronia, Ph. (1990). Atalandi, *Archaeologikon Deltion, Chronika*, in press. (In Greek).

Fossey, J. (1990). *The ancient topography of Opuntian Lokris,* J. Gieben, Amsterdam.

Kilian, K. (1981). Ausgrabungen in Tiryns 1978, 1979. *Archaeologisches Anzeiger*, 149–194.

Mountjoy, P. (1986). *Mycenaean Decorated Pottery*. Studies in Mediterranean Archaeology LXXIII. Göteborg.

Oldfather, W. (1924). Kynos, *Real Encyclopaedia* **XII**, 1.

Philippson, A. (1950). *Die Griechischen Landschaften*. Frankfurt, v. Klosterman, part B1/2.

Popham, M. & Sackett, L. (1968). *Excavations at Lefkandi, Euboea, 1964–1966*. British School at Athens. London; Thames & Hudson.

Pritchett, W. (1985). East Lokris revisited. *Studies in Ancient Greek Topography* **V**, Univ. of California Publications, Classical Studies 31, 166–189.

Skuphos, T. (1894). Die zwei grossen Erbeben im Lokris. *Z. Erdkunde* **29**, 409–474.

Stiros, S. & Dakoronia, P. (1989). Ruolo storico e identificazione di antichi terremoti nei siti della Grecia. In (E. Guidoboni, Ed.) *I Terremoti prima del Mille in Italia e nell'area mediterranea. Storia, Archeologia, Sismologia*, 422–439. Bologna: ING — Storia Geofisica Ambiente.

Stiros, S. & Papageorgiou, S. (1989). Upper Holocene sea-level changes and some implications for the active tectonics of central Greece. *Bull. Geol. Soc. Gr.* **XXIII/1**, 259–269. (In Greek).

Earthquakes and Civil life at Gortyn (Crete) in the Period between Justinian and Constant II (6–7th century AD)

Antonino Di Vita

Italian School of Archaeology at Athens,
14 Parthenonos, Athens 117 42, Greece

Abstract

Archaeological excavations reveal that Gortyn, the capital of Roman and Early Byzantine Crete, suffered earthquake destruction in around AD 620, from which it recovered very quickly. Earthquakes took place at about the same time elsewhere in Crete and in various other parts of the Aegean. The disappearance of Gortyn in around 670, after almost a millennium of life, can be attributed to an earthquake rather than to an Arab raid. Extensive damage and replacement of the old underground water supply system by a new aqueduct may indicate previous seismic destruction in the town at around AD 560. Excavation data confirm destruction of important buildings and the walls of the town in around AD 100 and 31–30 BC, possibly associated with earthquakes as well.

Introduction

There is no doubt that earthquakes in the Aegean were not directly responsible for the arrival of the Avars and Slavs in the Aegean in the second and sixth/seventh decades of the 7th century. Nor were they responsible for the advance from the S of the Arabs to the suburbs of Constantinople, separating permanently the Eastern from the Western world and thereby starting the Middle Ages, as Pirenne (1937) proposed. Nevertheless, recent archaeological research has shown that earthquakes were able to play a 'catalyzing' role in such historic invasions, although the precise nature of this role may not be known. Certainly, any region of strategic importance in antiquity that was prone to natural disasters would have been vulnerable to external attacks, especially if they were well coordinated.

In the last years of Constant II's reign (641–668), the important city of Gortyn in Crete (Fig. 1) declined drastically, following a lifetime of a millennium. The Byzantine empire's exhaustion, the presence of the Arabs even on Crete where from 673 to 677 they assaulted Constantinople, as well as the commerce stopping with the W, are factors that certainly affected the life of Gortyn during Constant II's reign. However, the excavation record may suggest that an earthquake was also responsible for the devastation of Gortyn, since the findings accord with the following criteria proposed by Stiros & Dakoronia (1989) for the identification of seismic effects at archaeological sites: (1) an earthquake is feasible on geological-geophysical grounds, (2) local ground instability, for example a landslide, can be excluded as the likely cause of destruction, (3) there is good stratigraphic control which permits reliable dating of the destruction or series of destructions, (4) the hypothesis of an earthquake is consistent with the historical and archaeological evidence, and (5) the destruction is a large-scale effect and correlates with destructions at nearby sites or areas.

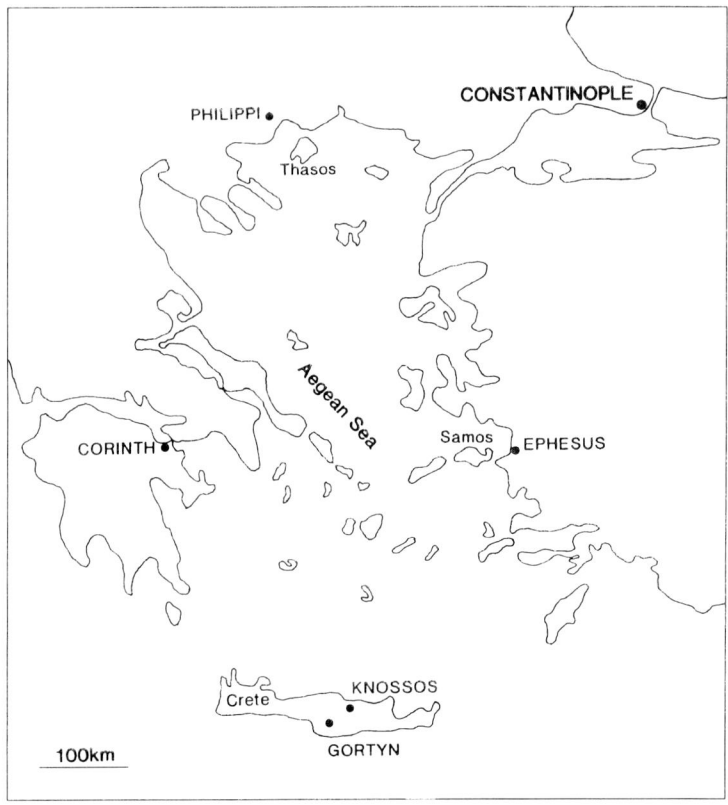

Figure 1. Location map.

The present writer believes, therefore, that it was due to an earthquake that the lower part of the city was abandoned by its inhabitants. As a result, they decided during the 7th century to move to the acropolis plateau, which was surrounded by walls during Heraclius' reign (610–641), and to the hills N of the area where they had originally come from one thousand four hundred years previously. This earthquake is not mentioned in the meagre historical sources of this period, except for a vague reference by the 11–12th century historian, Zonaras (II, 8), who reported serious seismic damage in many areas of the Byzantine empire during Constant II's reign.

Evidence for an earthquake *c.* 670
The available data, which come from two main excavations separated by about 500 m, concern Byzantine houses, the Praetorium and the Basilica of Metropolis (Figs 2–5) (Di Vita, 1979/80 a, b, c; 1984). The excavations reveal that the city was totally disturbed in the years after 666–668 but not much later, because first, the last identifiable coins found in the destruction layer all belong to Constant II's reign (641–668), and second, during the decades following the destruction, houses and a small monastery were built on the ruins. Although the destruction occurred during a politically turbulent period, there is no doubt that only a natural disaster could simultaneously have destroyed buildings of such good construction as those shown in Figs 2–5.

The case of Samos
There is a parallel for the destruction of Gortyn (Di Vita, 1979/80a). On the island of Samos Eupalino's underground aqueduct was used as a permanent refuge by the inhabitants during the first quarter of the 7th century as well as under Constant II: the waves of Avars, Slavs and Persians of the century's first decades and the Arabs, who were heading towards Constantinople in the years after 650, surely justify such a precaution. But it seems that the tunnel was no longer considered safe, and there are signs of its abrupt abandonment exactly at the time of the earthquake at Gortyn: the last coins date to 666, and anyway not later than Constant II. What is the reason for the Samians abandoning their shelter in which they had stored enough jars to hold 50,000 litres of water, just at the moment of major danger from Arabs between 668 and 677 (Hautumm 1981, 10–20)? One explanation may be the contemporary destruction of Gortyn: an earthquake. Convincing though this may appear, it does not satisfy Stiros & Dakoronia's (1989) criteria for the identification of earthquakes.

Figure 2. The great Christian Basilica of Metropolis at Gortyn. The columns between the first and the second aisle at the N belong to the second period Basilica that fell as a result of the earthquake of *c*. AD 670.

Figure 3. The great Christian Basilica of Metropolis at Gortyn. Floors laid upon one another in the main aisle; mosaics of the Justinian Basilica and large slabs of marble dated to the beginning of the 7th century.

The earthquake *c*. 620

The effect on Gortyn's life of another earthquake that hit the town a few decades earlier, around 618, was different. This date is again obtained from the extensive archaeological stratigraphic research in the Byzantine city: a small coin hoard in a house gives a *terminus post quem* of 616–617; another coin in a reconstruction stratum dates to 620–621. Altogether, the date of 618–621 for the destruction appears the most probable (Di Vita, 1979/80a).

Gortyn seems to have been totally rebuilt. Damage to the inhabited areas was extensive; in some cases the street paving was so disturbed that a thick road surface made of earth and fragments was put on it. The earlier of the two subsequent construction phases of the Basilica identified at Metropolis collapsed (Fig. 3). The Novum Praetorium, built at the end of the 4th century, collapsed and was rebuilt, and the Great Nymphaeum to the N of the Praetorium was reconstructed. The columns of the Nymphaeum bear the inscription of its constructor, Heraclius (Fig. 6). In 618–620 the resources of the Empire were far different from those in 670, and Gortyn, always remaining a provincial capital, was helped in its reconstruction by Heraclius.

On archaeological grounds it is likely that the earthquake around 620 identified at Gortyn was part of a series of major seismic destructions throughout the Aegean. Knossos was probably affected by the same event as well: the Basilica brought to light at the Venizelos Hospital area fell on a stratum dated by a coin ('follis') of Heraclius and Heraclius Constantine of 612–613 (Sanders 1982, 105–107). Ephesus was struck immediately after 612–616, Corinth in 619, and in the same year or a little later Thasos; furthermore, the Basilicas at Philippi fell in the first decades of the 7th century (for a review and references see Di Vita, 1979/80a). Since the archaeological evidence comes from these well investigated sites, there is no question that the destructions can be attributed to the Slavs, Avars and Persians, but on the other hand all of them probably took advantage of the difficulties that these series of earthquakes caused their traditional enemy: the Empire of Constantinople.

Figure 4. Street to the W of the Praetorium, with the collapsed columns of the last phase buildings following the destruction of *c*. AD 665. View from the S.

Figure 5. Street to the W of the Praetorium in its last period; view from the N. Fallen columns and other architectural members have been used again in the walls of houses of the end of the 7th and 8th centuries.

Figure 6. Columns of the Nymphaeum at the Praetorium, bearing inscriptions in honour of Heraclius who reconstructed the city after a seismic destruction dated *c*. 620 AD.

A possible seismic destruction during Justinian's times (527–565)

Going back in time, it becomes harder to identify confidently large-scale destructions in remote parts of the city of Gortyn. However, during the late Justinian era, excavations revealed extensive destruction in sector L, the sewer of sector I and the Byzantine houses of the Praetorium area. This event may be related to an important change in the life of the town: the construction of an arched aqueduct in the centre of the town (branch C: Fig. 7), dated 563–564 by a *decannumo* coin of Justinian. At least during the first years of the Roman domination, water was distributed through an extensive network of pipes which would have been vulnerable to seismic destruction. Two inscriptions, *I.C.* 461 and *I.C.* 465 (Codex Vaticanus Graecus 1759) found *in situ* in the Nymphaeum of the Praetorium, both dated to the second half of the 6th century, acknowledge a certain Georgios who brought the water again to the town (Di Vita 1988, 140, n. 32, 33; 1986/87, 478, n. 19).

Figure 7. Late aqueduct, built on arches (branch C, N of the Praetorium). This aqueduct was constructed to bring water to the town after the destruction of the older pipeline network, probably due to an earthquake that occurred shortly before AD 563 and was presumably associated with damage to various parts of the town.

Figure 8. Remains of the Hellenistic walls on the hills N of the city. During their reconstruction in 31–30 BC, all the walls were destroyed. This destruction correlates with the destruction of a prominent building of the city.

The circle of facts and hypotheses closes at this point: after an earthquake which destroyed the pipeline network leaving the town without water, the influential, richer citizens construct one or more branches of aqueduct on arches (Fig. 7) and bring the water back to the town.

Two older seismic events?

In this section attention is drawn to two earthquakes attested or confirmed by the recent excavations at Gortyn. The first one, already known from inscription *I.C.* 331 which deals with the reconstruction during Trajan's period (*c.* AD 100) of the Odeion *ruina conlapsum,* was confirmed in the 1989–1990 excavations: the grandiose first Praetorium of Gortyn seems to have been totally destroyed exactly during Trajan's period, after which its central part was rebuilt as thermal baths (Di Vita 1988–89, 469–471).

The second earthquake dates back to 31–30 BC when the Hellenistic walls on the northern hill of the town, which were being rebuilt at that time, completely collapsed (Fig. 8; Di Vita, 1986). It must also be mentioned that this destruction correlates with that of another very important building located at the foot of Pervolopetra hill: the circular building (Ecclesiasterion), on whose walls the famous laws of the town were inscribed (Willetts, 1967). After the destruction, the building was replaced by the well-known Odeion. It is tempting to attribute this destruction also to an earthquake.

References

Di Vita, A. (1979/80a). I terremoti a Gortina in età romana-proto-bizantina. Una nota. *Annuario della Scuola Archeologica di Atene e delle missioni Italiane in Oriente* **LVII–LVIII** (n.s. **XLI–XLII**), 435–440. Roma.

Di Vita, A. (1979/80b). Atti della Scuola 1980. *Annuario della Scuola Archeologica di Atene e delle missioni Italiane in Oriente* **LVII–LVIII** (n.s. **XLI–XLII**), 441–484. Roma.

Di Vita, A. (1979/80c). Atti della Scuola 1980. *Annuario della Scuola Archeologica di Atene e delle missioni Italiane in Oriente* **LVII–LVIII** (n.s. **XLI–XLII**), 485–507. Roma.

Di Vita, A. (1984). La città bizantina. In (A. Di Vita, V. La Rosa, M.-A. Rizzo, Eds) *Creta Antica*, 104–106. Roma: Scuola Archeologica Italiana di Atene.

Di Vita, A. (1986/87) Atti della Scuola 1986–87. *Annuario della Scuola Archeologica di Atene e delle missioni Italiane in Oriente* **LXIV–LXV**, n.s. **XLVIII–XLIV**, 435–534. Roma.

Di Vita, A. (Ed.) (1988) *Gortina I*. Monografie della Scuola Archeologica di Atene e delle Missioni Italiane in Oriente III. Roma.

Di Vita, A. (1988–89). Atti della Scuola, 1988–89. *Annuario della Scuola Archeologica di Atene e delle missioni Italiane in Oriente* **LXVI–LXVII** (n.s. **XLVIII–XLIX**), 427–484. Roma.

Hautumm, H. (1981). *Studien zu Amphoren der spätrömischen und frühbyzantinischen Zeit*, 10–20. Fulda.

Pirenne, H. (1937). *Mahomet et Charlemagne*. Paris.

Sanders, I. (1982). *Roman Crete*. Warminster; Aris and Philips.

Stiros, S. & Dakoronia, P. (1989). Ruolo storico e identificazione di antichi terremoti nei siti della Grecia. In (E. Guidoboni, Ed.) *I Terremoti prima del Mille in Italia e nell'area mediterranea. Storia, Archeologia, Sismologia*, 422–439. Bologna: ING — Storia Geofisica Ambiente.

Willetts, R. (1967). The law code of Gortyn. Kadmos, Supplement I. Berlin; Gruyer.

Evidence for an Earthquake at Mycenae

Elizabeth B. French

British School at Athens,
52 Odos Souedias, GR – 106 76 Athens, Greece

Abstract

Archaeologists of my generation, who attended university in the immediate aftermath of Schaeffer's great work (1948), were brought up to view earthquakes, like religion, as an explanation of archaeological phenomena to be avoided if at all possible. Thus it is only recently that the presence of an earthquake at Mycenae has begun to be a serious hypothesis. The areas discussed[1] are illustrated in Fig. 1.

The evidence can be summarized under three headings: the nature of the destruction, methods of construction and of repair, and cognitive implications.

The Destructions

The first indication came during the excavations of the Archaeological Society of Athens under the direction of Professor George E. Mylonas on the Panagia Houses in the first season in 1962. In House I a skeleton was found covered with fallen stones in the doorway of Room 5. This and other supporting evidence is clearly described by Ione Mylonas Shear (1987). Another such skeleton was found in another house excavated on the slopes of Mt. Hagios Elias at a spot called Plakes in 1975 (Mylonas, 1975a & b).

In these buildings and in others excavated by the Helleno-British team on the Citadel under the direction of Lord William Taylour (1981) the presence of a horizon of destructions where pottery and other artifacts had not been retrieved was identified. These destructions appeared to be contemporary with those of the houses containing the skeletons and this horizon has thus come to be called an earthquake horizon. This horizon can be dated to the middle of the LH IIIB period, *c*. 1250 BC.

Other areas destroyed at a similar time are often linked to this horizon, but the linkage is less secure archaeologically (Shear 1987, 155).

Building Methods

At the end of the LH IIIA2 period and the beginning of the LH IIIB period, i.e. *c*. 1300 BC, a programme of building was initiated at Mycenae which used heavy terraces as the foundation for support on the steep slopes of the site. Wright (1980) discusses the origins and intentions of this form of construction but does not link it specifically with precautions against earthquake.

Such terrace construction was not used in the Panagia houses (nor in the Plaka house) and neither was the system of tie beams linking the mudbrick superstructure to the stone foundation below[2] (Shear 1987, 8).

---

[1] This short paper covers the areas of Mycenae visited during the excursion following the conference and highlights the points discussed on that day.

[2] In Turkish villages today construction of mudbrick with wooden ties is considered particularly suitable in areas prone to earthquake shocks.

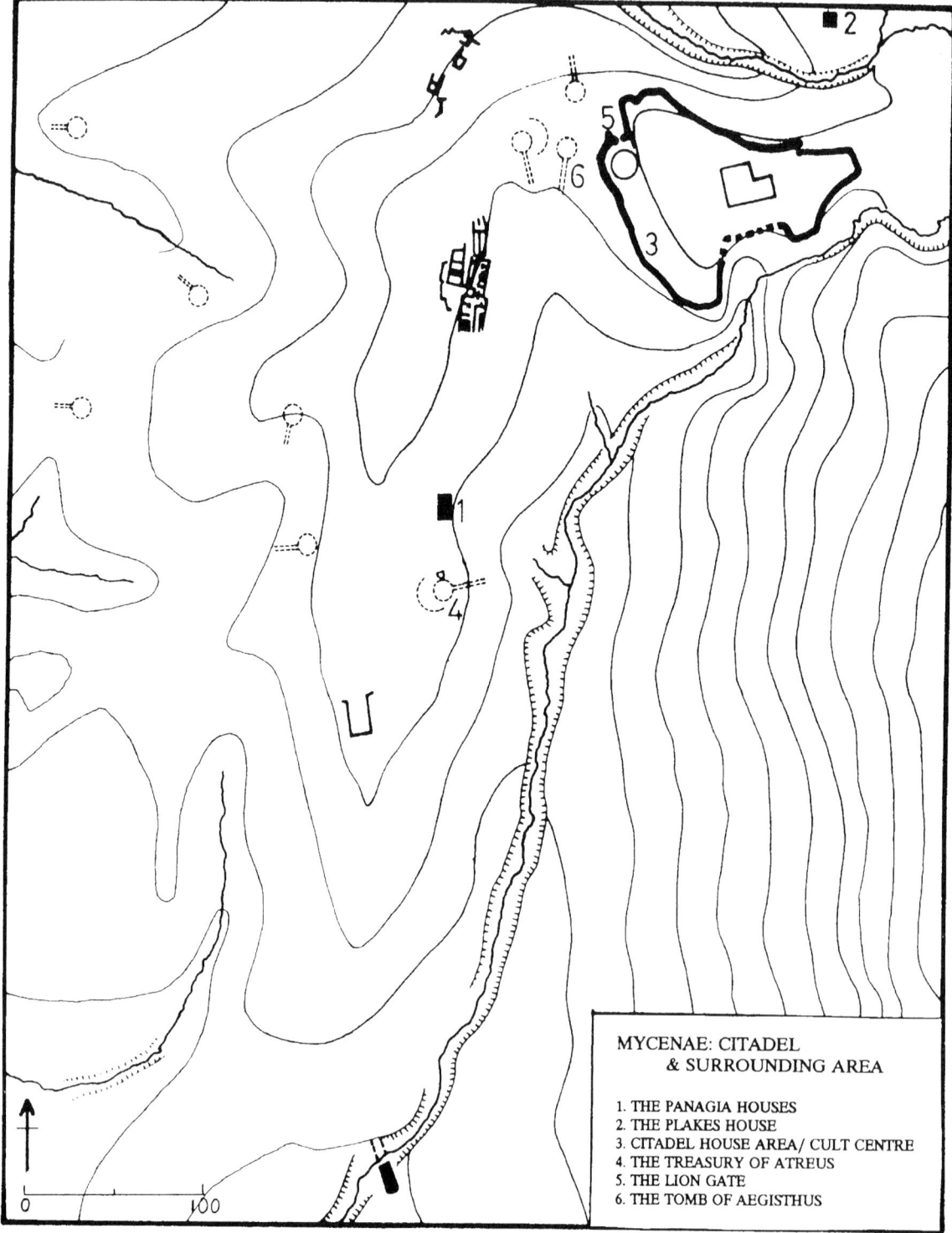

MYCENAE: CITADEL
& SURROUNDING AREA

1. THE PANAGIA HOUSES
2. THE PLAKES HOUSE
3. CITADEL HOUSE AREA/ CULT CENTRE
4. THE TREASURY OF ATREUS
5. THE LION GATE
6. THE TOMB OF AEGISTHUS

0   100

Figure 1. Plan of the Citadel Area at Mycenae.

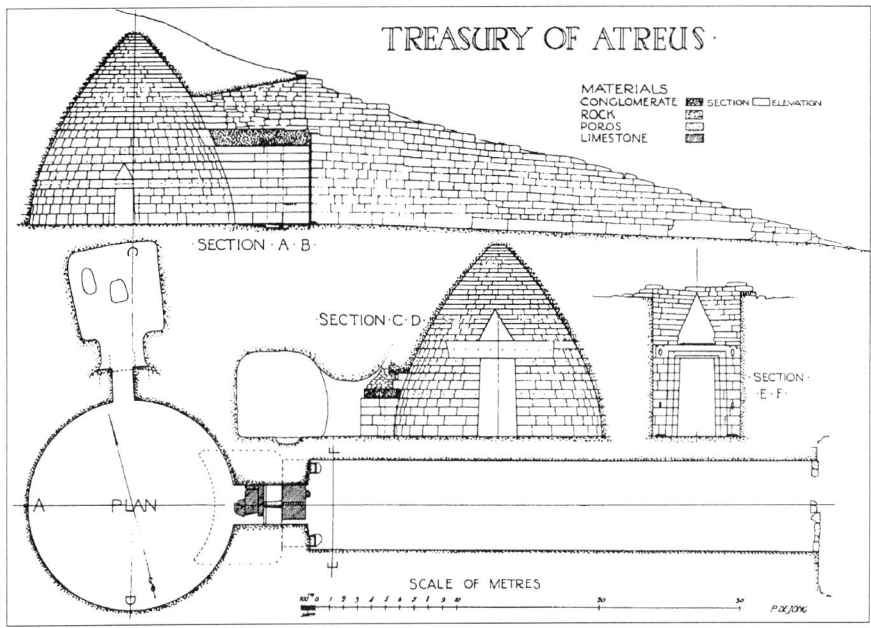

Figure 2. The Treasury of Atreus.

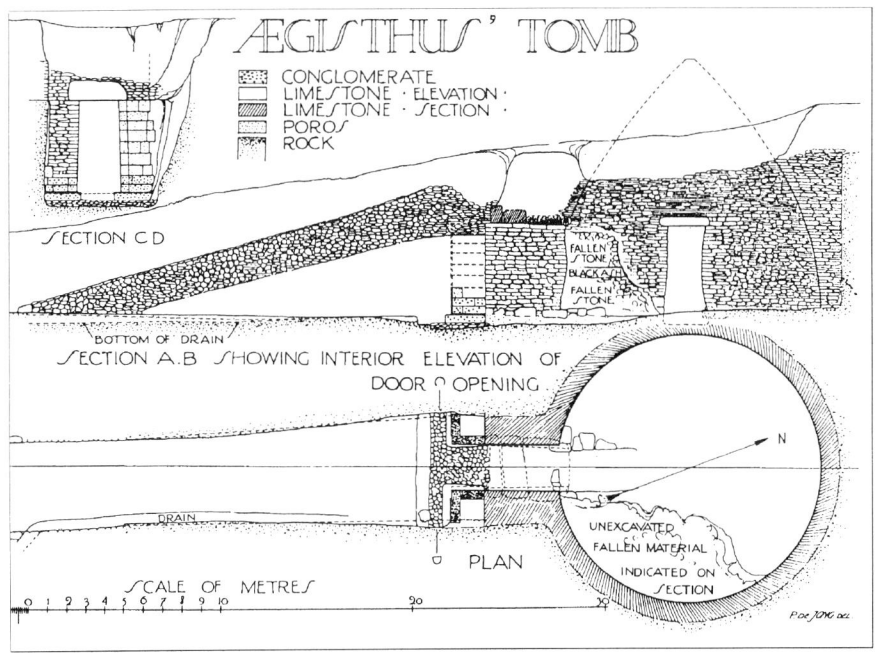

Figure 3. The Tomb of Aegisthus.

Following the 'earthquake', many measures to strengthen the Panagia houses and many alterations took place which are described in detail by Shear (1987, 154–155).

On the Citadel it was noted (Taylour *et al.*, forthcoming) that repairs following the 'earthquake' horizon had been executed in a new technique: pisé (mud poured like concrete into a moulded space instead of mud bricks) which allows repairs within a wall that is still partly standing.

Cognitive evidence

In the Cult Centre the damage caused by the 'earthquake' was dealt with in ways that indicate particular fear or awe. The storeroom behind the Temple was packed with votives often incomplete; the doorway was built up and then sealed with a layer of highly burnished plaster. In the Room with the Fresco the whole area was infilled and then areas around the walls where the majority of the votive offerings lay on the floor below were covered with slabs. Both these reactions to destruction are unusual though the sealing up of a storeroom behind a shine is parallelled at Phylakopi on Melos.

There is, however, some considerable counter evidence. A series of major monuments exists at Mycenae which would have been standing when this earthquake is supposed to have occurred. The Treasury of Atreus is immediately adjacent to the Panagia Houses. Its survival might be the result of its extremely sound construction (Fig. 2); indeed it has never collapsed. The Lion Gate can be considered similarly sound, though it is thought to have been built immediately before the supposed calamity. The Tomb of Aegisthus (Fig. 3) is of a quite different construction, much less stable. The collapse of its dome, however, is thought to have happened in two stages both subsequent to the Hellenistic reoccupation of Mycenae (Wace 1921/3, 296–316)[3]. It would, on this hypothesis, have been a standing structure at the time of the supposed earthquake and there is no evidence that it suffered damage at this time.

This then is the evidence both for and against the proposition that some destruction visible in the archaeological record at Mycenae can be assigned to an earthquake which would have taken place around the middle of the 13th century BC.

References

Mylonas, G. E. (1975a). Mycenae. *Ergon Archaiologikis Etairias* 95–111. (In Greek).

Mylonas, G. E. (1975b). Excavations at Mycenae. *Praktika Archaiologikis Etairias*. 158–161. (In Greek).

Schaeffer, C. F. A. (1948). *Stratigraphie Comparée et Chronologie de l'Asie Occidentale*. Oxford.

Shear, I. M. (1987). *The Panagia Houses at Mycenae*. Philadelphia.

Taylour, W. D. (1981). *Well Built Mycenae. The Helleno- British Excavations within the Citadel at Mycenae 1959-69, Fascicule 1, The Excavations* (W. D. Taylour, E. B. French & K. A. Wardle, Eds) Warminster.

Taylour, W. D., French, E. B. & Wardle, K. A. (forthcoming). *Well Built Mycenae, Fascicule 9, The South House and its Annex*.

Wace, A. J. B. (1921/3). Excavations at Mycenae. *Annual of the British School at Athens* 25.

Wright, J. C. (1980). Mycenaean palatial terraces. *Arch. Mitteilungen* 95, 59–86.

---

[3] It has also been free standing in its present unstable condition since 1922 when the stone collapse of the upper vault and the earth wash which filled it were removed.

Evidence for an Earthquake
in the Theatre at Stobi, *c.* AD 300

Elizabeth R. Gebhard

Department of Classics, University of Illinois at Chicago,
Box 4348, Chicago, Illinois 60680, USA

Abstract
An earthquake in the theatre at Stobi in the former Yugoslav province of Macedonia is suggested by the lateral movement of several large marble blocks in the auditorium and the failure of two outside walls in the scene-building. The event is dated *c.* AD 300 by pottery related to the subsequent rebuilding of the walls and other activities. Support for the conclusion that the destruction was caused by an earthquake comes from precautions taken by the later builders against weaknesses in the earlier foundations.

Introduction
The city of Stobi lies in the former Yugoslav Republic of Macedonia about 90 miles S of Skopje at the confluence of the Vardar and Crna Rivers, the ancient Axios and Erigon (Fig. 1a). Although founded in the Hellenistic period, the city expanded in the late 1st century BC and continued to flourish until the 6th century. The theatre was begun at the end of the 1st century AD or in the first years of the 2nd, but construction stopped before the building was completed. The plan of the theatre was then changed, and, in a second building phase, the structure was completed shortly after AD 150. After undergoing severe damage a century and a half later, the auditorium and scene-building were repaired and rebuilt with certain changes in their design.

The theatre continued in use until late in the 4th century. It was partially excavated in 1924–1928 by Baldwin Saria (1938), and clearance of the auditorium was completed in 1965–1969 by the Conservation Institute of Macedonia, Yugoslavia. New excavations at Stobi were undertaken in 1970–1981 by a joint Yugoslav-American team under the direction of James Wiseman and Gjordje Mano-Zissi. In the theatre I opened deep trenches in the scene-building, orchestra, and auditorium in order to find evidence for the complete plan of the structure, remains of the different phases that it underwent, and objects that would permit us to document its history. Detailed results are presented in my book, Gebhard (forthcoming); preliminary reports, Gebhard (1975; 1981a,b). For a recent summary of the site as a whole, see Wiseman (1984).

The theatre was built on flat ground at a distance of about 150 m from the modern bed of the Crna River (Fig. 1b). The auditorium was constructed in the Roman manner with radial walls linked by barrel vaults of poured concrete supporting rows of seats (Figs 2, 4). The slope that today appears behind the first section of seats was created after the theatre had gone out of use and was replaced by a large Episcopal Basilica. At that time the upper part of the cavea was demolished to provide a high artificial mound to raise the church above the surrounding city (Figs 2, 3).

The damage that appears to have been caused by earthquake(s) came rather late in the theatre's history. In its wake new walls were built in the scene-building and repairs were made in the auditorium. In addition, a certain amount of remodelling took place in both parts of the theatre, but that will not concern us here. A date

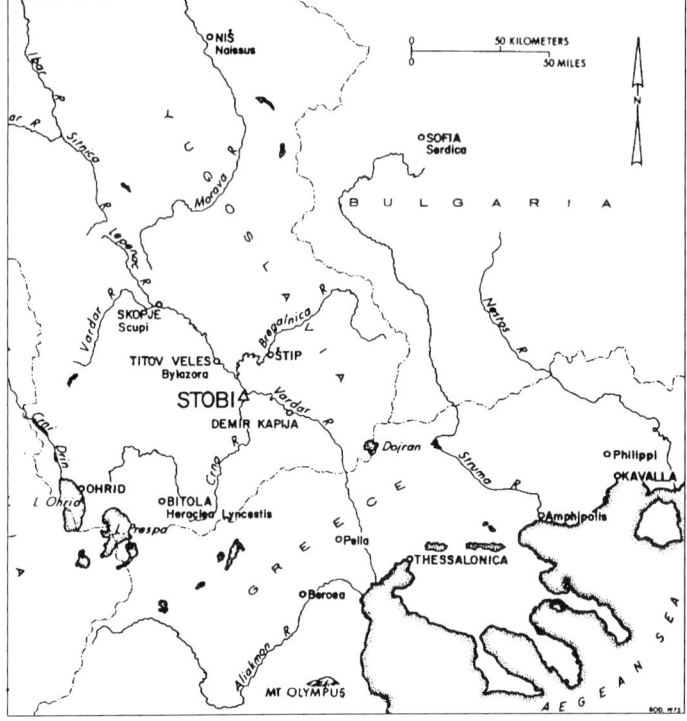

Figure 1a. Map showing the location of Stobi.

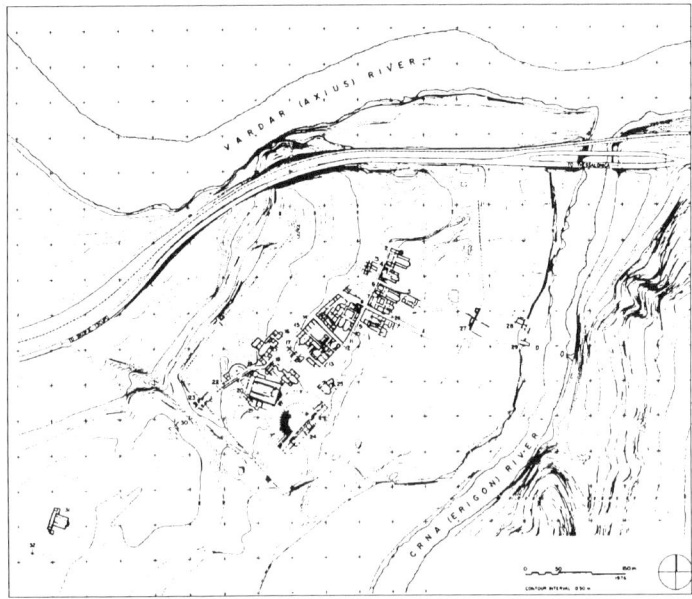

Figure 1b. City plan of Stobi.

for these changes at the end of the 3rd century or in the first years of the 4th is given by pottery beneath the floors of the final phase of the building. The case for an earthquake having struck the theatre rests largely on the considerable lateral movement of large marble blocks in the auditorium at the foot of the seats and in the retaining walls along the entrance corridors (Fig. 5). It is possible that natural settling of the subsoil caused the blocks to shift. On the other hand, Robert Folk, a geologist at the University of Texas, and Dusan Krcinovic, an engineer at the University of Illinois at Chicago, concluded that the sideways displacement of blocks, so massive and heavy, is best explained by the rippling motion of an earthquake. In the scene-building two exterior walls seem to have failed at about the same time and were rebuilt. Two interior walls that probably collapsed were not replaced because of changes in the plan. The builder took certain precautions that betray his concern for the integrity of the foundations belonging to earlier walls.

The Auditorium

At the foot of the seats next to the orchestra lay a passageway for spectators that was supported on a series of massive orthostates made of marble (Figs 4, 5). The third, fourth and thirteenth blocks from the W end have been shifted out of line from their original positions. When measured with respect to the blocks on either side, the amount of the shift is 0.10 to 0.13 m.

Marble blocks of such a size, *c*. 0.65 m thick, 0.97 m high, and up to 2 m long, would have needed considerable force to move them. Both above and below the orthostates, the crown and base courses were also shifted. At one place the movement left a gap of 0.26 m in the base

Figure 2. General view of the theatre at Stobi, looking N-W. Episcopal Basilica stands above and behind the theatre; River Vardar in background.

course (arrow in Fig. 5). No attempt appears to have been made to return the blocks to their original positions. Instead, the projecting portions of the orthostates and of the mouldings on the crown course were hacked off and the entire surface was painted. In the final phase the wall at the foot of the seats was heightened by the addition of a new wall built on top of the passageway. In Fig. 5 blocks that were shifted out of line before construction of the upper wall can be seen at the right side of the small doorway between the orthostates (arrow).

Another displacement of blocks in the same area of the auditorium occurs in the retaining wall along the western entrance passage. The lower end of this wall is seen at left in Fig. 5. The final block, triangular in shape, was shifted outward (toward the orchestra) for a distance of 0.23 m, and the three coping blocks above it slipped downwards. Considerable force would have been required to move a marble block of this size: 1.935 m long at the base, 0.79 m high (exclusive of the coping), and 0.49 m thick. In the comparable retaining wall along the eastern entrance passage, the one block that remains in the crown course is also shifted out of line.

Although the builder who repaired the theatre did not bother to replace the blocks, he does appear to have been concerned about the condition of the foundations supporting two major walls of the auditorium. When we excavated inside the western corridor beneath the seats (marked Radial Corridor 1 on Fig. 3; X in Fig. 7), we found that trenches at both sides of the passage had been dug through the floor (designated Floor 1 on the section in Fig. 6) to the level of the foundations for the walls lining the corridor. No alterations to the masonry took place, and it seems that the openings were made simply to inspect the condition of the footings. Some worry was apparently felt about their integrity at a time when the auditorium was undergoing repair. The trenches are contemporary with the rebuilding of walls in the scene-building (pottery in deposits 5 and 6, Fig. 6).

Scene-building

The E half of the rear wall of the scene-building and the E wall are not original with the building but were rebuilt at a later time. These walls were replaced without changing the plan of the building but with certain features that betray a concern for their strength. It is probable that the reconstruction followed a failure of the original walls. Pottery associated with the rebuilding places it in the same period as damage to the auditorium. Since that damage seems to have been caused by one or more earthquakes, it appears likely that the same shock(s) brought down walls in the scene-building. The plan in Fig. 7 shows the theatre after it was rebuilt and remodelled following the earthquake.

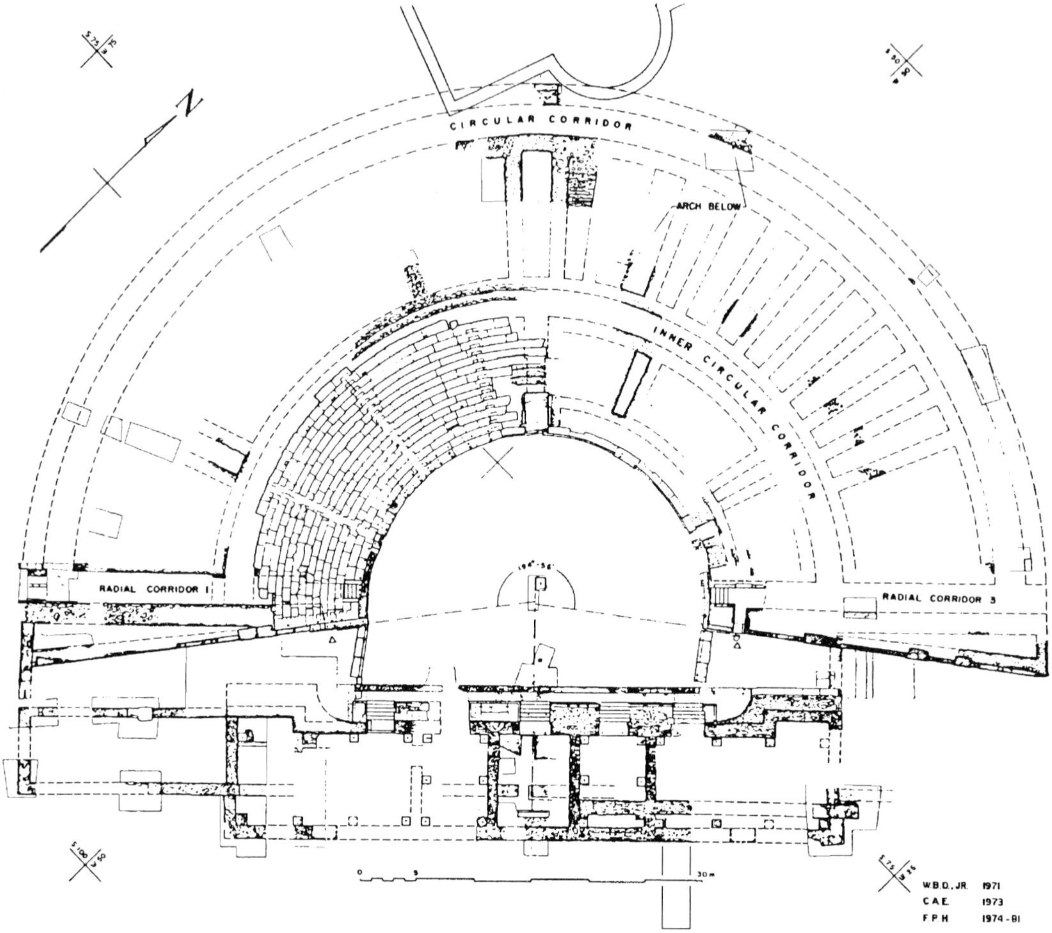

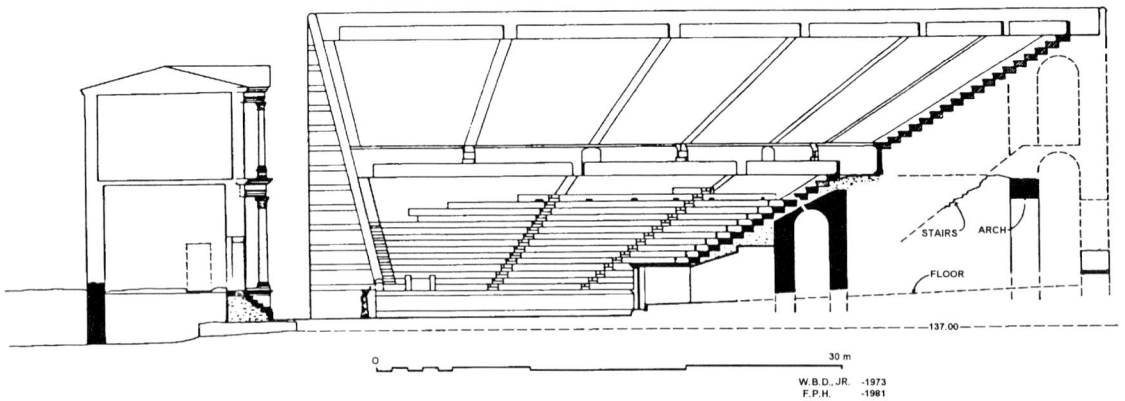

Figure 3. Actual state plan of the theatre.

Figure 4. Restored section of the theatre before the earthquake.

When the eastern half of the rear wall was replaced, the new portion (24.50 m long) was not built over the remains of the earlier wall but 1 m to the north of it, thus creating a jog in the line of the wall (Fig. 7). The relationship between the original rear wall and its replacement is clearly seen on the restored plan. This arrangement suggests that severe damage in the original wall caused the builders to worry lest its foundations were not sound. They did not want their new wall to be subject to failure due to hidden faults in the foundations, just as they were concerned about weakness in foundations along the western corridor in the auditorium. The thickness of the rear wall was increased (from 1.20 to 1.25 m), and it was bedded on foundations reaching over 2.50 m to bedrock. The S-E corner of the new scene-building was finished in a large buttress that, more than anything else, attests to the builder's concern about the ability of his structure to withstand future shocks (Figs 7, 8). The buttress, seen at the right of the arch in Fig. 8, extends 1.64 m beyond the end of the building. Although at present it stands only 0.96 m above ground level, it probably continued to the top of the wall.

An unusual feature of the new rear wall is the presence of two small arches carrying the wall across the foundations of previous walls that had been razed. The largest of these occurs at the corner, next to the buttress, where the rear wall crossed the original E wall of the building. The arch appears in Fig. 8 with the foundations of the first S-E corner in the foreground. The second arch is smaller. It is located at the jog in the rear wall (marked 'arch' on the restored plan in Fig. 7), where there was originally an interior cross wall (seen on the actual state plan, Fig. 3). In both places the builder appears to have thought it safer to use arches to span the earlier foundations than to rest the new wall on them. Similar arches are found in Early Christian churches

Figure 5. View of the auditorium and orchestra at the W side of the theatre. Western entrance passage at left. Arrows mark blocks that are out of alignment.

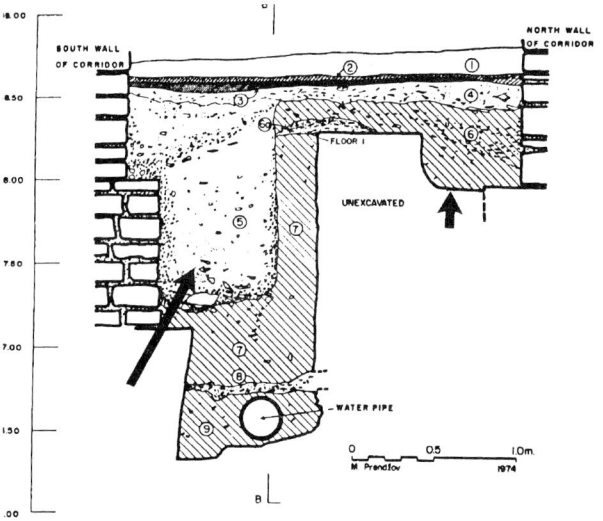

Figure 6. Section through the western corridor beneath the seats, looking W. At either side are inspection trenches (arrows) for the footing of the side walls. Trenches are filled by deposits 5 and 6 containing pottery of the late 3rd-early 4th century.

where a wall crosses a pre-existing tomb. The combination of the eastern arch and the buttress recalls in shape, though not in material, the 'flying' buttresses in the theatre at Corinth that were added to the eastern retaining wall of the auditorium after an earthquake (Williams & Zervos 1987, 23).

The eastern wall of the scene-building was also replaced, but the new wall appears to have been partially bedded on the foundations of the first one. The two walls are seen in section in Fig. 8, and it is apparent that

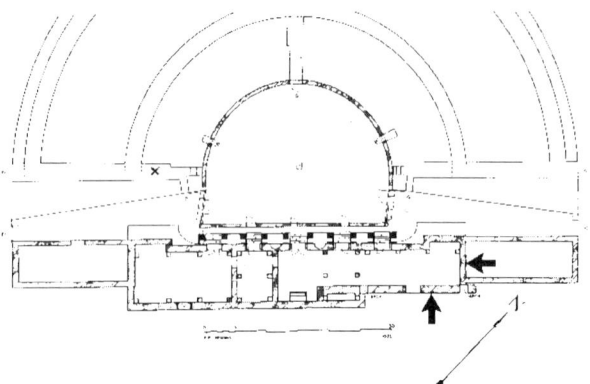

Figure 7. Restored plan of the theatre as it was rebuilt after the earthquake in *c*. AD 300. S-E and E walls of scene-building rebuilt (arrows). Note western corridor beneath the seats (X).

the later masonry (labelled 'E wall 3rd phase') was shifted about 0.30 m W of the line of its predecessor. Only the S end of the E wall has been excavated.

In the porches and colonnade of the facade signs of damage and repair are few. The absence of severe breaks or evidence of replacement among the 21 blocks remaining from the epistyle of the first storey (about 2/3 of the total) suggests that most, if not all, of that storey escaped serious injury (Fig. 4). From the epistyle of the second storey only eight blocks survive, and the majority of them are too fragmentary to show whether or not they were damaged prior to the final destruction. A capital of a style later than that seen in the capitals of the main floor was found at the W side of the orchestra. It may be a replacement piece for the second storey, although only its place of discovery associates it with the theatre. That the columns from the second storey might also be replacements is a possibility because of the darker colour of their marble and their slightly rougher finish in comparison with shafts from the first storey. On the other hand, the differences are not striking. The marble, though more heavily veined with gray and green, appears to have come from the same quarry as that used for the first storey.

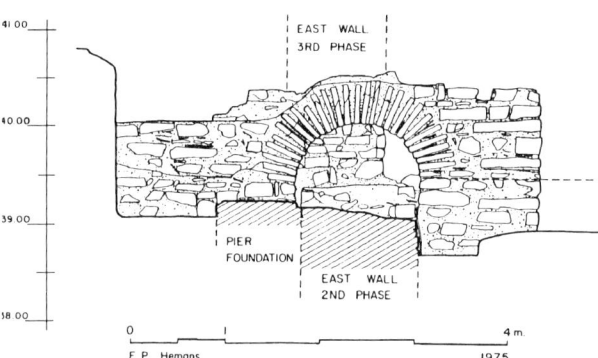

Figure 8. E end of rebuilt S wall of the scene-building with arch and buttress, looking N. Foundations for original E wall in foreground.

Summary

Changes to the scene-building that seem to have been made as a result of severe structural damage to the edifice are: (1) a new rear wall in the E half of the building; (2) a new E wall; (3) possible replacement of the second storey of the facade.

In the auditorium, large marble blocks were shifted from their original places, and trenches were opened inside a corridor to reveal the footings of two major walls. Deposits related to the repairs in both scene-building and auditorium contain similar pottery datable to the years around AD 300. It is thus likely that the damage was the product of a single or several disastrous shocks rather than general decay and subsidence over time. The identification of this event as an earthquake rests largely on the lateral displacement of massive blocks in the auditorium.

References

Gebhard, E.R. (1975). Protective Devices in Roman Theaters. In (J. Wiseman, Ed.) *Studies in the Antiquities of Stobi*. Beograd: Boston University and the National Museum of Titov Veles **II**, 43–6.

Gebhard, E.R. (1981a). The Theater at Stobi: A Summary. In (B Aleksova & J. Wiseman, Eds). *Studies in the Antiquities of Stobi*. Titov Veles: Macedonian Academy of Arts and Sciences and the National Museum of Titov Veles **III**, 13–27.

Gebhard, E.R. (1981b). The Scaenae-frons in the Theater at Stobi. In (B. Aleksova & J. Wiseman, Eds). *Studies in the Antiquities of Stobi*. Titov Veles: Macedonian Academy of Arts and Sciences and the National Museum of Titov Veles **III**, 197–201.

Gebhard, E.R. (forthcoming). *The Theater, Vol. 2 of Stobi: Results of the Joint Yugoslav-American Archaeological Investigations, 1970–1981* (J. Wiseman, Ed.). Princeton; Princeton University Press.

Saria, B. (1938). Das Theater von Stobi. *Jahrbuch des Deutschen Archaölogisches Instituts* **53**, 81–148.

Williams II, C.K. & Zervos, O.H. (1987). Corinth, 1986: Temple E and East of Theater. *Hesperia* **56**, 23–24.

Wiseman, J. (1984). History and Archaeology at Stobi. In (C. McClendon, Ed.) *Rome and the Provinces*, 567–582. New Haven; New Haven Society of the Archaeological Institute of America.

Earthquakes and Archaeological Context at 13th Century BC Tiryns

† Klaus Kilian[1]

Kommission für Algemeine und Verglichende Archäologie
Endenicher str., 41, 5300 Bonn 1, Germany

Abstract

Archaeological excavations indicate that the Mycenaean city of Tiryns suffered at least two catastrophes. The evidence consists of building remains with tilted and curved walls and foundations, as well as skeletons of people killed and buried by collapsed walls of houses. These destructions cannot be attributed to effects such as natural terrain shifts, but instead are more likely to be related to earthquakes datable to the end of Late Helladic IIIB1 and B2, concurrently with those that hit other Mycenaean centres as far as Macedonia and Troy. Changes in the style of building foundations can be regarded as a response to the earthquakes. The latter were not simply catastrophic events, but marked or made possible the reorganisation of settlements and changes in pottery style.

Introduction

One of an archaeologist's misfortunes is to find at his excavation certain findings for which science does not provide easy explanations. For instance, a common situation is for the excavator to bring to light remains of a house in which pottery objects are found destroyed beneath the collapsed walls, or remains of a house burnt with its remains covered by fallen walls and an ash layer. In both cases the available evidence simply permits one to conclude that a destruction marked the end of habitation in these houses. Our excavations of the Mycenaean site of Tiryns, however, brought to light destruction layers which can be assigned to earthquakes.

Evidence of earthquakes from observations of architectural remains

In a complex of rooms of the early LH III C period (*c*. 1190–1150 BC), outside the Acropolis in the Lower City (Unterburg), the walls of a building are not straight, but curved (Fig. 1). In a deeper stratum in the same house, a fireplace with sherds around it was found; the walls were also not rectilinear (Fig. 2). In both cases I think that the curvature of the walls is due to an earthquake, and not to foundation instability. In the Upper Acropolis, a perpendicular wall closing the opening of the Main Gate was again found curving, with the wall's component rocks thrown in front of it (Fig. 3). In a larger complex inside the Acropolis (Building X) the walls are not linear but curving, nor are they orthogonal where they meet (Fig. 4). The deformation of the walls in various directions, especially at the corners, is due to an earthquake. Building VI also provides evidence of earthquake destruction.

---

[1] This paper was prepared after the death of K. Kilian by S. Stiros in cooperation with Alkistis Papadimitriou. It is based on the amateur video recording of Kilian's presentation at the Meeting by A. Chasapis, his previous publications and the photographic archives of the Tiryns excavations in the German Archaeological Institute (DAI), Athens.

Figure 1. Room complex in the Lower City (Unterburg) of the early Late Helladic IIIC period. The walls are curved. German Archaeological Institute (DAI)–Athens, Tiryns photographic archives no. 76.5/42).

Figure 2. Same complex as in Fig. 1, but at a deeper level. The walls are again curved. German Archaeological Institute (DAI)–Athens, Tiryns photographic archives no. 76.5/15–16).

Figure 3. Main Gate of Upper Acropolis: the tranverse wall closing the Gate's opening is curved and collapsed. German Archaeological Institute (DAI)–Athens, Tiryns photographic archives no. 83.21/26).

Figure 4. Room complex inside the Acropolis. The walls are undulating and the corners are not at right angles. German Archaeological Institute (DAI)–Athens, Tiryns photographic archives no. 80.12/12–13).

Figure 5. Building VI, staircase corridor, view towards the S. The eastern wall is tilted downhill (westwards, to the left), while the western wall beyond the corridor is tilted uphill (eastwards). German Archaeological Institute (DAI)–Athens, Tiryns photographic archives no. 80.72/15–16).

Figure 6. Skeletons of a woman and child killed and buried by fallen walls of Building X. Compare with Fig. 4. German Archaeological Institute (DAI)–Athens, Tiryns photographic archives no. 80.9/67–68).

A high wall was transformed into a mass of rocks and only its foundations were preserved. S of the fallen rocks, the walls on the terrace and on the other side of the corridor are tilted downhill (westwards) and uphill (eastwards) respectively, that is in a direction opposite to that of a possible slope move-ment (Fig. 5). Such antithetic tilting of nearby walls is not the result of landslides but of seismic disturbances. Disturbed walls can be found in the remains of the Early Mycenaean and Middle Helladic periods at Tiryns as well.

The earthquakes also caused loss of human life. A skeleton was found beneath the fallen walls of an early LH IIIB house (*c.* 1300–1260 BC), before the period of the last palaces, while the skeletons of a woman and child buried by the walls of Building X (Fig. 6, cf. Fig. 4), belonging to the period of the last palaces, have also been brought to light. The excavation data lead us to the conclusion that the earthquakes identified in the Middle Helladic and Mycenaean periods were not a unique, but a frequently recurring event in the area. The period between such events was at least one year, possibly five, ten or even more. This result is based on the dating of the changes in pottery style (Kilian, 1980; 1982; 1983a, b; 1986; 1988a, b).

There is evidence that after the earthquakes, the Mycenaeans realized that good foundations were a factor in reducing the seismic vulnerability of their houses. A discussion of the various foundation types in Tiryns has been presented by the writer (Kilian, 1990). It is worth noting that only the upper social strata had the opportunity of improving their houses' foundations, but while good foundations may have prevented deformation of the walls, they did not prevent the walls from collapsing during strong earthquakes.

Walls deviating from a straight line have been excavated in the Palace of Pylos, while in the main workshop (NE building) of the same complex the corners of the foundations had opened by about 1.4 m (Blegen & Rawson, 1966). These are clear instances of the effect of earthquakes.

Discussion

On what evidence should an archaeologist decide whether traces of earthquakes can be recognized in an excavation? Certainly, there are no written sources confirming the occurrence of earthquakes in the Mycenaean period. However, comparative study of buildings that have been affected by earthquakes in the last 100–120 years supports our conclusions that the observed deformation of excavated buildings are of seismic origin. If the evidence of earthquakes is examined in the context of the development of pottery style, it can be concluded

Figure 7. Sites for which there is archaeological evidence of earthquakes at the end of LH IIIB1 (squares) and end of LH
    IIIB2 (circles). P Pylos, S Sparta, K Kastanas, T Troy. The cluster of sites corresponds to Mycenae, Tiryns and Midea.
    Based on Fig. 10 in Kilian (1988b).

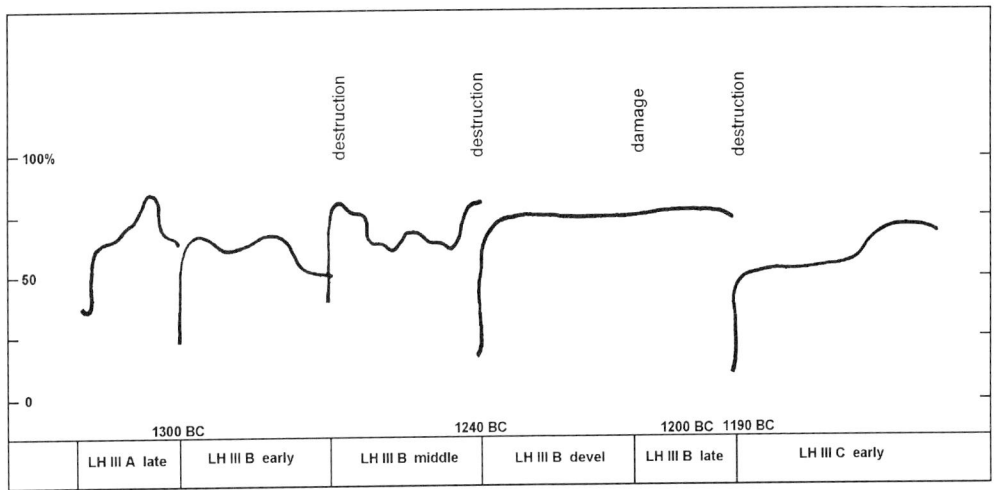

Figure 8. The floruit phases of Mycenaean painted pottery in LH IIIA late to LH IIIC early Tiryns in relation to building destructions (simplified after Kilian, 1988b).

that from the early palatial period (Late Helladic IIIA) earthquakes hit Tiryns as well as nearby and other settlements (Fig. 7; Kilian, 1980; 1983b; 1986; 1988b). It is important to note that the Mycenaean sites for which there is archaeological evidence of seismic activity coincide with areas that have been hit by earthquakes with a magnitude $M_s = 6.0$ or larger during the last two hundred years (IGME, 1989).

A final point is the consequence of earthquakes for the Mycenaean civilization. Fig. 8 shows the sequence of successive Mycenaean pottery styles in relation to the occurrence of earthquakes. This stylistic development is entirely based on stratigraphic data and is independent of any of the observations of seismic destruction discussed above. Earthquakes marked the beginning of a new phase and were related to, or even responsible for, changes in the organisation and planning of the site. We should not, therefore, simply regard Mycenaeans as earthquake victims. In the aftermath of an earthquake, a natural and necessary process of rebuilding and reorganisation took place.

References

Blegen, C. & Rawson, M. (1966). *The Palace of Nestor at Pylos in western Messenia. Vol. I: the Buildings and their contents*. University of Cincinnati, Princeton University Press.

IGME (Institute of Geology and Mineral Exploration) (1989). *Seismotectonic Map of Greece*, 1:500,000 scale. Athens.

Kilian, K. (1979). Ausgrabungen in Tiryns. *Archäologisches Anzeiger* **94**, 379–411.

Kilian, K. (1980). Zum Ende der mykenische Epoche in der Argolid. *Jahrbuch des Römisches-Germanischen Zentralmuseums Mainz* **27**, 166–195.

Kilian, K. (1982). Ausgrabungen in Tiryns 1980. Bericht zu den Grabunge*n. Archäologisches Anzeiger* **97**, 392–430.

Kilian, K. (1983a). Ausgrabungen in Tiryns 1981. Bericht zu den Grabungen. *Archäologisches Anzeiger* **98**, 277–328.

Kilian, K. (1983b). Civiltà micenea in Grecia: Nuovi aspetti storici ed interculturali. In *Magna Grecia e mondo miceneo, Atti del 22 convegno di studi sulla Magna Grecia, Taranto, 7–11 ottobre 1982*, 106–151. Taranto; Istituto per la storia.

Kilian, K. (1988a). Ausgrabungen in Tiryns 1982/3. Bericht zu den Grabungen. *Archäologisches Anzeiger* **103**, 106–151.

Kilian, K. (1988b). Mycenaeans up to date, trends and changes in recent research. In (E. B. French & K. A. Wardle, Eds) *Problems in Greek Prehistory*, 115–152. Bristol Classical Press.

Kilian, K. (1990). Mykenische Fundamentierungsweisen in Tiryns. In *L' Habitat Egéen Préhistorique*. Bull. Corresp. Hellénique, Supp. 19, 95–113. Paris.

Seismic Damage to the Monuments
of the Athenian Acropolis

Manolis Korres

A' Ephorate of Prehistoric and Classical Antiquities
Makriyianni 2–4, Athens 117 42, Greece

Abstract

Earthquakes have contributed much to the present-day ruinous state of the monuments on the Acropolis of Athens, and have caused distortions to their columns and walls. The study of these distortions has provided precious information on the seismic history of the area. At least one earthquake affected the Parthenon during the pre-Christian period; a large-scale distortion, which has been attributed in the past to the 1687 explosion, was associated with a large earthquake that occurred before the 12th or 13th century, while the collapse of a part of the retaining wall was caused by a shock in 1705. Some distortions of the Acropolis monuments, however, usually attributed to earthquakes, are the result of collision of fallen parts of the roof or the settling of foundations.

Introduction

The Acropolis monuments have suffered a great deal of damage over the centuries, chiefly due to human interventions, the most visible of which have been fire, bombardment and explosions, or systematic demolition to acquire and reuse building material from the monuments. Damage from natural causes is likewise evident, and has been caused by physico-chemical reactions due, amongst other things, to acid rain and certain micro-organisms. Natural damage, however, has also occurred due to mechanical forces, mostly by tensions inherent within the structures, by ground surface or foundation anomalies, and of course by seismic activity (for the **Parthenon**, see Michaelis 1871, 45–68; Travlos 1973, 218–236; Dinsmoor 1974, 132–155; Orlandos 1978, 464–470; Pavan 1983, 27–29, 169–176; Korres *et al*. 1989, 53–54, 64–65; Korres 1990, 17–44, 47–59; for the **Erechtheum**, see Paton *et al*. 1927, 478–581; for the **Propylaea**, see Tanoulas 1987, 413–483).

Earthquake damage is especially interesting for many and varied reasons. One need only point to the fact that it can provide us with the most exact material evidence not only for the seismic history of the monuments themselves, but also for that of Attica as a whole. It should also be noted that this damage provides an opportunity for gleaning much information, qualitative and quantitative, that can serve as a control in theoretical studies on the monuments' general seismic behaviour. This control is of exceptional value since it has not been possible until today to arrive at a really satisfactory in-depth understanding of the actual events, since research was confined to calculations and experimental data. There is no need to stress the utility of a programme that would examine the mechanical distortion of the monuments and of the ground on which they rest, recognise and record every measurable geometric movement, systematically classify all the information gathered, and finally conduct a documented study of the observations. Without such an understanding of the evidence to act as a basis for research, any interpretation of the data may be misleading.

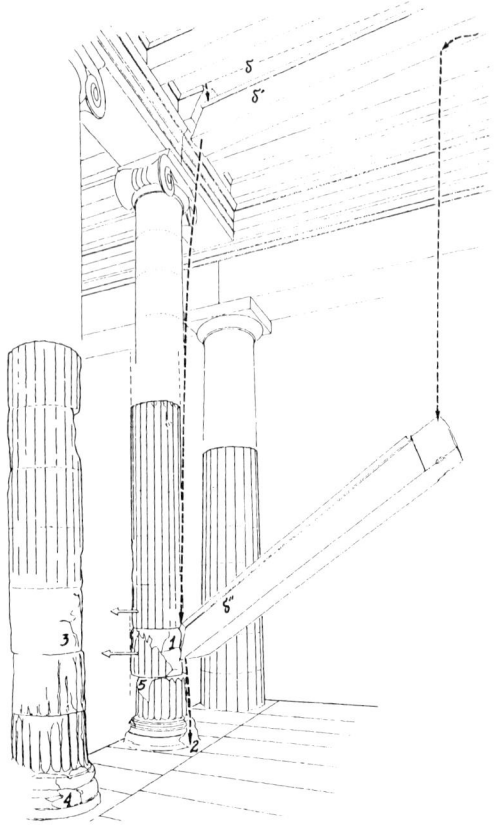

Figure 1. Our explanation for the distortion of the Propylaea columns. During the 1640 explosion, a 9-10 ton marble beam of the roof fell and hit two of the columns, causing a lateral offset (its direction is marked with arrows) and shattering of the marble (points 1 and 4). The itinerary of the beam is marked with dotted lines and arrows. Note that such drum offsets are usually attributed to rocking caused by earthquakes.

Pitfalls in the interpretation of distortions of monuments

Structural distortions of parts of the Acropolis monuments which in reality were the result of explosions may very easily be wrongly attributed to seismic activity. On the other hand, damage caused by contraction and expansion due to temperature fluctuations, observable at various points on the Parthenon, or by foundations settlement (e.g. at a few sections of the N wall running beside the Erechtheum, or in the Pinakotheke in the Propylaea) has likewise been misinterpreted as the result of explosions.

A good example is also provided by the westernmost column of the N inner colonnade of the Propylaea, where the column shaft has been displaced from the second drum upwards. This has often been attributed to the effects of an earthquake, as the writer has heard on at least one occasion at this conference. Careful observations, however, confirm that the column's pronounced displacement by 10 cm to the S was due to a forceful collision hitting the shaft from the N at the height of the second drum (Fig. 1). This drum presents a larger (14 cm) dislocation than the others, and a large section of it has been shattered and fallen away (point 1 on Fig. 1).

Although in most cases such drum offsets result from the rocking of columns caused by earthquakes, we suggest that the only satisfactory explanation is that this jolt at the Propylaea occurred during the collapse of one of the marble ceiling beams weighing 9–10 tons during the catastrophic explosion of the roof of the central wing of the Propylaea, dated to 1640 (see Tanoulas, 1987). The falling beam also caused part of the column base to shatter (point 2 in Fig. 1). Similar damage on a much smaller scale is discernible on the next column to the E (points 3 and 4 in Fig. 1).

This example also illustrates the difference between primary and secondary damage: the former is caused directly by the rocking of the columns themselves during earthquakes, while the secondary damage, which may be more important, is due to the collision of other moving (usually free-falling) structural elements with the columns.

Modelling Seismic Distortions of Ancient Monuments

During the restoration and stabilization works at the Acropolis, some hypotheses concerning the seismic behaviour of ancient monuments have been formulated, especially concerning the relationship between parameters of earthquakes and distortions in the structural members of ancient monuments.

This became possible because the area of Athens is not frequently affected by major shocks, the last one occurring in 1981 during our study period. Also, since the studied monuments are characterized by a large number of columns perfectly uniform and similar in their behaviour, and they were constructed with great accuracy and suffered limited distortion, observations on dislocations could be made with a precision of a tenth of a millimetre.

A first hypothesis concerns the magnitude of events causing distortions to the Parthenon. During the last 100 years, several earthquakes have hit Athens, but only that of 1981 of $M_s = 6.7$ at an epicentral distance of around 70 km from Athens caused a dislocation less than one centimetre of the corner columns of the E side of the monument. Five hours later, the major aftershock of the seismic sequence (with $M_s = 6.4$ at an epicentral distance of around 40 km from Athens) caused not the slightest shifting in the Parthenon. It is therefore likely that observed dislocations are associated with large, yet rare shocks that have hit Athens.

A second hypothesis is that despite the random nature of the dislocation of the individual blocks, the resultant dislocation of parts (columns, walls, etc.) caused by a specific earthquake is in the direction of the propagation of the seismic waves. As is analysed in the following paragraph, the dislocations of the Parthenon are in E-W and N-S directions, probably indicative of shocks originating from epicentres to the W (Corinth area) and N (Oropos area) of Athens. Thus, the small dislocations of the drums of the Parthenon columns, discussed below, which probably constitute the most important archive for the seismic history of the area, may also provide information on the seismic sources as well.

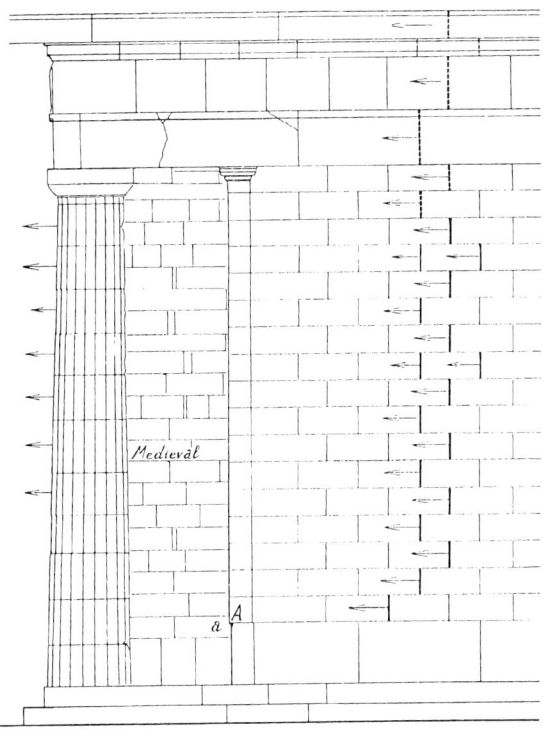

Figure 2. Dislocation of the western part of the S wall and columns of the Parthenon to the W, by about 2 cm (projection on an E-W vertical plane). Arrows indicate direction of movements, solid lines opened joints. Note that the lowermost course of blocks did not move. This dislocation was attributed to the 1687 explosion that ruined the temple. Our observations, however, revealed that this predates the addition of the Medieval wall, which is adjusted to the distorted shape of the wall of the cella (points a and A) and must be attributed to an earthquake that occurred before the 12th or 13th century.

Dislocations of Parts of the Parthenon

Our observations on the dislocations of the Parthenon are summarized as follows:

a) Dislocation of a large part of the E facade by 2.5 cm to the N. This occurred during antiquity, since repair attempts were executed with Classical building methods which are observable at various points on the displaced section. The similarity of the techniques applied in one of these repairs to those used in undamaged parts of the original building led us to conclude that the dislocation had been the result of the earthquake of 426 BC

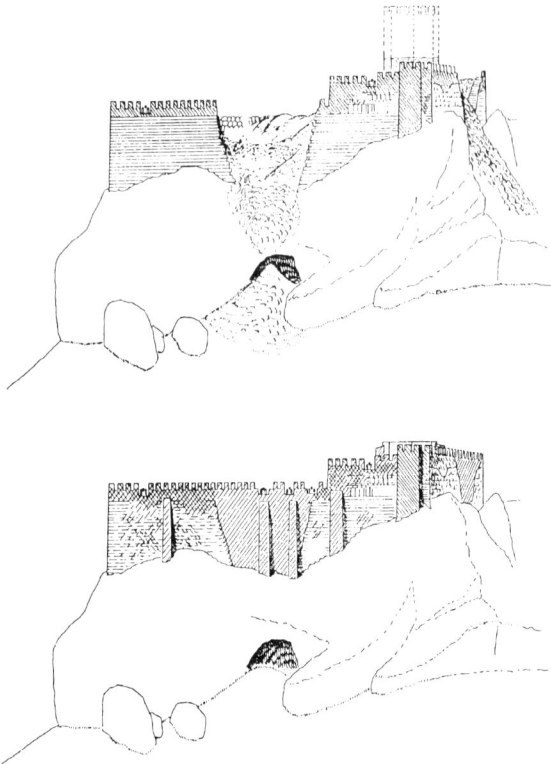

Figure 3. Above: Debris from the walls and the filling of the terrace of the Classical period, produced by the partial collapse of parts of the retaining walls of Acropolis in late 17th to early 18th century fell downhill and covered the mid-Byzantine and later strata.

Below: The situation in 1982, with most debris cleared and the walls repaired (walls with a different shading). Historical evidence suggests that this destruction is associated with an earthquake dated 1705. Dark shading indicates a cave.

(Korres & Bouras, 1983). Our more recent observations, however, made possible only during our recent intervention in this part of the temple, led us to the conclusion that the signs of damage do not all stem from the same period, and consequently the largest of these dislocations could have been caused by some other earthquake during the pre-Christian period.

b) Dislocation of a large part of the W facade by 2 cm to the N which is in general similar to that on the E facade and thus probably occurred at the same time.

c) Dislocation of the W wall and the western part of the N and S wall by 2 cm to the W, causing an opening of the joints of the N and S walls at a distance of 4 m from their W terminals. It occurred from the first block course upwards, while the orthostates remained in their place (Fig. 2). As a consequence, the corner columns of the W porch were also deformed.

In the past, it was believed that the important dislocation of the walls outwards could only have been due to the well-known gunpowder explosion of 1687 during the second Ottoman-Venetian war which ruined the building. However, the westward dislocation of the W part of the cella was not caused by this explosion, but is much older. This is evident from the manner in which the medieval staircase abuts onto the S-W corner of the cella (Fig. 2). The blocks filling in the gap between the column and the wall are accurately adjusted to the shape of the dislocated wall and column. This is especially clear at the point where the second course of the staircase blocks meets the undisplaced lower part (orthostate) and the displaced upper part of the W wall. The easternmost block of the stairway course (a in Fig. 2) has a kink carved into it which fits the corresponding irregular shape of the W edge of the original S wall (Fig. 2, point A).

Systematic examination of the material used for the staircase proved that it comes from the disassembly of a large part of the Philopappos monument, while a few blocks from the E wall of the Pinakotheke of the Propylaea were used as a complement. On the basis of this last piece of evidence, but also of the mortar used at the joints, the previous theory dating the stairway to the 12th century should now be reconsidered in favour of a 13th century date. Thus the large dislocation of the W part of the cella should be dated to before the 13th century, and consequently predates the introduction of explosives to Europe.

The scale of destruction testifies to the magnitude of the seismic shock that has evidently caused it. For eight or more centuries, the intensity of this shock seems to have remained unsurpassed, given that the damage caused to the W part of the temple was greater by far than that caused to the same part even by the 1687 explosion. This constitutes a most important material testimony for an earthquake prior to the 13th century, possibly the most destructive of all those that struck Athens since the Parthenon's construction. In all probability, it may have had its epicentre in W Attica or the Corinthian gulf.

The Collapse of the E Retaining Wall of the Acropolis

Another interesting testimony of a possible earthquake comes from the E wall of the Acropolis (Fig. 3). During excavations in 1982, it was ascertained that the surface of the S slope was covered with quite a characteristic succession of layers, of which the uppermost had resulted from debris thrown down during the early archaeological excavations on the Acropolis that started in 1840. Below this layer there was a palaeosol horizon, and immediately below, a thick layer consisting only of material from the Classical period, mostly large quantities of chips of hewn poros stone blocks, marble and rock from the Acropolis. This layer also included a few dozen large rectangular blocks which had the same inclination with the layer and the slope in general, and capped layers of the mid-Byzantine or more recent periods.

The most reasonable explanation is that the layer containing material and blocks of the Classical period results from the collapse and downthrow of a part of the wall and the fill behind it. This interpretation is supported by observations of the present condition of the wall's middle section, especially with its visible inner face. The latter consists of more recent, sturdy, roughly hewn limestone blocks, while none of the original large rectangular blocks is *in situ*.

At what date, however, did the ancient wall collapse and when were the appropriate repairs made? In 1982, when the excavations had reached some depth, it was ascertained that the layer immediately under that consisting of material of the Classical period reaches chronologically to the mid-Byzantine period and more recent times. Furthermore, the comparison of a 1898 plan of the Acropolis from 1687 drawn by Verneda (Omont, 1898, Fig. 42a, redrawn by Fanelli) with one of 1753 by J. Stuart (Stuart & Revett, 1787) shows that the collapse occurred between these two dates.

Although the Venetians, obliged to retreat from the Acropolis in 1688, had probably examined the possibility of sacking parts its walls, there is no indication that they have done so. The partial collapse of the walls must therefore be assigned to natural effects, most likely to an earthquake, since there is some historical evidence for that. Certain testimonies from Greek sources refer to an earthquake which affected the Acropolis fortifications at the beginning of the 18th century. According to Kambouroglou (1889, 60–67), based on a chronicle known as the *Anargyria phylla*, this earthquake took place in 1701 (see also Korres, 1990). Recent archival research of Turkish sources by Ambraseys & Finkel (1992) confirms the older testimonies and has uncovered the earthquakes's real date: 1705 (see also Ambraseys, this volume).

The investigation of the seismic damage to the E wall is presented here as a good example of the fruitful interaction of archaeological observations and historical accounts.

Acknowledgements
I would like to express my thanks to David Turner for the translation of the Greek text.

References
Ambraseys, N. & Finkel, C. (1992). The seismicity of the Eastern Mediterranean during the turn of the eighteenth century. *Istanbuler Mitteilungen des Deutsches Archaeologisches Instituts* **42**, 323–343.

Dinsmoor, D. (1934) The repair of the Athena Parthenos: a story of five dowels. *American Journal of Archaeology* **38**, 93–106.

Dinsmoor, W.B. Jr. (1974). New fragments of the Parthenon in the Athenian Agora. *Hesperia* **43**, 132–155.

Kambouroglou, D. (1889). *History of Athens*. Athens; A. Papageorgiou. (In Greek).

Korres, M. (1990). *Die Explosion des Parthenon*. Berlin; Antikenmuseum.

Korres, M. & Bouras, C. (1983). *Study for the Restoration of the Parthenon*, 658. Athens; Ministry of Culture. (In Greek).

Korres, M., Toganidis, N., Zambas, K., Skoulikidis, T., Theoulakos, P., Kouzelis, K., Belogiannis, N., Papakonstantinou, E., Charalambous, D., Doganis, I. & Moraitou, A. (1989). *Study for the Restoration of the Parthenon* **IIa**. Athens; Ministry of Culture. (In Greek).

Michaelis, A. (1871). *Der Parthenon*. Leipzig; Druck und Verlag Von Breitkopf und Härtel.

Omont, H. (1898). *Athènes au 17e siècle*. Paris.

Orlandos, A. (1978). *The Architecture of the Parthenon*, 3 vols. Archaeologiki Etaireia No 86, Athens. (In Greek).

Pavan, M. (1983). *L'Aventura del Partènone*. Firenze.

Paton, J. (Ed.) (1927). *The Erechtheium*. American School of Classical Studies, 2 vols. Cambridge, Mass.; Harvard Univ. Press.

Stuart, J. & Revett, N. (1787). *The Antiquities of Athens*, 2 vols. London; E. Stuart.

Tanoulas, T. (1987). The Propylaea of the Acropolis at Athens since the seventeenth century: their decay and restoration. *Jahrbuch des Deutsches Archaeologisches Instituts in Athen* **102**, 413–483.

Travlos, J. (1973). The burning of the Parthenon by Heruli and its repairs in emperor Julian's times. *Archaeologiki Ephemeris*, 218–236. (In Greek).

And the Walls Came Tumbling Down: Earthquake History in the Holyland

Amos Nur[a] & Hagai Ron[b]

[a] Geophysics Department, Stanford University, Stanford, CA 94305-2215, USA
[b] Institute for Petroleum Research & Geophysics (IPRG) PO Box 2286, Holon, Israel

Abstract

Geophysical, archaeological, and historical evidence, including biblical writings provide a unique history of earthquakes in the Holyland, going back 2000 years and more. These earthquakes are associated with the Dead Sea fault — the boundary between the African and Arabian plates. Specific earthquakes, with important historical, archaeological and biblical evidence happened in 1927, 1546, 749, 363, 31 BC and 760 BC. It is likely that Jericho's conquest by Joshua also involved an earthquake, as well as the catastrophe of Sodom and Gomorrah. Fallen columns and crushed skeletons provide unique proof for the occurrence of these earthquakes. The clear relation between damage and seismogenic faults in this relatively simple area may be used to unravel the archaeological earthquake evidence in more complex areas such as in western Turkey or Greece.

Earthquakes and tectonics

On July 11, 1927, a strong earthquake shook the town of Jericho in the Holyland, causing cracks and fissures in buildings and the ground, and great panic among its people. The shaking was not confined to Jericho itself: many cities and villages in Judea, Samaria, and Galilee suffered as well. The earthquake was large enough to be recorded at seismological stations then in existence in Europe, S Africa, N America, and the USSR (Ben-Menahem *et al.*, 1976). Although these records were few, they were sufficient to provide accurate arrival times for the compressional waves generated by the earthquake. From these, seismologists could determine the quake's epicentre — the point at which the earthquake rupture motion began — its time of origin and its magnitude. The epicenter was next to the River Jordan about 15 km N of Jericho, under the plain which extends N of the Dead Sea (Fig. 1). The amplitude of the recorded seismic waves indicated an earthquake of about 6.5 on the Richter scale.

The 1927 earthquake at Jericho was followed by a series of aftershocks, many of which were also strong enough for their epicentres to be located. These aftershocks cluster along a line through the origin of the main shock and continue S into the Dead Sea, suggesting that the fault runs approximately from N to S within the trough of the River Jordan (Freund *et al.*, 1970; Garfunkel, 1981; Nur & Reches, 1979; Salamon *et al.*, 1991). Analysis of the seismic records using modern methods has confirmed this hypothesis and specified further details of the motion across the fault: the land mass on the E side moved N, whereas the land mass on the W moved S during the earthquakes by perhaps as much as 50 cm.

This result fits other information supplied by geologists and geophysicists (Garfunkel *et al.*, 1981; Joffe & Garfunkel, 1987); the Jordan rift, together with the Gulf of Eilat to the S and the Bekkaa region to the N, forms the boundary between the Arabian plate to the E, and the African-Sinai plate to the W (Fig. 2). According to the theory of plate tectonics, which describes movements of plates of the earth's crust, Arabia is moving N

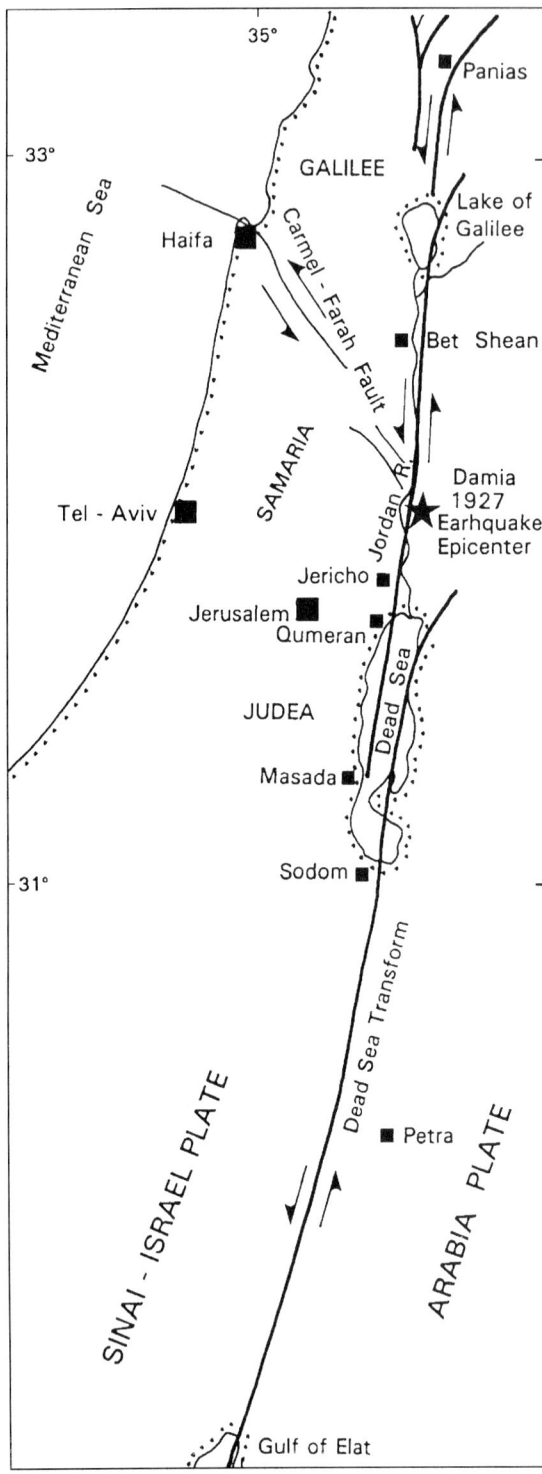

Figure 1. Location Map.

as the Red Sea opens in the S, and is colliding with Asia to produce the Zagros mountain belt in Iran. The Arabian plate moves northward relative to the African-Sinai plate at 0.5 to 1 cm per year. The 1927 earthquake is the only sizable event along this fault which has been recorded on instruments. It was only moderate in size and cannot alone be said to represent the long-term pattern of fault motion that plate tectonics predicts. But from this area we also have historical, biblical and archaeological evidence (Amiran, 1952; Russell, 1980, 1985; Degg, 1990; Ben-Menahem, 1979; Ambraseys & Barazangi, 1989). Unlike any other place on earth, the historical record here extends back about ten thousand years. By comparing this record with the effects of the modern earthquake, we may infer a great deal about seismic activity in the Jericho region (Karcz & Kafri, 1978; Willis, 1928; Arieh & Turcotte, 1988; Ben-Menahem et al., 1977).

An attentive observer can easily follow the Jericho fault along the Jordan plain (Reches et al., 1981). For example, it disrupts the flat sediments, and there is a line of springs along it. During the 1927 earthquake, the ground cracked in several places and water poured out; this phenomenon, caused by soil liquefaction, is common in earthquakes elsewhere. The pressure changes underground can change a wet, yet coherent soil or mud into a fluid that flows and can burst out onto the surface during the quake. In other cases, the water squeezes out of the soil as springs.

Past earthquakes

During the 1927 quake, chunks of mud slid into the River Jordan near Damiya, about 40 km N of Jericho, temporarily reducing its flow (Ben-Menahem et al., 1976). The quake and its associated phenomena destroyed numerous buildings in Jericho and caused lesser damage that was remarkably similar to the damage inferred from historical descriptions of past earthquakes. There have been about 30 earthquakes with a similar destruction pattern in this area during the past 2000 years or so.

Very important evidence for some of these earthquakes is found in historical writings, and archaeological excavations. In this respect two significant earthquakes are the AD 363 and the AD 749 events:

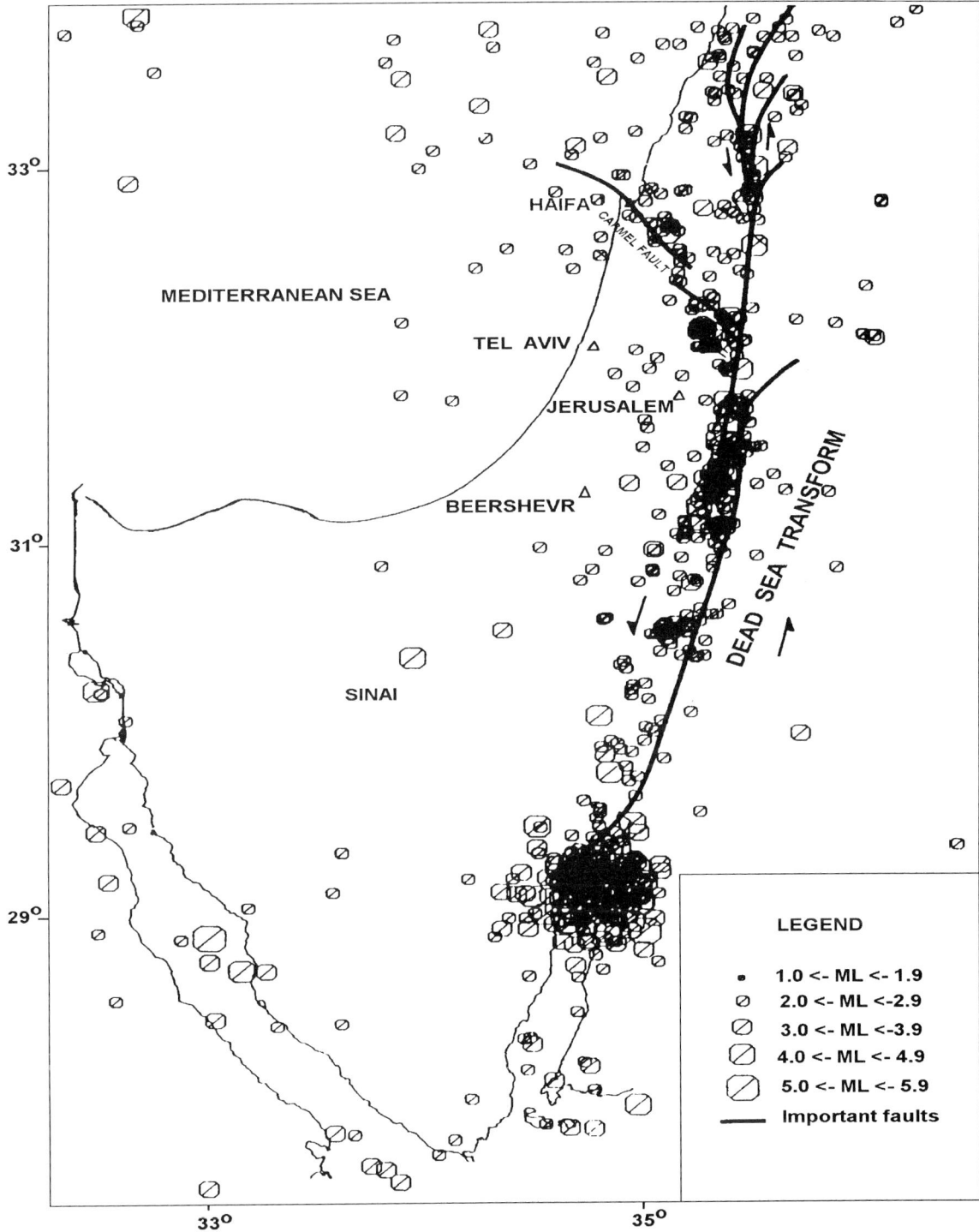

Figure 2. Recent seismicity of Israel, obtained from the IPRG networks.

Figure 3. The excavated main street of Bet Shean.

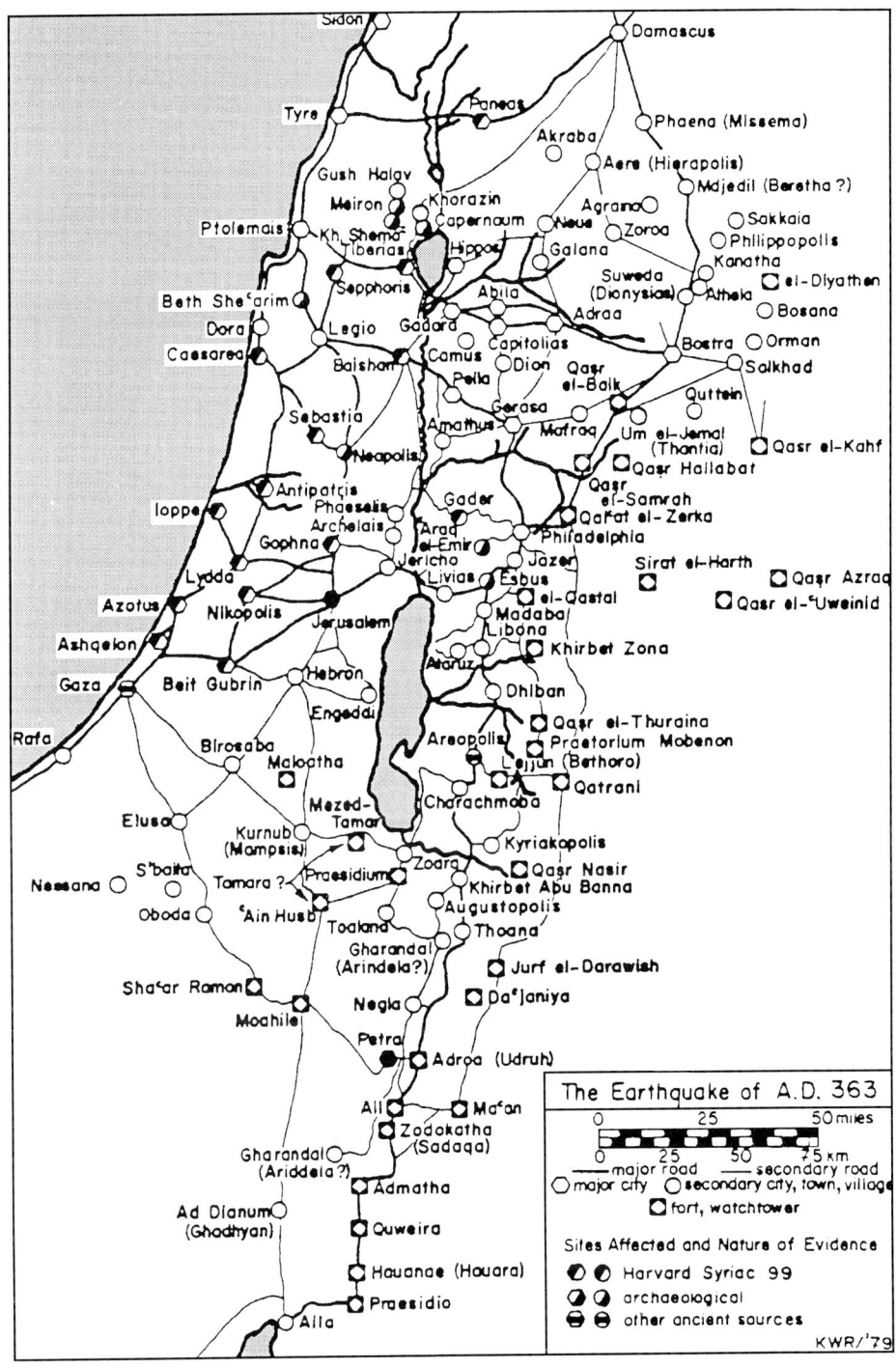

Figure 4. Russell's (1980) map of sites affected by the AD 363 earthquake, severe damage was found from Petra in the
S to Banias in the N, a distance of 350 km or so.

a) Kh. Shema

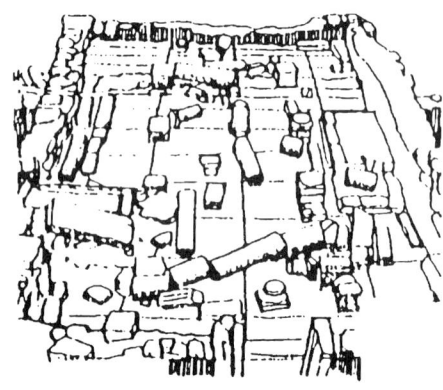

b) Qasrin Synagogue

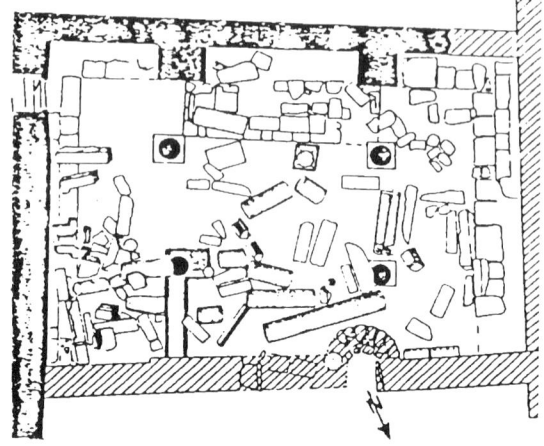

c) En - Nabratên

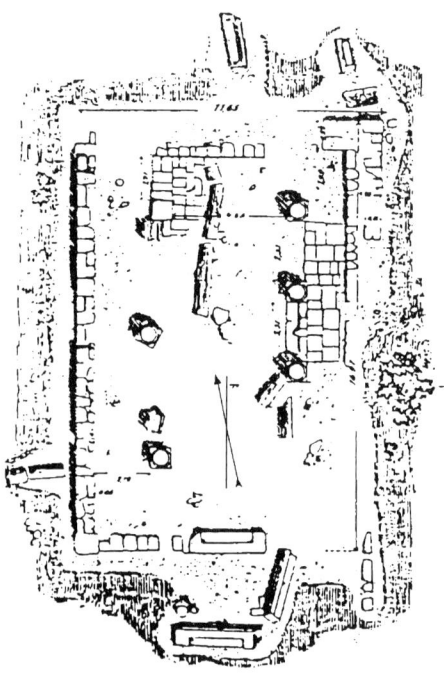

d) Kefr Bir'im

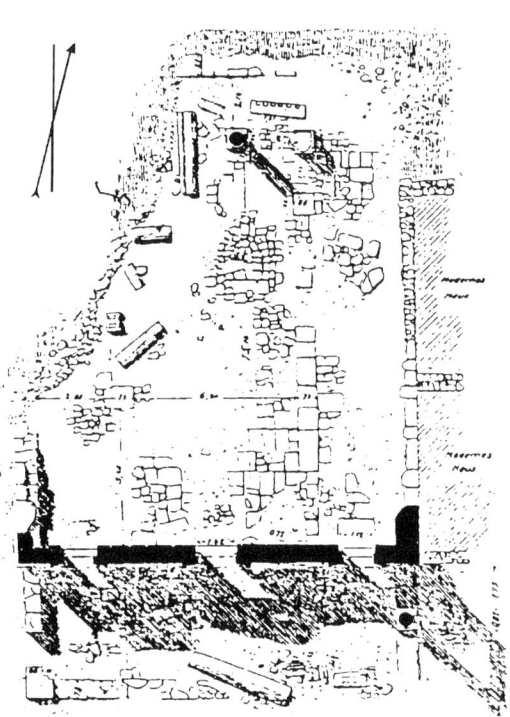

Figure 5. Spectacular examples of excavated synagogues destroyed by either the AD 363 or AD 749 earthquake. The systematic directions in which their columns collapsed is one focus of the proposed project: (a) Kh. Shema (Myers *et al.*, 1976); (b) Qasrin (Macoz & Killbrew, 1988); (c) En - Nabratên (Kohl & Watzinger, 1916); and (d) Kefr Bir'im, K., (Kohl & Watzinger, 1916).

the ancient Roman, Byzantine and Arab city of Bet Shean (Scitopolis) was destroyed by the AD 749 earthquake (Tzafrir & Foerester 1989), with its collapsed main street (Fig. 3) which remained untouched until it was excavated only in the past few years. This earthquake destroyed or damaged many other sites along the Dead Sea fault, with the magnitude estimated at 7 or more.

The AD 363 earthquake also destroyed Bet Shean, which was a Roman city at the time. Archaeological evidence reveals that the Byzantine builders used many of the Roman stones and columns as foundations and general building material for their reconstruction of Bet Shean. The damage of the AD 363 earthquake extended 300 km from Petra in the S to Panias in the N (Russell, 1980) (Fig. 4), suggesting an unusually large magnitude. This earthquake also destroyed dozens of synagogues in Galilee (Macoz & Killebrew, 1988; Meyers *et al.*, 1990; Meyers *et al.*, 1976; Nur *et al.*, 1989; Kohl & Watzinger 1916, 610). Because of their common columnar design, and geographical orientation, it is possible to infer from the direction in which these columns fell, the ground motion during this earthquake (Fig. 5). In most of the investigated sites which are W of the Dead Sea fault, columns fell northwesterly, whereas in sites E of the fault, columns fell southwesterly. Assuming that these more or less free-standing columns fell in a direction opposite to the initial horizontal strong ground motion, the directions may yield in the future the direction of fault rupture propagation. The most conclusive archaeological evidence for these two historical earthquakes are skeletons of people trapped and killed by collapsed structures. For the AD 749 event, skeletons were found both in Bet Shean and in the Hisham Palace near Jericho, as shown in Fig. 6.

The awesome fortification of Masada in the Judean desert which towers over the Dead Sea served as the last Jewish stronghold against the Roman armies until AD 73, when its 960 inhabitants committed mass suicide after surviving a prolonged siege. The conquering Roman army breached the citadel, but an earthquake along the Jericho fault, perhaps the one in 363, may have been responsible for the final destruction of Masada. The ruins show that the storehouse walls of Masada apparently collapsed as a single unit, as would be caused by an earthquake, rather than people.

In 31 BC, a major upheaval on the Jericho fault destroyed the town of Qumran, where the Dead Sea scrolls were found a few decades ago. A remarkable and detailed description of this event appears in the writing of the Jewish historian Josephus:

'At this time it was that the fight happened at Actium between Octavius Caesar and Anthony in the seventh year of the reign of Herod and it was also that there was an earthquake in Judea, such a one as has not happened at any other time and which earthquake brought a great destruction to the cattle in that country. About 10,000 men also perished by the fall of houses, but the army which lodged in the field recorded no damage by this sad accident' (Josephus Flavius; *Antiquities of the Jews*, Book XV, Chapter 5, Verse 2).

The earthquake destroyed the building and ruptured the water system of Qumran, which probably forced the inhabitants to abandon the town for several decades. The 2,000 year-old fault rupture in the stairs of the cistern, unearthed by archaeologists some years ago, appears as fresh as if it had happened yesterday.

Going further back in time, the Bible records Zechariah's prophecy, based upon the description of a large earthquake which occurred during the reign of King Uzziah around 760 BC:

'...and the Mount of Olives shall cleave in the midst thereof toward the E and toward the W, and there shall be a very great valley; and half of the mountain shall remove toward the N, and half of it toward the S. And ye shall flee...like as ye fled from before the earthquake in the days of Uzziah King of Judah' (Zechariah, Chapter 14, Verse 4–5).

This earthquake happened probably somewhere E of Jerusalem, most likely along the Jericho fault. Apparently, the offset of the rocks across it was great enough to reveal the northward slip of the eastern side relative to the southward slip of the western side. This motion is remarkably similar to the motion observed in the 1927 Jericho earthquake, and is, of course, consistent with the N-S movement of the plates in this area.

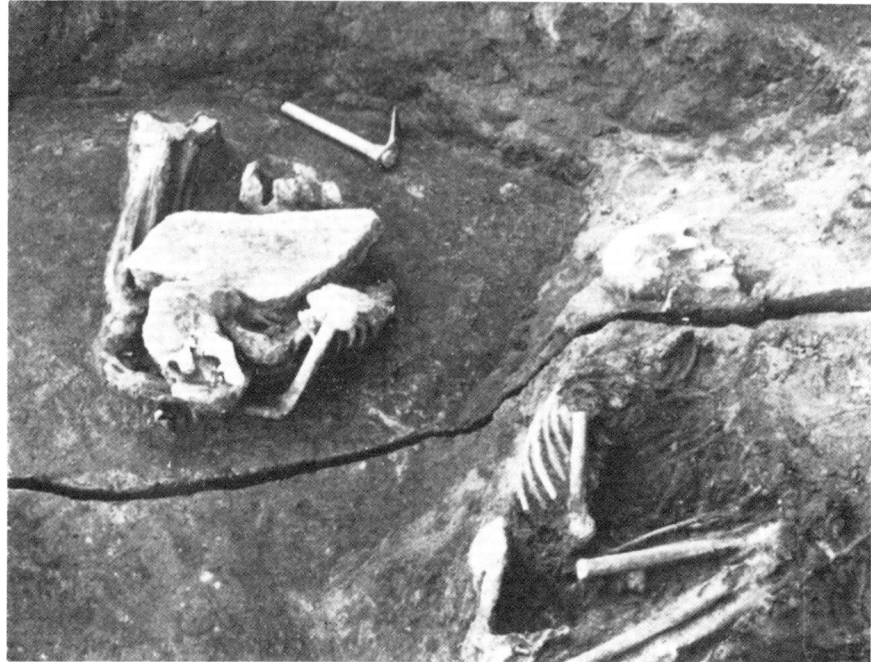

a.

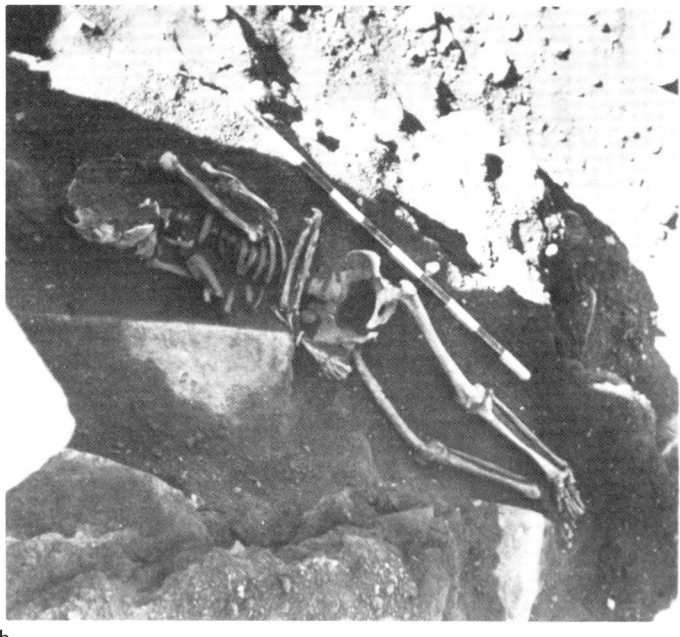

b.

Figure 6. Skeletons of (a) two people destroyed by a major earthquake in Jericho *c.* 1400 BC (Garstang & Garstang, 1940), and (b) a person destroyed by the AD 749 earthquake at Kh. Mafjar near Jericho (Photographic Collection, Rockefeller Museum, Jerusalem, Israel).

Joshua's Jericho and Sodom and Gomorrah

Earlier, around 1020 BC, an earthquake hit Judea during the battle waged by King Saul and his son Jonathan against the Philistines at Michmas. But the biblical accounts of two even older, and simultaneous events strongly suggest ancient quakes: the crossing of the Jordan by the Israelites and the collapse of the walls of Jericho at the time of Joshua's siege around 1000 BC. There is little doubt that the walls of this city have collapsed in earthquakes several times in its 10,000-year history. It is very likely that an earthquake caused their collapse also during the siege by Joshua's army, especially because the flow in the River Jordan was cut off at that time. This is recorded in the Book of Joshua:

'and as they that bare the ark were come unto Jordan, and the feet of the priests that bare the ark were dipped in the brim of the water (for Jordan overfloweth all his banks all the time of harvest), that the waters which came down from above stood and rose up upon a heap very far from the city Adam, that is beside Zaretan: and those that came down toward the sea of the plain, even the salt sea, failed, and were cut off: and the people passed right against Jericho' (Joshua, Chapter 3, Verse 15–16).

Adam is now Damiya, the site of the mud slides that in 1927 cut off the flow of the Jordan. Such disruptions, typically lasting one or two days, have also been recorded in 1906, 1834, 1546, 1534, 1267 and 1160. The combination of the destruction of Jericho and the stoppage of the Jordan is so typical of earthquakes in this region that there is little doubt about the reality of earthquakes in Joshua's time.

Finally, two skeletons of people killed by the fallen walls of Jericho were discovered here (Fig. 6). These have been dated to around 3,400 years old, or 1400 BC — possibly sufficiently close to Joshua's time (Garstang & Garstang 1940, 200).

One other well-known passage from the Bible may also refer to an earthquake: the description of the destruction of Sodom and Gomorrah, in approximately 2000 BC.

'Then the Lord ... overthrew those cities, and all the plain, and all the inhabitants of the cities, and that which grew upon the ground' (Genesis, Chapter 20, Verse 24–25).

Although the exact location of these extinct cities is not known, it is quite likely that they lay in the plain N of the Dead Sea, and E of Jericho, very close to the line of the Jericho fault. Just as earthquakes in southern California produce great clouds of dust that rise from the dry ground, so an earthquake in Sodom and Gomorrah could have appeared to Abraham as great clouds of smoke:

'and Abraham ... looked toward Sodom and Gomorrah, and toward all the land of the plain, and beheld, and, lo, the smoke of the country went up as the smoke of a furnace.' (Genesis, Chapter 19, Verse 27–28).

Conclusion

The earthquake history and archaeology along the Dead Sea fault in the Holyland provide a unique example and model for the study of archaeoseismicity in general:

- The damaging earthquakes here can be directly associated with the well understood and relatively simple seismogenic fault system.
- Extensive archaeological excavations and historical writings provide an almost continuous record over 2,000 years.
- Systematic patterns of earthquake effects in time and in space such as fallen columns may be used to yield estimates of fault rupture propagation direction, and earthquake magnitudes.
- The skeletons under fallen structure are proof of earthquake damage. [14]C ages may provide dates for the responsible earthquakes.

The lessons learned from this relatively complete record and tectonically relatively simple area may be applied to more complex regions such as western Turkey and Greece, in which the written archaeological records are less continuous and systematic, and most important, where the tectonics are much more complex, with many active faults, instead of a simple plate boundary.

References

Ambraseys, N. N. & Barazangi, M. (1989). The 1759 Earthquake in the Bekkaa Valley; Implications for the earthquake hazard assessment in the eastern Mediterranean region. *J. Geophysical Research* **94**, B4, 4007–4013.

Amiran, D. H. K. (1952). A revised earthquake catalogue of Palestine. *Israel Explor. J.* **2**, 48–65.

Arieh, E. J. & Turcotte, T. (1988). Nuclear Power Plant – Shivta site: Preliminary safety analysis report. Appendix 2.5A. *Catalogue of earthquakes in and around Israel*. The Israel Electric Corp. Ltd., 29 September.

Ben-Menahem, A. (1979). Earthquake catalogue for the Middle East (92 BC - 1980 AD). *Bolletino Geofisica Teoretica i Applicata*, 245–310.

Ben-Menahem, A., Aboodi, E., Vered, M. & Kovach, R. L. (1977). Rate of Seismicity of the Dead Sea region over the past 4000 years. *Physics of the Earth and Planetary Interiors* **14**, 17–27.

Ben-Menahem, A., Nur, A. & Vered, M. (1976). Tectonics, seismicity and structure of the Afro-Eurasian junction — the breaking of an incoherent plate. *Physics of the Earth and Planetary Interiors* **12**, 1–50.

Degg, M. R. (1990). A database of historical earthquake activity in the Middle East. *Transactions, Institute of British Geographers*. New Series **15**, No 3, 294–307.

Freund, R., Garfunkel, Z., Zak, I., Goldberg, H., Weissbrod, T. & Derin, B. (1970). The shear along the Dead Sea rift. *Phil. Trans. Roy. Soc. London* A, **267**, 107–130.

Garfunkel, Z. (1981). Internal structure of the Dead Sea leaky transform (rift) in relation to plate kinematics, *Tectonophysics* **80**, 84–108.

Garfunkel, Z., Zak, I. & Freund, R. (1981). Active faulting in the Dead Sea Rift, *Tectonophysics* **80**, 1–26.

Garstang, J. & Garstang, J. B. E. (1940). *The Story of Jericho*. London; Hodder & Stoughton.

Joffe, S. & Garfunkel, A. (1987). Plate kinematics of the circum Red Sea — a re-evaluation. *Tectonophysics* **141**, 5–22.

Josephus, Flavius, *c.* 75AD. *The Jewish War*. Michigan; Zondervan Publ. House (1975).

Karcz, I. & Kafri, U. (1978). Evaluation of supposed archaeoseismic damage in Israel. *J. Arch. Science* **5**, 237–253.

Kohl, H. & Watzinger, C. (1916). *Antiken synagogue in Galilaea*. Leipzig; J. C. Hinrich.

Macoz, Z. U. & Killebrew, A. (1988). Ancient Qasrin: synagogue and village. *Biblical Archaeologist* **51**, 32–35.

Meyers, E. M., Kraabel, A. T., Strange, J. F. Thompson, J. F., Bullard, R., G., Hanson, R. S., Bates, M. L., Liebowitz, H. A. & Meyers, Carol L. (1976). Ancient synagogue excavations at Khirbet Shema, Upper Galilee, Israel 1970–1972. In (D. N. Freedman, Ed.) *Annual of the American Schools of Oriental Research* **XXII**, 112–117.

Meyers, E. M., Meyers, C. L. & Strange, J. F. (1990). Excavations at the ancient synagogue of Gush Valav. *Meiron Excavation Project* **V**. American Schools of Oriental Research: Eisenbrauns Winona Lake, Indiana.

Nur, A. & Reches, Z. (1979). The Dead Sea rift; geophysical, historical and archaeological evidence for strike slip motion. *Eos, Am. Geophys. Union Trans.* **60** (18), 322.

Nur, A., Ron, H. & Tal, D. (1989). Earthquake parameters inferred from archeological evidence. *Israel Geol. Soc. Annual Meeting*, Ramot, Israel, April, 56.

Reches, Z. & Nur, A. (1980). Holocene seismic and tectonic activity in the Dead Sea area. *Eos, Am. Geophys. Union Trans.* **61**, 1100.

Reches, Z. Hoexter, D. F., Freund, R., Garfunkel, Z. (1981). Holocene seismic and tectonic activity in the Dead Sea area, The Dead Sea fort. Selected papers of the International Symposium on the Dead Sea Rift. *Tectonophysics* **80**, 235–254.

Russell, K. W. (1980). The earthquake of May 19, 363 AD. *Bull. Am. Schools of Oriental Research* **238**, 47–64.

Russell, K. W. (1985). The earthquake chronology of Palestine and N-W Arabia from the 2nd through the mid-8th century AD. *Bull. Am. Schools of Oriental Research* **260,** 37–59.

Salamon, A., Hofstetter, A., Garfunkel, Z. & Ron, H. (1991). A new seismicity map of the Sinai subplate. *Israel Geol. Soc., Annual Meeting*, Acco, Israel. April 24–25.

Tzafrir, Y. & Foerester, G. (1989). The date of 'Raash Sheviit'. *Tarbiz* **V**. LVII, 3–4.

Willis, B. (1928). Earthquakes in the Holyland. *Bull. Seismological Soc. of America* **18**, 72–103.

A Seismic Destruction at Achinos
(Phthiotis, Central Greece)?

Maria-Photeini Papaconstantinou

14th Ephorate of Prehistoric and Classical Antiquities
The Castle, Lamia 351 00, Greece

Abstract

At Achinos (Phthiotis, Central Greece), where the remains of Ancient Echinos are found, excavations have brought to light the foundations of a well-constructed public building of Roman date. In the interior of the building a destruction layer of hewn blocks, ash and debris were found. This layer contained the head of a statue, while the body was found separately in excellent condition, covered and preserved by the fallen blocks.

A landslide or rockfall should be excluded as a possible explanation for this destruction; human agency cannot be easily accepted; an earthquake of the third quarter of the 3rd century AD, not referred to in the historical sources, is likely to be the cause of the destruction.

Introduction

Achinos village is built on two hills at the foot of Mt. Othrys, close to the N coast of Maliac Gulf (Fig. 1). It held a critical position on the coastal road connecting Thessaly with southern Greece, and has been inhabited as early as Middle Helladic (about 2000–1550 BC). The ancient name of the site was Echinos or Echinous, which was at the border of Achaia Phthiotis and Malis. Excavation data of the last years (Papaconstantinou, 1994a) give us much information concerning the topography of the ancient site during the time it flourished, which extends from Late Classical to Roman times. In the 4th century BC a robust wall was built on the higher hill, at the southern and western slopes of which was built the site. At the top of the hill was the acropolis with its own walls. The cemetery was on a lower hill to the SW. The centre of the town probably occupied the centre of the slopes of the eastern hill, where after a rescue excavation, a building discussed below was brought to light (Papaconstantinou, 1993b).

This paper presents a report on this building and the dating of its destruction. A first attempt is made to explore the causes of the destruction, while it is recognised that the ideas put forward may be revised later after a detailed and integrated study of the building.

Excavation data

The plan of the building was rectangular, 5 m x 7 m wide, with the larger dimension running N-S. Its elaborate podium is made of poros and limestone hewn blocks (Fig. 2). Foundations are of dry masonry on bedrock. In the interior, the building is divided by two perpendicular walls into three aisles, the central one paved with marble slabs. On the northern perpendicular wall a marble moulded pedestal (Orlandos 1967–1968, 119; Petrakos 1968, 147–148) of dimensions 2.5 x 0.5 x 0.33 m survives. The northern aisle, whose level is 0.55 m lower than the central one (Dinsmoor 1975, 329), was accessible from the E by a staircase leading to an

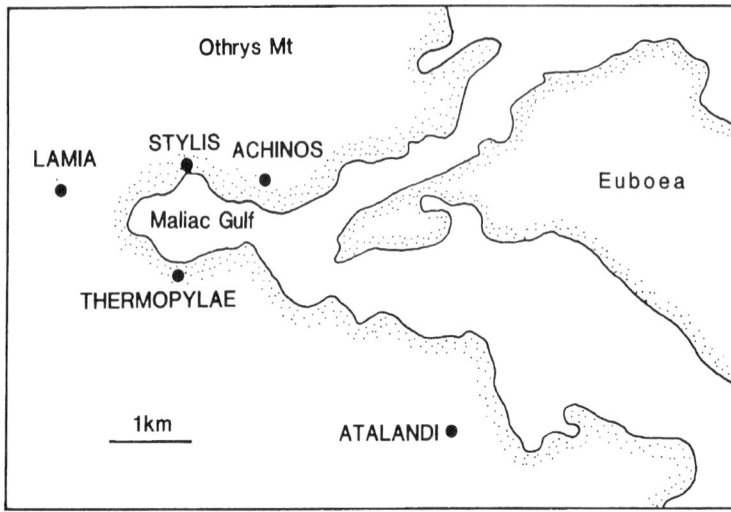

Figure 1. Location map.

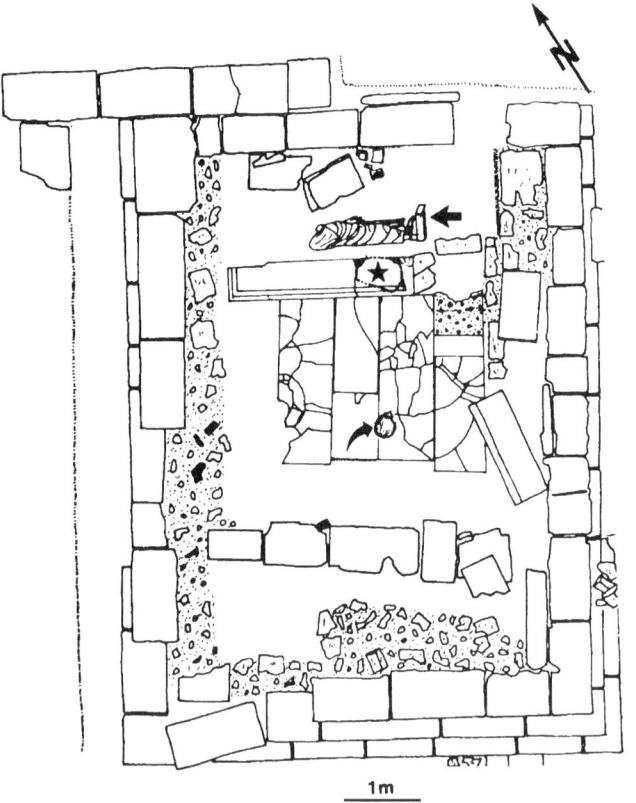

Figure 2. Plan of the building showing the decapitated statue and its head (marked with arrows) where they were excavated. The proposed original position of the plinth of the statue on the pedestral is marked by a star (drawing by A. Tsekoura).

entrance with a marble door (Dyggve *et al.* 1934, 338; Orlandos 1958, 12, Fig. 3, n. 10; 13, n. 10, Fig. 3). An older gravestone inscribed with names was used as a doorstep.

Sherds found during the excavation indicate that the building was erected during the Early Roman period (end of 2nd century BC – beginning of the 1st century BC). In the northern part of the building a destruction layer of hewn blocks, scattered roof tiles and burned soil were found (Fig. 3). Most blocks are slightly curved, and this indicates their use in a vaulted construction (Dinsmoor 1975, 329; Orlandos 1958, 347–353; Schazmann 1934, 115 Fig. 3, 121 Fig. 8). All other material of the superstructure of the building that could provide more information on the shape of the building and the cause of its destruction was moved away and used as a construction material in later, nearby constructions. The excavation revealed that the large fallen blocks (0.63–1.41 m long, 0.46–0.68 m wide and 0.46–0.65 m high) covered a headless male statue (Poulsen 1962, 54, n. 18, pl. XXVII) of life size, and functioned as a protective shield (Figs 4–5). The head of the statue was found S of the pedestal (Fig. 3), face down, and with limited damage. Originally it had been inserted into the body, and was cut obliquely across the neck. Near the head, a foot and support (Doenna 1938, Figs 27–29) of a marble table for offerings (Doenna 1938, 20) were found, while another foot of the same table was found behind the pedestal.

Pottery fragments (Fig. 6) and objects from the destruction layer provide information on the period of use and the dating of the building's de-

Figure 3. The destruction layer with the head of the statue at the foot of the marble table for offerings.

Figure 4. The body of the statue below the fallen blocks.

struction. Among them were two lamps of the second half of the 1st century BC – 1st century AD (Howland 1958, 121, type 37C, no 504) and three copper coins, the later one dated to the middle of 2nd century AD. Sherds of the middle of the 3rd century AD, on the other hand, provide a lowest date, and a *terminus post quem* for the destruction. The overall picture of this building gives evidence of a small shrine, a heroon (Dyggve *et al.*, 1934; Schazmann 1934, 110–127; Dinsmoor 1975, 329) for the worship of the dead person represented in the statue. Before any hypothesis about the fall of the statue is presented, the problem of its position and equilibrium conditions should be clarified. The most likely spot would be the E end of the pedestal, directly on which the plinth of the statue was placed, for reasons unknown, without any support (Fig. 7). In support of this hypothesis are the following data:

(i) the absence of any other base,
(ii) the locations of the fallen body and the head of the statue,
(iii) the possible position of the statue in relation to the axis of the building,
(iv) the absence of signs of support in the lower surface of the plinth,
(v) the large fissure and damage in the E part of the pedestal that coincide with the shocks at the corners of the plinth (Figs 8–9), and finally,
(vi) the oblique cutting in the E side of the pedestal at the height of the moulding, which would have followed the corresponding side of the plinth, probably after the statue was placed in position (Figs 8–9).

If we accept this hypothesis for the initial position of the statue, its possible orbit during its fall was: first, an oscillation from S-E to N-E, and provisional stabilization; then, inclination towards the N-E followed by

Figure 5. The statue *in situ*, after the blocks were removed.

Figure 6. Sherds from the destruction layer.

Figure 7. Copy (plaster cast) of the plinth of the statue in its possible original position.

Figure 8. Back and side view of the E part of the pedestal. The fissure, the damage from collision and the oblique cut on its E side at the height of the moulding are shown.

Figure 9. Copy (plaster cast) of the plinth of the statue in its possible original position (detail of Fig. 7).

fall, probably because of the weight of marble concentrated on this side. That the fall was in this direction is also deduced from the damage at the lower N-E corner of the pedestal (Figs 8–9). Finally, the statue rotated 180 degrees towards the N before it fell to the ground, in the position it was found. Alternatively, the statue was for some reason already lying on the ground when the large blocks collapsed and buried it.

The probable cause of the destruction

The fall of the statue could have been the result of a seismic shock, but its decapitation, which happened before its fall, may have been due to debris fallen from the superstructure. The body then fell and was buried by large blocks. A fire followed.

The robust construction of the excavated building, in combination with the information deduced from the study of the destruction layer, indicates a violent destruction which may be due to human effects (war, local revolt, fire) or a natural cause.

Discussion

Echinos was a small town, rarely referred to in ancient sources, whose history follows that of the wider region. If this destruction occurred after the middle of the 3rd century AD as the findings indicate, it is difficult for it to be associated with any war in Central Greece. The invasion of Costoboci in the times of Marcus Aurelius in 161 (Vortselas 1973, 213–214; Cook *et al.* 1936, 354 & 565) and their ascent up to Elateia, near Atalandi, is too early, while Goths who attempted three raids in the second half of the 3rd century AD were not successful in conquering fortified cities and were limited to desolating the country (Platis 1973, 48; Vortselas 1973, 215–216). Furthermore, no signs of an attack or struggle have been found in the destruction layer. For the same reason, the possibility of a local revolt, for which there is no additional (independent?) evidence, cannot be supported. Despite the high gradient of the relief, landslides and rockslides do not appear as possible causes of the destruction; foundations are on limestone and intact, and materials not related to the building have not been found. A seismic event in the third quarter of the 3rd century AD may appear as the most reasonable explanation for the destruction, since the area has been affected by several destructive earthquakes in the 5th and 3rd century BC (Bequignon 1937, 72–73), AD 106 (Orosius VII, 12–15; Eusebius Hieronymous II, 162) and the 6th century AD (Bequignon 1937, 72).

References

Bequignon, Y. (1937). *La vallée du Spercheios*. Paris.

Cook, S. Adcock, F. & Charlesworth, M., Eds (1936). *The Imperial Peace. AD 70-192*. The Cambridge Ancient History **XI**. Cambridge.

Dinsmoor, W. B. (1975). *Architecture of Ancient Greece*. London, Batsford.

Doenna, A. (1938). *Le mobilier Délien*, Délos **XVII**. Paris.

Dyggve, E. Poulsen, F. & Romaios, K. (1934). *Das Heroon von Kalydon*. Kobenhavn.

Howland, R. (1958). Greek lamps and their survivals. In *The Athenian Agora* **IV**. Princeton: The American School of Classical Studies at Athens.

Orlandos, A. (1958). *Construction materials of ancient Greeks*, A, 2. Athens. (In Greek).

Orlandos, A. (1967–68). *Arcadian Alipheira and its monuments*. Athens. (In Greek).

Papaconstantinou, M.-Ph. (1993b). (Excavations at) G. Alexiou House, *Archaeologikon Deltion*. Chronika **43**, 213. (In Greek).

Papaconstantinou, M.-Ph. (1994a). The South and West part of Achaia Phthiotis from Classical to the Roman Times. In: *Actes du Colloque International d'Archeologie 'La Thessalie'*, Lyon 1990. Athens; Ministry of Culture (TAP), 233. (In Greek).

Petrakos, V. (1968). *Oropos and the Amphiaraos Shrine*. Athens. (In Greek).

Platis, G. (1973). *Lamia*. Lamia; Municipality of Lamia. (In Greek).

Poulsen, V. (1962). *Les portraits Romains* **I**. Glyptotheque Ny Carlsberg.

Schazmann, P. (1934). Das Charmyleion. *Jahrbuch des deutschen Archaeologischen Instituts* **XLIX**.

Vortselas, J. (1973). *Phthiotis*. Reprint of the 1907 edition. Athens; Castalia. (In Greek).

The 1296 Earthquake and its Consequences for Pergamon and Chliara

Klaus Rheidt*

German Archaeological Institute, Istanbul Section, Ayazpaşa Çamii Sk. 48,
80090 Istanbul (Gümüşşuyu), Turkey

Abstract

The earthquake of AD 1296 in western Asia Minor is reported in detail by Byzantine authors. The recent excavations at Pergamon uncovered a densely-settled Byzantine settlement with the evidence of sudden damage in the last years of the 13th century, without doubt caused by this earthquake. The Byzantine descriptions, together with the archaeological evidence, allow a detailed reconstruction to be made of the situation before and after the destruction, as well as a reliable estimate of the strength of the quake and its influence upon the development of the city.

Introduction

In the summer of 1296 the densely populated Byzantine cities of Pergamon and Chliara in Asia Minor (western Turkey) were shaken by a severe earthquake (Wirth 1966, 398; Ducellier 1980, 106). The chronicler Georgios Pachymeres reports the date as the first day in the month of Maimakterion, i.e. June 1 (Pachymeres, 233; for date, cf. Tannery 1920, 228; Voltz 1895, 547; Schmid 1958, 85; Grumel 1958, 176. 481). This was also the occasion of damage to the Church of All Saints in Constantinople, where the harm done to a statue of the emperor Michael in particular was interpreted as an ominous sign by the superstitious because his son, the emperor Andronikos II, had left the city (Gregoras, 202; Perrey 1850, 19; Heisenberg 1908, 19; Downey 1955, 600; Downey 1955/56, 302; Nicol 1972, 118; Müller-Wiener 1977, 406). The shock to the theme of Neokastra, newly organized under the Comnenes to incorporate the cities of Adramyttion, Pergamon, and Chliara (Fig. 1; Rheidt 1986, 225ff. 241f. Beil. 6), was apparently strong enough to be felt even in the capital, more than 250 km away, where not only tremors, but some scattered damage as well, were reported.

Historical Reports

The chronicler Georgios Pachymeres described at length the effects of the earthquake in the province in order to underscore, so to speak, the symbolically interpreted incidents in the capital:

'The earth was shaken like the throbbing of the pulse in the human body, with alternating convulsions of contraction and expansion. Those who report this earthquake say that this type is particularly devastating and terrible because the very foundations of the earth are virtually thrust outward and torn apart' (Pachymeres, 233).

* present address: Deutsches Archäologisches Institut, Zentrale, Dienstgebäude & Lieferanschrift, Podbielskiallee 69–71, 14195 Berlin (Dahlem).

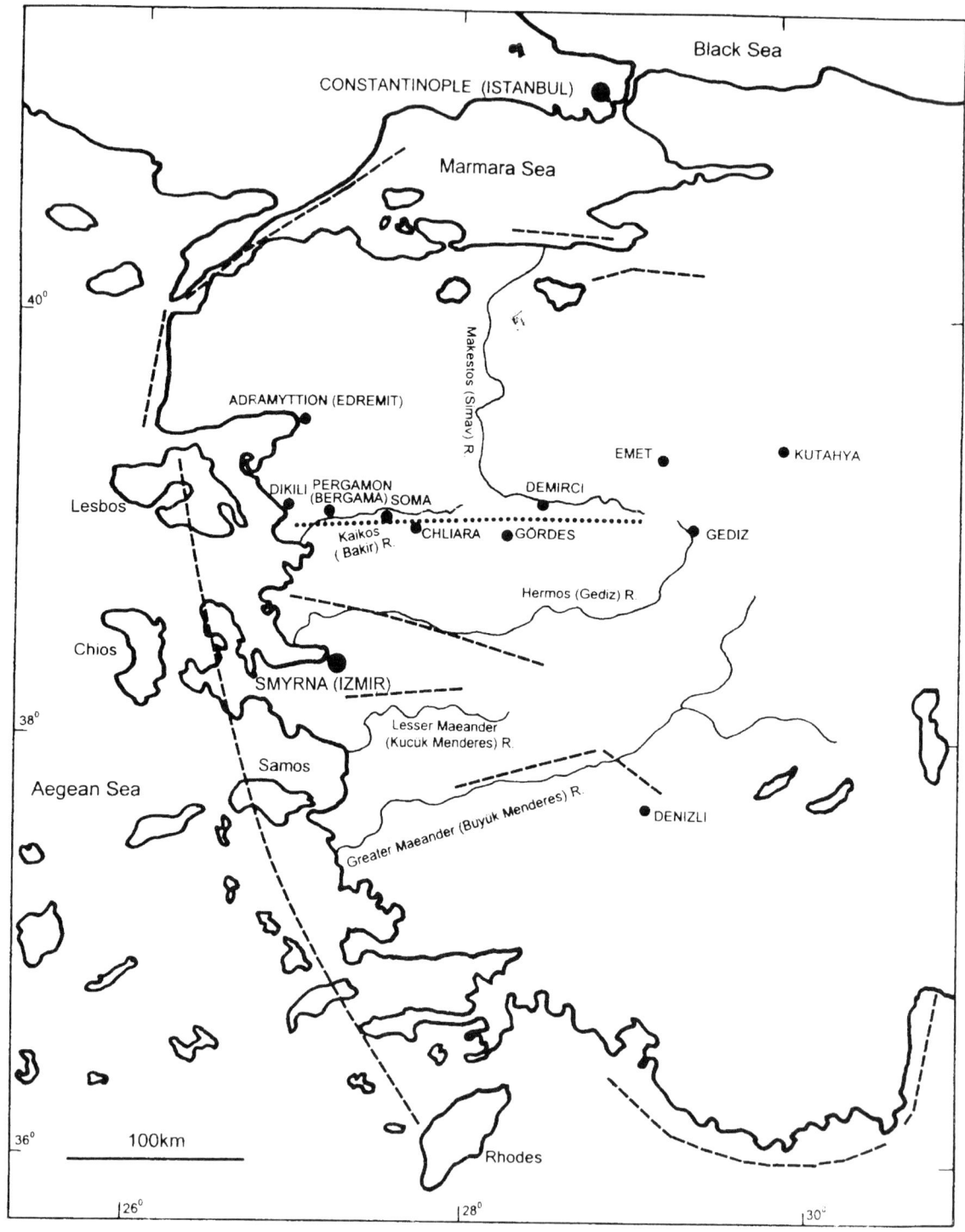

Figure 1. Location map. Earthquake lines (discontinuous lines) after Weismantel (1891) and the line corresponding to the 1296 earthquake (dotted line) are shown.

Here the chronicler had obviously been inspired by the description of an earthquake given by Pausanias, who likewise employed the metaphor of the human pulse. Pausanias (VII, 24, 11) wrote that earthquakes push from 'directly under the buildings and force the foundations upward just as molehills are cast out of the ground.' Following his general characterization of this type of earthquake, Pachymeres addressed the specific happenings in Neokastra:

'Following the 17th of July the tremors were, although longer in duration, weaker in intensity; in the E, notwithstanding, stronger and more intensive than the previous. The calamity began at Pergamon, however, and spread directly over Chliara even into areas in the Persis. At many locations the ground was rent open; at others water was sprayed out of the depths' (Pachymeres, 233; cf. Rheidt 1986, 227 n. 33).

The earthquake thus shifted eastwards from the Aegean coastal zone, striking Pergamon and Chliara with repercussions throughout the Region of present-day Gördes and Demirci as far as the 'Persis', the Anatolian plateau S of Kütahya, where severe recent earthquake damage occurred in 1970 (Weber 1969, 201; Naumann 1979, XI; Ambraseys 1988, 59). Since 1900 several severe quakes have been recorded along this line (at Soma 1919, 6.9; Dikili/Bergama 1939, 6.5; Saphane 1944, 6.0; cf. Ambraseys 1988, 30f., 39, 44; Salomon-Calvi 1940, 46ff.), each resulting in considerable destruction. An earthquake in 1895 had caused stretches of the then still erect northern flank of the Byzantine fortifications at Pergamon to collapse (Conze *et al.* 1912–1913, 307f.; Szalay *et al.*, 1937, 4); and another strong quake occurred at Emet/Kütahya in 1896 (*Türk Ansiklopedisi* XIII 1966, 86). Thus an additional line may be added to the chart of historical earthquakes which Otto Weismantel compiled as early as 1891 (Fig. 1; Weismantel 1891, 3ff.). The line coincides roughly with the courses of the Bakir and the Simav Rivers (Fig. 1) northward of and parallel to the rift valleys of the Greater and Lesser Maeander Rivers and the Gediz River (Salomon-Calvi 1940, 108). Even today there are many thermal springs along these zones of seismic activity (Philippson 1968, 154f. 177; Salomon-Calvi 1940, 50f.).

Commenting on the considerable damage wrought by the quake of 1296 upon the houses and fortifications of the medieval cities, the chronicler reports:

'The foundations of the fortress near Chliara were destroyed; the churches also, and other buildings renowned for their stability, were levelled to the ground. In this region, moreover, many tall and massive structures, their stability verified by their long endurance, fell in at the first convulsion of the earth; and many new structures collapsed. Walls enclosing wide open areas and those of masonry without mortar fell over rings round, so that any observer might justifiably have assumed that the neatly lined-up stones had been arranged by a stonemason about to begin his task' (Pachymeres, 233).

Buildings at Chliara and Pergamon

Chliara, apparently in a state of nearly total destruction, may have been deserted and left lying in ruins; in any case, it seems to have been of only minor significance during the 14th and 15th centuries (Rheidt 1986, 228). Its fate remains uncertain due to the lack of archaeological research. In Pergamon, on the other hand, the excavations carried out by the German Archaeological Institute since 1973 (see reports by Radt in Archäologischer Anzeiger for years 1974–1982 and 1985–1992; see also Filgis & Radt 1986, 8ff.; Rheidt 1991b, 10f.) have revealed evidence of sudden damage suggestive of horizontal impact at several locations within the densely settled Byzantine residential district (Rheidt 1991b, 36ff.). Through numerous coins recovered, the damage can be dated to the final years of the 13th century (Rheidt 1991b, 35ff.; Voegtli 1993, 8ff.). There can be no doubt that the destruction throughout this stratum was occasioned by the earthquake described above. The earlier excavators of Pergamon had encountered this same destruction level — although without the finds to date it securely — many times over (Dörpfeld 1909, 82f. 89; Rheidt 1991b, 152).

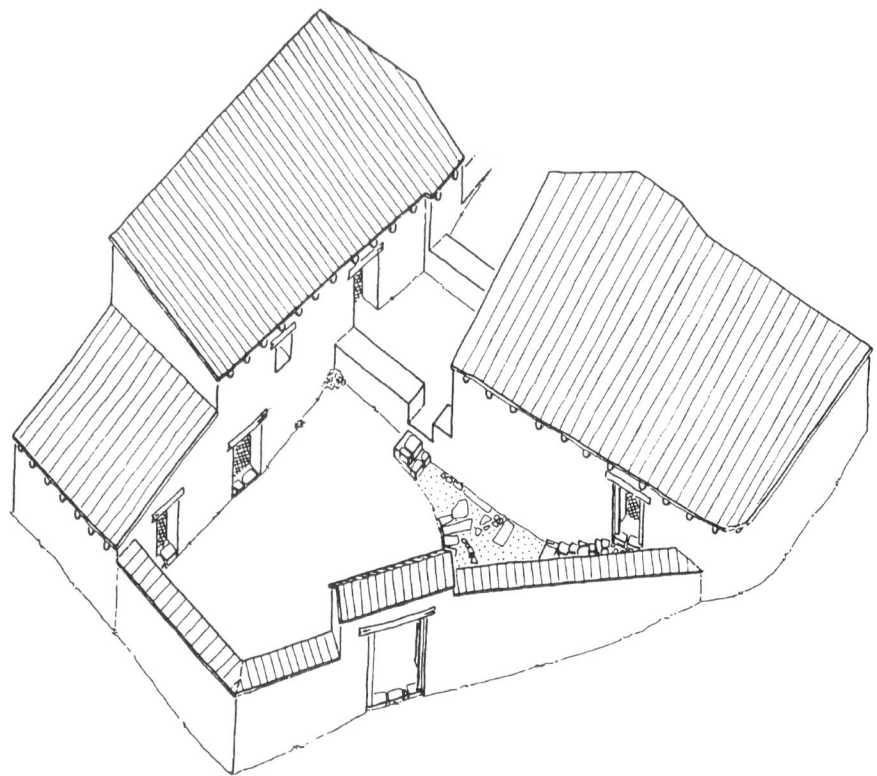

Figure 2. Pergamon, 1973–80 excavation. House 4, late 13th century, schematic reconstruction.

Since the end of the 12th century the humble Byzantine dwellings of Pergamon had gradually developed into a loose-knit community, mainly agricultural in character, clustered upon the S slope below the acropolis wall (Rheidt 1991b, 198f. pls. 2–6). The structure of the settlement resembled to a great extent that of a rural village today; indeed the layout of the individual houses affords a good comparison with present-day rural architecture (Müller-Wiener 1986, 470; Rheidt 1990, 195ff.; Rheidt 1991b, 208f.). Thus we are struck by very obvious parallels — both in plan and in general layout — between a Byzantine farmstead (Fig. 2; Rheidt 1991b, 43ff. fig. 13; Rheidt 1990, 202. fig. 6) and a present-day farmhouse to the N of Pergamon (Fig. 3). Such construction techniques as employed in these simple buildings and walls around the yards could hardly have withstood the assailant force of the earthquake (cf. also Salomon-Calvi 1940, 57f. 114ff.).

The house walls were usually a conglomerate of stones and pieces of brick; in place of mortar, suitable soil was employed. As a rule there were no headers whatsoever to bond the two outer surfaces of the wall. One example (Fig. 4), relatively well built and therefore not completely destroyed, illustrates particularly well the characteristic damage caused by the horizontal impetus. The two opposite faces of the wall, by no means statically bonded, separate; and with either surface too flimsy to support its own weight (Rheidt 1991b, 21ff.), long stretches of the wall simply collapse as described by Pachymeres. Such a breach can be seen in the wall in Fig 4, subsequently repaired with a patchwork of smaller material (Rheidt 1991b, 108. pl. 13,3; Rheidt 1991a, 188f. fig. 3).

The roofs, 'shingled', so to speak, with ceramic tiles (cf. Wiegand 1928, 21f. fig. 10; Szalay *et al.*, 32; Radt 1978, 217; Özyiğit 1990, 168ff.; Rheidt 1991b, 30ff. fig. 10. pl. 14; Rheidt 1991a, 189ff.) simply fell into the rooms at the onslaught. The straw-tempered tiles, quite large in format, broke into several fragments (Fig. 5; cf. Rheidt 1991a, 191ff. fig. 9. 13). The inhabitants, therefore, sparing themselves the effort of clearing the debris, often laid a new floor directly upon the layer of broken tiles and earth.

The extent of the damage to individual houses can be assessed by observing the alterations made in rebuilding, as illustrated by the examples in Fig. 6. Quite conspicuously, some parts of the houses underwent only minor alteration; as in Complex 7, for example, the two rooms set within solid ancient walls remained unchanged in the new configuration. Other constructions as well, such as 9, 16, and 20 with their relatively sturdy walls, were so little damaged that they could be incorporated in the reconstruction with practically no changes. Other structures, however, especially in the areas 5, 17, 18, and 19, had obviously suffered such severe damage that they were either deleted from the plan entirely or rebuilt in a very different manner (cf. Rheidt 1991b, 35ff.).

After the earthquake

Transferring these individual situations onto a more comprehensive plan, we can reconstruct the general condition — albeit sketchy and lacking in some details — of the settlement immediately after the catastrophe. The loosely knit rural community which

Figure 3. Contemporary farm beside the so-called 'Kleiner Aquädukt' N of Pergamon.

Figure 4. Pergamon, 1973–80 excavation. House 20, S-E wall repaired after earthquake damage (DAI Istanbul, PE 80/14–7, E. Steiner 1980).

Figure 5. Pergamon, 1973–80 excavation. Collapsed roof in quadrate 4060/26 (DAI Istanbul, PE 84/27–6, E. Steiner 1984).

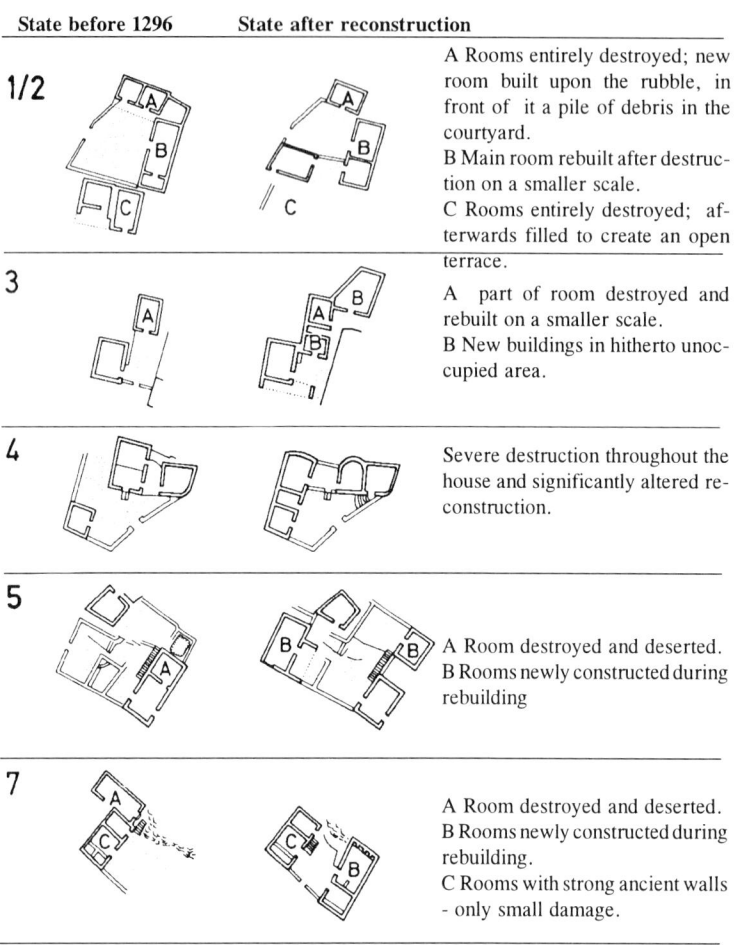

State before 1296	State after reconstruction	
1/2		A Rooms entirely destroyed; new room built upon the rubble, in front of it a pile of debris in the courtyard. B Main room rebuilt after destruction on a smaller scale. C Rooms entirely destroyed; afterwards filled to create an open terrace.
3		A part of room destroyed and rebuilt on a smaller scale. B New buildings in hitherto unoccupied area.
4		Severe destruction throughout the house and significantly altered reconstruction.
5		A Room destroyed and deserted. B Rooms newly constructed during rebuilding
7		A Room destroyed and deserted. B Rooms newly constructed during rebuilding. C Rooms with strong ancient walls - only small damage.

Figure 6. See caption and continuation of figure on page opposite.

had existed on the S slope of the acropolis before the earthquake (Fig. 7; Rheidt 1991b, pl. 6) had been almost totally destroyed. The walls which were reused after the disaster and those archaeologically attested heaps of rubble probably to be associated with it (cf. Rheidt 1991b, 36f. 100) have been drawn in on Fig. 8. Major changes in the plan, those involving alteration in the size and layout of the residential complexes, occur primarily along an approximately five-meter thick stratum of tuff which, sandwiched between two plates of andesite, joins the surface in a line across the centre of the area excavated (Rheidt 1991b, 46. 48. 51. 58. 100f.; in general, Philippson 1911, 87ff.; Conze *et al.* 1912–1913, 45ff.). It is likely that more pronounced shifting occurred along the boundaries between the soft tuff and the harder andesite (Rheidt 1991b, 100 n. 552).

The earthquake was also responsible for considerable damage outside the area of the residential quarter excavated. The Byzantine defences near the northern point of the fortress were repaired with a poorer quality masonry following the earthquake destruction (Szalay *et al.* 1937, 6. pl. 22a), and the patching of a breach in the southern flank of the upper acropolis fortifications (Fig. 9), to judge by the masonry technique, may date to the beginning of the 14th century as well (cf. Klinkott 1980, 53). The earthquake may also have been

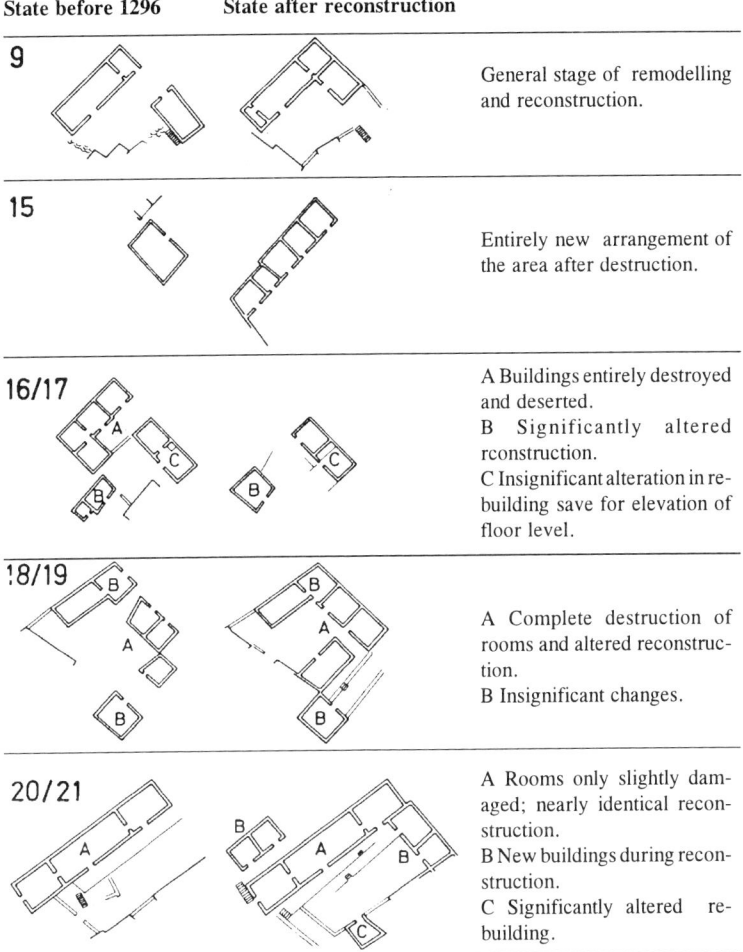

State before 1296   **State after reconstruction**

9 — General stage of remodelling and reconstruction.

15 — Entirely new arrangement of the area after destruction.

16/17 —
A Buildings entirely destroyed and deserted.
B Significantly altered reconstruction.
C Insignificant alteration in rebuilding save for elevation of floor level.

18/19 —
A Complete destruction of rooms and altered reconstruction.
B Insignificant changes.

20/21 —
A Rooms only slightly damaged; nearly identical reconstruction.
B New buildings during reconstruction.
C Significantly altered rebuilding.

Figure 6. State of Byzantine houses in Pergamon before the 1296 earthquake and after the rebuilding; brief explanation of damage, and repair, reconstruction or alteration.

responsible for the collapse of the impressively high dome on the Oberer Rundbau in the Asklepieion of Pergamon, praised for its magnificence by Georgios Kedrenos as late as the 12th century (Kedrenos, 299; Rheidt 1991b, 193).

Pachymeres' description, together with the archaeological evidence, permits a fairly reliable estimation of the intensity of the quake, the epicentre of which must have been quite near Pergamon. The levelling of the simple buildings within the settlement, in addition to the considerable damage inflicted upon the sturdy fortifications and the solid constructions standing since antiquity, allow us to estimate a maximum intensity (Io) of IX, which may denote a magnitude of 7.0 on the Richter scale (cf. Rapp 1982, 44). To judge from the destruction, the earthquake would seem to have been nearly as strong as that which occurred at Gediz in 1970, when many villagers' houses were levelled and solid ancient buildings damaged as well, such as the Temple of Zeus and the facade of the theatre at Aizanoi (Naumann 1971, 214ff.; Naumann 1973, 155ff.).

Reconstruction at Pergamon following the disaster of 1296 proceeded speedily; the houses soon supported roofs of newly produced tiles (Fig. 10). Imperial efforts to strengthen the defences of the empire were at this

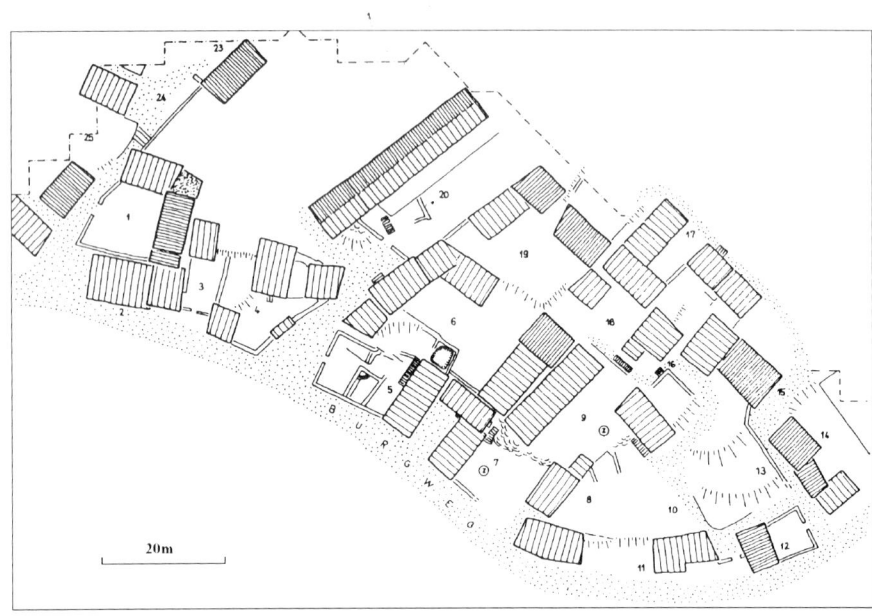

Figure 7. Pergamon, 1973–80 excavation. Byzantine settlement shortly before the 1296 earthquake. Reconstruction sketch.

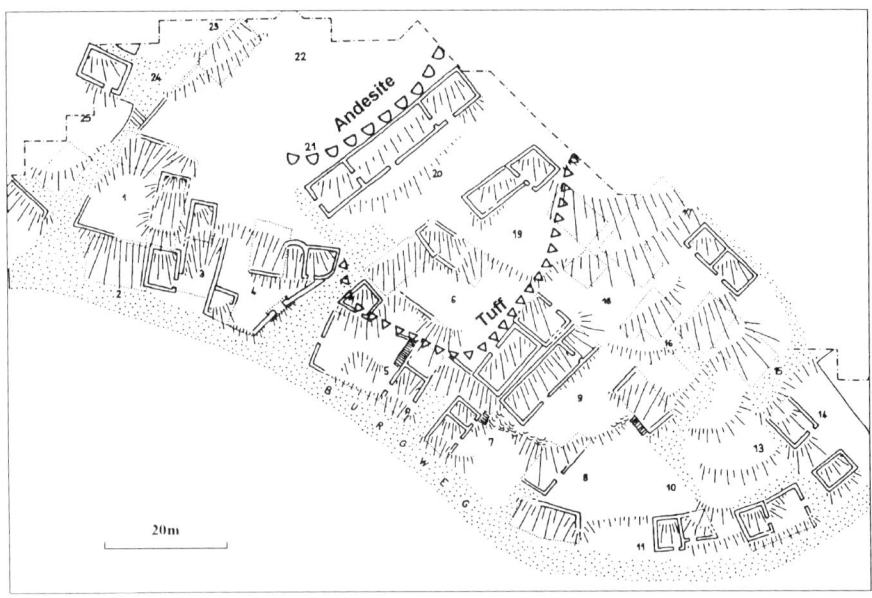

Figure 8. Pergamon, 1973–80 excavation. Byzantine settlement immediately after the 1296 earthquake. Reconstruction sketch.

Figure 9. Pergamon, southern stretch of the Byzantine acropolis fortification wall. Gap probably due to the 1296 earthquake, subsequent repair and elevation of the wall in the early 14th century (DAI Athen, Inv.nr. 1427).

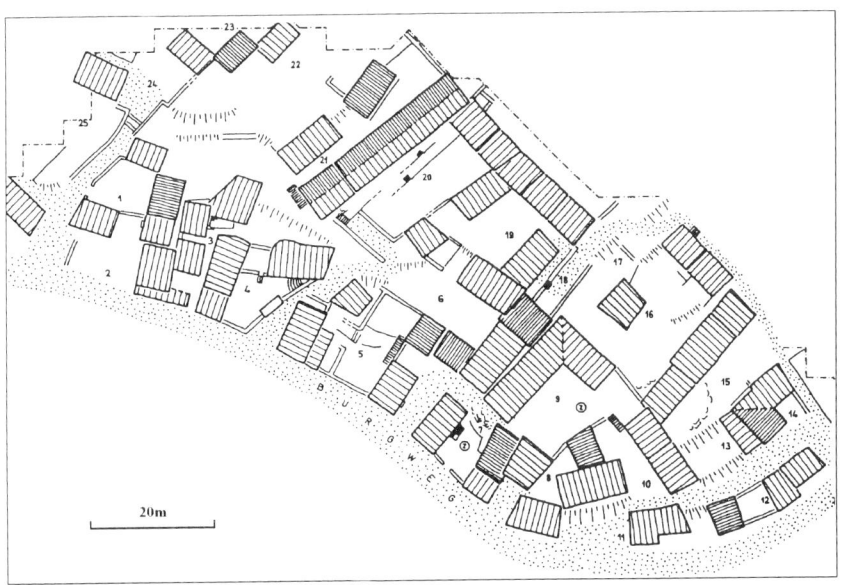

Figure 10. Pergamon, 1973–80 excavation. Byzantine settlement as rebuilt after the earthquake (about 1300). Reconstruction sketch.

time ensuring that the strategically important city of Pergamon would achieve a corresponding material prosperity as well (Pachymeres, 389f.; Laiou 1972, 87ff. 118f.; Rheidt 1991b, 200, 250f. pl. 7). The rebuilding of the settlement was marked, not only by the incorporation of recessed hearths, flagged floors, and built-in storage vessels, but also by totally new structures which served to broaden and facilitate the existing complexes. The Byzantine community thus appeared better equipped after this reconstruction phase than it had in the phases immediately preceding the quake. The new masonry, however, shows no alteration in technique to the older structures; there are obviously no signs of strengthening or reinforcing the new structures against future earthquakes. Figures 4 and 9 show that the new constructions are, despite the richer equipment inside the houses, even weaker, consisting of small stones, again lacking the headers to bond the surfaces of the walls.

Thus, at least for Pergamon, the earthquake represented a caesura in the community's development only upon an external, visible plane. No break can be seen in the historic development of the city; indeed the structure of the rebuilt settlement, despite the many modifications in detail, demonstrates no basic change in respect to the use, size, plans or building technique of the structures (Rheidt 1991b, 200; Rheidt 1990, 197).

It was not for several more years, until the beginning of the 14th century, that distinct changes are to be observed, marked by the construction of the city fortifications on the S slope (cf. Klinkott 1980, 50ff). It was, above all, the endless stream of immigrants from the surrounding countryside seeking refuge within the newly built defences who, from the beginning of the 14th century onwards, dramatically influenced the standard of living and the lifestyle of the community (Rheidt 1991b, 200f, 251).

The earthquake of 1296 and the wake of destruction it left behind has thus provided the archaeologist with a well-defined stratum most convenient for dating. As far as the inhabitants of Pergamon shortly before the Turkish conquest of about 1315 were concerned, it represented, despite its considerable impact, no more than a transient episode with little influence upon the overall development of the city.

References

Ambraseys, N. N. (1988). Engineering Seismology. *Earthquake Engineering and Structural Dynamics* **17**, 1–105.

Conze, A., Berlet, O., Philippson, A. & Schuchhardt, C. (1912–1913). Stadt und Landschaft. *Altertümer von Pergamon* **I**. Berlin.

Dörpfeld, W. (1909). Tagebuch der Ausgrabungen in Pergamon 1909. Unpublished report, in the Pergamon Excavation House.

Downey, G. (1955). Earthquakes at Constantinople and Vicinity, A.D. 342–1454. *Speculum* **30**, 596–600.

Downey, G. (1955/56). The Church of All Saints (Church of St. Teophano) near the Church of the Holy Apostles at Constantinople. *Dumbarton Oaks Papers* **9/10**, 301–305.

Ducellier, A. (1980). Les Séismes en Méditerranée Orientale. *Act. du XVe Congrès International d'Etudes Byzantines* **IV**. Athens.

Filgis, M. N. & Radt, W. (1986). Die Stadtgrabung, Teil 1: Das Heroon. *Altertümer von Pergamon* **XV** 1. Berlin.

Gregoras, Nikephoros, Ed. Bonn 1829, Vol. I.

Grumel, V. (1958). *Traité d'Etudes Byzantines I: La Chronologie*. Paris.

Heisenberg, A. (1908). *Grabeskirche und Apostelkirche*. Leipzig.

Kedrenos, Georgios, Ed. Bonn 1838, Vol. I.

Klinkott, M. (1980). Bericht über die Arbeit an den byzantinischen Verteidigungsanlagen Pergamons. Koldewey-Gesellschaft, Bericht über die 30. Tagung für Ausgrabungswissenschaft und Bauforschung 1978, 49–54.

Laiou, A. (1972). *Constantinople and the Latins*. Cambridge.

Müller-Wiener, W. (1977). *Bildlexikon zur Topographie Istanbuls*. Tübingen.

Müller-Wiener, W. (1986). Von der Polis zum Kastron. *Gymnasium* **93**, 435–475.

Naumann, R. (1971). Wirkungen eines Erdbebens an den antiken Bauten in Aezani. *Archäologischer Anzeiger* 1971, 214–221.

Naumann, R. (1973). Restaurierungen und Untersuchungen in Aizanoi. *Türk Arkeoloji Dergisi* **20**, 155–162.

Naumann, R. (1979). *Der Zeustempel von Aizanoi*. Berlin.

Nicol, D. M. (1972). *The Last Centuries of Byzantium*. London.

Özyiğit, Ö. (1990). Alaturka kiremidin olusumu. *Arkeoloji-Sanat Tarihi Dergisi* **5**, 168–179.

Pachymeres, Georgios, Ed. Bonn 1835, Vol. II.

Perrey, A. (1850). Mémoire sur les tremblements de terre ressentis dans la péninsule turco-hellénique et en Syrie. *Mémoires couronnés et mémoires des savants étrangers publiés par l'Académie royale de Bruxelles* XXIII.

Pausanias, Liber VII 24, 11, Ed. Hitzig, H. - Bluemner, H. (1904). Vol. II 2. Leipzig. 746ff. 834.

Philippson, A. (1911). Reisen und Forschungen im westlichen Kleinasien. *Petermanns Mitteilungen Ergänzungsband* **36**, Nr. 167, 1–104.

Philippson, A. (1968). Kleinasien. *Handbuch der regionalen Geologie* **22**, V 2. (Repr.) New York.

Radt, W. (1978). Die byzantinische Wohnstadt von Pergamon. *Diskussionen zur Archäologischen Bauforschung* **3**, 199–223.

Rapp, G. (1982). Earthquakes in the Troad. *Troy, Supplement Monograph* **4**, 43–58. Princeton.

Rheidt, K. (1986). Chliara. Ein Beitrag zur spätbyzantinischen Topographie der pergamenischen Landschaft. *Istanbuler Mitteilungen* **36**, 223–244. Taf. 61–65. Beilage 6.

Rheidt, K. (1990). Byzantinische Wohnhäuser des 11. bis 14. Jahrhunderts in Pergamon. *Dumbarton Oaks Papers* **44**, 195–204.

Rheidt, K. (1991a). Bautechnik und Bautradition im byzantinischen Pergamon. *Diskussionen zur Archäologischen Bauforschung* **5**, 187–196.

Rheidt, K. (1991b). Die Stadtgrabung, Teil 2: Die Byzantinische Wohnstadt. *Altertümer von Pergamon* **XV** 2. Berlin.

Salomon-Calvi, W. (1940). *Untersuchungen über Erdbeben in der Türkei*. Ankara.

Schmid, P. (1958). Zur Chronologie von Pachymeres, Andronikos L. II - VII. *Byzantinische Zeitschrift* **51**, 82–86.

Szalay, A., Boehringer, E. & Krauss, F. (1937). Die hellenistischen Arsenale. *Altertümer von Pergamon* **X**. Berlin.

Tannery, P. (1920). Les Noms des Mois Attiques chez les Byzantines. *Rev. Arch.* **9**, 1887, 23ff. In *Mémoires Scientifiques IV, Sciences exactes chez les Byzantins 1884–1919*. Paris; Cauthier-Villars.

Türk Ansiklopedisi **XIII**, 1966, s.v. *deprem*. Ankara.

Voegtli H. (1993). Pergamon. Die Wohnstadtgrabung 1973–1981. Die Fundmünzen. *Pergamenische Forschungen* **8**.

Voltz, L. (1895). Bemerkungen zu byzantinischen Monatslisten. *Byzantinische Zeitschrift* **4**, 547–558.

Weber, H. (1969). Der Zeus-Tempel von Aezani – ein panhellenisches Heiligtum der Kaiserzeit. *Athener Mitteilungen* **84**, 182–201.

Weismantel, O. (1891). Die Erdbeben des Vorderen Kleinasiens in geschichtlicher Zeit. *Königliches Gymnasium zu Wiesbaden*, Programm Nr. **391**, 3–29.

Wiegand, Th. (1928). Bericht über die Ausgrabungen in Pergamon 1927. *Abhandlungen der Preussischen Akademie der Wissenschaften, Phil.-Hist. Klasse* Nr. **3**, 1–22.

Wirth, P. (1966). Zur 'byzantinischen' Erdbebenliste. *Byzantinische Forschungen* **1**, 393–399.

Earthquakes and Temples in Late Antique Corinth

Richard M. Rothaus

Department of History, Oklahoma State University,
Stillwater, Oklahoma 74078-0611, USA

Abstract

Destructions in Late Antique Corinth have long been attributed to seismic activity. Among the buildings subjected to the traumas of the period were the pagan temples of Corinth. At least three of these were thrown into utter disrepair and, whether for lack of resources or interest, were never restored. In this sense, earthquakes in the late 4th century AD delivered a substantial blow to classical pagan cult in the city, and we might wonder if this blow was a factor in the demise of pagan cult in Corinth equal to or even greater than the advent of Christianity.

The exact chronology of the 4th century earthquake(s) deduced from archaeological and historic data is uncertain. It appears that there were at least two major seismic events, one around 365 and another closer to AD 400.

Introduction

Christians and earthquakes have occasionally been blamed for the destruction of temples in the Peloponnese. For years the final collapse of the temple at Nemea was attributed to an earthquake (Hill 1966, 8). Careful examination of the evidence by Stephen Miller has now revealed, however, that an earthquake was not the culprit after all (Miller, 1986). In the 6th century of our era, and perhaps later, the Christian community at Nemea systematically undermined the columns of the temple causing the collapse of the superstructure.

The city of Argos underwent great destruction at the end of the 4th century (Brommelaer & Grandjean 1972, 197, 224). Among the structures damaged were the Aphrodision and a temple identified as that of Artemis or Athena. The cause or causes of the destruction remains unknown (Daux 1969, 1009; Vollgraff 1920, 220). Perhaps Alaric was to blame, but this is far from certain and perhaps unlikely given the severe nature of the damage. One may wish to posit earthquake damage in Argos in the late 4th century, and Christian attacks upon the temples cannot be ruled out.

In the Corinthia the Christians do not seem to have attacked the temples. The destruction of at least three major temples in Corinth, the temple of Poseidon at Isthmia, and the so-called sanctuary of Isis at Kenchreai may have been caused by earthquakes; Christianity and zealous Christians seem to have played little role in the initial demise of these edifices. If earthquakes in the late 4th century delivered a substantial blow to classical pagan cult sites in the city, one might wonder if this blow, more than the advent of Christianity, was the decisive factor in the end of pagan cult in Corinth. No monumental theory based on environmental determinism is intended here. The 4th century saw other crises, including the activity of Alaric, and was a period in which political, social, religious and economic transformations were under way. These transformations and changes underlie the reactions to the visible reactions to physical destruction. The earthquakes were less a cause than a catalyst. Nevertheless, seismic activity, unlike other aspects of change in 4th century Corinth was sudden, tangible and had immediate results.

Literary sources

Literary evidence records three earthquakes that may have struck the Peloponnese in late antiquity. The sources vary in value and reliability, however, and their reports of earthquakes can never be accepted uncritically or at face value. Ammianus Marcellinus (26.10.17–18) reports that an earthquake and tsunami struck the Eastern Mediterranean on the 21st of July 365. He supports this by describing a ship he personally viewed in Methone that had been thrown almost two miles inland. There is no reason to doubt the general veracity of Ammianus' report. It must not be assumed, however, that an earthquake causing damage in some or even much of the Peloponnese also struck the Corinthia. Truly large earthquakes cannot occur in Greece and the area affected by a given seismic activity is limited (Ambraseys, this volume). Ammianus does not specifically mention Corinth in his account of seismic activity near Methone and there can be no certainty that Corinth was among the suffering regions.

Zosimos (4.18) states that an earthquake struck all of Greece except Athens shortly after the death of Valentinian I in 375. It seems, however, that Zosimos (or more probably Eunapios, his source) has exaggerated or perhaps even fabricated this earthquake as a rhetorical flourish. Late antique authors liked to associate natural disasters with the passing of emperors. Eunapios may have desired just such an event to correspond to the death of Valentinian, and he may not have seen it amiss to create or move an earthquake to accompany this event. It seems probable that Eunapios has shifted the 365 earthquake to 375 in order to fit his rhetorical structure.

Libanios, in his funeral oration for Julian, reports that shortly after Julian's death in 363 all of Greece was devastated by an earthquake 'except for one city'. Libanios certainly is using a rhetorical *topos* here, and there is no reason to accept his account at face value, although one may wish to join his reference to Ammianus' account of the earthquake in 365. Eunapios has picked up this *topos*, and perhaps even his account of the 375 earthquake from Libanios; the parallel is too strong to be coincidence. Eunapios takes the *topos* one step further than Libanios, however, and instead of saying 'all of Greece except one city', he says 'all of Greece except Athens'. Eunapios often singles out Athens as a city especially beloved by the gods, and his exclusion of this favoured pagan city from those suffering damage is closely paralleled by his report that only Athens was spared from Alaric; a report that excavations in the Agora seem to indicate is false (Frantz 1988, 53–56). Eunapios exaggerates the extent of the earthquake in order to emphasize the blessed position of Athens in the eyes of the gods. To assume from Zosimos' problematic account of the 375 earthquake that Corinth suffered at this date is methodologically unsound. It seems more likely that Eunapios is engaging in a literary *topos*, and he may, in fact, have absconded the earthquake of 365 for rhetorical purposes. The literary evidence for an earthquake in 375, if not dismissible, is extremely unreliable.

Finally, two late sources mention 4th century earthquakes. Marcellinus Comes (*MGH Auctores Antiquissimus* 64) mentions an earthquake in 395 that 'shook the whole world', and Glykas (Ed. Bonn 478) mentions a 'universal earthquake' that struck in 395 or 396. These accounts are so vague, however, that they are difficult to evaluate. The possibility of a 395 or 396 earthquake in Corinth is left open, but it is certainly not demonstrated.

The literary sources tell us nothing about the effect of earthquakes in Corinth. While an earthquake did hit the Peloponnese in 365, any effect this might have had on Corinth cannot be answered from the literary records. The same holds true for the alleged quakes of 375 and 395 (or 396); if these later earthquakes did occur, their effect on Corinth remains unclear. Furthermore, earthquakes may have struck the Corinthia that receive no mention in the literary sources.

Archaeological evidence

Earthquake damage at Corinth must be ascertained from the archaeological record. This is not an easy task, however. The reports of earthquakes by Ammianus and Zosimos were noted early in the twentieth century by excavators at Corinth. Unfortunately it became the tendency to assign any damage that could be roughly dated to the late 4th century to one or both of these events, with 375 being the preferred date (the *locus classicus* for the Corinth publications is Broneer (1935, 58 n. 1). A mention of earthquake damage in the Corinth publications cannot, therefore, be accepted uncritically. Earthquake damage must be identified on the basis of the archaeological record alone. General damage from unknown causes may be associated with earthquakes, as may repairs, but only after such earthquakes have been firmly established.

Four structures provide evidence for late 4th century damage that almost certainly resulted from earthquakes: the Julian Basilica, the Great Bath on the Lechaion Road, the West Shops, and the Sanctuary of Isis at Kenchreai.

The Julian Basilica

The Julian Basilica shows the clearest evidence of earthquake damage. The excavators report that the walls of this structure fell from the E to the W, and that material from the upper floor collapsed into the lower. Debris accumulated in this structure to a depth of 0.40 m, and coins in this debris indicate that the collapse of this structure occurred at an indeterminable time prior to, but probably not much before, 395. There is little doubt that this damage resulted from an earthquake (Weinberg 1960, 52, 57).

The Great Bath

The Great Bath on the Lechaion Road likewise suffered catastrophic damage that should be attributed to an earthquake or earthquakes. At some point in the late 4th century the marble blocks of the facade fell from the structure. An attempt to repair the structure was made, but soon abandoned. Room I of this structure also suffered a calamity at some point prior to 383, necessitating the remodelling of the room and the filling of the pool therein. Massive destruction is also evident in Room 3, the pool of which was partially filled in and floored over. The calamity or calamities that befell this structure cannot be precisely dated, but the magnitude of the damage make seismic activity a probable culprit (Biers 1985, 4, 31–32, 37, 42, 48, 50, 62).

The West Shops

The West Shops also show evidence for damage that probably should be attributed to earthquakes. At some point, presumably but not certainly the late 4th century, two of the capitals in this structure fell and broke. They subsequently were clamped together and restored in place. It seems likely that the capitals were dislodged by an earthquake (Williams & Zervos 1990, 335–336).

Damage in the South Shops should also be mentioned at this point. The stratigraphy in this area is unclear, but pieces of marble revetment and seats from a latrine were found amidst destruction debris that had collapsed into the drain. Numismatic evidence gives a *terminus post quem* of 379–395 for this destruction. The original excavator attributed this wreckage to Alaric, but it seems unlikely that Alaric would have gone to the trouble of demolishing a latrine, if he even attacked Corinth. The damage may very well have resulted from an earthquake, and, if this is the case, we have evidence for an earthquake later than 379 (Broneer 1958, 153).

The Sanctuary of Isis

The sanctuary of Isis at Kenchreai, one of the ports of Corinth, clearly was destroyed by seismic activity. The structure, built on a promontory, collapsed and was submerged, preventing any attempts at repair (Scranton *et al.* 1978, 75–76; Hohlfelder 1976, 225–226). Unpublished ceramic material (most notable a Peloponnesian version of Yassi-Ada II amphorae) has provided a date near 400 for this seismic event. One may also want to associate uplift at Lechaion, the other harbour of Corinth, with late 4th century earthquakes. (S. Stiros, pers. comm.).

Discussion

Given the evidence from these structures, it is probable that at least two earthquakes struck Corinth in the late 4th century. The archaeological evidence is not precise enough to establish exact dates for the seismic events. The evidence from the Great Bath indicates a date prior to 383; the evidence from Kenchreai and perhaps the latrines points to another event closer to 400. The record seems, therefore, to indicate at least two discrete damaging seismic events in the 4th century.

Fortunately epigraphical evidence clarifies the matter somewhat. Two inscriptions (Kent 1966, nos. 504 and 505) indicate repairs undertaken at the behest of Valentinian I who died in 375. One of these inscriptions was found at the entrance facade to the South Basilica, the other at the West Shops, where most probably there was earthquake damage. If we associate these imperial sponsored repairs with the earthquake damage, as seems probable, then the repairs must be for damage resulting from an earthquake dating before 375. I will use 365 as a date of convenience; there is no convincing evidence precisely linking the seismic event in Corinth to that in Methone, only coincidence. One can be certain, however, that Valentinian could not have been notified and responded to an earthquake in 375 before his death, especially as Eunapios, our only source for this earthquake, states that the event occurred after Valentinian's death. Eunapios' unreliable report and the epigraphic evidence do not support the 375 earthquake so often referred to in the Corinth publications.

Rather than forcing the evidence to produce precise dates and demanding more from the literary records than they are able to give, it seems prudent to assert merely that there was one earthquake near 365. The damage at Kenchreai occurred too late to have been part of this seismic activity near 365 and another event closer to 400 must be posited. The possibility remains, of course, of other earthquakes in this period. Any attempt to identify discrete seismic events spaced by only thirty or forty years approaches the limits of archaeological science, and such questions, while important, should not detract from considerations of broader issues. It is certain that there were damaging earthquakes in the 2nd half of the 4th century in the Corinthia. Two discrete events seem to be identifiable, one *c.* 365, the other *c.* 400.

Other cases of destruction

Other examples of destruction from earthquakes in the late 4th century can be tentatively identified. It must be emphasized, however, that only the examples already given clearly indicate damage by earthquake. Other damage can be associated with the earthquakes, but the relationship is not certain. Serious damage that can be dated no more precisely than the late 4th century is evident at the West Shops, the South Basilica, the Odeion, the Demeter and Kore sanctuary, the Southwest Forum, Temple Hill, East of the Theater, the Central Shops, the Gymnasium Area and the Theater. There is also damage at the North Market, South Basilica, Mosaic House, East of the Theater, and the Anaploga Villa that seems to be late enough in the 4th century that we may want to associate it with seismic activity near 400 (Appendix). Corinth was heavily damaged in the late 4th century; the exact chronology and causes are not clear, but earthquakes seem to have been a major contributor.

Among the buildings damaged in the late 4th century were some of Corinth's most important religious structures: the Asklepieion, the structure designated by Dinsmoor the 'largest temple in the Peloponnese', Temple E, and the Temple of Poseidon at Isthmia. All of these structures share the characteristic of being so thoroughly destroyed that their blocks were completely removed for reuse shortly after their destruction.

The Asklepieion

The Asklepieion was destroyed sometime prior to 408. The blocks from this structure were completely removed and many probably were reused in Corinth's late Roman fortification wall. The excavator reports that a layer of burned debris 0.70 m deep covered the bedrock foundations and there are numerous coins in this layer that date from 363 to 450. Rather than a particularly thorough Christian destruction of this temple, as was suspected by the original excavator, it seems more likely that this temple was so heavily damaged by the late 4th century earthquakes that its stones were available for immediate and easy reuse. Demolition of buildings tends to take time and rarely was a temple so completely stripped as was the Asklepieion. Poros and marble chips distributed in the overlying debris indicate that the stones were being reworked on the site in the late 4th and early 5th centuries. A catastrophic destruction of this temple helps to explain the total removal of the structure (DeWaele 1933, 417–451; Roebuck 1951, 160–161).

The 'Largest Temple'

The same scenario seems to fit the so-called 'Largest Temple in the Peloponnese'. This immense structure was so thoroughly dismantled that, while many architectural members have been found, its original location has not. Again, it seems possible that this structure was felled by the 4th century earthquakes and its stones were put to immediate use; many found their way into the Late Roman fortifications of the city (Dinsmoor 1949, 115).

Temple E

Temple E was destroyed sometime after 361 and stones began to be removed by 408. Evidence from early excavations, most notably in the form of a lion's head spout shattered where it fell, makes it clear that the structure collapsed, perhaps as a result of the earthquakes. Again the overlying fill contained marble chips, indicating that stones were being reworked on the spot in the late 4th and early 5th centuries, and perhaps again in the Byzantine period. The capitals were reused in later Byzantine walls (Stillwell *et al.* 1941, 183; Williams & Zervos 1990, 356). In the case of Temple E, we cannot be sure that the reused blocks were incorporated into the late Roman wall; the presence of capitals in the Byzantine walls perhaps, but not necessarily, implies that the pieces of Temple E did not travel far.

Earthquakes and the Transformation of Corinth into a Byzantine city

I offer the following scenario as a possibility. Corinth was hit by at least one devastating earthquake near 365, and another around 400. Among the buildings damaged were some of the larger and more important temples in the city, including that of the immensely popular god Asklepios. These temples were literally shaken to their foundations and their stones littered the grounds where they once stood. There was no attempt at restoration. Rather, the stones were almost immediately put to reuse, many being reworked on the spot and many going into the late Roman fortification wall that was to surround the city.

This scenario of destruction will work well for the Temple of Poseidon at Isthmia (Broneer 1971, 103–160). This temple is still under study by the University of Chicago Excavation team directed by Prof. Elizabeth Gebhard so what I say about this structure may be superseded as more evidence becomes available. Evidence for destruction by earthquake at the sanctuary has, however, recently been uncovered at the Roman Bath at Isthmia. The eastern side of this structure was completely robbed out for use in the early 5th trans-Isthmian wall (Gregory 1992); the rest of the Bath remained standing until a later period. There is substantial evidence, however, that the Bath was damaged and abandoned for a ten to fifteen year period before this wall was robbed out. Silting in the N-E rooms of the Bath indicates that water was entering the building from the N-E corner. Such a situation could only have occurred with damage to the walls of the structure.

New evidence, as yet unpublished, indicates that this abandonment took place in the last decade of the 4th or perhaps the first decade of the 5th century. It seems probable that the walls of the Bath were damaged in the earthquake that occurred near AD 400. Fissures in the still standing walls, although not datable, perhaps indicate the type of damage the building suffered and the means by which the water and silt gained access to the building. In the first or second decade of the 5th century, a decade or so after the structure was damaged, the constructors of the trans-Isthmian wall availed themselves of the material of the E wall. As much of the Temple of Poseidon also found its way into this fortification wall, it seems that it too may have been severely damaged or destroyed in the late 4th century earthquakes.

Thus we have the temples laid low not by Christian zealots, but rather by a natural disaster. But why were they not restored? Restoration certainly was a possibility. The temple of Zeus at Apamea was destroyed by zealous Christians in the late 4th century, and a limited restoration was immediately undertaken (Theodoret, Hist. Eccl. 5.21; Herington *et al.* 1958, 30–62). Why did such restorations not take place at Corinth? There is no certain answer, but a lack of financial backing and the changing focus of benefactions probably played a significant role. The need for materials to build the fortification wall played a part in the dismantling of the temples. But other buildings, damaged in the same time period were repaired or reused rather than stripped. The temples seem to have been specifically singled out for use in the late Roman wall. It is this complete dismantling of temples which is of note. That the temples were allowed to be stripped bare for the fortification wall re-emphasizes the lack of interest in reconstruction or repair of these structures.

Buildings in late antique Greece were almost always funded by wealthy individuals or by the provincial governor. Given the religious enthusiasms of the late 4th century emperors it is doubtful that any emperor would have suffered the use of imperial funds for the reconstruction of an edifice that could serve no purpose other than to house pagan cult. The restorations of shops is one matter, that of temples another.

With imperial funds ruled out, repair for earthquake damage would have been financed by affluent citizens of Corinth. Wealth and wealthy individuals were far from absent in the 3rd through 6th centuries in Corinth. Monumental architecture was still an aspect of Corinth into the 6th century, and large villas began to bloom in the 4th century and continued to flourish through the 5th and 6th centuries. The wealthy citizens, however, chose not to invest in or contribute to the temples. One possible explanation for the lack of attention to the temples could be that such actions would have been looked askance at. Certainly local officials trying to impress the emperor could not brag of such accomplishments. It is possible that the majority of Corinthians no longer attached any great importance to the temples. Whatever the reason, temples were unable to recover from the disasters and earthquakes of the late 4th century. Classical pagan cult could not function without temples, and the devastation of these monuments must have meant the destruction of pagan public worship.

The devastation at Corinth in the late 4th century was particularly thorough, but it need not be seen as a completely negative event. Rather, as Scranton, the author of the volume on medieval Corinth, has noted, the catastrophes hastened and assisted the transformation of the late antique city into a Byzantine city (Scranton 1957, 5). Part of this transformation included the transition from paganism to Christianity. How long pagan cult at Temple E, the 'largest Temple in the Peloponnese', the Asklepieion, Kenchreai and Isthmia might have continued had these temples not been destroyed is a question that can be asked, but not yet answered. We can be sure, however, that the earthquakes played a role in the end of cult at these sanctuaries.

Appendix
Areas of 4th Century Destruction by Uncertain Causes:
West Shops: Scranton (1951, 131); Williams *et al.* (1974, 9).
South Basilica: Weinberg (1960, 76).
Odeion: Broneer (1936, 147).
Demeter & Kore: Slane (1991, 5, n. 15); Pemberton (1989, 191); Stroud (1965) 1–24; Bookidis & Fisher (1972, 284).
Southwest Forum: Williams & Fisher (1975, 14); Williams (1976, 132; 1977, 62–3).
Temple Hill: Robinson (1976, 220).
East of Theater: Williams & Zervos (1983, 23–4); Williams (1984, 101).

Central shops: Broneer (1935, 57).
Gymnasium: Wiseman (1970; 1972).
Theater: Shear (1926, 454); Stillwell (1952, 140); Williams & Zervos (1987, 31).
North Market: Scranton (1951, 192).
Mosaic House: Weinberg (1960, 76).
Anaploga Villa: Miller (1972, 333 n.6).

Acknowledgements

C. K. Williams II and T. E. Gregory have given graciously of their time and knowledge and provided valuable assistance. Complicity, however, should not be assumed. Two anonymous reviewers have also provided comments and helped to make this revised paper substantially better than the version presented in Athens. I regret that I have not been able to address all of the issues they have raised.

References

Ambraseys, N. (this volume). Material for the Investigation of the Seismicity of Central Greece.

Biers, J. C. (1985). *Corinth XVII: The Great Bath on the Lechaion Road*. Princeton: American School of Classical Studies at Athens.

Bon, A. (1952). *Le Péloponnèse byzantin*. Paris.

Bookidis, N. & Fisher, J. (1972). The Sanctuary of Demeter and Kore on Acrocorinth. Preliminary Report IV: 1969–1970. *Hesperia* **41**, 284–231.

Brommelaer, J.-F. & Grandjean, J. (1972). Recherches dans le quartiers sud d'Argos. *Bull. Corresp. Hellénique* **96**, 155–228.

Broneer, O. (1935). Excavations in Corinth, 1934. *Am. J. Archaeology* **39**, 53–75.

Broneer, O. (1936). *Corinth X: The Odeum*. Cambridge Mass.; Harvard University Press.

Broneer, O. (1958). *Corinth I, iv: The South Stoa and its Roman Successors*. Princeton: American School of Classical Studies at Athens.

Broneer, O. (1971). *Isthmia I: The Temple of Poseidon*. Princeton: American School of Classical Studies at Athens.

Daux, G. (1969). Chronique des Fouilles: Argos. *Bull. Corresp. Hellénique* **93**, 966–1025.

DeWaele, F. (1933). The Sanctuary of Asklepios and Hygieia at Corinth. *Am. J. Archaeology* **37**, 417–451.

Dinsmoor, W. B. (1949). The Largest Temple in the Peloponnese. *Hesperia* Supp. 8, 105–115.

Gregory, T. E. (1992). *Isthmia V: The Hexamillion and Fortress*. Princeton: American School of Classical Studies at Athens.

Frantz, A. (1988). *The Athenian Agora XXIV: Late Antiquity A.D. 267–700*. Princeton: American School of Classical Studies at Athens.

Herington, C. J., Goodchild, R. G. & Reynolds, J. M. (1958). The Temple of Zeus at Cyrene. *Papers of the British School at Rome* **26**, 30–62.

Hill, B. H. (1966). *The Temple of Zeus at Nemea*. Princeton: American School of Classical Studies at Athens.

Hohlfelder, R. L. (1976). Kenchreai on the Saronic Gulf: Aspects of its Imperial History. *Classical Journal* **71**, 217–216.

Kent, J. H. (1966). *Corinth VIII, iii: The Inscriptions 1926–1959*. Princeton: American School of Classical Studies at Athens.

Miller, Stella G. (1972). A Mosaic Floor from a Roman Villa at Anaploga. *Hesperia* **41**, 332–356.

Miller, S. G. (1986). Poseidon at Nemea. *Philia Epi* **1** (Festschrift G. Mylonas), 261–271. Athens.

Pemberton, E. G. (1989). *Corinth XVIII, i: The Sanctuary of Demeter and Kore, the Greek Pottery*. Princeton: American School of Classical Studies at Athens.

Robinson, H. S. (1976). Excavations at Corinth: Temple Hill, 1968–1972. *Hesperia* **45**, 222–223, 237–238.

Roebuck, C. (1951). *Corinth XIV: The Asklepieion and Lerna*. Princeton: American School of Classical Studies at Athens.

Scranton, R. L. (1951). *Corinth I, iii: Monuments in the Lower Agora and North of the Archaic Temple*. Princeton: American School of Classical Studies at Athens.

Scranton, R. L. (1957). *Corinth XVI, Medieval Architecture in the Central Area of Corinth*. Princeton: American School of Classical Studies at Athens.

Scranton, R. L. Shaw, J. & Ibrahim, L. (1978). *Kenchreai: Eastern Port of Corinth*. Leiden; E. J. Brill.

Shear, T. L. (1926). Excavations in Corinth, 1926. *Am. J. Archaeology* **30**, 444–463.

Slane, K. W. (1991). *Corinth XVIII, ii: The Sanctuary of Demeter and Kore, the Roman Pottery*. Princeton: American School of Classical Studies at Athens.

Stillwell, R. (1952). *Corinth II: The Theater*. Princeton: American School of Classical Studies at Athens.

Stillwell, R., Scranton, R. L., Freeman, S.E. & Askew, H. E. (1941). *Corinth I, ii: Architecture*. Cambridge, Mass.; Harvard University Press.

Stroud, R. (1965). The Sanctuary of Demeter and Kore on Acrocorinth. Preliminary Report I: 1961–1962. *Hesperia* **34**, 1–24.

Vollgraff, W. (1920). Fouilles d'Argos, 1912. *Bull. Corresp. Hellénique* **44**, 219–226.

Weinberg, S. S. (1960). *Corinth I, v: The Southeast Building, the Twin Basilicas, the Mosaic House*. Princeton: American School of Classical Studies at Athens.

Williams, C. K. II, Macintosh, J. & Fisher, J. E. (1974). Excavations at Corinth, 1973. *Hesperia* **43**, 1–76.

Williams, C. K. II & Fisher, J. C. (1975). Corinth 1974, Forum Southwest. *Hesperia* **44**, 1–50.

Williams, C. K. II (1976). Corinth 1975, Forum Southwest. *Hesperia* **45**, 99–162.

Williams, C. K. II (1977). Corinth 1976, Forum Southwest. *Hesperia* **46**, 40–81.

Williams, C. K. II & Zervos, O. H. (1983). Corinth 1982, East of the Theater. *Hesperia* **52**, 1–47.

Williams, C. K. II & Zervos, O. H. (1984). Corinth 1983, The Route to Sikyon. *Hesperia* **53**, 83–122.

Williams, C. K. II & Zervos, O. H. (1987). Corinth 1986, Temple E and East of the Theater. *Hesperia* **56**, 1–46.

Williams, C. K. II & Zervos, O. H. (1990). Excavations at Corinth, 1989: The Temenos of Temple E. *Hesperia* **59**, 335–336.

Wiseman, J. (1970). The Fountain of the Lamps. *Archaeology* **23**, 216–225.

Wiseman, J. (1972). The Gymnasium Area at Corinth. *Hesperia* **41**, 1–42.

Cases of Earthquakes at Mycenaean and Pre-Mycenaean Thebes

Adamantios Sampson

Ephorate of Palaeoanthropology-Spelaeology
Ardittou 34b, Athens 116 10, Greece

Abstract

The older excavations of the Mycenaean palace at Thebes have revealed that it was totally destroyed in the 13th century BC (LH IIIB period), concurrently with other Mycenaean centres (Mycenae, Tiryns, Asine, Pylos, etc.), probably as a result of foreign invasions. A recent excavation in a palatial workshop at Thebes, however, proved that this destruction was associated with the collapse of a two-storey building, which killed and buried a woman. This finding is likely to indicate that an earthquake is the likely cause of the destruction, as is probably also the case in most other Mycenaean centres.

Skeletons of at least two people, killed and buried by collapsed walls, testify to another, probably also seismic, destruction that occurred at the end of the 3rd millennium BC (EH period) in Thebes. This destruction was probably contemporary with destructions in several other centres, and may reflect another wave of large earthquakes.

Introduction

The Kadmeia is the prominent hill in the centre of modern Thebes which has been occupied since EH II at the beginning of the 3rd millennium BC. It owes its name to Kadmos, who according to the myth established his palace there making Thebes one of the most important centres of Mycenaean Greece. In the course of archaeological excavations two successive destructive layers were uncovered among the strata of Early and Late Bronze Age date. Long-standing arguments attribute the catastrophes to fire destructions by new comers. However, new excavation data give a new point of view which considers the destructions as a result of earthquakes.

LH IIIB Excavation Data

Few excavations have so far taken place in the area of the Kadmeia, and so our knowledge about the Mycenaean palace of Thebes is incomplete (Keramopoulos, 1909; Symeonoglou, 1973; Demakopoulou, 1974; Spyropoulos, 1971). Most research has concentrated on the surrounding rooms and especially the workshop area of the palace.

The excavation we had the opportunity to take up in the eastern wing of the Kadmeia in 1980 resulted in the discovery of part of a LH IIIB building belonging to the palatial workshop (Sampson, 1980). It was found at about 3 m depth, while architectural remains of two other Mycenaean phases and a MH building (Sampson, 1985) were uncovered within the upper and lower layers respectively (Fig .1). The Mycenaean building was very carefully constructed and had massive external walls, which indicate that a second floor existed as well.

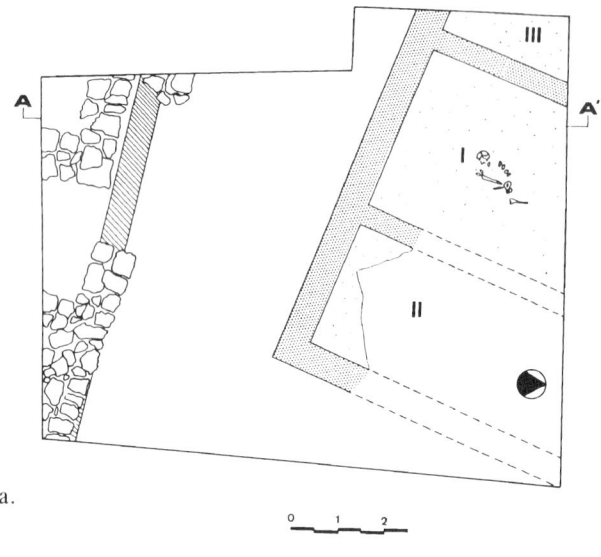

a.

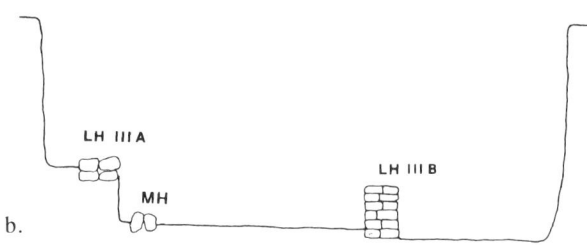

b.

Figure 1(a). Plan of the excavated part of the LH building at Kadmeia, Thebes. In Room I the skeleton remains *in situ* are shown. (b) Cross section along axis AA' in (a), showing the walls of the various building phases.

Its superstructure consisted of unbaked mudbrick, whose inner face was plastered and whose upper part was possibly strengthened by timberwork. Since most of the building extends under nearby properties, only parts of three rooms could be excavated. Two deposits of the Byzantine period and the effects of a bulldozer had caused considerable damage to Room II of the building. It is fortunate that in Room I the deposits were left undisturbed, which enabled us to discern the way this building, and consequently the whole palace of Kadmos, were destroyed.

Excavations in the Kadmeia commonly bring to light a thick destruction layer, the natural result of a long-lasting fire. In the Mycenaean building, the layer was more than 1 m thick, which is also indicative of a second floor. The roof must have been two-sided and covered with tiles. They were found within the upper levels of the destruction layer, among carbonised parts of wood which would initially have supported the roof. Unbaked mudbricks coming from the fallen walls of the building were found in different levels; some of them were later baked by the fire.

The destruction was immediate, obviously caused by a sudden earthquake succeeded by fire of long duration which consumed the inflammable structural materials. Moreover, the fact that the Mycenaean building contained workshops of ivory and possibly of carpentry (Sampson, 1985) accounts for the long-lasting burning which gave deposits 0.50–0.60 m thick. Carbonised wood, broken mudbricks and several objects that were in the room lay within the ashes (Fig. 2).

A human skeleton lying 0.70 m above the room floor was the unexpected find of the excavation. The skeletal remains were within the destruction layer; since it was overlain by a much harder stratum of erosion, a common feature in the surrounding trenches, it cannot postdate the destruction layer. The remains were found well above the ground floor which suggests that the person was on the first floor at the dreadful moment of the destruction, could not escape and was finally trapped among the ruins. Although a few traces of burning are visible, the skeleton was not carbonised. It is possible that the building did not collapse immediately because of its light mudbrick structure, but only after several subsequent vibrations. A careful anthropological study suggests that the skeleton belongs to a young female of about 20 to 25 years old and 1.55 m in height. Injuries are evident on the skull, but what caused death was a fatal depressive detaching fracture in the middle of the cranium vault (Foundoulakis, 1986), very likely produced by a very violent blow from a sharp structural material — probably a roof beam — which hit the woman suddenly.

The destruction itself is chronologically defined by the relatively abundant ceramics found either within the ashes or, more commonly, as objects that had fallen from adjacent shelves and furniture onto the floor. The typical decorative motifs date the unit to LH IIIB1, namely the mid-13th century BC (Figs 3, 4).

Discussion

This is the first time a skeleton has been found in the destruction layer of Mycenaean Thebes. As such, it is comparable to those discovered at Mycenae (French, this volume), Koukounaries Paros (Schilardi, 1979) and Anemospilia, near Knossos, Crete (Sakellarakis & Sapouna-Sakellaraki 1987, 74).

Although the skeleton is as yet a single find at Thebes, it does provide us with additional evidence to support the argument that the disaster at Thebes and indeed the LH IIIB Mycenaean palaces elsewhere were due to earthquakes and not to seamen's (or Sea People's) incursions or to newcomers invading from the N, as was formerly believed. Kilian (1985, 74; in press)

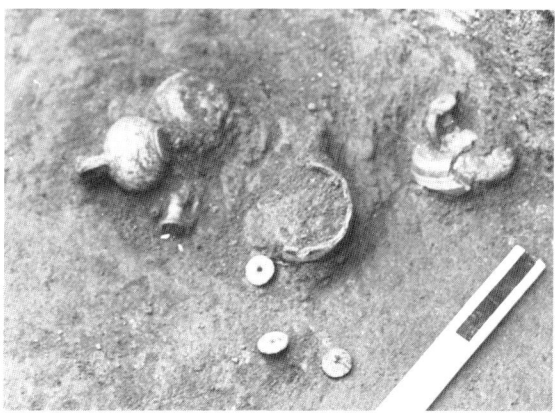

Figure 2. Kadmeia, Thebes. Mycenaean vases and other finds on the floor of Room II.

has also proposed that environmental changes and seismic effects account for many of these catastrophes. Among the sites where LH IIIB destructions have been identified are Mycenae (Taylour *et al.* 1981, 8), Tiryns (Kilian 1980, 177–182, Fig. 7), Korakou (Rutter 1974, 536), Midea and Profitis Elias in the Argolid, Menelaion in Sparta (Catling 1980/81, 18), Pylos (Blegen, 1966) and Troy VIa (Schachermeyr 1950, 189). Gla in the Kopais Basin in Boeotia (Iakovidis, 1983) is the example of destruction geographically closest to Thebes.

It should however be made clear that the factors bringing about these destructions cannot in themselves account for the decline and fall of such a prospering civilisation. The catastrophes were possibly succeeded by local rebellions which caused confusion and challenged the despotic authority of the absolute ruler. The fact that palaces widely separated in distance were destroyed at about the same time can be satisfactorily explained by the hypothesis of a number of major earthquakes occurring over short time period (see Papadopoulos, this volume). A present-day parallel is the spate of earthquakes that affected in a period of only eight years Thessaloniki (1978), Volos (1980), Corinth, Athens and Thebes (1981) and Kalamata (1986).

The evidence for earlier seismic destructions at Thebes can now be considered. There is none for the end of MH which is marked by a thick layer of burning (Sampson, 1980), but the situation is different for Early Helladic.

EH Excavation Data

We now turn to the middle and late EH period when many settlements are ascertained to have been destroyed by fire. Until recently, this phenomenon has generally been attributed to invasion, this time new people coming from the N or the E. The destructions occurred twice, at the end of EH II and EH III; there is clear evidence for them at the Kadmeia.

In a plot to the S of the Kadmeia N. Papadopoulou found recently five human skeletons within a destruction layer. Three of them had rolled away from their initial position, but the other two, which belong to a male and a female of old age, were lying *in situ* and under a MH floor. One of the two was found in a position suggesting that the person was trying to avoid the blow: a big stone was close to the head and moreover the hand was raised to the head. This find is exceptional. According to the excavator, the associated ceramic finds belong to the EH period and especially to phase Lefkandi I. Two other buildings at Thebes were destroyed during the same period (Touloupa, 1964; Demakopoulou, 1975).

Figure 3. LH III vases from the destruction layer.   Figure 4. LH III pottery from Room II.

In another plot at Thebes (Aravantinos, 1985; 1986) EH buildings were found ruined by fire, and they are dated to the end of EH II, contemporary with the destruction of the 'House of Tiles' at Lerna.

Discussion

In the same way that the Mycenaean period came to an end in the wake of a series of major catastrophes, the flourishing Early Helladic culture terminated after many settlements had been destroyed, giving way to the 'Middle Ages' of prehistory, the Middle Helladic period. At the end of EH II, *c.* 2500–2400 BC, not only Thebes, but also Lerna, Eutresis, Voidokoilia of Pylos suffered from destructions (see Zachos, this volume). A hundred years later, at the end of EH III (Lefkandi phase I — Manika phase 3) again Thebes, Eutresis, Ayios Kosmas and Tiryns were destroyed by fire. Destruction layers have also been observed at Orchomenos and Salganeus, dating to the end of EH III (Spyropoulos, 1970; Sampson, 1973/74), but not it appears at Lithares (Tzavella-Evjen, 1985) which is strange since it is situated not far from Thebes. Neither Lefkandi (Popham & Sackett, 1968), nor the EH settlement of Manika, which was peacefully abandoned (Sampson, 1985a; 1988), seem to have been affected by the catastrophes perhaps because the intensity of the shock in question was much smaller on Euboea.

The well-established hypothesis that newcomers invaded Greece from the N, albeit a valid hypothesis for decades (Konsola 1981, 57), is now strongly disputed. It is therefore necessary that a more persuasive and practical explanation be sought for the EH destructions. These destructions did not apparently occur uniformly either chronologically or spatially throughout central and southern Greece, and yet despite this and even in the absence of independent evidence that the period in question was one of intense tectonic activity (as was the case, it seems, in the 13th century BC) a logical explanation would be the effect of earthquake followed by fire.

In conclusion, earthquakes followed by fires can account for the EH and LH catastrophes of the Kadmeia. This proposal is consistent with the seismic history of the area: at the beginning of this century and even recently Thebes was half-destroyed.

References

Aravantinos, V. (1985). Nuove elementi sulle catastrophi nella Tebe Micenea. In (D. Musti, Ed.) *Le origini dei Greci.*, 349–355. Bari; Laterza.

Aravantinos, V. (1986). Tebe e il ruolo dei centri Elladici nel commercio Egeo in eta Premicenea. In (M. Marazzi, S. Tusa & L. Vagnetti, Eds) *Traffici Micenei nel Mediterraneo*, 215–231. Taranto; Instituto Gramsci Siciliano.

Blegen, C. W. (1966). *The Palace of Nestor I*. Princeton; Princeton Univ. Press.

Catling, H. W. (1980/81). *Archaeological Reports for 1980–81*, in British School at Athens, 16–20.

Demakopoulou, K. (1974). Mycenaean palace workshop in Thebes. *Archaeologika Analekta Athinon* **VII**, 162–173. (In Greek).

Demakopoulou, K. (1975). News from Thebes: An Early Helladic apsidal house. *Archaeologika Analekta Athinon* **VIII**, 192–199. (In Greek).

Foundoulakis, M. (1986). Human remains from Thebes. *Annals of Anthropology and Archaeology* **1**, 123–132. (In Greek).

French, E. (this voloume). Evidence for an earthquake at Mycenae.

Iakovidis, S. (1983). Late Helladic Citadels on Mainland Greece. In (E. J. Briel, Ed.) *Monumenta Graeca et Romana* **IV**. Leiden.

Keramopoulos, A. (1909). The House of Kadmos, *Archaeologiki Ephemeris*, 57–122. (In Greek).

Kilian, K. (1980). Zum Ende der Mykenischen Epoche in der Argolis. *Jahrbuch Römisch-germanisches Zentralmuseum Mainz* **27**, 166–195.

Kilian, K. (1985). La caduta dei palazzi mycenei: aspetti archeologici. In (D. Musti, Ed.) *Le origini dei Greci*. 73–115. Bari; Laterza.

Kilian, K. (in press). The destruction of Mycenaean palaces of continental Greece. *Proc. of the Congress on Orchomenos*. (In Greek).

Konsola, N. (1981). *Premycenaean Thebes*. University of Athens: Unpublished PhD Thesis. (In Greek).

Papadopoulos, G. (this volume). An earthquake engineering approach to the collapse of the Mycenaean palace civilization on the Greek mainland.

Popham, M. & Sackett, L. (1968). *Excavations at Lefkandi, Euboea, 1964–1966*. London; Thames and Hudson.

Rutter, J. (1974). *The LH IIIB and IIIC period at Korakou and Gonia in the Corinthia*. Univ. of Pennsylvania. Ann Arbor. PhD Thesis.

Sakellarakis, I. & Sapouna-Sakellaraki, E. (1987). Neolithic and Minoan Crete. In (N. M. Panagiotakis, Ed.) *Crete, History and Civilization*, **I**. Herakleion. (In Greek).

Sampson, A. (1973/74). Ecxavation Report. *Archaeologikon Deltion, Chronika* **29**, 447. (In Greek).

Sampson, A. (1980). Ecxavation Report. *Archaeologikon Deltion, Chronika* **35**, 218–220. (In Greek).

Sampson, A. (1985). Un atelier palatial Mycenien à Thebes. *Bulletin de Correspondance Hellénique* **109**, 21–29.

Sampson, A. (1985a). *Manika I, An EH town in Chalkis*. Athens; Etaireia Evoikon Meleton. (In Greek).

Sampson, A. (1988). *Manika II, The EH settlement and cemetery*. Athens; Etaireia Evoikon Meleton. (In Greek).

Schachermeyr, F. (1950). *Poseidon und die Entstehung des griechischen Gotterglaubens*. München; Leo Lehnen Verlag.

Schilardi, D. (1979). Excavation at Paros. *Praktika Archaeologikis Etaireias*, 236–248. (In Greek).

Spyropoulos, T. (1970). *Archaeologikon Deltion, Chronika* **25**, 222–224. (In Greek).

Spyropoulos, T. (1971). Topography of the palace of Kadmos. *Archaeologika Analekta Athinon* **IV**, 32–37. (In Greek).

Symeonoglou, S. (1973). *Kadmeia I. Mycenaean finds from Thebes*. Studies in Mediterranean Archaeology 35, Göteborg.

Taylour, W. D., French, E. B & Wardle, K. A. (1981). *Well built Mycenae, fasc. 1: The Excavations*. Warminster, England; Aris and Phillips.

Touloupa, E. (1964). Excavation Report. *Archaeologikon Deltion, Chronika* **19**, 194–195. (In Greek).

Tzavella-Evjen, H. (1985). *Lithares*. Athens; Minister of Culture (TAP). (In Greek).

Zachos, K. (this volume). Tracing a destructive earthquake in southwestern Peloponnese during the Early Bronze Age.

Contribution to a Study of the Configuration of the Coast of Pylia, Based on the Location of New Archaeological Sites

Ilias Spondilis

Ephoreia of Marine Archaeology,
Kallisperi 30, 117 42 Athens, Greece

Abstract

The formation of the Methoni-Sapienza region in southern Greece has been the subject of extensive research. Recent archaeological finds and studies of the area suggest that, independently of the mechanisms at work today in the formation of the shoreline, such as rapid erosion, at some time in the past the coasts of this region have been subject to the effects of tectonic movements.

Specifically, a number of sites, chiefly prehistoric, have been discovered — one of them submerged — whose present condition gives a different picture of the mechanism of erosion that has taken place in the area. Furthermore, finds from more recent periods help towards a closer estimation of the time of formation of the present shoreline at certain places.

In view of this new evidence, therefore, it would be worth re-examining the interpretation of a number of known archaeological sites in the general area.

Introduction

The region of Pylia in the province of Messenia attracted early on the attention of archaeologists and was the scene of important discoveries that have greatly furthered scientific knowledge. Interest in the diachronic evolution of the region was further stimulated as part of a campaign to achieve a better interpretation of the archaeological data (McDonald & Rapp, 1972).

There is a large bibliography regarding the formation of this region, including specialized studies of the region (Flemming *et al.*, 1973a, b; Kraft & Aschenbrenner, 1977; Kraft *et al.*, 1975; Kraft *et al.*, 1980), with the proviso that one bears in mind the reservations expressed by each author in stating his views. These reservations were succinctly put by Loy (1967, 57): 'Each problem [of geomorphology] must be solved, if it is to be solved, locally with local evidence'. How specialized, however, must a study be to win acceptance in the interpretation of a specific problem? This question came to my mind while I was working for the Ephoreia of Marine Archaeology at Pylos Castle in the years 1982–1986. During that time, I located a number of previously unknown archaeological sites. I came across them either in the course of my tours of duty, guided by the published data, whilst familiarizing myself with the region, or during visits to the sites for my own amusement. Here I shall mention only those whose history I have tried to interpret on the basis of relatively recent studies dealing with limited areas of S-W Pylia.

Erosional and Depositional Processes along the Pylia Coast

The more specialized of these works (Flemming *et al.*, 1973b; Kraft *et al.*, 1977) consider the decisive factors in the formation of the shoreline to have been the gradual rise of mean sea level caused by the progressive melting of the polar ice and the secondary consequences of this process. For the Methoni district in particular (Kraft & Aschenbrenner, 1977) it is accepted that the secondary consequence of this process was the rapid erosion of the friable rocks of the area. As a result, the shoreline retreated at the points where the erosion took place, and the products of the erosion were transported to and deposited at other points, extending as far as the locality of Finikous (Kraft & Aschenbrenner 1977, 33). This process was set in motion by the rise in mean sea level, which already by the 4th millennium BC had submerged the rocky limestone projection, in the form of a barrier, that joined the Eocene rocks of the Ag. Nikolaos – Ai-Thanasis – Methoni line to the corresponding rocks on Sapienza Island. The same process explains the separation from the mainland of the rocky islet of Nisakouli (Fig. 1), where Middle Helladic finds have been found (Choremis, 1969), which resulted from the erosion of the neck of land joining it to the shore.

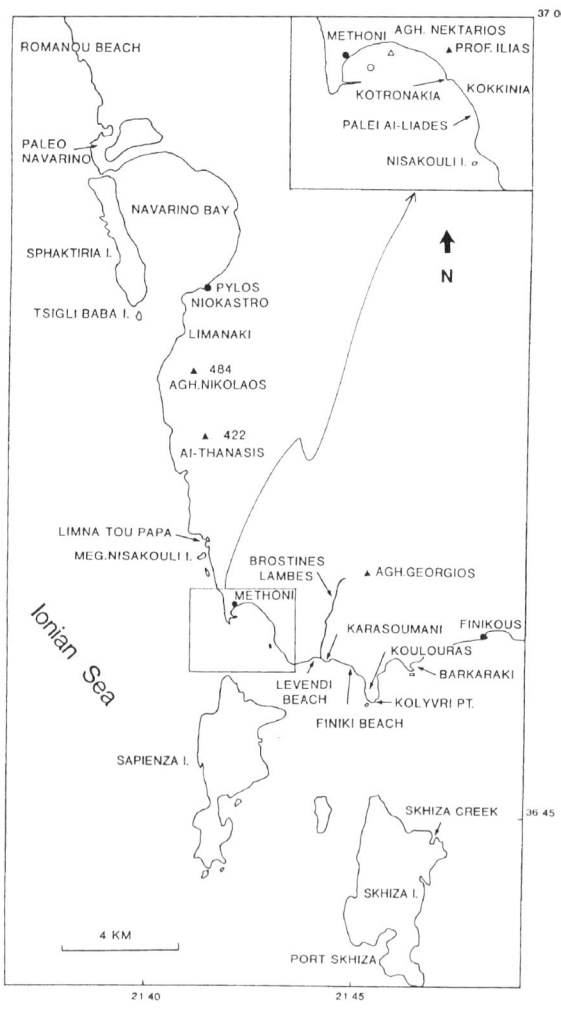

Figure 1. General map of the coastal area of southwestern Pylia.

New Observations on the Erosion of the Pylia Coast

Recent observations appear to confirm this theory at different places along the coast. We see, for example, at Palei Ai-Liades how the ground and the mosaic floor crumbled away after a heavy sea storm. I also observed considerable changes between the years 1983 and 1989 on the raised beach below the hill with the recent chapel of Profitis Ilias, at the place mentioned in Kraft & Aschenbrenner (1977, 22) (this should not be confused with Palei Ai-Liades: Profitis Ilias stands on a low elevation some 25 m high 1 km E of the cemetery of Aghios Lazaros at Methoni, while Palei Ai-Liades is some distance further E in the locality also known as Kokkinia). The archaeological deposit is rapidly disappearing due to the retreating shoreline caused by erosion. The 'Roman wall with bricks' (Fig. 2) was already overhanging in 1988, and it could be seen that the structure had a floor made of *kourasani* (powdered brick). It may have been part of a cistern or, in view of the abundance of bones in the earth fill, a tomb. Today it helps to retain the earth, together with some makeshift works carried out in the immediate vicinity, because the whole width of the coastal road is in danger of being washed away. Other ancient walls can also be seen on the shore, but they are not so solidly built and consequently parts of them have broken away, and they are either disintegrating or else remain *in situ* on the shore or in the shallows (up to 2.5 m) in the area lying between the little bridge E of the public camping ground and the rocky spit

Figure 2. Methoni: Profitis Ilias, Roman wall with bricks.   Figure 3. Methoni: part of the aqueduct.

of Kotronakia (Fig. 1). Even the older section of this bridge, which was built of stones and mortar, could not withstand the fury of the waves in 1988. It was swept away, leaving only the more modern part, half the length, which was constructed of reinforced concrete on the landward side. The bridge spans the mouth of a small torrent at the eastern end of the natural beach barrier of sand and pebbles bounding the southern side of the marshy area that used to be salt-pans in the time of the Venetian occupation. Remains of an aqueduct incorporating clay pipes (Fig. 3) were found on the shore in this locality, running E of the small bridge westward in the direction of Methoni, and visible for some 150 m. According to the local people, before World War II at least two arches belonging to the aqueduct still survived in the vicinity of the mouth of the main river bed at Methoni. The parts still visible have also suffered damage from the sea as well as by human agency, since the beach is much frequented.

Observations in the area make it clear that the worst destruction is caused by heavy seas coming from a general southerly direction and not from the N-W, as has sometimes been suggested. Also the natural shore barrier, which at some time in the past rimmed a lagoon like that of Rivari at Paleo Navarino, was not man-made. It would certainly once have been wider and stronger, and the aqueduct would not have been built on the edge of the sea, but at a safe distance from the waves. The line of the aqueduct, which today diverges progressively from the land as it proceeds towards Methoni, provides useful evidence for the contemporary shoreline.

A site, probably Mycenaean in date, that was found on a low spit between the localities of Brostines Lambes, or Alyki, and the sandy beach of Levendi (Fig. 1) by the mouth of the torrent that runs through the valley W of the heights of Ag. Georgios, does not change the picture of the erosion process.

Evidence for Seismic Activity on the Pylia Coast

My doubts began when I came across a site that is almost certainly Early Helladic in date in the locality of Karasoumani. This is a blunt headland forming the southern-most extension of the Ag. Georgios heights and separating the Levendi beach from the long beach of Finiki, which is not to be confused with Finikous (Figs 1 and 4).

The geological stratigraphy, which is visible on the abrupt southern side and in the deep section exposed on the N side of the cutting made for the passage of the so-called MOMA road, although it does not differ much from the description of the Nisakouli area in the survey by Kraft & Aschenbrenner (1977), appears to be more

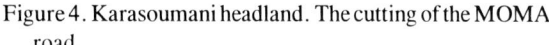

Figure 4. Karasoumani headland. The cutting of the MOMA road.

Figure 5. Barkaraki: the point and the island from the W.

resistant. The hard sandstone strata are thicker with fewer altered siltstone intrusions. Its surface forms a terrace 30 m above the sea measuring some 250x150 m. Many walls are visible, built of sandstone blocks without mortar, a construction material still used today in the district. The whole site is covered with numerous sherds and obsidian flakes or blades. The sherds are EH and MH, and they occur, though in fewer numbers, for another 200 m N of the MOMA road. Some 500 m still further to the N, around the chapel of Ag. Georgios, there is another archaeological site, on which the sherds are Hellenistic.

At the southern end of the terrace the walls are cut by the edge of the cliff. On the beach a nearly horizontal layer of hard rock forms a 'gangway' all along the S shore. At a very slightly lower level the same rock forms an extensive submerged platform some 60 m wide, beyond which the bottom gradually shelves. The impression it thus gives is that the southern, missing section of the headland was violently broken away from the remaining body that we see today.

Another prehistoric site was located in the locality of Barkaraki or Mavrovouni (Fig. 1). This is a small headland with an islet off its tip (Fig. 5), about 6 km directly S-E of Methoni. On its W side are cliffs, and on the E there is a small gully ending in a rocky inlet. The headland slopes from N to S and from W to E, but the surface levels out at the southern end. The islet off the southern tip slopes from S to N and from E to W. The channel between the point and the islet is shallow (2 m) and strewn with large boulders, some of which jut out of the water.

Many sherds were found over the whole surface of the headland, but they were less frequent and more worn on the N side. On the southern side walls are visible projecting above the ground (Fig. 6). The building material used was the tabular rock of the district, without mortar. Between them is a pure archaeological fill with EH and MH sherds (Fig. 7), bones and blades or flakes of flint and more rarely obsidian.

On the islet opposite, at the highest point on its eastern side, a wall of similar construction was found (Fig. 8). In the thin archaeological stratum at this point there are many sherds from pots broken *in situ* and belonging to the same period. The position of the finds and the nature of the geological substratum (hard sandstone) exclude the possibility that the island was cut off from the headland by the action of the sea. Evidence that the area has undergone seismic activity is suggested, to my mind, by the fact that this wall is parallel to the flat but not horizontal surface of the ground. Another reason against the original neck of land having been eroded away by the sea is the fact that on top of the rock (Fig. 5), near its northern edge, enough earth has survived to support plant life in an area of about one square metre; and even this contains prehistoric sherds. If the power of the waves had been sufficient in this place to cut off the island from the mainland, it would have certainly

Figure 6. Barkaraki: walls on the southern side of the point.

Figure 7. Barkaraki: S shore; a sherd near the walls.

broken right over the rock and swept it bare centuries ago. Along the eastern and southern shore the bottom shelves steeply into deep water with a series of steps formed of hard rock.

Between the last two sites the promontory of Kouloura juts out, ending in Kolyvri point (Fig. 1). Off its southwestern tip lies the rocky islet of Neraides, where we also find a shallow channel 3–5 m deep with a rocky bottom. The rock follows the same line in an imaginary extension of the islet towards the S-W, forming an extensive shoal 150 m long and 1.5 m deep, at the southern end of which fragments of Hellenistic-Roman amphoras were found in 6–11 m of water during a reconnaissance in 1990, indicating the presence of a wreck of that period. This is further evidence that the shoal and therefore the general configuration of this coast at that time was close to the present one.

In the Bay of Methoni, some 300 m from the public camping ground and at a depth of 3.5–5.5 m there are extensive clusters of building remains (Fig. 1, inset, marked with an open circle). The walls are preserved in places to a height of four courses and are as a rule made of flat stones. They are of double construction except where irregular blocks were used, when there is only a single row. The ground on which these structures were built is siltstone, like that on the shore, with a rapid rate of erosion, the sand forming only a thin stratum. Besides many remains of rectangular buildings, there are also buildings with curved plans. One of these, with a preserved length of some 10 m, has an apsidal end (Fig. 9). A wall about 3.5 m long divides the long section from the apsidal end, which has a length of roughly 2 m. The building recalls a church in plan, except that the apse is at the W end. It is bounded on the W and partly on the N by a very strong wall, which still stands quite high. In the same locality two completely circular buildings are visible, one with a diameter of 4 m (Fig. 10) and the other 5.5 m (Fig. 11); the wall of the latter is up to 80 cm thick. It is tempting to suppose that the building remains belonged to a second island, the one illustrated by Braun & Höhenberg in 1574 (Kraft & Aschenbrenner 1977, 25–26; Lianos 1987, 131–132), but this hypothesis will not stand. To begin with, no kind of mortar was found in the wall construction; and in the second place, if in the intervening years since the print was made there had been enough subsidence in this place to submerge the hypothetical island to its present depth, then the harbour works at Methoni would have to lie at a much greater depth (Flemming *et al*. 1973b, 21; Lianos 1987, 130) than they do today, unless of course it is suggested that the tract of limestone rock was not affected at all (Loy 1967, Fig. 1). Also, from the picture I formed when excavating the underwater EH settlement at Platiyali Astakou (Delaporta & Spondylis, 1987; Delaporta *et al.*, 1990), I believe that these are the remains of prehistoric walling. And lastly, important evidence in favour of a prehistoric date is afforded by a wall with herringbone masonry running W from a large circular edifice (Fig. 12). The sherds and larger

Figure 8. Barkaraki: wall on the highest part of the E side of the islet.

Figure 9. Methoni: apsidal building.

Figure 10. Methoni: small circular building.

Figure 11. Methoni: large circular building.

fragments of pots of the late Roman period that are present in the locality and are the only diagnostic ones, clearly derive from the erosion of the beach and were washed down there. Furthermore, not only the hill of Profitis Ilias, the lower part of which has been heavily eroded, but also the whole slope of the heights N and E of it as far as the chapel of Ag. Nektarios (Fig. 1), on the asphalt Methoni-Finikous road, are covered with Roman and possibly Hellenistic sherds.

The submergence of the building remains at Methoni cannot be regarded as the result of eustatic change like the simple subsidence or erosion of the beach, because in that case everything should have vanished (Kraft *et al.* 1985, 68–71). For the same reason a tectonic subsidence of around one or two metres per millennium (Flemming *et al.* 1973a, 47, 61; Flemming *et al.* 1978, 156; van Andel & Shackleton 1982, 447), which may be rapid in geological terms but is too slow for the archaeological data, is hardly likely to have been the cause. The degree of preservation of these remains can only be explained by a very rapid vertical tectonic movement, undoubtedly accompanied by a corresponding seismic activity; such an activity is not uncommon in this region (Flemming 1969, 81, Fig. 15), which coincides with an area of high tectonic activity (Flemming *et al.* 1973a, 48, Fig. 1; Pirazzoli, 1988; Psychoyos 1988, 11). It should be remembered that in the sea S of Methoni and W of Pylos there are depths of around 5,000 m, the greatest found in the Mediterranean.

Figure 12. Methoni: wall of herringbone construction.

Figure 13. General view of Limna tou Pappa. It shows the circular cove, the beacon tower on the southern tip and Megalo Nisakouli further S.

Near the building remains in the Bay of Methoni (Fig. 1 inset, marked with an open triangle) there is another piece of evidence that may tell us more about the speed of recession of the shoreline. These are the remains of the wreck of a wooden ship laden with spherical stone cannon-balls, some 30 in number, the largest having a diameter of 35 cm; these now form an elongated stack of triangular section and do not lie in a scatter. The evidence from the wooden construction shows that the ship sank parallel to the shore at a depth of 2.5 m. It is not suggested that the ship is contemporary with the period when these cannon-balls were in use; the wreck is probably that of a much later vessel, and may well have been one of the ships set on fire by the Greek fleet during the War of Independence, the cannon-balls having been used as ballast. But even this suggests that the sea at that time had roughly the same depth at this point as it does today.

Other useful archaeological evidence for the general area is the EH site at the cave of Mavri Trypa on the now uninhabited island of Skhiza (Valmin 1930, 162; 1953, 44, pl. II 3; Chadzi 1981, 156) and the new site of probably the same period in the cove of Karavostasi, or Skhiza Creek, on the N-E side of the same island, which was found in 1990 during a survey in which I took part. There are a number of wrecks on the seabed around the entrance to the cove, mostly Roman in date.

A little to the N of Methoni on the W coast there is an almost circular inlet known as Limna tou Pappa (Fig. 1) with a very narrow entrance channel from the sea (Fig. 13). Along the vertical cliff on the N side of the channel traces of series of successive submerged shorelines are apparent in the limestone at depths of 1–7 m. On the southern point of the entrance on the side facing the islets of Nisakoulia (not to be confused with the Nisakouli at Methoni), a solid round tower still stands to a height of some 2.5 m (Fig. 14), built of roughly worked stones with mortar and packed with sherds, dating to late Antiquity or the early Middle Ages. It was probably a beacon tower, since it is visible from Methoni on one side and the peak of Ai-Thanasis (the southern tip of the Ag. Nikolaos heights) on the other, and since on the summit of Ag. Nikolaos the trigonometric marker of the Army Survey is surrounded by a circular structure of similar construction; from this point there is direct visual communication with Paleo Navarino. One might have expected the beacon tower to have been built on Megalo Nisakouli, since this is more clearly visible on the Methoni — Ai-Thanasis line, has fresh water at the bottom of a natural cutting on the eastern side, and a few prehistoric sherds have been noted on its surface. The reason it was not used is probably because the submerged spit that extends from the southern point of the entrance channel to the northern tip of Megalo Nisakouli at a depth of no more than 2 m was already submerged at the time the tower was built.

Figure 14. The beacon tower of Limna tou Pappa. View from the S.

Figure 15. The barrier of beach rock in a cove on the Romanos coast.

In the same district, S of Limna tou Pappa, there is a long inlet suitable as a temporary shelter for craft, in the middle of which there are numerous fragments of Hellenistic amphoras at a depth of 6 m, which probably came from an old shipwreck. Sherds of the same period are found on the neck of the point, while the eastern shore of Limna tou Pappa is skirted by the foundations of a strong wall built of roughly worked stones that follows the curve of the shore. This wall might have been used as the source of building material for the beacon tower, and at first sight appears to be Hellenistic in date. If this is the case, then this particular stretch of coast must have had the same configuration in that period as well.

Further N, in the cove of Limanaki, or Glyfa Nera (Fig. 1), where there are underwater springs, just S of Niokastro (Pylos), fragments of concreted Hellenistic commercial amphoras were found in the rocky shallows (up to 3 m) on its southern shore, apparently from an ancient shipwreck in this place. Here I will only mention the MH sherds, an indication of habitation, on what is today the precipitous, inaccessible and unfriendly islet of Pylos, or Tsigli Baba (Korres 1981, 240), S of Sphaktiria, and pass on to the prehistoric sherds that have been found on a low hill on the beach of Romanou (Fig. 1), in the vicinity of the survey mark, on the red earth that is visible in places under the modern dunes.

This hill commands a small cove closed on the seaward side by a formation of beach-rock (Fig. 15) that projects at least 60 cm above the surface of the sea for its greater part. There is no archaeological evidence for the time when this barrier was formed, but some indication of the rate at which it formed in the locality of Rivari further to the S is given by the imprint of a modern beer can which was observed in the surface layer of the rock. It may be noted that this area too has been the subject of a special palaeomorphological study (Kraft *et al.*, 1980).

Discussion

What the above archaeological evidence and observations suggest is that in spite of the undoubted fact of the rapid erosion that occurred at certain points along the shoreline, there are also strong indications of seismic activity, and this must have played a decisive part in the formation of the basic lines of the present map of the region. Furthermore, the sites described conform to the necessary preconditions postulated by Flemming (1969, 85) for similar sites in the Western Mediterranean.

According to the archaeological data cited here, this seismic activity can be dated between the end of the MH period and the end of the Hellenistic to the beginning of the Roman period, and should not be confused with more recent seismic phenomena in this region (Pirazzoli, 1986).

I hope that this paper will stimulate wider scientific collaboration and research in this archaeologically-rich but still little known region of Messenia. I hope that such a collaboration will further confirm the truth of Blackman's remark (1973, 136): 'Flemming has shown how much use the geomorphologist can make of archaeological evidence for sea-level change. It is for the archaeologist to be aware of the value and limitations of such evidence and to supply data to the geomorphologist, who in return can aid the archaeologist's understanding of coastal sites.'

The results will constitute the answer to my original question, following the dictum of Masters and Flemming (1983, 603), who at the Symposium at the Scripps Institution of Oceanography on 26–29 October 1981 declared that 'archaeological interpretation, on the other hand, typically requires accuracy of the order of 1.0 m. To obtain this resolution each site area must be studied specifically to determine the local sea level-time relationship.'

Acknowledgements

I visited most of the sites during this time with Mrs A. Argiraki, archaeologist and assistant lecturer in the Department of History and Archaeology at the University of Athens; I would like to take this opportunity to thank her for her assistance. I also wish to thank the head custodian of antiquities at Methoni, Mr D. Sardelis, who also happens to be an amateur fisherman and hunter. Mr Sardelis, in each of these capacities, is an expert in the topography of the region. I am indebted to him for the local place names and for much useful information about the area.

References

van Andel, T. H. & Shackleton, J. C. (1982). Late Paleolithic and Mesolithic Coastlines of Greece and the Aegean. *Journal of Field Archaeology* **5**, 445–454.

Blackman, D. J. (1973). Evidence of sea level change in ancient harbours and coastal installations. In (D. J. Blackman, Ed.) *Marine Archaeology*, Colston Papers, 115–139. London; Butterworth.

Chadzi, G. (1981). Tours - Location of Antiquities, Nomos of Messenia. *Archaeologikon Deltion* **36**, B1 Chronika, 155–156. (In Greek).

Choremis, C. (1969). MH Altar on Nisakouli, Methoni. *Archaeologica Analekta Athenon* **2**, 10–14. (In Greek).

Delaporta, C. P. & Spondilis, I. (1987). Un habitat Helladique Ancien II à Platiyali Astakos. In (H. Tzalas, Ed.), *Tropis II, 2nd International Symposium on Ship Construction in Antiquity*, 127–134. Delphi: Hell. Inst. for the Preservation of the Nautical Tradition.

Delaporta, A., Spondilis, I. & Baxevanakis, Y. (1990). Platiyali - Astakos: a submerged Early Helladic site in Akarnania. *Enalia Annual* **1** (1989), 44–46.

Flemming, N. C. (1969). Archaeological Evidence of Eustatic Change of Sea Level and Earth Movements. In *The Western Mediterranean during the last 2,000 years*. Colorado: The Geological Society of America, Special Paper 109.

Flemming, N. C., Czartoryska, N. M. G. & Hunter, P. M. (1973a). Archaeological Evidence for Vertical Earth Movements in the Region of the Aegean Islands Arc. In (N. C. Flemming, Ed.) *Science Diving International*, 47–65.

Flemming, N. C., Czartoryska, N. M. G. & Hunter, P. M. (1973b). Archaeological Evidence for eustatic and tectonic components of relative sea level change in the south Aegean. In (D. J. Blackman Ed.) *Marine Archaeology*, Colston Papers, 1–66. London; Butterworth.

Flemming, N. C., Raban, A. & Goetschel, G. (1978). Tectonic and Eustatic Changes in the Mediterranean Coast of Israel in the last 9,000 years. In (J. Barto Arnold III Jr., Ed.) *Beneath the Waters of Time*, 129–165. Austin, Texas; Texas Antiquities Committee, Publ. 6.

Korres, G. St. (1981). Excavation at Voidokilia. *Praktika Archaeologikis Etairias* **A´**, 194–240. Athens. (In Greek).

Kraft, J. C. & Aschenbrenner, S. E. (1977). Paleogeographic Reconstruction in the Methoni Embayment in Greece. *Journal of Field Archaeology* **4**, 419–444.

Kraft, J. C., Kayan, Il. & Aschenbrenner, S. E. (1985). Geological Studies of Coastal Change applied to Archaeological Settings. In (G. Rapp Jr & J. A. Gifford, Eds) *Archaeological Geology*, 57–84. London; Princeton Univ. Press.

Kraft, J. C., Rapp Jr, G. R. & Aschenbrenner, S. E. (1975). Late Holocene paleogeography of the coastal plain of the Gulf of Messenia, Greece, and its relationships to archaeological settings and to coastal change. *Geological Society of America Bulletin* **86**, 1191–1208.

Kraft, J. C., Rapp Jr, G. R. & Aschenbrenner, S. E. (1980). Late Holocene Paleogeomorphic Reconstruction in the Area of the Bay of Navarino: Sandy Pylos. *Journal of Archaeological Science* **7**, 187–210.

Lianos, N. (1987). A study of the ancient harbour works of Methoni. Pub. Ministry of Culture. In *Restoration - Conservation - Protection of Monuments and Complexes*, 129–135. Athens. (In Greek).

Loy, W. G. (1967). *The Land of Nestor: A Physical Geography of the Southwestern Peloponnese*. Office of Naval Research Report no. 34. Washington D.C.

McDonald, W. A. & Rapp, G. R. Jr. (1972). *The Minnesota Messenia Expedition: Reconstructing a Bronze Age Regional Environment*. Minneapolis; University of Minnesota Press.

Masters, P. M. & Flemming, N. C. (1983). Summary and Conclusions. In (P. M. Masters & N. C. Flemming, Eds) *Quaternary Coastlines and Marine Archaeology*, 601–629. London; Academic Press.

Pirazzoli, P. A. (1986). The Early Byzantine Tectonic Paroxysm and its influence on coastal sites in the Eastern Mediterranean. In *Cities on the Sea-Past and Present*, Summaries 1st International Symposium on Harbours, Port Cities and Coastal Topography, 149–152. Haifa.

Pirazzoli, P. A. (1988). Sea-level Changes and Crustal Movements in the Hellenic Arc (Greece), The Contribution of Archaeological and Historical Data. In (A. Raban, Ed.) *Archaeology of Coastal Changes*. BAR International Series 404, 157–182. Oxford.

Psychoyos, O. (1988). *Déplacements de la ligne de rivage et sites archéologiques dans les régions côtières de la mer Egée au Néolithique et à l'age du Bronze*. Studies in Mediterranean Archaeology Pocket-book 62. Jonsered.

Valmin, N. (1930). *Etudes Topographiques sur la Messénie Ancienne*. Lund; Carl Blom.

Valmin, M. N. (1953). Malthi-epilog. *Opuscula Atheniensia* **1**, 29–46. Lund.

Identification of Earthquakes
from Archaeological Data:
Methodology, Criteria and Limitations

Stathis C. Stiros

Institute of Geology and Mineral Exploration (IGME)
70, Mesoghion Street, 115 27 Athens, Greece

Abstract

Structural damage and abandonment of ancient buildings and sites in various areas and periods have for long been assigned by archaeologists to earthquakes. The latter, however, were regarded more as *Deus ex machina* than scientific explanations of the observed effects. Recent regional studies covering a wide time span have revealed that, in spite of the fragmentary and sometimes inconclusive character of archaeological findings, it is possible to present a typology of earthquake effects in architectural works corresponding to different architectural and structural styles. It is possible too to discriminate between traces of earthquakes from those of other natural and anthropogenic effects, and also to recognize the way of thinking of ancient architects and builders who were trying to minimize the seismic vulnerability of their works. A list of criteria is presented for the identification of earthquakes from ancient remains, if certain conditions are satisfied. This approach certainly leaves unexplained a number of cases of destruction and abandonment of ancient ruins, but contributes to more solid foundations for Archaeoseismology.

Introduction

Very few ancient architectural works survive today. Most were destroyed either because of the ageing of their materials, or deliberately, during wars, or because of architectural innovations. In seismically active areas there are also numerous ancient constructions which were demolished or simply damaged suddenly in a way that excludes human agency. The characteristic structural damage of some of them has for long being assigned to earthquakes. The architect, W.B. Dinsmoor, for instance, speaking about the Temple of Zeus Olympius at Acragas (Agrigento) in Sicily (Fig. 1) suggested that 'the south wall of the cella lies flat on the floor, with the blocks in their proper positions, just as it was upset during an earthquake' (Dinsmoor 1985, 105). The archaeologist, Carl Blegen, assigned the catastrophe that marks the end of the VIth city of Troy to an earthquake, since no signs of a generalised conflagration, hostile attack or post-destruction change in the organisation, economy, foreign relationships and culture of the city was observed; the mass of structures that were hurled down 'point to a force beyond the power of human hands in an age before the invention of explosives and modern machinery of destruction' (Blegen, 1963). Finally, the geologist, N. Kritikos, assigned the sinusoidal offset of two drums of the columns of Hephaisteion (Theseion) temple in Athens (Fig. 2) to earthquakes, and concluded that the city is not earthquake-safe, as was hitherto believed (see Galanopoulos, 1956).

While in these cases the effects of earthquakes in ancient constructions were recognised, or even certain associated methodological problems were confronted, Sir Arthur Evans (1928), inspired by an earthquake that

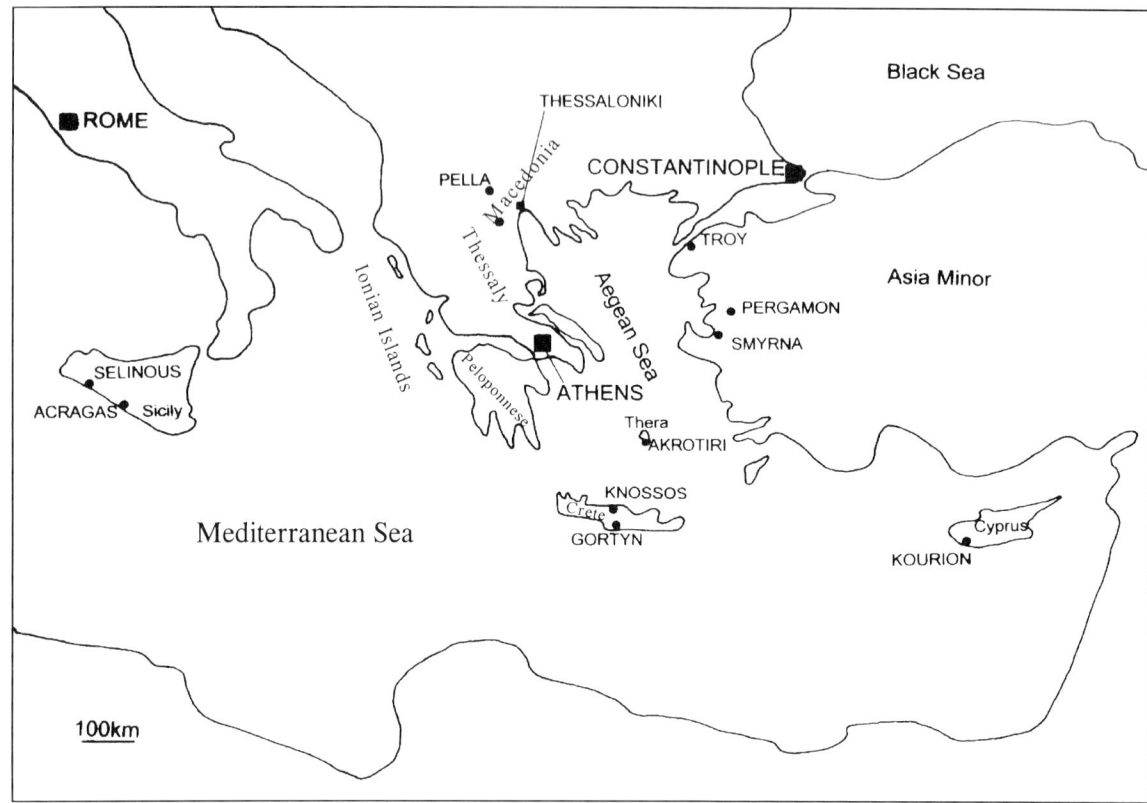

Figure 1a. Location map.

hit Knossos in Crete during his excavations in 1926, went a step ahead. Based on evidence of a destruction layer, he established the tradition of regarding earthquake horizons as benchmarks in archaeological stratigraphy and chronology. Following this tradition and in the light of modern experience of earthquake effects (for instance, Naumann, 1971), historical data and numerous inscriptions reporting earthquake damage and fatalities (for example, Robert, 1978; Guidoboni, 1989), modern archaeologists assign many of the destructions of ancient constructions to earthquakes. Some have gone further, proposing that seismic events had a catalysing, historical role in the evolution and death of ancient societies (Marinatos, 1939; Kilian, 1980; 1986).

Among the numerous archaeological earthquake hypotheses a few are well documented (for instance, Sakellarakis & Sapouna-Sakellaraki, 1981; Sorren & Davis, 1985; Sorren, 1988); in most cases the existing evidence is at best inconclusive (for instance, fallen rocks or tilted walls, conflagration or a modern earthquake in the area) and a seismic destruction simply appears as a *Deus ex machina* to explain the destruction of a building or the abandonment of a site. Others generated long-lasting debates; the discussion on the authenticity of the Trojan War and the possible role of earthquakes in destroying the walls of the Mycenaean city of Troy (Easton, 1985) is one of the most fascinating examples of such debates. In spite of the familiarisation of the archaeological community with earthquake hypotheses, the systematic and scientific approach of this matter has only appeared in recent years, leading to the birth of Archaeoseismology as an interdisciplinary field of research (Naumann, 1971; Karcz & Kafri, 1978; Rapp, 1987; Stiros, 1988b; Nikonov, 1988; Kirikov, 1992).

Deciphering earthquakes from archaeological data

One of the first aims of archaeoseismic research was to formulate diagnostic criteria for a reasonably secure recognition of traces of ancient earthquakes from ancient remains. The first results on this subject have been presented by Karcz & Kafri (1978), Nikonov (1988) and Stiros & Dakoronia (1989). An updated version of these criteria and a typology of seismic damage in ancient architectural remains are included in this paper (Appendix 2).

To document an ancient seismic destruction it is necessary to show that (i) the observed effects can unhesitatingly be assigned to an earthquake, and (ii) any other cause can be excluded; in many cases, however, such a conclusion will not be without reservations unless some independent evidence (for example, results from a nearby excavation) is available. The identification of an earthquake challenges the investigator to further answer a number of questions: when did the earthquake occur? What were its parameters? How is it related to geological features and surface deformation? How is it related to other destructions or destruction layers? What were its historical implications? Any of these questions may lead to a pitfall. It is therefore a prerequisite of any presentation of diagnostic criteria of ancient earthquakes to discuss in a simple way some methodological problems of the archaeological and archaeoseismic research. A short section on how earthquakes work is included for those who may be unfamiliar with this topic.

Figure 1b. Location map.

How earthquakes work

As textbooks on Seismology or Geology describe, the rigid cover of the earth (the lithosphere) is not stable, but consists of a great number of fragments of different sizes (plates, at the size of continents, to tectonic blocks up to few kilometres or even less). In tectonically and seismically active areas these lithospheric fragments move relative to each other along fractures called faults. The latter are discontinuities up to hundreds of kilometres long, up to ten or more kilometres deep, and sometimes cut through the surface; in this case their most usual geomorphic expression is escarpments flanking mountains.

The rough surface of faults prevents the blocks from moving relative to each other easily, and the rocks along the fault surfaces initially deform because they are to some extent elastic. If the stress due to the relative

Figure 2. Sinusoidal offset of drums of columns in the 5th century BC Hephaisteion (Theseion) temple in Athens, indicative of seismic deformation according to N. Kritikos (after Galanopoulos, 1956). See also Figs 3 and 6.

Figure 3. Colona Antonina in Rome: rotations and displacements of around 15 cm, observed on the 4 m wide drums of this 40 m high column are clearly seen in the offset sculptures. The similar Colona Traiana, about 700 m away, is in a perfect state of preservation (see Sinopoli, 1989a; Funiciello *et al.*, 1989 and Figs 2 and 6).

movement of the blocks is maintained for long enough, the deformation may exceed the elastic strength of the rocks which fracture along the faults. At the moment of fracture, the rocks regain their original shape but to a new position. It is during the sudden movement of the rocks back to their original shapes, after the stress is released, that the ground 'shakes'. This results in the propagation of waves which move away from the focus (i.e. the point on the fault where the seismic waves are generated, at some depth beneath the surface, vertically below the epicentre), as waves spread out on a pond from a stone dropped into the water.

An earthquake is a complicated process, and is better described as an earthquake sequence, that is a major shock preceded and followed by numerous other smaller shocks (originating from the same or neighbouring foci) and by different types of seismic waves.

Earthquake scales

The magnitude of the earthquake depends on the amount of elastic energy released, the latter obviously depending on the dimensions of the seismogenic fault. The magnitude of earthquakes is estimated from seismograms and is usually measured on the Richter scale. On this logarithmic scale shocks with magnitude 5 or 8, for instance, are associated with an elastic energy release 33 times larger than earthquakes of magnitude 4 and 7 respectively. Similarly, the amplitude of ground motions (or of seismic waves) increases by a factor of 10 for each unit of increase of the magnitude of the shock. The maximum known magnitude of earthquakes is 8.9.

Another very useful measure of the strength of an earthquake is its intensity, which measures the amount of shaking of the ground or damage in a specific site (see Rapp, 1987). Intensity depends on the magnitude of the earthquake, the distance from the epicentre and the depth of the focus, as well as the geological background of an area; recent unconsolidated sediments for instance tend to magnify intensities. For this reason, intensities can vary considerably even at nearby sites. Discussed below is the case of Colona Antonina and Colona Traiana in Rome. These two columns are only about 700 m apart, but the extent of shaking and deformation at their base from the same shock was different, and this at least partly explains their different response to seismic shocks and different states of preservation (see Funiciello *et al.*, 1989; here Fig. 3).

Archaeoseismic data are obviously more suited to the estimation of seismic intensities. If, however, there is available information for intensities in different areas, the magnitude of the earthquake can be estimated.

Recurrence intervals of earthquakes

Various seismological and geological studies reveal that not all areas are hit by earthquakes with the same frequency. Some areas, for example the Corinth area, Thessaly and the Ionian Islands in Greece, are hit by strong earthquakes every few tens of years. In other areas the corresponding period of return of major earthquakes is larger, a few hundred or even a few thousands of years, i.e. periods for which no recordings in seismographic stations, nor memories of seismic disasters exist. This is the explanation why, for instance, the area of Sparta was regarded by ancient writers as an area of high seismic risk (Strabo, VIII,8,4 = C389), but not other areas of the Peloponnese like Messenia or Elis. Any modern map of epicentres of earthquakes in the areas, based on seismograph recordings covering a period of less than a century, shows exactly the reverse situation!

Effects of earthquakes

Ground shaking

This is the major result of earthquakes, and is due to a combination of travelling seismic waves. The effects of ground shaking on various architectural works are analysed in other sections of this paper.

Surface faulting and surface tectonic deformation

Earthquakes are associated with deformation of the deep seismogenic layers along seismic faults and involve displacement of blocks on one side of a fault relative to the other in a vertical or horizontal sense, or their combination. Seismic faults rarely cut through the surface (surface faults). In most cases, the uppermost strata deform plastically (are usually buckled) and prevent faulting from reaching the surface (blind faults). Surface faults can be recognised from vertical and/or horizontal offsets in characteristic natural features (slopes, streams, etc.), and even man-made constructions (fences, road pavements, lines of equally spaced trees, etc.) with an amplitude of up to a few metres for each seismic event (the San Andreas Fault, California, for instance, is the most well-studied case; Wallace (1990) gives a well-illustrated presentation). The cumulative displacement of surface seismic faults produces the faults seen on the surface as scarps, usually several tens of metres high. Most of them, however, are not active (seismogenic) any more.

Some active faults cross areas inhabited (or exploited) since prehistoric times. Therefore, a number of anthropogenic remains are cut and offset by surface seismic faults and testify to their reactivation. The best example is the Great Wall of China, offset by the 1739 fault by about 3 m in the vertical and horizontal senses (Zang *et al.*, 1986). Smaller offsets of ancient constructions have been reported by Trifonov (1978), Stiros (1988a, b) and Stiros & Dakoronia (1989). Three characteristic deformed constructions are shown in Fig. 4. While cases of deformed ancient constructions are frequent in the archaeological literature, not all offset or deformed structures testify to seismic faulting or associated deformation; local ground instability effects may be responsible for the changes in their shapes. Yet, some of the latter may have been caused by earthquakes. For instance, in the palace of Vergina in ancient Macedonia (northern Greece), three parallel minor walls are

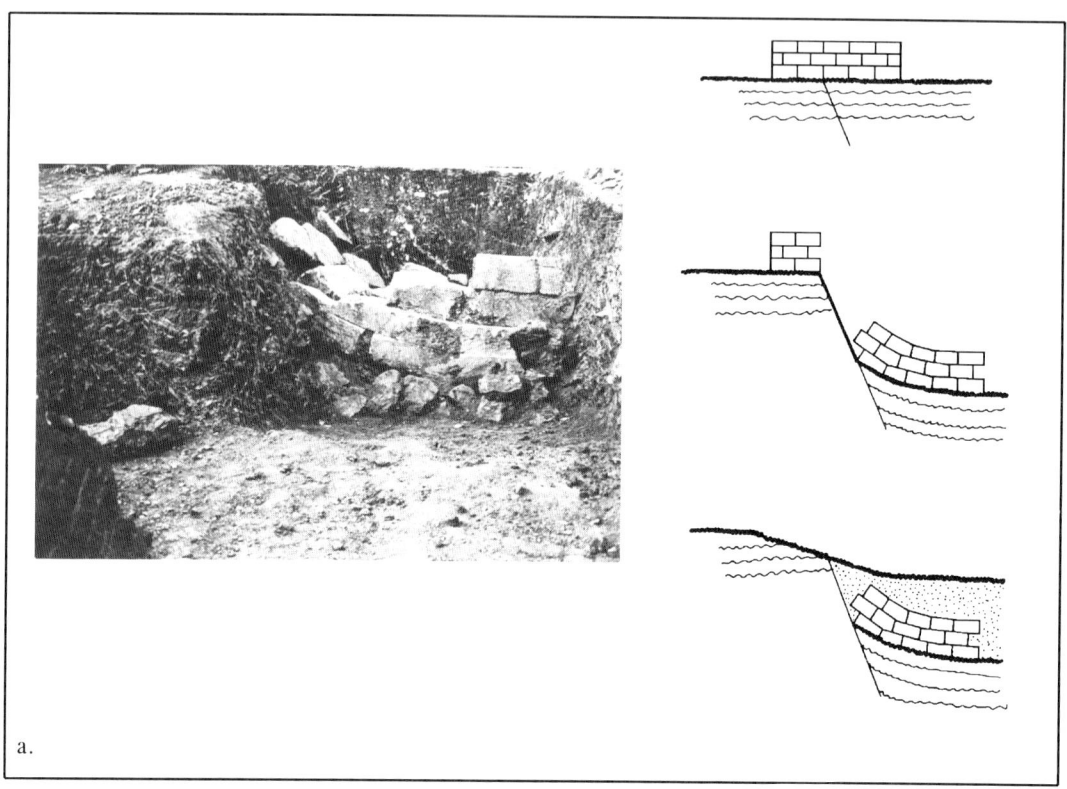

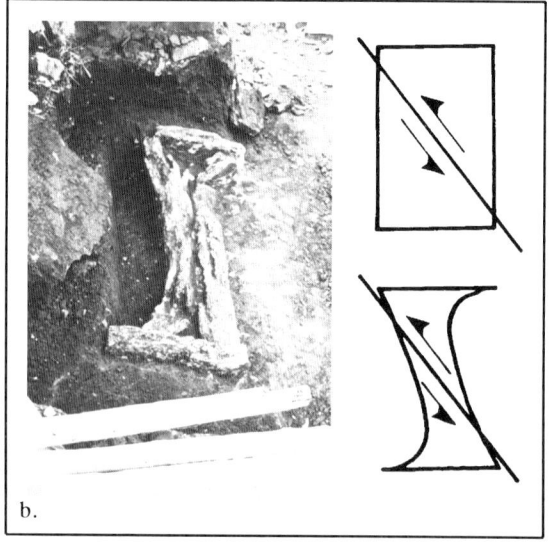

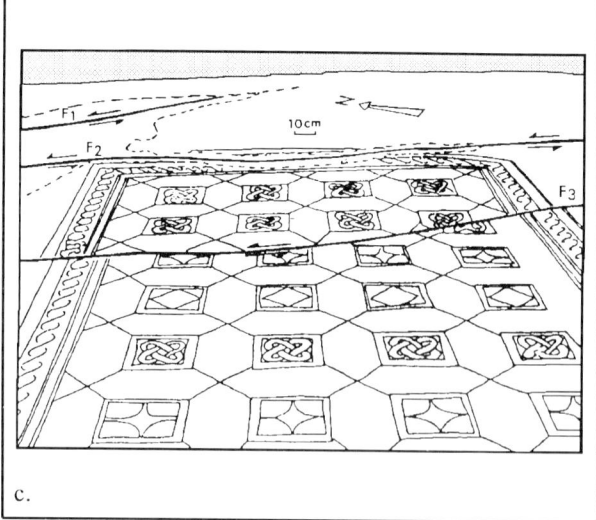

Figure 4. Ancient remains offset and deformed by seismic faulting. (a) Atalandi, central Greece, earthquake *c.* 450 BC; (b) Lamia central Greece; (c) Tunis (for references see Stiros, 1988a, b; Stiros & Dakoronia, 1989).

systematically laterally offset along a well-defined line (Bakalakis & Andronikos, 1969), but it is difficult to explain them as indicative of seismic surface faulting. Geomorphological changes associated with blind or seismic surface faults, for example coastal uplifts (Pirazzoli, this volume), uplifts in the hinterland hindering the flow of rivers and giving birth to (transient) lakes (Meghraoui *et al.*, 1988), or coastal subsidence (Stiros & Dakoronia, 1989) have also been documented.

Secondary effects

The shaking of the ground may produce permanent secondary but locally very destructive effects like landslides, liquification or compaction of unconsolidated sediments, changes in the rate of flow of sources, etc. Landslides may destroy buildings or even whole towns (see Marinatos, 1960), hinder the flow of rivers and cause flooding (Rapp, 1987; Nur & Ron, this volume). Liquification or compaction of unconsolidated sediments may deform the ground of buildings and cause their collapse. Landslides offshore or faulting of the seabed may produce tsunamis, i.e. seismic sea waves which can sweep coastal areas up to a height of tens of metres (Ambraseys, 1962; cf. also Dakoronia, this volume). Zangger (1993) discusses the case of the seismic destruction of a dam due to which a part of the town of Tiryns in the Argolid was buried under flood deposits 3–5 m thick.

In summary, the seismic damage is caused by (1) seismic waves (shaking of the ground), (2) surface faulting and tectonic deformations and (3) secondary effects, landslides, tsunamis, etc. Obviously, the bulk of seismic damage on human constructions is associated with shaking of the ground, though permanent deformations of the latter due to deep tectonic or secondary effects may locally be very important.

Response of constructions to earthquakes — structural considerations

In principle, the effects of seismic waves on an construction manifest themselves in two forces: one horizontal force exerted at the top of the construction, and a vertical force exerted at its foundations. These forces are not constant in amplitude, and they are alternating in direction. Their result is to tend to deform (momentarily) rectangular shapes to parallelograms (pure shear; Fig. 5). In the case of a tall, slender column, the effects of these forces is to make these structures oscillate around a vertical axis (Fig. 6). If the strength of the structure is adequate, the seismic deformation will be quickly attenuated, otherwise a permanent deformation (Fig. 8), or even the collapse of the structure of some of its parts, will occur.

The response of a construction to an earthquake depends on the parameters of the earthquake, such as its magnitude, and the structural characteristics of the building. For instance, according to observations of M. Korres, the first main shock of the 1981 seismic sequence in the Gulf of Corinth produced offsets in columns of the Parthenon in Athens, but not the second main shock of the same sequence that occurred a few hours later! Constructions, whether in wood or of hewn blocks held together by the forces of gravity and friction (so-called ductile constructions), such as ancient Egyptian and Greek temples, can accommodate small deformations between their elements. Furthermore, they respond to an earthquake in a way different from constructions made of rocks cemented with strong mortar not permitting an internal deformation without failure (brittle constructions, such as many Roman and Byzantine buildings).

The effects of earthquakes depend also on their orientation relative to the direction of propagation of the seismic waves; the effect of a seismic force acting in the direction of a wall is illustrated in Fig. 5a. By contrast, a seismic force perpendicular to a wall will tend to separate it from any transverse walls (Fig. 7a), bend and fracture it along a horizontal line near its foundations and finally topple it. This last effect is not observed in stocky walls, nor close to corners made with interbonded rocks etc. Consequently, the factors of design and scale are among those controlling the seismic response of buildings.

Modern analytical engineering techniques permit a detailed modelling of present-day constructions made of reinforced concrete and other materials, but they are not appropriate to ancient buildings. The latter

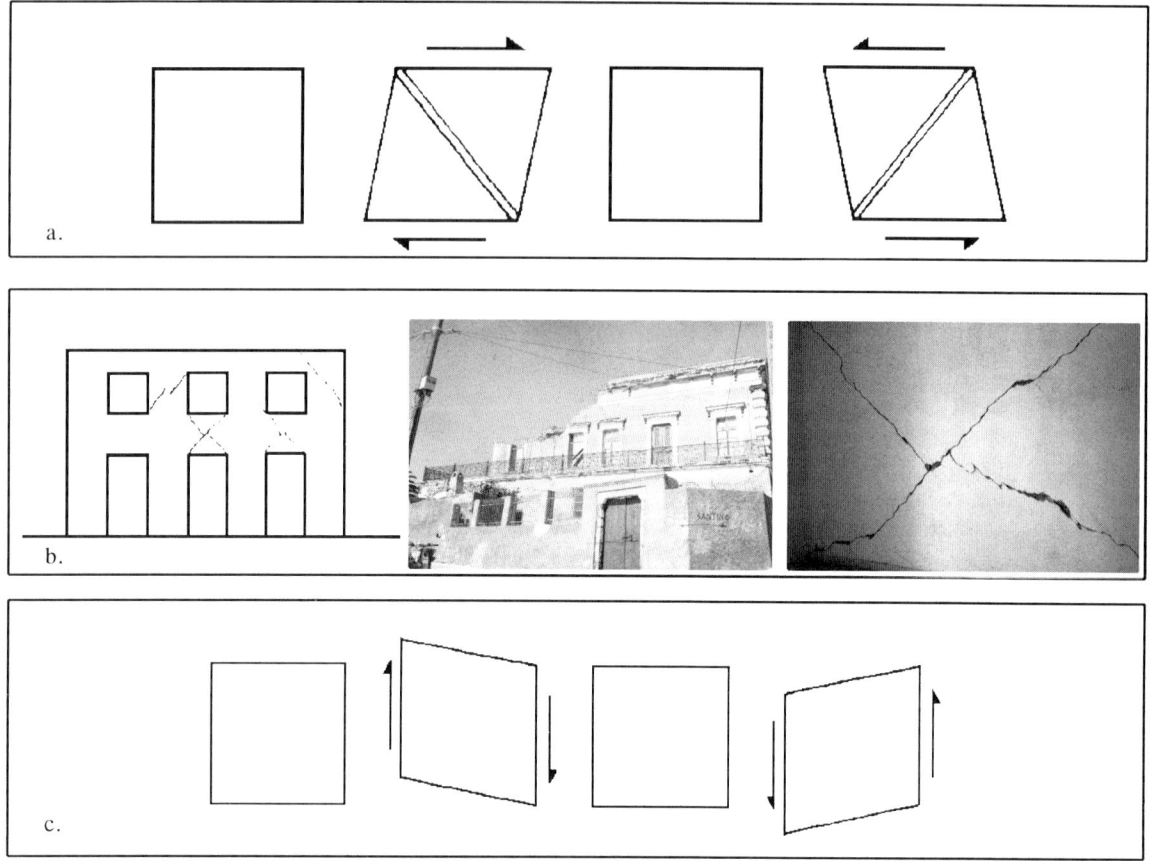

Figure 5(a). The effect of a horizontal seismic acceleration (or force) is to oblige a structure to oscillate (better expressed in columns and other slender constructions, see Fig. 6a), tending to deform a rectangle to parallelograms. Under its influence, a rigid structure (a structure made with strong mortar like a Roman or Byzantine wall) tends to fail and diagonal fissures tend to form. In the case of ductile structures (structures of dry masonry, of wood, and to a lesser degree of mudbrick) the deformation is distributed and accommodated by the opening and closure of joints; a permanent deformation may, however, remain (cf Fig. 2 in Korres, this volume).

(b) Typical occurrence of seismic fractures in buildings: left: modelling; fissures are often near openings and in corners; middle: a house at Messaria, Thera, after the 1956 earthquake and right: diagonal fractures in the brick-and-mortar filling walls of a modern building in the village of Sergoula, near Naupaktos, after the $M_s = 5.1$ earthquake on February 11, 1985 in the Gulf of Corinth. The reinforced concrete frame was not harmed.

(c) Effect of a vertical seismic force (vertical acceleration) in a rectangular shape.

correspond to different structural styles, are made with different materials, and in most cases their detailed structure behind the decorations are not known. For example, it is not possible to know what exactly lies at the foundations of the Parthenon, inside the dome of the Pantheon in Rome or inside the piers of Aghia Sophia of Constantinople (Istanbul). On the other hand, earthquakes that occurred during the last few decades and are recorded on seismograms are probably not representative of the earthquakes that have hit monuments erected hundreds or thousands of years ago. In spite of all these difficulties, it is possible to describe certain characteristic cases, and these are given in Appendix 1.

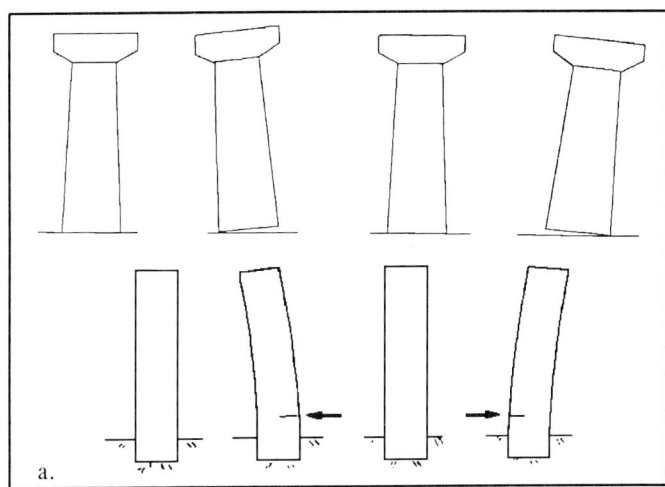

Figure 6(a). Seismic oscillation of a slender, free-standing monolithic column around its base corner edges (above) and of another column clamped to the ground (below). In the latter case a large amplitude oscillation produces strong extensional stresses at the bases of the columns; such stresses cannot be accommodated by mortar and other material whose tensile strength is very small. As a result, the columns fracture at the points marked with arrows and topple down.

(b). Seismic oscillation of a colonnade of a temple consisting of free standing blocks (ductile structure). Note that during oscillations the structure tends to take the shape of a parallelogram.

(c). Seismic oscillation of a multi-block column consisting of drums simply resting on top of one other. When the oscillating parts of the column (or the whole column) return to the vertical position, they collide with the rigid ground surface, and because of this impact a translation also occurs (based on Sinopoli, 1989a, b; 1991; Augusti & Sinopoli, 1992; compare with Figs 2 and 3). It is obvious that a, if not the, reason for metal or wood reinforcements in the columns, shown in Fig. 10 (in fact, a matter of debate among specialists, see Dinsmoor 1985, 172) was to prevent or minimise sliding following impact.

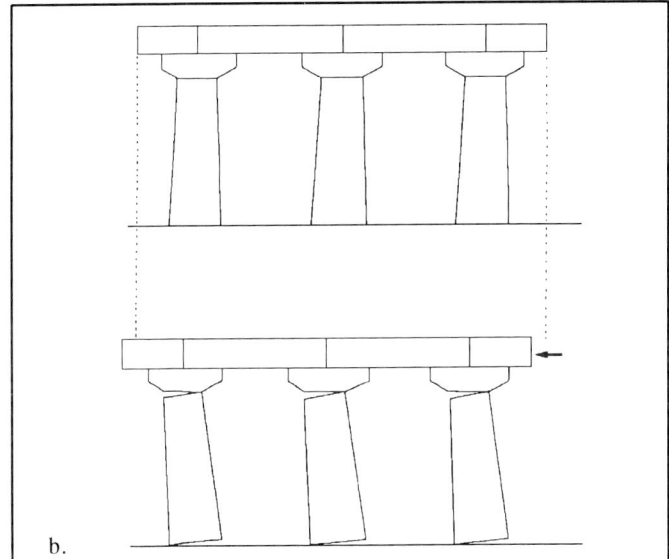

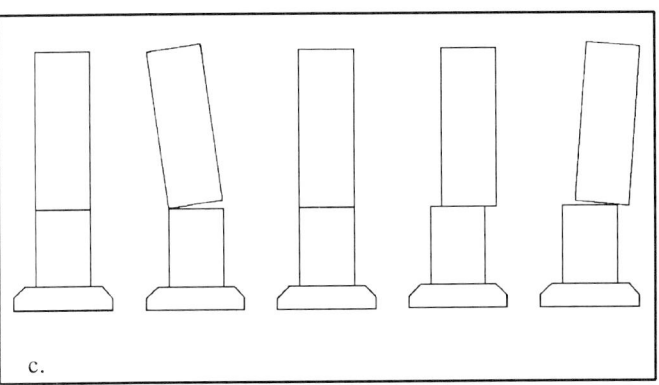

b.

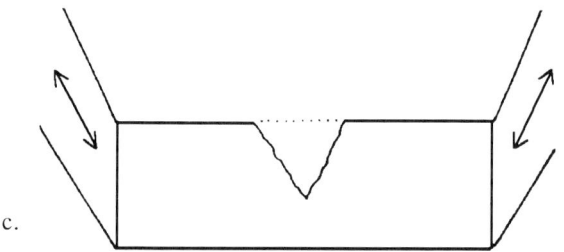

a.   c.

Figure 7(a). Church at Kalamata (S-W Peloponnese), affected by the 1986 earthquake. A seismic force in the direction of the arrows resulted in the separation of the walls through vertical cracks along the corner, in order to facilitate the oscillation of the wall normal to its direction. The shock was not, however, fatal, and the wall did not collapse.
(b). To prevent collapse of separated walls, as in (a), especially if these accommodate loads (for instance, from the roof), buttresses are usually built; the example here is the Monastery of Osios Loukas, near Delphi, Central Greece.
(c). If the corner is strongly built (for instance with interbonding well-hewn rocks), the formation of vertical cracks along the corners is not possible. But if the walls are large relative to their height and of rather poor construction (if low strength mortar and no perimetric reinforcing layers are used), a seismic force in the direction of the arrows will tend to produce the collapse of a triangular section.

The characteristic frequency of a structure

Maximum deformation is obtained when the frequency of the seismic waves is close to the value of the characteristic natural frequency (or period) of oscillation of the structure. This period (or frequency) depends on the geometrical and structural characteristics of each structure and will be changed if alterations to the structure itself are made. For instance, the fundamental period of the 36 m high minaret of the Rotonda of Thessaloniki was 0.8 sec before and 0.97 sec after an internal reinforced concrete jacket was inserted at the top of the minaret (Penelis *et al.*, 1993). This indicates that structural interventions may expose monuments to risks different from those to which they were previously exposed. The Rotonda minaret survived without damage four centuries exposed to earthquakes and thunderstorms, yet in its present condition it is untested against such hazards.

The characteristic, natural frequency of oscillation of the various structures is responsible for their selective response to various types of earthquakes. Generally speaking, a small earthquake only generates short wavelength waves which do not travel very far; such an earthquake can be destructive to low (short-wavelength) constructions close to its epicentre, but in principle can cause no harm to tall buildings. Strong earthquakes generate long-wavelength waves as well which may affect distant, long-period tall buildings like columns and minarets, but not their adjacent, low constructions. An example is the 1985 earthquake in Mexico City which caused the collapse of multi-storey buildings, but did not harm modest dwellings. For this reason, the large distant earthquakes which can cause damage to a large number multi-storey buildings in modern cities, would have practically no effect on low (short-period) ancient buildings (Ambraseys, 1971).

Two conclusions from this analysis can be arrived at. First, there is no ground for hypothesising 'universal' earthquakes (like that of AD 365) which devastated most of the ancient world. And second, archaeological data generally record local earthquakes, whose epicentres were up to a few tens of kilometres away from the affected areas; minarets, tall slender columns and certain towers are an exception to this rule. Another conclusion is that the selective response of various types of constructions to earthquakes reported and modelled by modern engineers (Housner, 1963), and the manner of seismic damage to ancient constructions in particular, observed by archaeologists (Naumann, 1971), were not unknown to ancient builders. The latter, operating on the 'trial and error technique', probably developed their construction styles not only on the grounds of aesthetics and static efficiency, but on the dynamic strength of their works as well. It can therefore be assumed that the evolution of certain architectural styles was to some degree influenced by the seismicity of certain areas, a hypothesis analysed elsewhere.

Static and dynamic effects

The partial or total failure of a building can be caused by static or dynamic effects. A *static failure* is that caused by the weight of a construction itself, or of its parts, without any external abrupt loading. Static failure can result from overloading, bad design, gradual weakening or even deformation of a structure due to its ageing (leaking mortar, dissolved bricks, rotten timber, etc.) or foundation weakness (differential settlement, tilting, etc.). For certain types of ancient monuments designed to last indefinitely, a static failure is rather improbable: Greek temples, for instance, are made of marble or other good quality rocks, and due to the large dimensions of their structural elements their stress level is relatively low, and cannot, usually, be responsible for cracks or their static failure (Sinopoli, 1989b; 1991).

A *dynamic failure*, in contrast, is caused by external violent loads, such as those caused by earthquakes, winds, explosions, rock falling downhill, bombs, floods, and thunderstorms, and have some specific effects. An explosion, for instance, at the base of a medieval rampart would produce quasi-vertical fissures, cutting bricks and rocks along its path. The effects of earthquakes, on the other hand, have already been discussed. While the mechanisms of static and dynamic deformation and failure are quite different, as is for example illustrated in Fig. 8, the discrimination between static and dynamic loads as agents for the partial or total failure of ancient constructions is not an easy task, especially since the destruction of ancient constructions is usually due to their combination, or even to chain effects. The discrimination of the various dynamic effects from their results is also a problem without any ready solution. Two examples from the Acropolis of Athens discussed by Korres (this volume) and from the nearby Temple of Olympian Zeus illustrate these problems. At the Propylaia, a huge marble beam fallen from the ceiling (not necessarily because of an earthquake) hit a column and produced an offset similar to that caused directly by earthquakes. The sliding of a part of the S wall and columns of the Parthenon along horizontal joints was assigned to the 1687 explosion (i.e. another dynamic effect), until it was found that this deformation predated the construction of a 12th century wall and must merely be assigned to an earthquake (Korres, this volume). A column from the Temple of Olympian Zeus fell during a storm in the last century, and its drums have the domino-type arrangement, usual in seismic destructions (see Fig. 9).

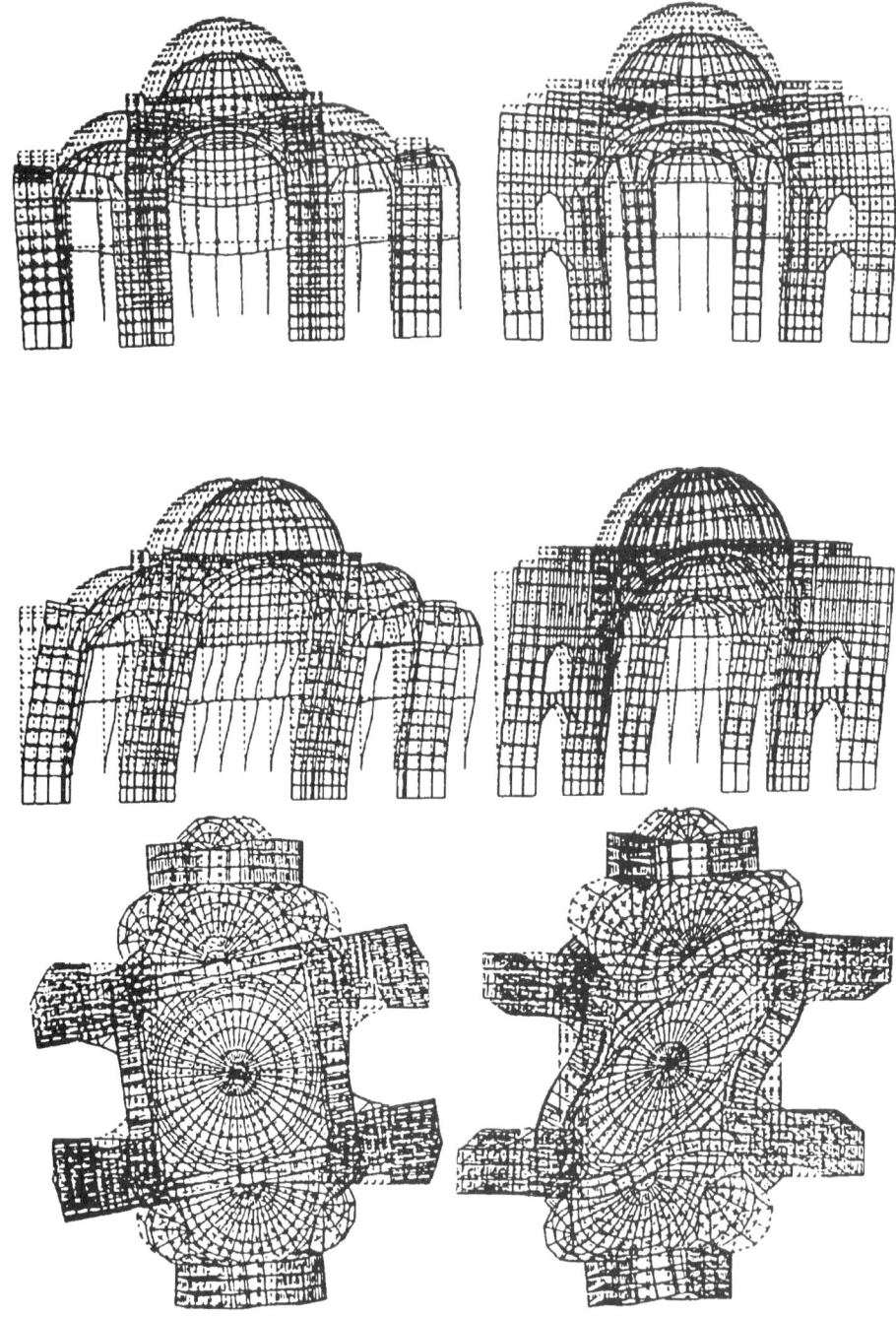

Figure 8. An example of the difference between a static and a dynamic deformation of a monument. Model for the deformation of Aghia Sophia of Constantinople (Istanbul) from its own (above) and from seismic loads (middle and below). After Erdik & Durukal (1993). The pattern of deformations depends on the modelling of the structural characteristics of the constructions and the characteristics of the earthquake.

Foundations and superstructure

In several cases, tilted and cracked ancient walls have been regarded as evidence of seismic damage. This has led to criticism from geologists (e.g. Karcz & Kafri, 1978) who assigned such effects to ground instability such as local sliding and differential compaction, that is to factors not (necessarily) related to earthquakes. This criticism is absolutely reasonable, although the earthquake shaking may be responsible for deformations of the ground surface on which the ancient structures are founded. However, if the geological background consists of solid rocks (for example, limestones), or the foundations are not deformed and the damage is confined to the superstructure of the buildings, any weakness in foundations should be excluded as an explanation for the observed damage. The 5th century BC temple at Vassai in the W Peloponnese is a characteristic example: it is founded on limestone, but with an artificial filling of variable

Figure 9. One of the parallel fallen columns of the 5th century BC Temple of Zeus at Olympia (W Peloponnese) with a characteristic domino-style arrangement of its drums. This temple was destroyed by an earthquake, probably in the Byzantine period (see Dinsmoor, 1985).

thickness between the surface of the rock and the foundations. Because this filling was locally partly removed, mainly due to leaking rainwater, the foundations subsided locally, and this is partly responsible for the observed damage (Andronopoulos *et al.*, 1977). Another characteristic case is the contrast in the deformation of two famous columns in Rome: relative sliding of the drums is clearly observed in the Colona Antonina (Fig. 3), but not in its nearby, almost identical Colona Traiana. A study by Funiciello *et al.* (1989) revealed that the soft sediments beneath the Colona Antonina cause a local amplification of seismic oscillations and temporal horizontal displacements more than 12 cm from the vertical. The amplitude of oscillations is much smaller in the Colona Traiana, founded directly on bedrock, and this partly explains its near-perfect state of preservation.

Seismic sequence and oriented destruction

As already mentioned, instead of a single earthquake, it is better in most cases to think of an earthquake sequence as the possible cause for the destruction or abandonment of a building or a site. The catastrophic effects of earthquakes are not usually due to a single major shock, but to the cumulative effect of the strongest shocks of a seismic sequence. The main shock may simply weaken the strength of a building to which a relatively weak aftershock, with a relatively different mechanism and focal parameters (epicentre, etc.), may give the final shot. To make matters more complicated, any large earthquake must be regarded as the sum of different types of waves, each of them causing damage to different 'weak' points of a structure. This explains why the fallen structural elements of buildings may not show a predominant preferred direction of fall. Thus, while parallel fallen columns (Karcz & Kafri 1978, Fig. 8; Nur & Ron, this volume) can be regarded as evidence of a seismic destruction, their absence is not a reason to exclude an earthquake as an agent for it. A second reason for a 'chaotic' arrangement of structural elements of a building fallen during an earthquake is that its failure under a seismic load is an extremely complicated process, with numerous factors, including defects in design, material and craftsmanship and chance playing a role. Even in the most geometrically well-defined classical temples, there are factors which prevent a uniform behaviour of their structural elements. In the Parthenon, for instance, the foundations conditions are different beneath its N and S columns (the northern ones are founded on bedrock while the southern one on top of a 18 m high artificial terrace), probably causing local amplification of seismic intensities in its S part.

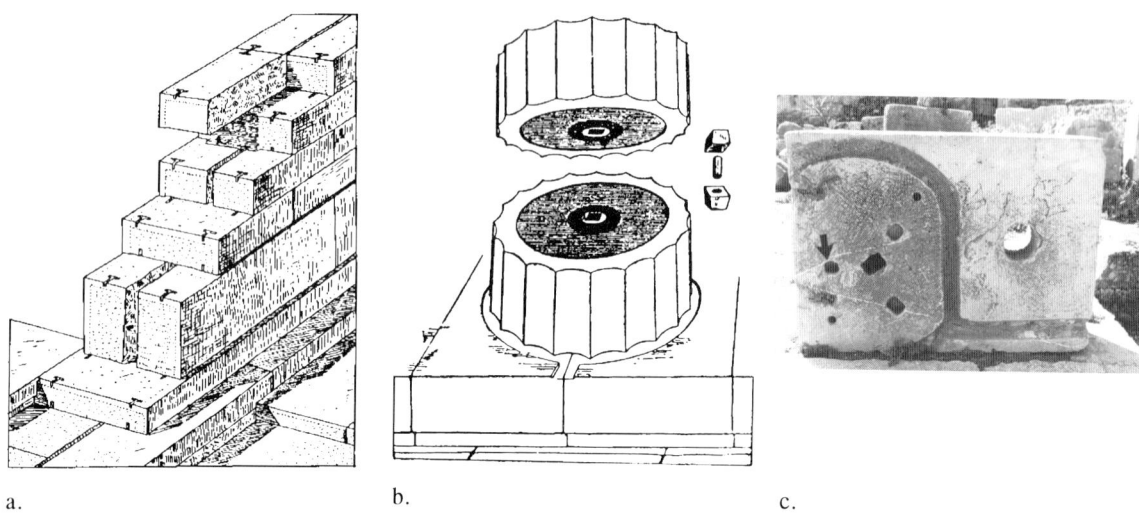

a.   b.   c.

Figure 10. (a) Metal reinforcement in a wall of the Parthenon (after Martin, 1965), (b) single and (c) multiple clamps between drums in a column.

Archaeological Considerations

Dating uncertainties

Archaeological data can usually provide a relative dating of destructions and therefore of earthquakes, usually as *terminus ante quem* and *terminus post quem*. The accuracy and precision of the archaeological dating usually range between a few centuries (a value compatible with that of radiocarbon dating) and a few years. Even this extremely precise dating makes difficult the correlation of destructions even in nearby buildings and sites, or the correlation of destructions with historical events. Particularly problematic is the situation in areas where the recurrence intervals of earthquakes are short, of the order of a few tens of years, in Corinth for instance (see Rothaus, this volume).

Single and cumulative effects

The difficulty of correlating a destruction with an earthquake known from historical data or with other nearby destructions is not the only one caused by the limitations in archaeological dating techniques. Sometimes it is difficult to identify whether a certain damage or destruction is the product of a single effect, an earthquake for instance, or is the cumulative effect of anthropogenic and/or natural processes, the sequence and impacts of which cannot be determined. Offset drums of ancient columns, for instance, can usually be assigned with much certainty to earthquakes, but may have been the result not of a single earthquake, but the cumulative effect of several earthquakes. The following hypothetical but realistic example emphasises some other aspects of this problem. Let us assume that an earthquake hit an isolated building and left it in semi-ruinous condition, but still free standing; some or many years later, the weakened structure collapsed owing to a relatively minor event such as a storm or weak seismic shock, and the ruins covered some coins that were issued after the first, destructive earthquake. The unsuspecting excavator will probably find no evidence of the destructive earthquake, but based on numismatic evidence will assign both the weakening and the collapse of the structure to a later either non-existent or exaggerated event.

Recorded and reported information on destructions

An archaeological excavation is a slow process, sometimes lasting for decades or longer, and depending on the main focus of the excavator, the recorded or preserved evidence will change over time. In the recovery of, say, fine statues from the excavation of a building, it may appear perverse for the archaeologist to place emphasis in the building's description on a post-seismic repair or a skeleton of what can be proved to be an earthquake victim. Consequently, the lack of information on possible seismic destruction (observations and reports) cannot be taken to signify that the specific site was free of seismic damage, especially since the traces of this damage may have disappeared during reconstruction works in older periods.

Natural, seismic and anthropogenic causes of destruction

Destructions of fortification walls and large buildings, or even town-wide, deliberate destructions are not unknown in the historical record, for instance the destruction of Thebes by Alexander the Great. However, there are numerous cases in which the scale of the destruction and the lack of signs of fire and looting make unlikely any anthropogenic effect. A nice example is the destruction at around 90 BC of the city of Pella, the capital of ancient Macedonia (Northern Greece): in an area more than several hundreds of metres wide, the public and private buildings abruptly collapsed, among them numerous workshops burying thousands of precious products and arti-

Figure 11. Horizontal brick layers in a tower of the early Byzantine walls of Constantinople (Istanbul).

facts, some of them aligned in a particular direction. All these buildings were constructed of brick and wood, but no sign of conflagration was observed. On the contrary, there is evidence that after the destruction some quickly built buttresses or timber beams were erected, presumably to support unstable walls (J. Akamatis, pers. comm.). It is therefore difficult to propose an explanation for this destruction, other than that proposed by Akamatis (1985), namely an earthquake. Independent support for this interpretation comes from a sector of this city, where a group of eleven people was found buried by debris next to the entrance of a house (Siganidou, 1981).

Social and historical impacts of ancient earthquakes — Historical role

The possible historical role of ancient earthquakes is a matter of study and debate, and a point addressed by several authors in this volume (e.g. Kilian, Dakoronia, among others) and is only marginally discussed here. Although we agree with Ambraseys (1971) that earthquakes should not be regarded as an easy solution for the explanation of civilization and cultural gaps observed in certain regions, it is well documented that under certain circumstances earthquakes may play a certain historical role. For instance, the 464 BC earthquake that destroyed Sparta triggered a revolt of slaves and oppressed tribes, and a war that could have ended with the disappearance of the Spartan state. The important town of Gortyn in Crete, on the other hand, survived the earthquake *c.* AD 620 probably due to the financial and other assistance from the central government; yet when this support dried up, Gortyn disappeared as an organised town after the later earthquake of *c.* AD 670 (Di Vita, this volume). The recovery of a town or province from a seismic destruction should not therefore be examined without reference to the social, political and economic context of the period and the region (see Helly, 1989; Guidoboni, 1989).

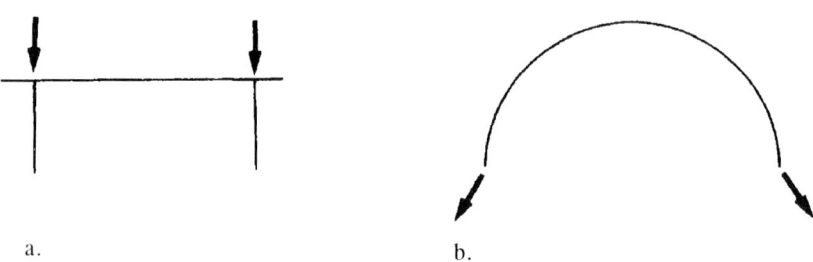

Figure 12. Forces in (a) a column-and-horizontal-beam system and (b) an arch-on-column (or vault, dome, etc.) system. In the second case, the component of horizontal force ('thrust') at the base of the arch should be compensated by lateral buttresses or by the ground in case of a buried structure, in order for the arch, vault or dome to be stabilised.

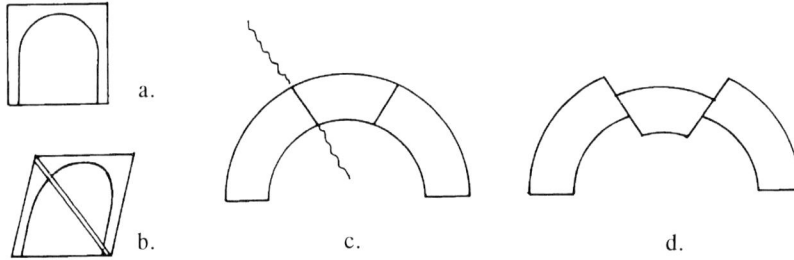

Figure 13. An arch (vault or dome) under the influence of a seismic force is stretched, and not stable, for the thrust is not (momentarily) compensated by lateral forces expressed by buttresses, etc. As a result, joints open in a dry masonry structure, and the keystone (or even the uppermost voussoirs) slides down; in a rigid structure, a crack forms. As a consequence the total or partial collapse of the structures occurs.

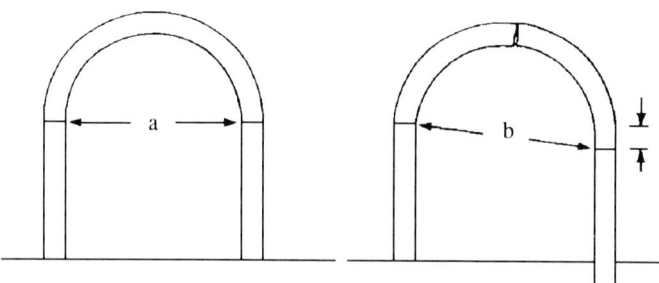

Figure 14. Arched and similar constructions are very sensitive to ground settling which produce effects similar to those of earthquakes. After settling, the opening at the base of the arch becomes larger, and this stretching produces cracks or joint openings at the upper parts of the arch, as in Fig. 13.

Earthquake victims

Earthquake victims were numerous in the past, and at least in the ancient Greek vocabulary there was a term to describe them (*seismatias*). Sometimes, however, seismic destructions were of a scale that forced survivors to abandon victims trapped under the ruins of houses, shrines, and other buildings. This may indicate an ideological and cultural disorganisation, even physical destruction of communities, since the formal burial of the dead was a fundamental ritual in most ancient societies. The identification of skeletons of earthquake victims is a rare occurrence archaeologically (for two exceptions, see Sakellarakis & Sapouna-Sakellaraki, 1981; Sorren, 1988), while the significance of unburied earthquake victims was not appreciated by most excavators, and their occurrence is rarely only included in archaeological reports (see Michaelidou-Nikolaou, 1985; French, Kilian, Nur & Ron & Sampson, this volume). To make matters more complicated, in at least one case, the death and burial of people and animals by debris from fallen walls has been assigned to anthropogenic events (Schilardi, 1980).

Remodelling

Historical sources and excavations from Pergamon in Asia Minor indicate a radical remodelling of the town following the AD 1296 earthquake (Rheidt, this volume). Remodelling of Troy followed a destruction that was assigned to an earthquake by Blegen (see Introduction), and the same took place at Tiryns according to Kilian (this volume). In all these cases the towns were rebuilt without any innovative techniques. On the other hand, when Smyrna was rebuilt after the 1688 earthquake, new, and what can be regarded as 'anti-seismic' techniques were introduced (Simopoulos, 1984). There is some evidence that a similar situation can be inferred for Akrotiri on Thera (Santorini) prior to its burial by pumice about 3,500 years ago (Palyvou, 1988).

Discussion

In spite of the difficulties and limitations outlined above, we are sufficiently optimistic to propose a typology of seismic effects, or certain criteria for a secure recognition of seismic effects from archaeological, *senso lato*, data. These criteria are listed in Appendix 2. Some points must, however, be emphasised.

First, these criteria are of value only if certain conditions demonstrably exist: that the foundations are intact (to exclude the possibility of local ground instability), that effects like rockfalls and explosions can be excluded as reasons for the observed damage (to exclude the possibility of dynamic effects other than earthquakes) and that the destruction took place in a short time interval (to exclude in some cases the possibility of slow destructions).

Second, even if clear evidence of an earthquake exists, not all observed effects at a specific site need be assigned to one single earthquake: the observed effects may be the cumulative result of various seismic and non-seismic factors.

Third, convincing evidence of an earthquake cannot provide the characteristic deformation of either a particular structural element or even a whole structure (because such deformations may have various causes), but the consistent and repetitious pattern of deformed elements and structures; on statistical and probabilistic grounds such a pattern is indicative of a seismic effect. For example, the domino-style arrangement of the fallen drums of column of the Temple of Olympian Zeus in Athens, as already discussed, was associated with the collapse of the column during a thunderstorm; yet, only earthquakes can be responsible for the numerous parallel fallen columns with the domino-style arrangement of their drums of the Temple C at Selinous (Selinunte) in Sicily or the Temple of Zeus at Olympia (Fig. 9); graves 'squeezed' like the one in Fig. 4 can be found everywhere and are usually indicative of local ground instability or anthropogenic effects; yet, the systematic pattern of such graves discussed by Stiros (1988b) and Stiros & Dakoronia (1989) can only have a seismic origin (if, of course, large-scale ground instability effects can be ruled out).

Fourth, the larger the number of such criteria is satisfied and the wider the area affected, the stronger the earthquake hypothesis becomes. In other words, isolated tilted, cracked or collapsed masonry walls are not regarded as a secure indication of an earthquake; the death of a person by falling rocks at an isolated site, or the collapse of a house with precious objects abandoned beneath its ruins are regarded as inconclusive evidence of an earthquake. By contrast, the collapse of a temple with nearly all its columns lying parallel to its other, their drums in a domino-style arrangement and its foundations in perfect condition are a reliable indicator of a seismic destruction. Following this approach, the data base of cases of seismic damage deduced from observations of ancient buildings and sites becomes much narrower. A large number of cases of destruction and desertion of buildings and sites which are left unexplained, and abandoning the concept of earthquakes as *deus ex machina* are two necessary sacrifices to a scientific approach to the problem of ancient earthquakes. Under these circumstances, the reservations expressed by Karcz & Kafri (1978) can be removed, and the interdisciplinary Archaeoseismological research can be regarded as an independent technique to serve both archaeology and earth sciences.

Acknowledgements

The experience reported here has accumulated through cooperation with numerous archaeologists in Greece and participation in field-trips in other countries; for the latter I am indebted to Dr M. Mouty (Syria), Prof. E. Karaesmen and Dr F. Eke (Turkey), Prof. R. Funicielo (Italy), and Dr M. Miele (Egypt). The author has benefited from examination of unpublished material and discussions with M. Korres, A. Sinopoli, Ph. Dakoronia and numerous other archaeologists. Careful review by R. E. Jones is acknowledged. Encouragement and support, especially in the early stages of this research by R. E. Jones, H. W. Catling and A. M. Snodgrass must also be acknowledged. This is a contribution to the Active Geodynamics (IGME-DE-8661704) and the Hellenic Organisation for Antiseismic Planning and Protection (OASP) research projects.

References

Ambraseys, N. (1962). Data for the investigation of the seismic waves in the Eastern Mediterranean. *Bull. Seism. Soc. Am.* **52**, 895–913.

Ambraseys, N. (1971). Value of historical records of earthquakes. *Nature* **232**, 375–379.

Andronikos, M. (1984). *Vergina. The royal graves and the other antiquities.* Athens; Ekdotiki Athinon.

Andronopoulos, B., Koukis, G. & Tzitziras, A. (1977). Specific engineering geology study in the area of the Temple of Apollo Epicurios (IInd phase of the study). *Engineering Geology Investigations*, no. 6, IGME, Athens. (In Greek).

Akamatis, J. (1985). Clay matrices from Pella. Contribution to the study of Hellenistic pottery. PhD thesis, Thessaloniki University. (In Greek).

Augusti, G. & Sinopoli, A. (1992). Modelling the dynamics of large block structures. *Meccanica* **27**, 195–211.

Bakalakis, G. & Andronikos, M. (1969). Excavations at Vergina. *Archaeologikon Deltion* **24**, 390–395. (In Greek).

Bakirtzis, Ch. (1983). What happened in Thassos at the beginning of the 7th century AD? *Philia Epi eis G. Mylona* **3**, 339–341. (In Greek).

Blegen, C. (1963). *Troy and the Trojans.* London; Thames and Hudson.

Dakoronia, P. (this volume). Earthquakes of the Late Helladic III period (12th century BC) at Kynos (Livanates, Central Greece).

De Maisonneuvre, P., Ferrigni, F. & Helly, B. (Eds) (1990). *La protection du bâti ancien dans les zones à risques sismiques* PACT 28. Louvain.

Dinsmoor, W. B. (1985). *The architecture of ancient Greece.* London; Batsford.

Di Vita, A. (this volume). Earthquakes and civil life at Gortyn (Crete) in the period between Justinian and Constant II (6–7th century AD).

Easton, D. (1985). Has the Troyan War been found? *Antiquity* **59**, 188–196.

Erdik, M. & Durukal, A. (1993). Ayasofya'nin Deprem Davranisi. In: *Proceedings of the Seminar 'Protection of Architectural Heritage against earthquakes'*. Ankara; Ministry of Public Works and Settlement.

Evangelatou-Notara, F. (1993). *Earthquakes in Byzantium from the 13th to the 15th century: historic examination*. Athens, Parousia, Annex 24.

Evans, A. (1928). The *Palace of Minos II*. London.

French, E. (this volume). Evidence for an earthquake at Mycenae.

Funiciello, R., Boschi, E., Di Bona, M., Malagnini, L., Marra, F., Rovelli, A. & Salvi, S. (1992). Local seismic amplifications in the city of Rome inferred from observations of damage in monuments of Imperial age: ground motion estimates based on subsurface geology data. Paper presented in the Int. Symp. on the effects of surface geology on seismic motion, ESG.

Galanopoulos, A. (1956). The seismic risk at Athens. *Praktika Akadimias Athinon* **31**, 464–472. (In Greek).

Guidoboni, E. (Ed.) (1989). *I terremoti prima del Mille in Italia e nell'area Mediterranea. Storia, archeologia, sismologia*. Bologna; SGA — ING.

Helly, B. (1989). La Grecia antica e i terremoti. In: Guidoboni, E. (Ed.), *I terremoti prima del Mille in Italia e nell'area Mediterranea, Storia, archeologia, sismologia*, 75–91. Bologna; SGA — ING.

Housner, G. (1963). The behavior of inverted pendulum structures during earthquakes. *Bull. Seism. Soc. Am.* **53**, 403–417.

Karcz, I. & Kafri, U. (1978). Evaluation of supposed archaeoseismic damage in Israel. *J. Archaeological Science* **5**, 237–253.

Kilian, K. (1980). Zum Ende der mykenischen Epoche in der Argolis. *Jahrbuch des Römisch-Germanisch Zentralmuseums Mainz* **27**, 166–195.

Kilian, K. (1986). La caduta dei palazzi micenei continentali: aspetti archeologici. In (D. Musti, Ed.) *Le origini dei Greci. Dori e mondo Egeo*, 73–116. Rome and Bari.

Kilian, K. (this volume). Earthquakes and archaeological context at Tiryns (Late Helladic Period).

Kirikov, B. (1992). *Earthquake resistance of structures: from antiquity to our times*. Moscow; Mir.

Korres, M. (this volume). Seismic damage to the monuments of the Athenian Acropolis.

Marinatos, S. (1939). The volcanic destruction of Minoan Crete. *Antiquity* **13**, 425–439.

Marinatos, S. (1960). Helice: A submerged town of classical Greece. *Archaeology* **13**, 186–193.

Martin, R. (1965). *Manuel d'Architecture Grecque. I Materiaux et Techniques*. Paris; Picard et Cie.

Meghraoui, M., Jaegy, R., Lammali, K. & Albarede, F. (1988). Late Holocene earthquake sequences on the El Asnam (Algeria) thrust fault. *Earth and Planetary Science Letters* **90**, 187–203.

Michaelidou-Nicolaou, I. (1985). Evidence for an unknown earthquake in Paphos. *Proc., 2nd Cyprological Congress*. Nicosia; Society of Cypriote Studies, 357–362.

Naumann, R. (1971). Wirkungen eines Erdbebens an den antiken Bauten in Aezani. *Archäologisches Anzeiger* **86**, 214–221.

Nikonov, A. (1988). On the methodology of archaeoseismic research into historical monuments. In (P. Marinos, & G. Koukis, Eds), *The Engineering Geology of Ancient Works, Monuments and Historical Sites, Preservation and Protection*, 1315–1320. Rotterdam; Balkema.

Nur, A. & Ron, H. (this volume). And the walls came tumbling down: Earthquake history in the Holyland.

Palyvou, C. (1988). *Akrotiri, Thera: Building techniques and morphology in Late Cycladic Architecture*. PhD Thesis, Athens Polytechnic University. (In Greek).

Papastamatiou, D. & Psycharis, I. (this volume). Numerical simulation of the seismic response of megalithic monuments: preliminary investigations related to the Apollo Temple at Vassai.

Penelis, G., Papayanni, I., Stylianidis, K., Ignatakis, C. & Athanasiadis, L. (1993). Strengthening intervention of a 400 year old Ottoman Minaret. In: Programme- Abstracts, *Int. Seminar 'Historical and monumental structures in seismic regions'*, Santorini, Greece. Council of Europe, European Centre on Prevention and Forecasting of Earthquakes.

Pirazzoli, P. (this volume). Uplift of ancient Greek coastal sites: study methods and results.

Rapp, G., Jr. (1987). Assessing archaeological evidence for seismic catastrophies. *Geoarchaeology* **1**, 365–379.

Rheidt, K. (this volume). The 1296 earthquake and its consequences for Pergamon and Chliara.

Robert, S. (1978). Documents d' Asie Mineure. V. Stèle funéraire de Nicomedie et seismes dans les inscriptions. *Bulletin de Correspondance Hellénique* **102**, 395–408.

Rothaus, R. (this volume). Earthquakes and Temples in Late Antique Corinth.

Sakellarakis, Y. & Sapouna-Sakellaraki, E. (1981). Drama of death in a Minoan temple. *National Geographic* **159**, 205–222.

Sampson, A. (this volume). Cases of earthquakes in Mycenean and pre-Mycenean Thebes.

Schilardi, D. (1980). The destruction of the LH IIIB citadel of Koukounaries on Paros. In (J. Davis & Cherry, Eds) *Papers in Cycladic Prehistory,* Monograph XIV, Institute of Archaeology, Univ. of California, Los Angeles, 158–179.

Siganidou, M. (1981). Excavation report, Pella, section I, square 2. *Archaeologikon Deltion* **36**, B2, 318. (In Greek).

Simopoulos, K. (1984). *Foreign Visitors in Greece, 1700–1800* **II**, 4th Ed., Athens.

Sinopoli, A. (1989a). Effetti sismici su strutture monumentali lapidee: una puntualizzazione. In (E. Guidoboni, Ed.), *I terremoti prima del Mille in Italia e nell'area Mediterranea. Storia, archeologia, sismologia*, 256–259. Bologna; SGA — ING.

Sinopoli, A. (1989a). Kinematic approach in the impact problem of rigid bodies. *Applied Mechanics Revue* **44**/2, S233–S244.

Sinopoli, A. (1991). Dynamic analysis of a stone column excited by a sine wave motion. *Applied Mechanics Revue* **44**/2, S246–S255.

Sorren, D. & Davis Th. (1985). Seismic archaeology at Kourion: the 1984 campaign. *Rep. Dept. Antiquities of Cyprus*, 193–301.

Sorren, D. (1988). The day the world ended at Kourion — Reconstructing an ancient earthquake. *National Geographic* **174**, 30–53.

Stiros, S. (1988a). Earthquake effects in ancient constructions, In (R. E. Jones & H. W. Catling, Eds). *New aspects of archaeological science in Greece*, Occasional Paper no 3 of the Fitch Laboratory, British School at Athens, 1–6.

Stiros, S. (1988b). Archaeology, a tool to study active tectonics — The Aegean as a case study, *Eos, Trans. Am. Geophys. Union* **13**, 1636, 1639.

Stiros, S. & Dakoronia, Ph. (1989). Ruolo storico e identificazione di antichi terremmoti nei siti della Grecia, In (E. Guidoboni, Ed.). *I terremoti prima del Mille in Italia e nell' area Mediterranea. Storia, sismologia, archeologia*, 422–439. Bologna; SGA — ING.

Trifonov, V. (1978). Late Quaternary tectonic movements of western and central Asia. *Geological Society of America Bulletin* **89**, 1059–1072.

Varoufakis, G. (1992). How the iron clamps and dowels of the temples of the Athenian Acropolis resisted to the century-long corrosion? *Archaeologia* **45**, 14–19. (In Greek).

Wallace, R. (1990). Geomorphic expression. In (R. Wallace Ed.). *The San Andreas Fault System, California*. U.S. Geological Survey Professional Paper 1515, 15–60.

Zambas, C. (1988). Principles for the structural restoration of the Acropolis monuments. In (P. Marinos & G. Koukis, Eds). *The Engineering Geology of Ancient Works, Monuments and Historical Sites. Preservation and Protection*, 1813–1818. Rotterdam; Balkema.

Zang, B., Liao, Y., Guo, S., Wallace, R., Bucknam, R. & Hanks, T. (1986). Fault scarps related to the 1739 earthquake and seismicity of the Yinchuan graben, Ningxia Huizu Zizhiqu, China. *Bull. Seismological Society of America* **76**, 1253–1287.

Zangger, E. (1993). *The Geoarchaeology of the Argolid. Argolis II.* Deutches Archäologisches Institut Athen. Berlin: Ge. Mann Verlag.

Appendix 1
Characteristic cases of response of ancient constructions to earthquakes

Dry masonry columns and columnades. When a seismic load is exerted on an isolated column, this will start to oscillate around the vertical (Fig. 6a). If the strength of the column is adequate, the oscillation (rocking) will quickly die out; otherwise it will be damaged, or overturned. The response of a column to an earthquake depends on its geometrical and structural characteristics: whether it is monolithic or multi-block, slender or stocky, simply lying on the ground or clamped, etc. A slender column simply lying on the ground (the type of columns in classical Greece) for instance, will rotate around its base corner edges, as shown in Fig. 6a. In the case of a colonnade, all columns tend to oscillate in a uniform way (Fig. 6b).

Another effect associated with the rocking of a column is the impact. When the drums of columns of Fig. 6c, rocking around their base edge, return to their vertical position, they collide with the rigid ground surface. After the impact, apart from rotation, sliding occurs. This sliding introduces an additional cause of failure, and is observed both at the base of rigid monolithic columns, and between the drums of multi-block columns (Figs 2, 3; Papastamatiou & Psycharis, this volume; Sinopoli, 1989a, b; 1991). The translation induced after the impact seems to be the primary cause for the overturning of a multiblock column, for the excessive sliding leads to the loss of the initial geometric configuration of the column (Sinopoli, 1989a, b; 1991; Augusti & Sinopoli, 1992). This is probably the case with Temple of Zeus at Olympia and Temple C at Selinous (Sicily), where the columns of the southern colonnade fell parallel to each other, with their drums in a domino-style arrangement (Fig. 9), although this arrangement is not a safe indication of a seismic destruction in the case of a single column (see the case above of the Temple of Olympian Zeus in Athens).

Walls in dry masonry buildings. As shown in Fig. 5, seismic forces tend to deform rectangular shapes to parallelograms. In the case of a colonnade in a classical temple, the structural style is very ductile and the seismic deformation is accommodated by the instantaneous opening and closure of joints (Fig. 6b). The walls of buildings made without mortar also tend to deform to parallelograms in response to seismic forces parallel to their orientation. In this case the total deformation is obtained as an accumulation of small deformations of blocks: certain blocks slide relative to each other along horizontal joints, while vertical joints open and close according to the directions of the seismic forces; some permanent deformations may however remain (Fig. 2 in Korres, this volume; Naumann 1971, Figs 5, 6). In the case of a seismic force normal to a wall, this will tend to oscillate around an axis roughly coinciding with its trace on the ground. The oscillation of such a wall seen in cross-section is to a first approximation similar to that of a column (Fig. 6) and tends to separate this from transverse walls (Fig. 7a).

Clamps and dowels. The horizontal relative sliding of structural elements of mortarless constructions was a relatively common occurrence and was undoubtedly a problem for ancient architects. The solution developed through the centuries, based on the trial and error technique (obviously after observations like those of Naumann, 1971), and almost universally adopted (see Dinsmoor, 1985; Martin, 1965), was to use metal or wood clamps covered with lead between the various structural elements of the constructions (Fig. 10).

This solution permitted first, a higher friction between the elements; second, protection against the corrosion of metal clamps; third, a quick absorption of energy because of the plasticity of lead (the air bags in modern cars are based on the same principle); fourth, unlimited functioning of the system due to the reversible deformation of lead during every earthquake, and fifth, protection of the expensive marble elements from failure due to the thermal expansion and seismic excitation of less malleable clamps and dowels. In support of this, Varoufakis (1992) has found that metal reinforcements in the Parthenon consist of sulphur-free iron obtained from certain ore bodies, and had a special structure to protect them against corrosion. Lead, therefore, was primarily used for its mechanical and not its chemical properties.

The metal and wood reinforcement of certain ancient buildings thus reflects an apparently genuine and brilliant anti-seismic reinforcement technique developed through millennia (see also Sinopoli, 1989b; Kirikov, 1992). The principles of this technique, the structural significance of which has not been acknowledged by most workers, have been adopted in the present-day restoration of the Acropolis monuments (Zambas, 1988). On the other hand, the poor imitation of this technique on the Acropolis early this century — the use of common iron reinforcements not covered by lead, and consequently not protected from corrosion — had catastrophic effects on the marble even in the absence of earthquakes. It is of interest to note that the technique of lead-sealed metal elements was in use even in the last century, especially for connecting non-structurally significant elements.

Walls in rigid constructions. If a wall made with mortar (for example in a Roman, Byzantine or later construction) is excited by seismic waves parallel to its direction, it will tend to take the shape of a parallelogram at the expense of its structural integrity; diagonal cracks will form (Fig. 5), especially around the openings for windows and in corners, and because of this whole triangular parts of masonry may be removed from the corners (Fig. 5). If the direction of the seismic force is nearly perpendicular to a wall, this will be forced into an oscillation. But since the construction is rigid and the possibility of accommodating small deformations is practically nil, the wall will tend to fracture along a line parallel and close to its trace on the ground and will topple down, occasionally with masonry fallen in parallel lines, or in a 'slices of salami' arrangement (see Rapp, 1987; Karcz & Kafri, 1978). This is, of course, possible only if the wall is not anchored to transverse walls, for example, where only small rocks at the corners and weak mortar are used. In such cases sub-vertical cracks separating the walls with a direction normal to the seismic force from those parallel to the seismic force are formed (Fig. 7a). These effects become more important in the case where the walls accommodate horizontal forces from roofs etc. As a remedy, buttresses that prevented the collapse of walls and whole structures were usually erected, and sometimes these appear integrated into the architectural design of the buildings (see the church of Osios Loukas in central Greece, Fig. 7b).

Where a wall normal to the seismic force is anchored to transverse walls and piers no free oscillations (as in Fig. 7a) are possible. If, however the length of the part of this wall between anchor points is several times larger than their height, the collapse of a usually triangular section may occur (Fig. 7c). As far as modern constructions are concerned, the effect of rather free oscillations and collapse is observed in filling walls not anchored to frames of reinforced concrete. It can be deduced from observations in areas free of seismic shocks that vertical cracks along the corners, tilted walls and imbricate disposition of fallen masonry in buildings made of small stones and rather weak mortar may not be associated with earthquakes; they may result from the ageing of the structure and other factors like shrinking mortar, leaking and freezing rainwater, foundation instability, pressure from roots or branches of trees. Ancient builders were conscious of this weakness of mortar walls, especially those made of small or rounded stones, and as a remedy, boulders were included in the masonry, well-hewn interbonded blocks were used at the corners, and buttresses or exterior walls thickening downwards or metal reinforcements were employed. Another technique was the regular use of rows of bricks, well coupled to each other, arranged around the structure. In later periods this technique evolved to simple decorative layers.

Apart from rows of bricks, rows or a frame of timber were also used, a technique not unusual in traditional local houses in various parts of Greece, reminiscent of the techniques at Akrotiri 3,500 years ago (Palyvou, 1988). As discussed elsewhere, there is evidence that an (if not the) aim of these techniques was to offer anti-seismic protection. In certain cases, such as the Aegean islands, the structural weakness of isolated structures was remedied by the construction of a cluster of adjoining dwellings, with each wall supported by perpendicular walls of adjacent houses. There is historical evidence that this technique was assumed to offer anti-seismic protection (Notara-Evangelatou, 1993; see also de Maisonneuve *et al.*, 1990).

Fortification walls. In addition to seismic deformations described for ordinary walls, fortification walls, because of their length, are affected by vertical seismic forces as well (Fig. 5c). This vertical movement is amplified at sites where local inhomogeneities in the geological background exist. Ductile constructions — walls made of large, hewn blocks without mortar — respond to this type of seismic excitation by the opening and closure of their joints. Walls made with strong mortar fracture, and mainly sub-vertical cracks form. The characteristic of such fissures is that because they are high acceleration effects cut also smaller rocks they cross. Similar effects can, however, be produced by explosions at the base of the walls; traces of such explosions cannot be easily identified if the holes were repaired with the same techniques and material as the original masonry. Settling of foundations can also produce sub-vertical and inclined cracks, but their pattern can more easily be recognised. Another particular feature of fortification walls of various periods is that they are usually composed of two faces of walls and filling, with or without mortar between them. Such constructions are obviously exposed to the risk of buckling due to their own weight and the lateral pressure of the filling, as well as the risk of collapse if a small hole is opened. For this reason, horizontal layers of a few rows of well-built bricks covering the entire surface of the wall were introduced at regular intervals (Fig. 11). The contribution of this technique to the earthquake resistance of the walls is evident.

Arched, domed and vaulted constructions. Although these rigid constructions are usually made with mortar, dry masonry arches in walls, the Mycenaean tholos (cantilevered or pseudo-domed) tombs (Dinsmoor, 1985), the royal Macedonian vaulted tombs (Andronikos, 1984), or small shepherds huts are among the most well-known exceptions to this rule. A feature of these constructions is that they exert to their supporting columns, piers and walls not only vertical, but horizontal forces ('thrusts') as well (Fig. 12). These forces become extremely large in large openings, and for this reason an arch requires massive buttresses or other types of lateral support to be stabilised (for instance, arches must be incorporated in a wall or the vaults must be buried in the ground). Earthquake loads are superimposed on these horizontal forces (thrusts), and for this reason these constructions are extremely sensitive to earthquakes.

A seismic load in the direction, or better in the plane, of an arch counterbalances the force exerted at one of its bases (or its lower part on one side) and the structure is found momentarily without lateral support. In a dry masonry structure, the keystone slides downwards, while in a rigid one a crack will form (Fig. 13). If a surface of weakness exists between a rigid arch, made, for example, of bricks and mortar, and its base (monolithic or masonry column), the system may respond to the horizontal seismic load as a ductile system, with the arch behaving as a monolithic beam (see Fig. 6b). However, this deformation may easily lead to the total failure of the system. If the seismic force is in a direction normal to the plane of an arch composing a rigid system with its masonry columns, the system seen in cross section will behave as a rigid wall (see above), and will tend to be fractured at the base of the columns and will topple down, sometimes without internal deformation (see also Bakirtzis, 1983).

An earthquake force in a direction normal to the axis of a dry or mortar masonry vaults will have effects similar to those described for an arch, but in three dimensions, with opened joints and cracks crossing the whole structure along its upper parts, parallel to its axis. The situation with domes or cupolas is somewhat similar, with seismic forces tending to produce cracks along circles passing usually from their upper parts. Buttresses, partial cupolas or external arches to support domes (for instance in the Aghia Sophia of Constantinople; see also Fig. 7b), metal beams at the base of arches (usual in late Byzantine and Ottoman architecture) or metal girdling rings at the base of domes (in later constructions) are some of the measures taken to compensate for the thrusts and reinforce these structures against earthquakes. Arches, domes and similar constructions are very sensitive to small settling effects of the foundations as well. These settlings tend to elongate the radii at the base of arches and domes and generate cracks at their tops (Fig. 14), that is they produce effects similar to earthquakes.

Appendix 2
Criteria for the identification of earthquakes from archaeological data (in keeping with the reservations expressed in other sections of this text).

1. Ancient constructions offset by seismic surface faults.

2. Skeletons of people killed and buried under the debris of fallen buildings.

3. Certain abrupt geomorphological changes, occasionally associated with destructions and/or abandonment of buildings and sites.

4. Characteristic structural damage and failure of constructions:
- Displaced drums of dry masonry columns
- Opened vertical joints and horizontally slided parts of walls in dry masonry walls
- Diagonal cracks in rigid walls
- Triangular missing parts in corners of masonry buildings
- Cracks at the base or top of masonry columns and piers
- Inclined or subvertical cracks in the upper parts of rigid arches, vaults and domes, or their partial collapse along these cracks
- Downslided keystones in dry masonry arches and vaults
- Several parallel fallen columns
- Several fallen columns with their drums in a domino-style ('slices of salami') arrangement
- Constructions deformed as by horizontal forces (rectangles transformed to parallelograms)

5. Destruction and quick reconstruction of sites, with the introduction of what can be regarded as 'anti-seismic' building construction techniques, but with no change in their overall cultural character.

6. Well-dated destructions of buildings correlating with historical (including epigraphic) evidence of earthquakes.

7. Damage or destruction of isolated buildings or whole sites, for which an earthquake appears the only reasonable explanation.

New Evidence of Earthquake Destructions in Late Minoan Crete

Despina Vallianou

Ephoreia of Prehistoric & Classical Antiquities,
Herakleion, Crete, Greece

Abstract

The destruction of the Minoan palatial and residential centres in Crete has been assigned by many workers to the eruption of the Santorini and probably another, nearby volcano, as well as the related phenomena of earthquakes and tsunamis. Recent excavations at two different sites of different periods seem to support this hypothesis.

In the first case, a huge, two-storey villa in the area of Pitsidia in southern Crete was destroyed and abandoned in the LM IB period (15th century BC). No signs of either hostile intervention or fire exist, while the overall destruction patterns are likely to indicate a seismic destruction, before which the inhabitants had enough time to take away their most valuable items. This destruction is not an isolated event, for a concurrent desertion of the wider area has been documented.

In the second case, a coastal settlement at Gouves, not far from the Minoan centre of Knossos, was probably destroyed by a tsunami in the LM IIIB period (*c.* 13th century BC). Evidence for that comes from a potter's workshop, in which all the tools are found *in situ*, thrown in the same direction and covered by pumice, the thick layer of which is capped by material from the collapsed walls. There is historical evidence for a similar destruction in the 17th century AD, as well.

Introduction

The successive destructions which occurred in Minoan Crete from the Old Palace period (20th–18th centuries BC) and onwards, both at palatial and residential centres, have been one of the most controversial issues of Minoan Archaeology. They have been mainly attributed to natural, geological phenomena, especially devastating earthquakes which were associated with the trench offshore Crete, but mainly with the eruption of the volcano on Thera (Marinatos, 1939).

Recent excavations and surface surveys in Central Crete have brought to light new evidence which strengthens the view that earthquakes and tsunamis, possibly following volcanic eruptions, have hit the area repeatedly, not only at the end of the Neopalatial period (LM IB, 15th century BC), but later as well, during LM IIIB period (13th century BC).

This view is supported by the results of our investigations in the Pitsidia area, near Phaistos, on the S Cretan coast and the Gouves area, near Heraklion, on the N coast of the island (Fig. 1).

Evidence from the Pitsidia area
Neopalatial Villa
In the broader area of Phaistos, N of the village of Pitsidia, on a plateau slightly inclined to the S, a Neopalatial

villa has been under excavation since 1988. The ground in the area is chalky marl and is extracted in slabs, 'plakes' in Greek, hence the name of the location — Plakes.

The building, 20.70 x 13 m, with more than twenty rooms set along the exterior sides and around corridors in a typical Minoan layout (Fig. 2), is one of the largest Minoan villas to be investigated in Central Crete. Two staircases, on the E and N sides, a great deal of building material, and other evidence attest to the fact that the villa had a second floor, and the inclination of the ground was exploited to form underground storage areas (Fig. 3).

The walls of the building are built of stones with a thick clay mortar. Big, rectangular, oblong blocks were used for the construction of the exterior walls. Some of these blocks were oversized, while smaller, rough stones were used for the interior walls. Quite noticeable is the extensive use of wood. Impressions on clay and wall niches provide evidence for the existence of both horizontal beams and vertical props in approximately the mid-section of the interior and in less solid walls. Also wooden were the door jambs and the panelling of the wall front of the E staircase, as fitting traces on the stone thresholds and the holes of the stone base show. One observes, therefore, the practice of anti-seismic construction which had been used at neighbouring Phaistos since the Old Palace period (Phase IB).

The whole building collapsed simultaneously and was finally abandoned in LM IB, probably following a tremendous earthquake, as excavation evidence (particularly from the villa destruction), concurrent destructions and desertion in the broader region of Pitsidia and Phaistos and the great seismicity of the region reveal.

Excavation Evidence

The fill of the excavated areas comprises successive layers of rubble, fallen from the superstructure, with soil (from crushed clay mortar) in between, along with sherds and stone tools. The floors of either stone slabs or thin layers of clay on the levelled rock or an older fill are all found on approximately the same level and belong to one phase, the final period before the destruction (Fig. 3).

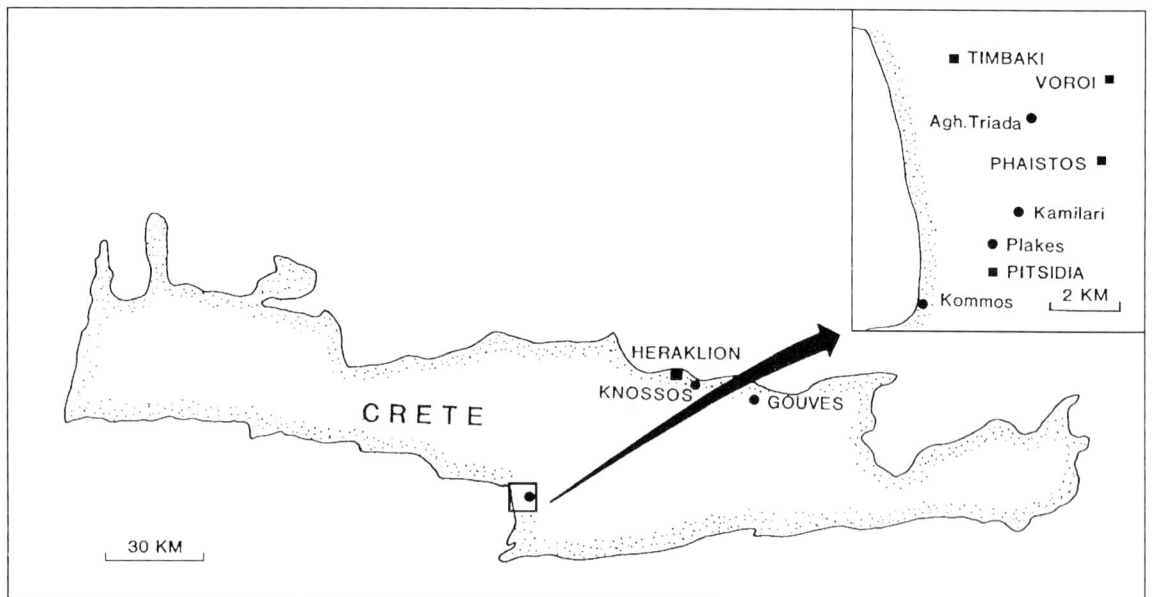

Figure 1. Location map.

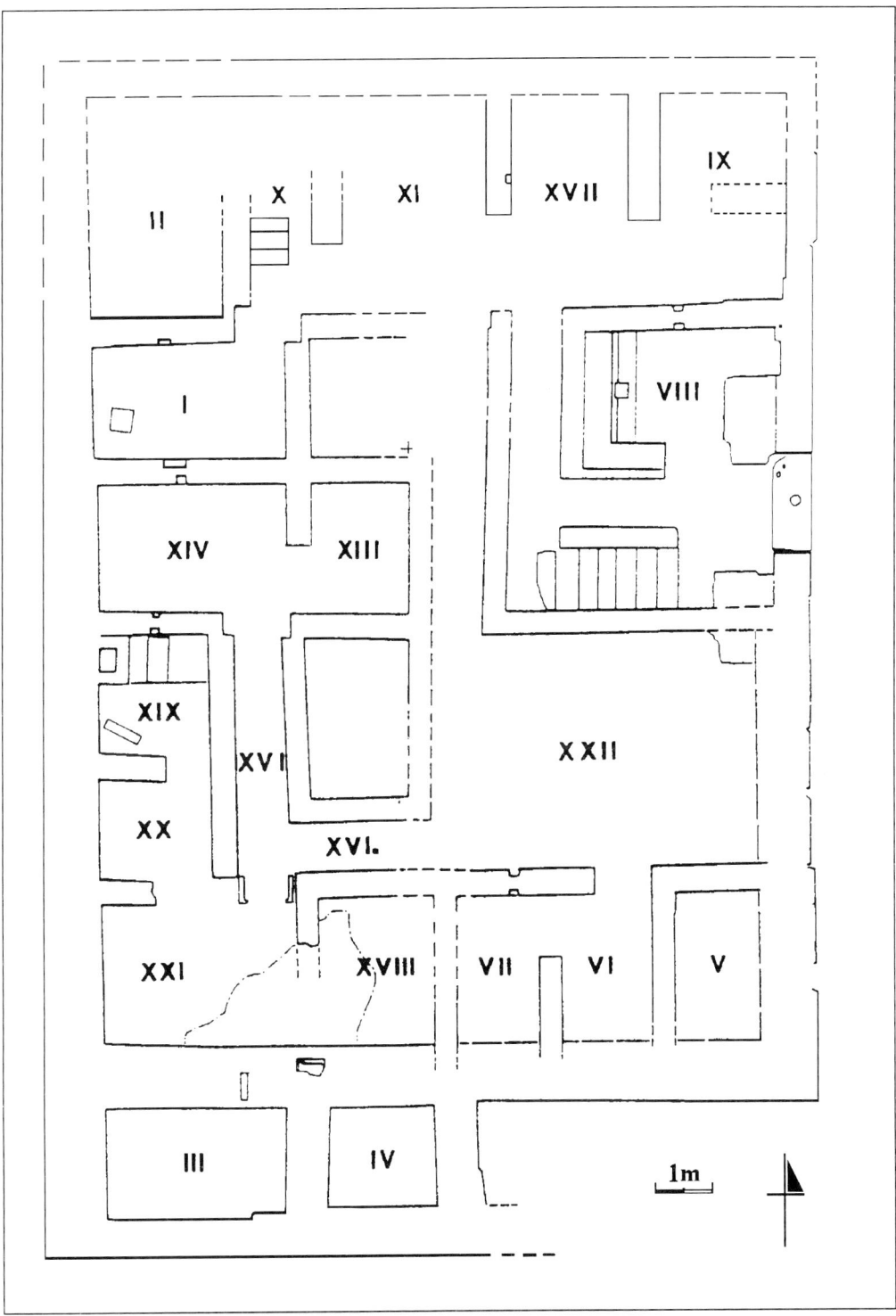

Figure 2. Plan of the Minoan Villa at Pitsidia.

Figure 3. General view (looking W) of the Minoan villa at Pitsidia.

Figure 4. Pottery fragments and debris from the destruction of Room XIV. This is the only place where signs of fire have
   been identified.

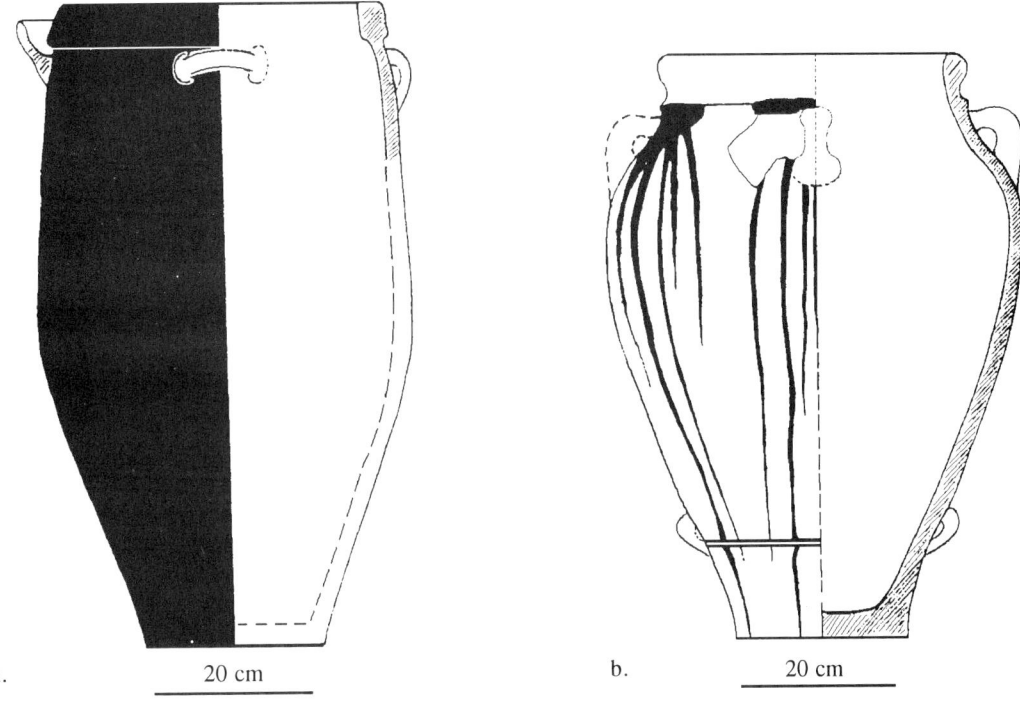

a.   20 cm   b.   20 cm

Figure 5. Pithoi from the destruction layer of Rooms XVII (a) and VI (b).

The direction of the fall of stones and of other objects is from W to E and less so from N to S. The walls are preserved to heights of 1–1.20 m in the W of the building and only at threshold heights or at the euthenderia in the E. The E staircase is damaged and its wall front has an eastward inclination. In the middle of Room IX, at the NE corner of the building, a series of fallen stones, possibly part of a disintegrated pillar, has collapsed also from W to E. The wall between Rooms I and XIV, on the W side, presents an S-shape inclination.

Despite the use of wooden frameworks, a clear layer of fire destruction has yet to be established, with the exception of Room XIV where the wooden beams seem to have fallen and burnt (Fig. 4). Scattered vases were found both in higher layers of the fill and near the floors. Also, vases intact or broken and trapped *in situ* among the stones were very seldom found. Sherds from the same vases were scattered all over the excavated rooms even in various layers. Those in the upper layer, probably fallen from rooms on the upper floor, were scattered in an area larger than a single room. Besides broken pottery — mainly big storage vases — and a number of stone tools, no valuable items were found. This fact testifies to their timely removal before the destruction, perhaps the result of previously acquired experience in earthquake situations. Thus, these excavations provide undeniable evidence for violent destruction throughout the whole building, which was not caused by fire (arson) and seems to have allowed ample time for the occupants to evacuate the building taking with them their moveable valuables. Earthquake destruction seems the most likely explanation, there being no reason to suggest that it is a result of vandalism followed by the abandonment of the building, as was probably the case with the mansion at Pseira and Building 5 at Palaikastro (MacGillivray & Sackett 1991, 132).

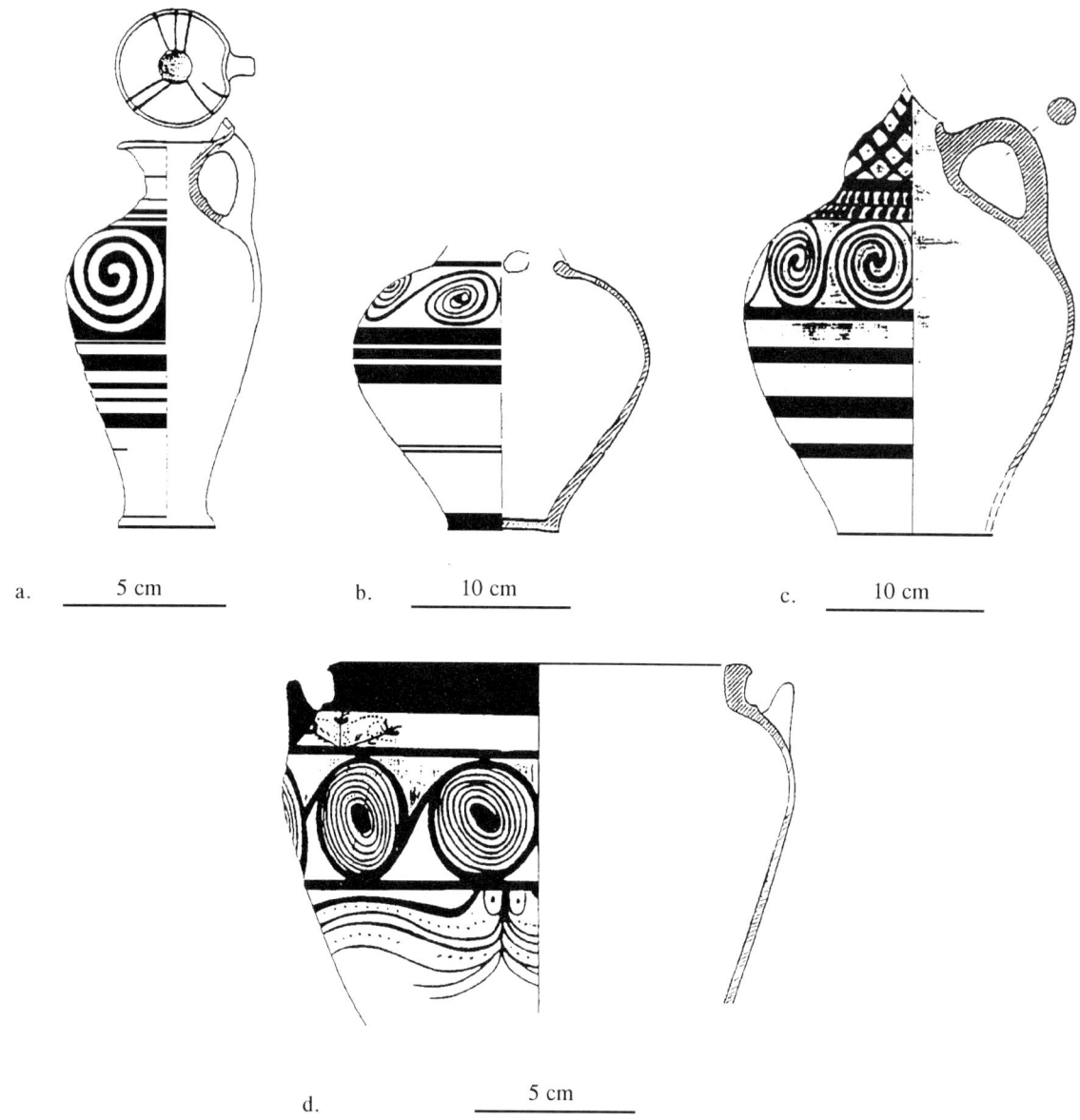

a.   5 cm   b.   10 cm   c.   10 cm

d.   5 cm

Figure 6. Pottery from the destruction layer of Rooms IX(a), IV(b), XXII(c), and XVII(d).

Dating the Evacuation & Destruction of the Villa
Since both the excavation and the laboratory processing of the findings are still in progress, the dating of the final destruction and evacuation of the building is based on current excavation data; the study of the restored pottery is very problematic.

A few restored vases, dating to the LM IA period or the MM IIIB–LM IA transition, have been found in the overall destruction layer. Examples are the ewers, from Rooms IX and I, and the spouted pithos from Room

XVII (Fig. 5). The ewers, with white-on-dark spiral decoration (Fig. 6a–c), are similar to, but more elegant than, those from the Temple Repositories at Knossos (Betancourt 1985, 105–6, pl. B J, 14 B J) and especially those from Ayia Triadha (Di Vita *et al.* 1984, 178, 262). The pithos has a striking resemblance to pithos WP 68 from House N at Palaikastro which, although it dates to the MM III period according to the excavators (Sackett & Popham 1970, 220, pl. 65 and fig. 16), remained in the storeroom from the first residential period to the final destruction in LM IB.

There was also some pottery in the LM IA tradition with typical Floral Style decoration and particularly with dark brown bent reeds on a light ground found within the destruction layer in several rooms. This pottery is very similar to that from the destruction layer of House N and Area DD at Palaikastro, e.g. NP 117 and PK/62/133 (Sackett & Popham 1970, 215f, 231, pl. 59c, 238, pl. 65c), but is particularly close to vases from Phaistos and Ayia Triadha (Di Vita *et al.* 1984, 155, 178, figs 210, 263).

However, the typical LM IB pottery found scattered everywhere, along with the preceding vases, both in the upper layers and on the floors of excavated rooms, provides the dating of the final destruction and desertion of the villa at Pitsidia. Indicative are examples of restored vases with spiral decoration, geometric patterns and other motifs of the LM IB Standard Tradition as well as the Floral and the Abstract and Geometric styles (Fig. 7b) (see Betancourt 1985, 137 ff. pl. 19d, 21d, figs. 103, 104, 109, and Popham

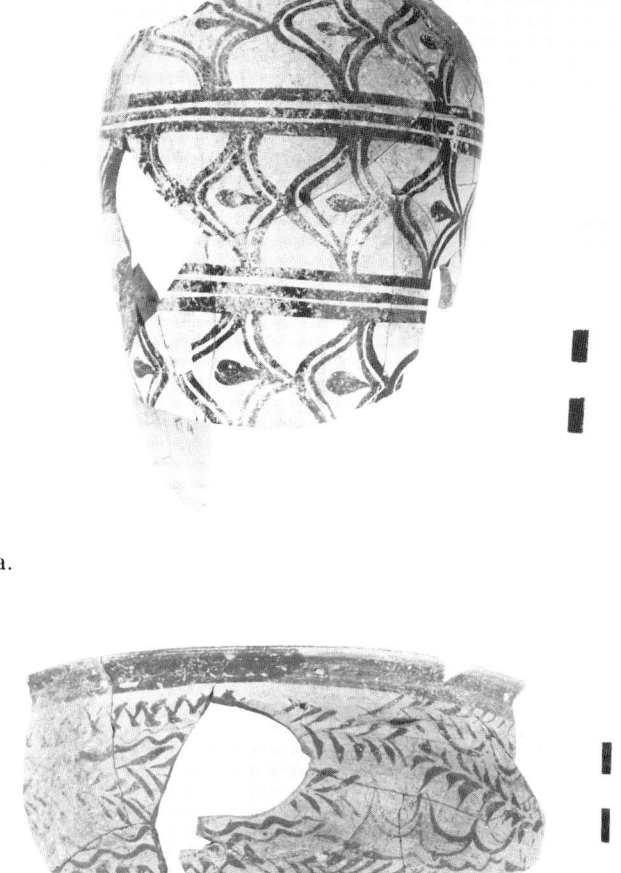

a.

b.

Figure 7. Sherds of a LM IB rhyton (a) and cup (b) from the floor of Room XIV. Scale division cm.

1967, 340, figs 2,7). These and the sherds of an ovoid rhyton from a Knossian workshop (Fig. 7a) from the floor of Room XIV constitute the best evidence for dating the destruction and desertion of the building to the LM IB period (Popham 1967, 340, figs. 2, 12 and pl. 81c).

Thus what has been said of other areas, especially eastern Crete (Palaikastro, Gournia, Mochlos, Pseira, Zakros), may apply to the villa at Pitsidia: that either the tradition and characteristics of LM IA continue when LM IB Knossian pottery has spread all over Crete, or a number of LM IA ceramics survived intact into LM IB. For example, we know that several large vases (pithoi, amphoras, etc.) were used for many years, a phenomenon observed time and again both for Minoan and modern Cretan pithoi. If we accept both this view and the recent evidence that the Theran eruption belongs to LM IA (Renfrew, 1990), irrespective of the higher

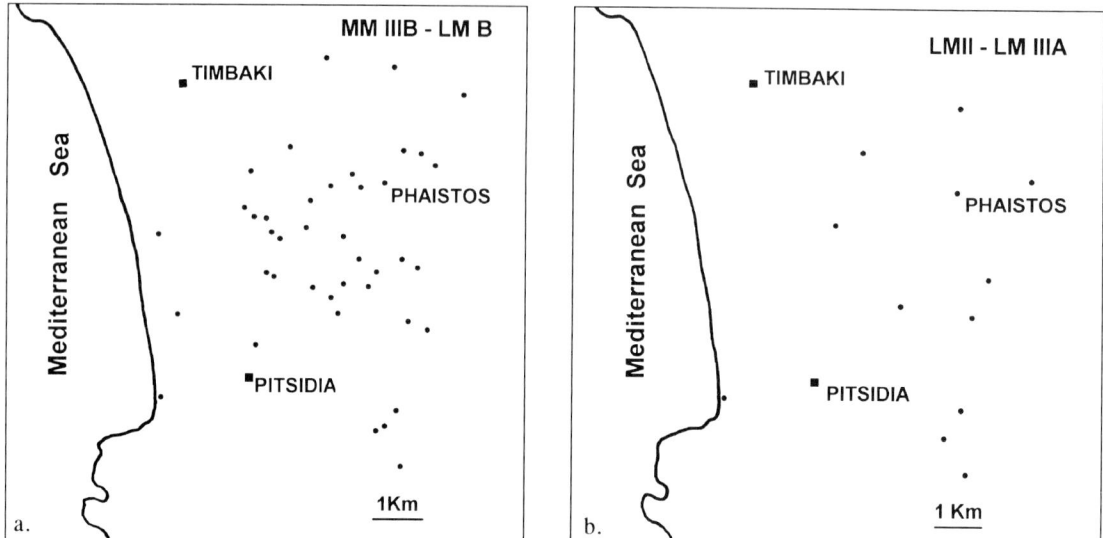

Figure 8. Distribution of the sites of the MM IIIB–LM B (a) and LM II–LM IIIA (b) periods in the Phaistos-Pitsidia area. These diagrams indicate that the destruction and abandonment of the villa at Pitsidia in LM IB is not an isolated case but was followed by the desertion of old sites, even the desertion of the area.

(1645 or 1628 BC; Betancourt, 1987; 1990; Michael, 1976; Baillie & Munro, 1988; Kuniholm, 1990) or the lower absolute dates (1500–1520 BC; Marinatos, 1939; Warren & Hankey 1989, 137), the destruction of the villa should be subsequent to that eruption.

To conclude, we could claim that:

(i) The villa at Pitsidia was built as a residential building in the Neopalatial period on earlier foundations. Excavation of control pits, not discussed here, suggest these foundations date to the Old Palace period or before.

(ii) It was destroyed and abandoned completely in LM IB, concurrent with many other residential and palatial centres of Crete and of the broader region (Kythera, Kea, Rhodes, Kos, Telos, Miletos, Iassos, Asia Minor) of the eastern Mediterranean (Betancourt 1985, 133–135; Warren & Hankey 1989, 78–81).

(iii) The building was not repaired and the area was not re-inhabited until much later, during historic times.

Desertion of the Phaistos-Pitsidia area

During LM IB there were destructions mainly in northern and eastern Crete, from Chania to Palaikastro and Zakros. But the situation in the western Mesara and the Phaistos-Pitsidia area was different. This region was densely populated particularly at the end of the Neopalatial (MM IIIB–LM IB) period. In addition to the large centres of Phaistos, Ayia Triadha, Kommos, and farm houses of Kousses (Marinatos, 1925), Selli-Camelarion (Di Vita *et al.* 1984, 196), Cannia-Gortyn (Levi 1959, 237ff), a large number of sites (Fig. 8a) have been detected in a recent systematic survey (Watrous *et al.*, 1993). The desertion of old sites, apart from Ayia Triadha, Phaistos and Kommos, even the desertion of the area as a whole (Fig. 8b), is observed at the end of LM IB (from LM II until LM IIIA).

Seismicity of the Region

Besides the effects of the Thera eruption, which have been particularly stressed in recent years, the great seismicity of Crete itself seems to have played an important role in shaping the cultural horizon of the island. Recurring strong earthquakes, which have been recorded and described in ancient and modern sources, have hit Crete with devastating effect during antiquity as well as in modern times. Catalogues of these earthquakes have been published by Platakis (1950), Di Vita (1980 and this volume), and Dracopoulos *et al.* (1983) for ancient and modern, Roman and Early-Byzantine, and for modern times respectively. According to the seismotectonic map of Dracopoulos *et al.*, the area of Pitsidia from 1959 to 1972 was the epicentre of four major earthquakes. The major one was of intensity VIII on the Merkali scale and destroyed the larger part of the traditional village. Its inhabitants remember even today the 'muddy and agitated spot' on the nearby Kommos coast.

Conclusion
Taking into account the analysis above and the absence of evidence for the villa at Pitsidia having been totally destroyed by fire in LM IB (except Room-Cellar XIV which was probably burnt by a lit lamp during the collapse of the building), as well as the fact that there is no evidence of hostile intervention, we may suggest that the building was destroyed by an earthquake, whether localised or widespread, subsequent to a volcanic eruption.

Evidence From The Area of Gouves
During the last few years the NW part of a Late Minoan settlement has been excavated at a distance of 30–90 m from the present-day winter sea-line near the small harbour at Gouves, 14 km E of Heraklion.

Excavation of the Settlement & Potters' Workshop
Within three excavation periods two blocks of buildings (A and B), a megaron and potter's workshops with two kilns have been uncovered. The buildings are preserved at low heights (1–rows of stones) and the kilns only at the lowest hewn section of the rock. The walls, built with small and medium-sized rough stones and clay mortar (Fig. 9), were founded on the natural, rather unstable limestone, and in very few cases on a thin layer of soil. Piles of fallen stones are everywhere, but the exact cause of destruction and desertion of the building cannot be determined since recent excavation works and configurations completed the destruction.

The Pumice Deposits
Nevertheless, inside the whole excavated area (approx. 8 acres) a large quantity of pumice, occasionally in thick layers of 10–20 cm, was found. A particularly large mass of pumice was found along the N exterior walls of megaron B and Area VIII, N and W of Room I (Block A), as well as in Room XI in the N.E. and of the same block, that is outdoors and proximal to the sea-line areas. The layer of pumice, along with soil and the fallen objects it covers, is located below the layer of fallen stones and above the floors made of flattened bedrock and thin soil layer (Fig. 10).

Indicative is Room XI where, below the layer of pumice, all tools and accessory items of a potter's workshop were found *in situ*: the stone base of a potter's wheel with a clay basin near the NE wall, a clay wheel 2 m from the centre of the room, a water pithos (NE corner), fallen to the W, while two small vases, and most of the pumice, were found in front of the SW wall (Fig. 11). In addition, a deep bowl (Fig. 12a) trapped inside a stone 'barrier' in the NW corner was also found. All objects, including the pumice, appear to have a direction from N-NE to S-SE. Pumice fragments, with worn-rounded surfaces, are of different sizes: mainly small-medium but also larger ones from the area of the N wall and the area of Room XI and megaron B.

From the direction of dispersed objects, as well as from the shape and mass of the pumice, we gain the impression that the buildings were destroyed after they had been flooded; the objects were violently dislocated and broken. Subsequently, the walls fell and the construction materials covered the layer of destroyed objects and pumice.

Although there has not been an analysis of the pumice, we believe that Gouves may be the first clear instance of a Minoan installation destroyed by a tsunami, probably following an eruption of the Thera or Yali volcanoes, or of an underwater volcano (Keller, 1980) and the subsequent earthquakes.

Figure 9. General view of the excavated settlement of Gouves. The bay of Gouves is seen on the upper, right corner of
the photograph.

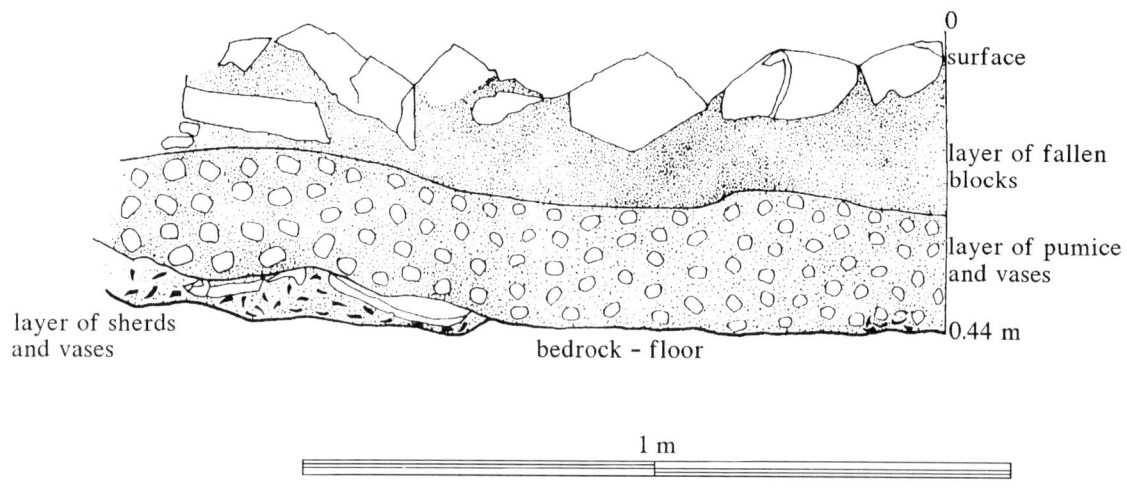

Figure 10. Stratigraphic section of the layer in Room XI.

Figure 11. Gouves: Room XI. The layer of pumice, under the fallen stones of the wall, covers the floor, tools and implements of the potter's workshop, fallen from N-NE to S-SW.

Dating the Evacuation & Destruction

Our dating of the destruction and evacuation of the building and potter's workshop is based, for the time being, on pottery which was found in abundance, especially near the kilns. Although only a small part has been restored and the excavation is still in progress, we can say that, with the exception of a small percentage of pottery dating from LM IIIA2 (1385–1350/40 BC, see Betancourt 1985, 121; or 1370/1360–1340/130, Warren & Hankey 1989, 169), the main body of pottery from the destruction layer of the excavated buildings belongs to LM IIIB (1350/40–1190 or 1340/1330–1190), in particular to its beginning. The forms, the decoration and the technique of coarse and decorated vases (Fig. 12a–f) are similar to those of well dated vases from Knossos and other areas of Crete (Kanta, 1980; Popham 1969, 1970).

The Causes of Destruction

Destructions in LM IA Crete have been attributed to a tsunami following the huge Thera eruption. Small quantities of pumice and Theran ash have been found at Nirou Khani (Platon, 1954), Knossos (Warren & Puchelt 1990, 71), Kato Zakros (Vitaliano & Vitaliano, 1976), Pseira (Betancourt & Davaras, 1988; 1990), Mochlos (Soles & Davaras 1990, 89) and Palaikastro, while huge quantities of seaborne pumice were found at the Amnisos villa (Marinatos, 1932), Chania and Malia and, volcanic ash at Myrtos (Cadogan & Harrison, 1978). All of these were associated with the LM IA destruction layers and were attributed to the known eruption of the Thera volcano.

Volcanic ash and seaborne pumice deposits have also been encountered on Rhodes and Kos (Marketou, 1990), Anafi, Paros, Lemnos, Samothrace and as far away as Israel (Francaviglia, 1990; Keller, 1980). They have been mainly associated with the LM I A eruption on Thera, but possibly also to a later, as yet unidentified eruption of a volcano in the SE Aegean which has entirely collapsed into the sea (Francaviglia, 1990).

D. VALLIANOU

a.

b.

c.

d.

e.

f.

Figure 12. Pottery from the destruction layer of the LM IIIB period at Gouves. Scale bar 20 cm.

The LM IIIB destruction of Gouves might be associated with the latter eruption and its related phenomena of earthquakes and tsunamis. It is recalled that such phenomena have repeatedly occurred at different times in the past and moreover have been recorded by contemporary writers. For instance, Marinos Tzane Bounialis gives us a complete picture of the Heraklion area destruction by a tsunamis subsequent to the Thera volcano eruption, during the siege of Chandax (the Medieval Heraklion) by the Turks in 1650 (Platakis 1954, 480–490):

'It was Sunday they looked at the sun, the twenty-ninth of September,
its rays turned dark, as if it would not shine.
On Melos lightning fell, and there was a stench of Sulphur;
and all people wept because of those omens,
and it all was manifestations of demons.
Right then the castles started a war all on their own,
the sea vanished and the bottom became visible.
From Melos, fire fell upon Santorini,
again and again lightning they threw on Kyseri.
Thunder and lightning illuminated the world,
that shook Crete and the sea trembled but no foams was there,
sometimes it diminished by its own, other times it grew larger,
until it toppled the walls as when the enemy moves in.
It blew up and bent itself with no breath of wind,
the ships it violently pulled, to drag them into its depths.
Ships and galleys all departed forcibly,
and stopped only as they reached the opposite coast of Dia.'

A similar natural phenomenon could have caused the destruction and final desertion of the settlement at Gouves. A wave of destruction and desertion occurred throughout Crete in LM IIIA2–B: in the N (Nirou Khani, Amnisos, Gazi, Malia, Katsambas, Ayia Pelagia, Knossos, Archanes, Stamnio), E (Palaikastro, Gournia), W (Chania, Perivolia, Stylos, Armenoi) and S (Kalohorafites, Ayia Triadha, Kommos, Gallia, Hondros Viannou) (Betancourt 1985, 171; Warren & Hankey 1989, 88–90; Kanta 1980, 324). The destructions are not associated with volcanic debris nor are they concurrent (although the stylistic differences in the pottery are small (Popham 1967, 347)).

It is during this period, particularly at its end, that widespread destructions occurred throughout much of the eastern Mediterranean. The Mycenaean centres were similarly affected at this time (see this volume). The destructions have been variously attributed to a number of factors including natural disasters, such as earthquakes, and invasion and internal unrest. Pomerance (1970) strongly held the view that the destruction of coastal towns and consequent loss of life in the Aegean and the Mediterranean was caused by a huge tsunami, subsequent to the Thera eruption, that is during the 12th century BC. Do the finds at Gouves support this theory? Only careful research on an interdisciplinary basis at other coastal Aegean sites, a review of the documentation from older excavations, and archaeometric research can provide more solid answers to this question.

References

Baillie, M. G. L. & Munro, M. A. R. (1988). Irish tree rings, Santorini and volcanic dust veils. *Nature* **332**, 344–346.

Betancourt, P. (1985). *The History of Minoan Pottery*. Princeton.

Betancourt, P. & Michael, H. N. (1987). Dating the Aegean Late Bronze Age with radiocarbon. *Archaeometry* **29**, 45–49; 212–213.

Betancourt, P. & Davaras, K. (1988). Excavations of Pseira 1985–1986. *Hesperia* **57**, 207–225.

Betancourt, P., Goldberg P., Hope Simpson, R. & Vitaliano C. J. (1990). Excavations at Pseira: The evidence for the Theran Eruption. In (D. Hardy & A. C. Renfrew, Eds) *Thera and the Aegean World* III , 96–99. London: The Thera Foundation.

Cadogan, G. & Harrison, R. K. (1978). Evidence of tephra in soil samples from Pyrgos, Crete. In (C. Doumas, Ed.) *Thera and the Aegean World* I, 235–255. London: The Thera Foundation.

Doumas, C. & Papazoglou, L. (1980). Santorini tephra from Rhodes. *Nature* **287**, 322–324.

Francaviglia, V. (1990). Sea-borne pumice deposits of archaeological interest on Aegean and Eastern Mediterranean beaches. In (D. Hardy & A. C. Renfrew, Eds) *Thera and the Aegean World* III, 127–134. London: The Thera Foundation.

Hood, S. (1973). The eruption of Thera and its effects in Crete in Late Minoan I. *Proceedings of the 3rd Int. Cretological Congress*, 111–118.

Hood, S. (1978). Traces of the Eruption outside Thera. In (C. Doumas, Ed.) *Thera and Aegean World* I, 681–690. London: The Thera Foundation.

Kanta, A. (1980). *The Late Minoan III period in Crete. A survey of sites, pottery and their distribution*. Studies in Mediterranean Archaeology 58. Göteborg.

Keller, J. (1980). Prehistoric pumice Tephra on islands. In (C. Doumas Ed.) *Thera and the Aegean World* II, 49–56. London: The Thera Foundation.

Kuniholm, P. I. (1990). Overview and assessment of the evidence for the date of the eruption of Thera. In (D. Hardy & A. C. Renfrew, Eds) *Thera and the Aegean World* III, 13–18. London: The Thera Foundation.

Levi, D. (1959). La Villa rurale minoica di Gortina. *Bolletino dell' Arte*, 2374.

Levi, D. (1976/1981). *Festos e la Civilta minoica*, I–II. Roma.

MacGillivray, J. A., Sackett, L. H., Driessen J. Farnoux, A. & Smyth D. (1991). Excavations at Palaikastro 1990. *Annual of the British School at Athens* **86**, 121–147.

Manning, S. (1988). The Bronze Age eruption of Thera: Absolute dating, Aegean chronology and Mediterranean cultural relations, *Journal of Mediterranean Archaeology* **1**, 17–82.

Marinatos, S. (1924/25). Middle Minoan house in Kato Mesara. *Archaeologikon Deltion* **9**, 53–78. (In Greek)

Marinatos, S. (1939). The volcanic destruction of Minoan Crete. *Antiquity* **13**, 425–439.

Marinos, G. & Melidonis, N. (1971). On the strength of seaquakes (tsunamis) during the prehistoric eruptions of Santorini. ACTA of the 1st International Scientific Conference on the Volcano of Thera, 277–282. Athens: Archaeological Services of Greece.

Marketou, T. (1990). Santorini Tephra from Rhodes and Kos: Some chronological remarks based on the stratigraphy. In (D. Hardy & A. C. Renfrew Eds) *Thera and the Aegean World* III, 100–113. London: The Thera Foundation.

Michael, H. N. (1976). Radiocarbon dates from Akrotiri on Thera, *Temple University Aegean Symposium*, 7–9.

Page, D. L. (1970). The Santorini volcano and the destruction of Minoan Crete, *Journal of Hellenic Studies*, Suppl. **12**.

Platakis, El. (1950). Earthquakes of Crete, *Kritika Chronika* **4**, 463–503. (In Greek).

Platon, N. (1954). Minoan house shrines. *Kritika Chronika* **8**, 428–483 (In Greek).

Platon, N. (1973). La chronologie des receptacles des tresors du sanctuaire. The Temple Repositories et des autres depots contemporains du palais, *Proceedings of the 3rd Int. Cretological Congress*, 241–253.

Pomerance, L. (1970). *The final collapse of Santorini*. Studies in Mediterranean Archaeology 26, Göteborg.

Popham, M. R. (1969). The Late Minoan goblet and kylix. *Annual of the British School at Athens* **64**, 299–304.

Popham, M. R. (1970a). Late Minoan chronology. *American Journal of Archaeology* **74**, 226–228.

Popham, M. R. (1970b). Late Minoan IIIB pottery from Knossos. *Annual of the British School at Athens* **65**, 195–202.

Renfrew, C. (1990). Summary of the Progress in Chronology. In (D. Hardy & A. C. Renfrew, Eds) *Thera and the Aegean World* III, 242. London: The Thera Foundation.

Sackett, L. H. & Popham, M. R. (1970). Excavations at Palaikastro. *Annual of the British School at Athens* **65**, 203–242.

Soles, S. & Davaras C. (1990). Theran ash in Minoan Crete: New excavations on Mochlos. In (D. Hardy & A. C. Renfrew, Eds) *Thera and the Aegean World* III, 89–95. London: The Thera Foundation.

Vallianou, D. (in press). Minoan potter's workshops. An ethnological approach based on new data. *Proceedings of the 6th Cretological Congress*. (In Greek).

Vitaliano, C. J. & Vitaliano, D. B. (1974). Volcanic tephra on Crete. *American Journal of Archaeology* **78**, 19–24.

Di Vita, A., La Rosa, V., & Rizza, A. (1984). *Creta Antica*. Rome.

Warren, P. M. (1987). Absolute dating of the Aegean Late Bronze Age. *Archaeometry* **29**, 205–211.

Warren, P. M. & Hankey, V. (1989). *Aegean Bronze Age Chronology*. Bristol.

Watrous, L. V., Chatzi-Vallianou, D., Pope, K., Mourtzas, N., Shay, J., Shay, T. C., Bennet, J., Tsoungarakis, D., Angelomati-Tsoungarakis, E., Vallianos, C. & Blitzer H. (1993). A survey of the western Mesara plain in Crete: Preliminary Report of the 1984, 1986 and 1987 field seasons. *Hesperia* **62**, 191–248.

Tracing a Destructive Earthquake
in the Southwestern Peloponnese (Greece)
during the Early Bronze Age

Kostas Zachos

Ephoreia of Prehistoric & Classical Antiquities,
6, 25th March Square, 452 21 Ioannina, Greece

Abstract

Excavation data from the Early Bronze Age (3200–2050 BC) site of Ayios Dhimitrios, in S-W Greece, indicate a violent destruction without the inhabitants having had time to save valuable items; some of the latter give the impression that they fell from shelves. A somewhat similar destruction is reported at the site of Voidokoilia, about 60 km away from Ayios Dhimitrios. Since the similarity of the pottery assemblage at the two sites is striking and suggests that within the limits of archaeological, stylistic dating the two destructions are contemporary, as well as reports of earthquakes that have affected both sites during possibly the last centuries, it is concluded that an earthquake is responsible for the destruction of these two Early Bronze Age sites.

Introduction

The western Peloponnese, together with the Ionian islands, has shown a high incidence of earthquake activity during the last 100 years (for example, Galanopoulos, 1940; 1947). The violent earthquakes of 1986 at Kalamata and 1993 at Pyrgos constitute the most recent examples. Although the situation was apparently not different in historical and prehistoric times, the ancient written sources concerning earthquake activity in Elis and Messenia are sporadic (Ammianus Marcellinus 25.10.17–18; Pachymeris, *History* II; Bonn 1835, 393, 3; neighbouring Sparta was devastated by the earthquake of 464 BC: Thucydides I.101, Plutarch, *Cimon* 16.4). Yet there are many cases in which the monuments themselves speak of violent earthquake destructions in antiquity. For example, the replacement of the reclining female Lapiths of the western pediment of the temple of Zeus at Olympia by replicas of Pentelic marble has been attributed to the effects of disastrous earthquakes (Dinsmoor 1975, 153–154, n. 3; Ashmole & Yalouris 1967, 22). The present position of the fallen drums of the same temple speaks dramatically for the violent earthquakes of the 6th century AD, which levelled one of the most glorious monuments of ancient Greece (Gardiner 1925, 3–5). Excavation data, however, can provide evidence of earthquakes that are likely to have hit the area during earlier periods, when human constructions were modest and their remains poorly preserved. The aim of this paper is to try to document an earthquake that has probably hit two sites in the western Peloponnese. Evidence for this earthquake is provided by the excavated destruction layers of two contemporary structures containing a massive amount of clay vessels and other artifacts indicating their sudden and unanticipated abandonment by their occupants.

The earliest architectural remains of the southwestern Peloponnese which can possibly inform us about seismic activity in this part of Greece are dated to the Korakou culture of the Early Helladic period (hereafter EH, about 2650–2200 BC). Although the western Peloponnese has been intensively investigated thanks to the

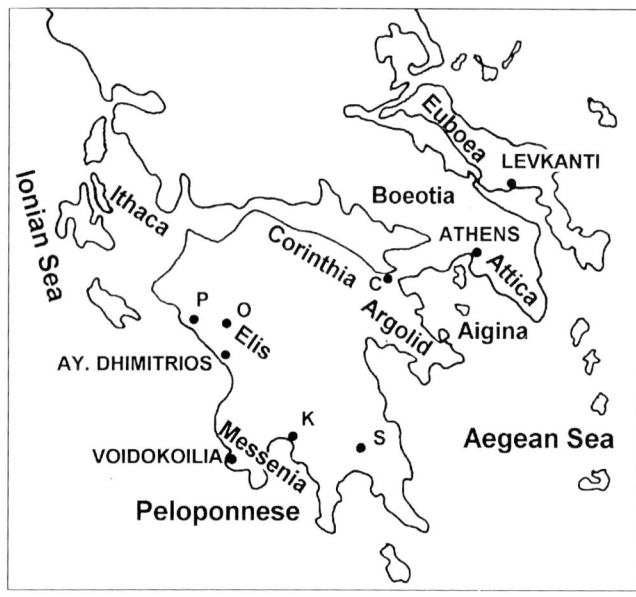

Figure 1. Location map: C=Corinthos, K=Kalamata, O=Olympia, P=Pyrgos and S=Sparta.

University of Minnesota Messenia Expedition, the number of known Early Bronze Age sites is surprisingly small compared to those from the eastern Peloponnese. Most of the settlements are concentrated along the Pamissos river valley, while the rest are very widely scattered mainly along the western seashores (McDonald & Hope-Simpson 1969, 172). Two recently excavated EH sites in the western Peloponnese, namely Ayios Dhimitrios in Triphylia and Voidokoilia in Messenia (Fig. 1) furnish evidence for a probable destruction by violent earthquake.

The case of Ayios Dhimitrios

The prehistoric site of Ayios Dhimitrios in Triphylia is located on a hill below the Classical acropolis of Lepreon (Figs 1,2). Excavations there revealed deposits of the Final Neolithic and the Early, Middle and Late Bronze Age (about 4500–3200 BC, 3200–2050 BC, 2050–1550 BC, 1550–1100 BC, respectively). Two successive phases of the Early Bronze Age have been recognized: phases Ayios Dhimitrios IIa and IIb, both certainly dated to the EH II period. The architectural remains of both these phases are very poorly preserved. From phase IIb, which chronologically belongs towards the end of the EH period, the lower layers of the stone foundations of a house (House A) have been preserved. This is a rectangular house oriented N to S with three rooms along its long axis. The foundation walls are resting on bedrock and consist of two rows of unworked stones. The space between the stones is filled with mud and smaller stones. The average thickness of the walls is 65–75 cm. This type of foundation is a common feature of the architecture of the EH period in southern Greece and it served as a base for the superstructure which in most cases was made of mudbricks. At Ayios Dhimitrios only traces of mudbricks were preserved; in other settlements of this period, however, like Strefi in Elis, Ayios Kosmas in Attica, Lerna and Berbati in the Argolid, mudbricks were entirely preserved.

The deposits of Rooms I and II of House A were poorly preserved due to building activity on the hill during the Frankish period. The deposits in Room III were better preserved and allow some conclusions regarding the causes of the destruction of House A. Only the S and part of the eastern foundation walls of this room were preserved. The floor of the room, which was 30 cm below the floor of the neighbouring rooms, was made of beaten yellow clay. Near the centre of the room an almost circular hearth was found, made of flat stones. On top of the stones a mixture of reddish earth, carbonized material, animal bones, pottery sherds and a fragment of a denticulated blade of whitish flint had accumulated. Another fragment of the same blade, joining the first, was found outside of the hearth. A collar-necked jar bearing traces of burning was found within the reddish earth of the hearth (Fig. 11, n. 4). A clay bellows nozzle (tuyère) was plugged in the N-W side of the hearth (Fig. 8, n. 5). E of the hearth was found a millstone with its grinder on top and, scattered on the clay floor around it, animal bones of sheep or goat. Over the entire surface of the room, on top and around the hearth, lay debris of earth and stones mixed with the equipment of the house. Many fragments of vases were found upside down as they had fallen from shelves fixed on the walls (Fig. 3). Some vases could be mended entirely, others partially, from many sherds scattered all over the area of the room. The repertory of the vases includes a rich variety of

AYIOS DHIMITRIOS - LEPREON
site plan

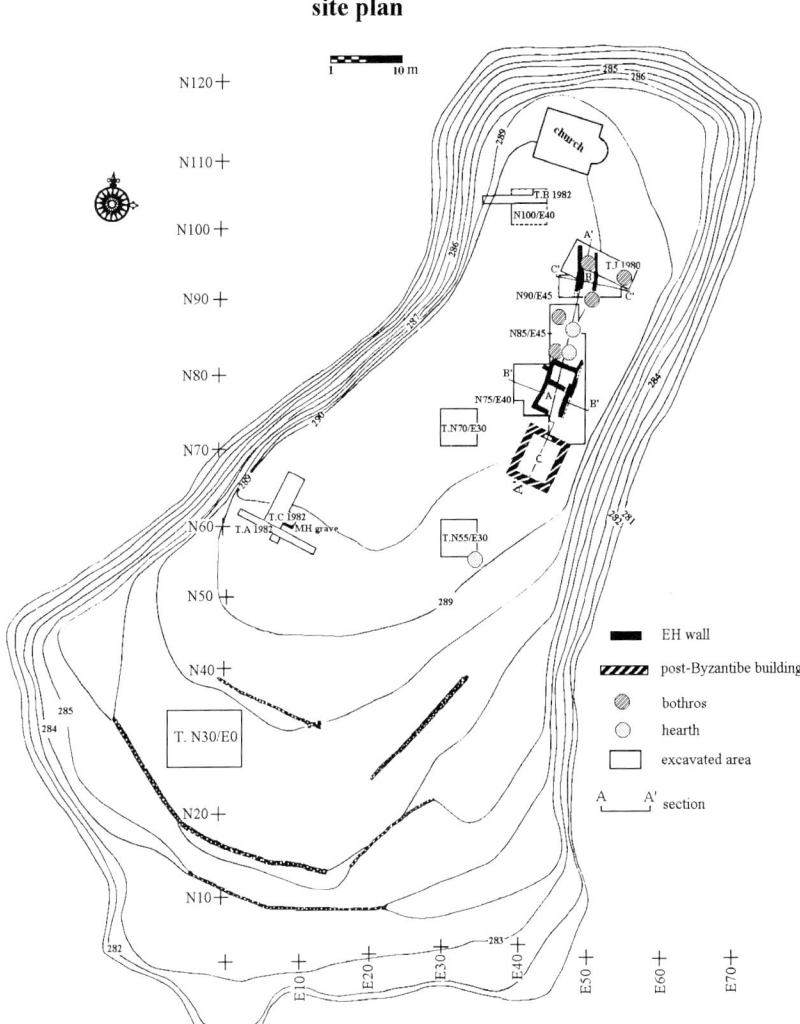

Figure 2. Site plan of Ayios Dhimitrios.

forms for carrying, storing, preparing and serving food, like pithoi, basins, cooking pots, jars, baking pans, jugs, askoid jugs, fruitstands, bowls, saucers, sauceboats, and a small double-vase (Figs 5–11). In addition to the animal bones, various other food remains were found, including snail shells and crab's claws. A boar's tusk found in the debris most probably was carried into the house as a valuable item as well as some *Dentalium* and *Patela* sea shells, the former being very popular as ornaments among the EH people. Near the N-W corner of the room were found a clay sealing and a fragment of a hearth rim with incised decoration (Fig. 11, n. 10; Fig. 8, n. 6). Towards its N-E corner two lead spools and a clay spindle whorl were resting on the floor (Fig. 8, nos 4, 7–8). Obsidian tools and debitage were scattered all over with a greater concentration towards the eastern part of the room. Three more millstones, in addition to the one near the hearth, were also found (for the description of the House A see also Zachos 1986, 31–33; 1987, 161–166).

Figure 3. Pottery *in situ* from the destruction level of House A Room III at Ayios Dhimitrios.

Figure 4. Pottery *in situ* from the destruction level of N-N-E sector at Voidokoilia.

The description of the destruction layer of Room III was presented above in detail in order to transmit to the reader an impression of the puzzle presented by the finds. It is clear that the accumulation of debris was not the result of an abandoned and slowly demolished empty house but rather the result of an unexpected event. The inhabitants abandoned the house without taking any of the equipment, not even the valuable lead spools (which most probably functioned as a kind of ingot).

The case of Voidokoilia

The picture presented by the destruction layer of a room at the EH settlement of Voidokoilia in Messenia led me to the conclusion that it was due to the same event that caused the destruction at Ayios Dhimitrios; in both cases massive amounts of broken pots were found, some entirely preserved in an inverted position giving the impression they had fallen from shelves.

The EH settlement of Voidokoilia in Messenia, excavated by G. Korres, is located on a hill on the N side of the Gulf of Voidokoilia. A large part of it is overlaid by a Middle Helladic tumulus and a Mycenaean tholos tomb previously discovered and partially investigated by S. Marinatos.

Within the cavities of the bedrock, where the foundations of the EH houses were resting, pottery sherds typical of the Final Neolithic period of the Peloponnese were collected. From the excavation reports published by Korres, it is clear that the EH settlement of Voidokoilia has a long sequence from a transitional phase of the EH I to EH II period until the end of the EH II period (Korres, 1977; 1978; 1979; 1980a; 1980b; 1981; 1982). The erection of a tumulus during the Middle Helladic period and of a tholos tomb during Mycenaean times had a disastrous impact on the stratigraphy of the EH deposits. In some instances, however, the excavator distinguished closed, undisturbed deposits, and it is expected that the final publication of the site will clarify the succession of strata. In a destruction layer at the N-N-E sector the excavator (Korres 1979, 153) describes a closed deposit as follows:

> 'The pottery of the deposit included fragments of vases with counter-sunk bases and incurved rims. The main finds in the excavated area include large parts of a pithos scattered all over and at least a dozen inverted vases (an askoid jug, two sauceboats, and several saucers) which had fallen from a shelf. The askoid jug has a triple strap, wide mouth, ring base and a plastic cordon decoration on the body. Two sauceboats had vertical handles and the plethora of the saucers were of various types.'

(see here Figs 4 and 12, nos 1–4).

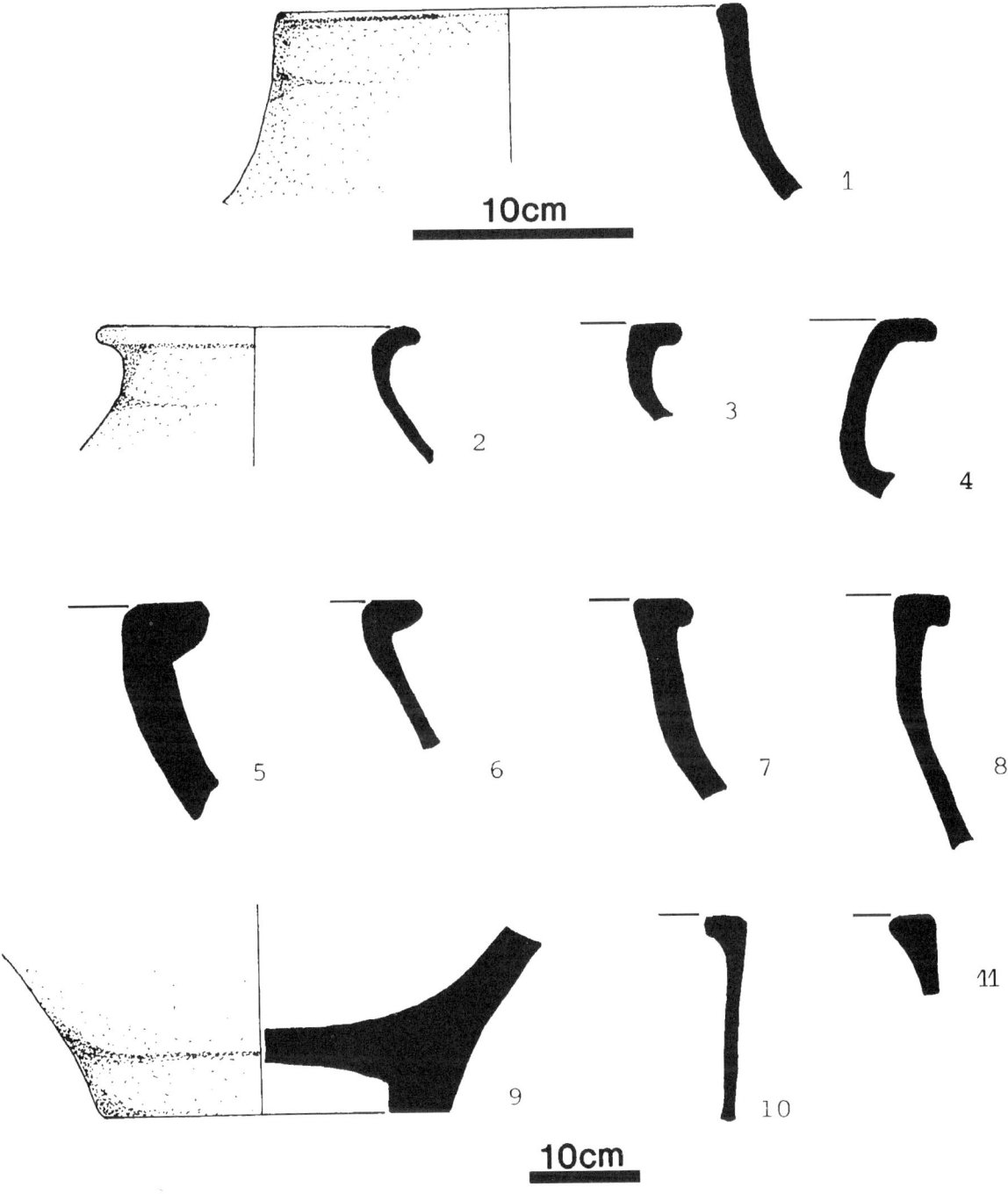

Figure 5. Pottery from Room III at Ayios Dhimitrios: Pithoi.

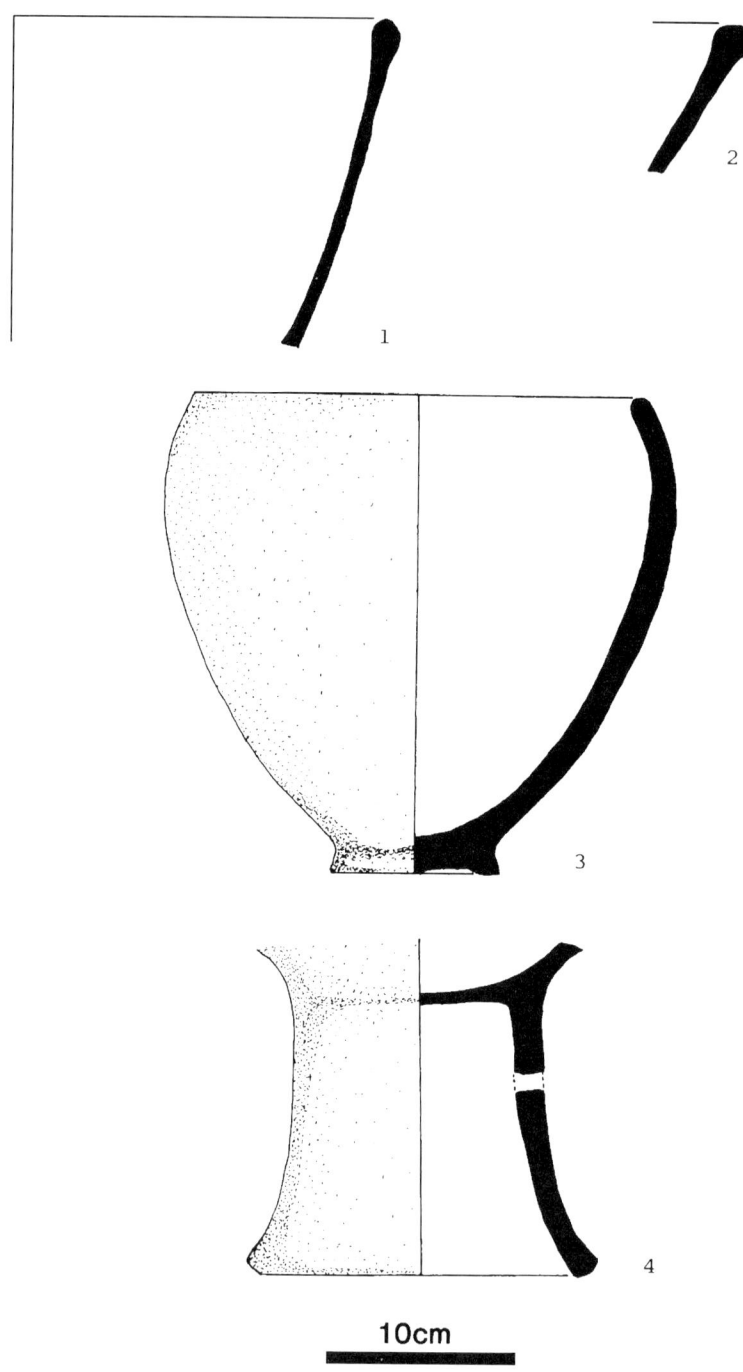

Figure 6. Pottery from Room III at Ayios Dhimitrios. Basins (1–2) Cooking pot (3), Base of fruitstand (4).

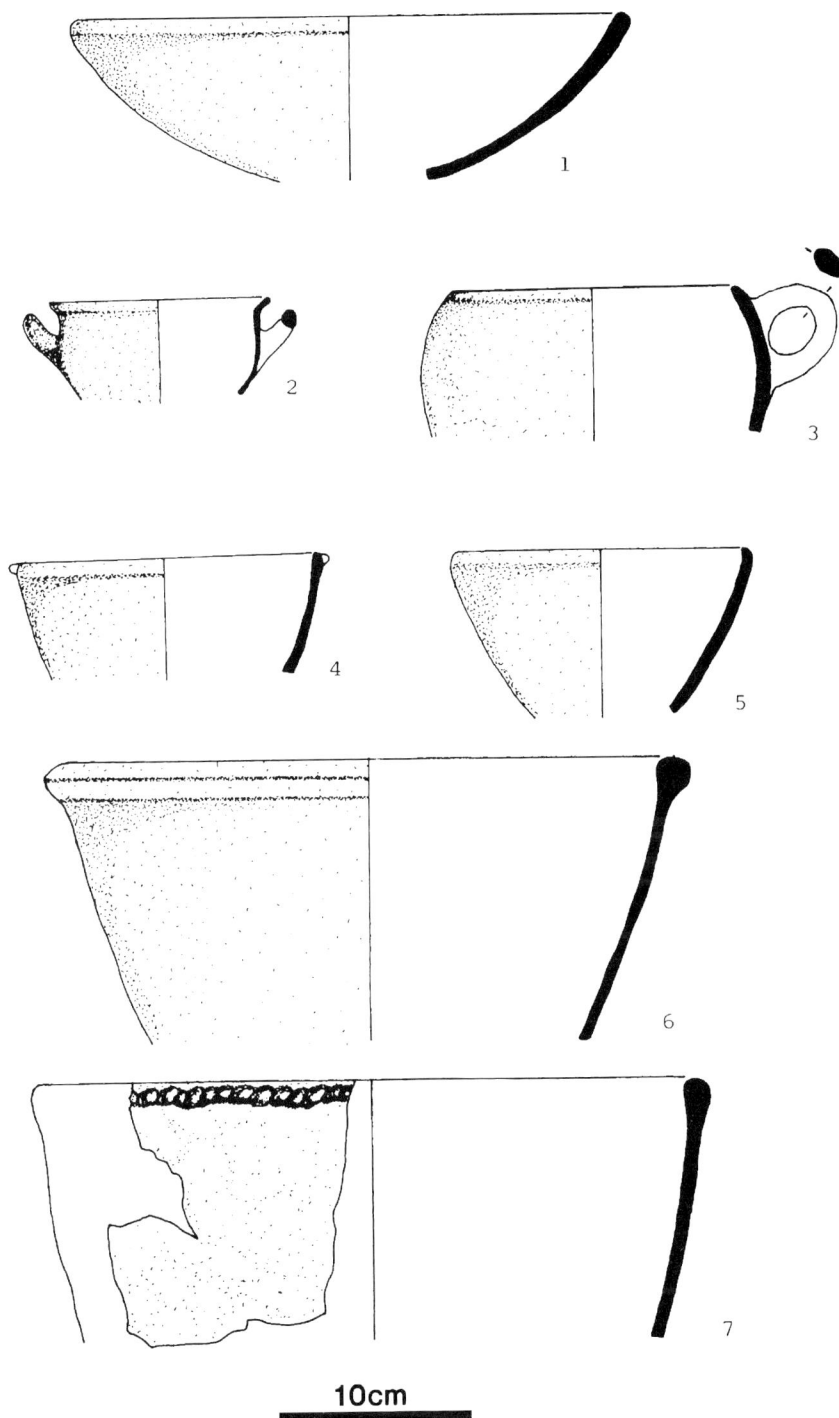

Figure 7. Pottery from Room III at Ayios Dhimitrios. Bowls (1–2, 4–5), Cup (3), Basins (6–7).

The pottery of the Korakou culture is characterized by a broad range of vase forms with a stylistic uniformity and limited decorative modes. The evolution of the shapes and decorative motifs is very conservative considering the great span of the period, lasting for several hundred years (Rutter 1993; Wiencke 1989, 496, n.2). Most of the excavated sites of this period in Greece have not produced a deep succession of strata, except Lerna and Tiryns in the Argolid. A short sample of the pottery from those sites has been presented in various preliminary reports. The above factors discourage attempts towards a stylistic analysis which could establish an evolution of shapes, centres of production and exchange patterns. Some basic characteristics concerning stylistic evolution and regional variation can, however, be demonstrated. Caskey & Wiencke have presented some characteristics of the evolution of particular shapes and painted decoration of the pottery of Lerna (Caskey, 1960; Wiencke, 1987; 1989, 496–497, n. 6). The same has been done by Weisshaar (1981, 1982, 1983) for Tiryns. Concerning regional stylistic variations, the shoulder-handled bowl with an everted rim is considered a Boeotian and Euboean feature, the flaring pedestal foot of open shapes a feature of central Greece (although it occurs in many Peloponnesian sites), and pattern-painted pottery a feature of eastern Attica and Argolid-Corinthia (Rutter 1993). Neutron activation analysis of EH pottery has suggested a ceramic exchange between sites in the Argolid-Corinthia during the EH period, but the scale of such exchange remains unknown (Attas, 1982; Pullen 1985, 341–344; Rutter, 1993).

The vases of the two destruction deposits at Ayios Dhimitrios and Voidokoilia share common features. This affinity determines their classification into the same ceramic region, in a developed stage of the ceramic evolution of the Korakou culture. The clay of the fine wares is soft and powdery, mostly unpainted, but when paint is applied it is light in contrast to the early stages of the period (Wienke 1989, 496, n. 6). The saucers with incurved rim and ring bases correspond typologically to Weisshaar's type IIb which at Tiryns appears in developed horizons of EH II lasting up into the 'Übergangs' phase (Fig. 9, nos 1–8, 10; Weisshaar 1981, 223–224, Fig. 68; 1983, 340, Fig. 10). To developed stages at Tiryns (Schicht VI which Weisshaar correlates with the House of the Tiles horizon at Lerna) correspond also the saucers with straight-sided profiles and dimple bases as well as saucers with vertical rim (Fig. 9, nos 9, 11–13; Weisshaar 1981, Fig. 80: 3, 7, 11). At Lerna the type of saucers from Ayios Dhimitrios and Voidokoilia belong to the period of the House of the Tiles, i.e. Phase D (Wiencke, 1987). The sauceboats from the destruction deposits in Messenia with deep cylindrical bodies and high spouts belong to Caskey's type III, which is placed in a late stage of the EH period (Fig. 10, nos 1–2; Fig. 12, no. 3; Caskey 1960, 290, Fig. 1; Wiencke 1989, 496–497, n. 6).

The askoid jug illustrated by Korres (1979, Pl. 113a; here Fig. 12, no. 4) is almost identical with the askoid jugs from the destruction deposit of Room III at Ayios Dhimitrios (Fig. 11, nos 6, 7, 9). The characteristic vase shape known in Aegean prehistoric research as the *askos*, should be considered, in my opinion, a sensitive regional and chronological marker during the EH period. Rutter has shown that during this period askoi are produced in as many as a half-dozen variants (Rutter, 1993). At Lerna itself, it seems that an evolution of the shape can be demonstrated. Caskey notes that askoid vessels are common in Lerna III and illustrates three different examples from stages that predate the House of the Tiles (Caskey 1954, 27, Pl. 11a; 1956, 169 Pl. 46e; 1959 204, Pl. 41e; 1960, 290). An askos with possible provenance from the 'Rundbau' at Tiryns resembles a fine polished and light-painted askos from Phase IIIC at Lerna (Müller 1938, Pl. IX. 7; Caskey 1956, 169, Pl.46e; Wiencke 1989, 496–497, n. 6; Fig. 12, nos 5, 6).

To my knowledge, the only example resembling the askoid-jugs from Messenia comes from an EH II deposit of area I at Pelikata in Ithaka (Heurtley 1935, 19, Pl. 6, no.42; here Fig. 12, no. 7). Commenting on this site Caskey (1971, 792) notes:

> 'Little remained of the houses, which had been demolished repeatedly by the earthquakes that afflict this region; the debris was often found to consist of stones from fallen walls, packed into hollows to level the ground. This tidy practice has been observed at other EH sites also. In spite of the ruinous state of the architectural remnants, none the less, it is clear that Pelikata was occupied in two of the

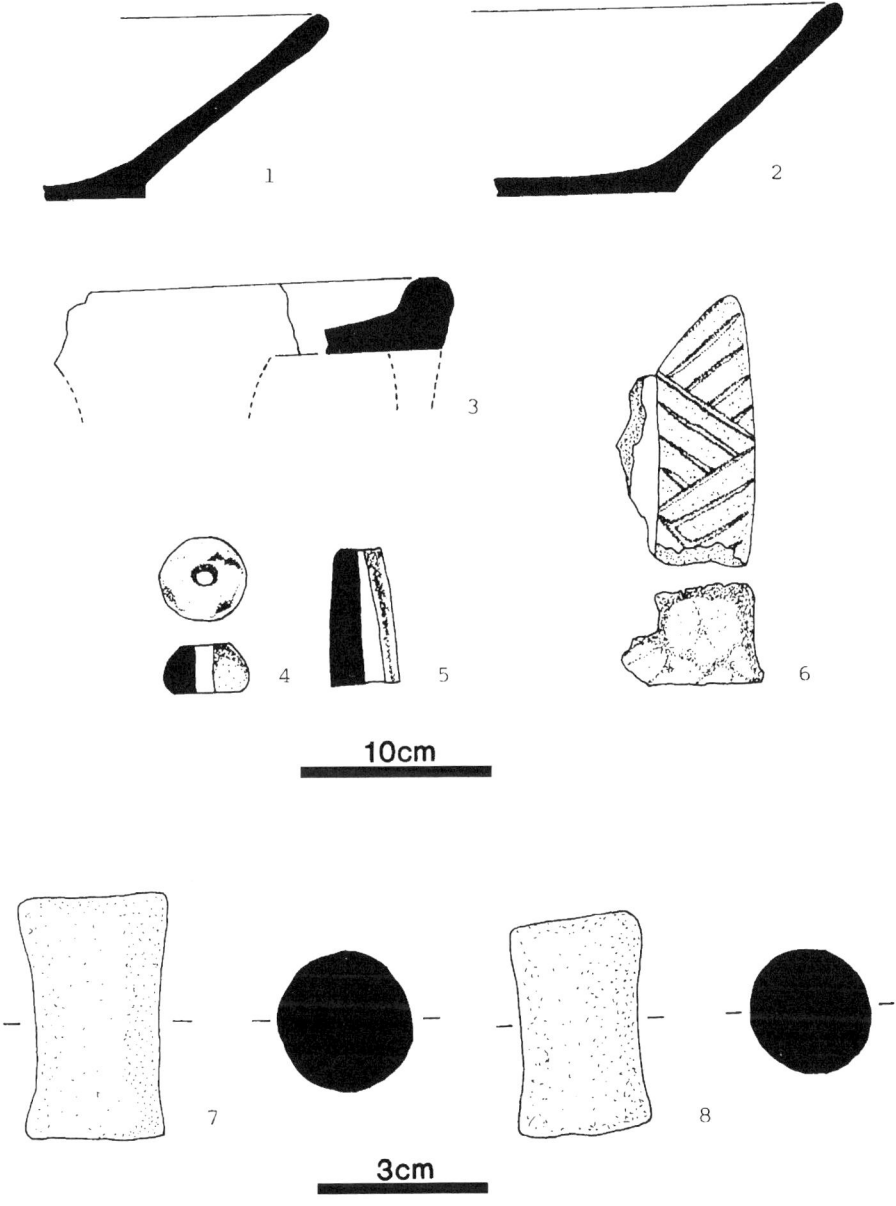

Figure 8. Artefacts from Room III at Ayios Dhimitrios. Baking pans (1–3), Hearth-rim fragment (6), Spindle whorl (4), Tuyère (5), Lead spools (7–8).

main phases that are known in eastern Greece. Certain of the areas examined produced pottery that must be assigned to the EH II: sauceboats, askoi, saucers, basins, and jars'.

On the basis of the excavation reports by Heurtley, it is unfortunately not possible to associate the context of the askoid jug no. 42 and the remainder of the pottery with a specific structure.

Vulnerability of Constructions of the EH Period

The degree of the destructive effect of an earthquake is related not only to the intensity of the earthquake but also to the construction and technique of a building. During the EH period in southern Greece, aside from the monumental buildings at Lerna, Akovitika in the Argolid, Thebes in Boeotia, Aigina, the 'Rundbau' at Tiryns and possibly at other sites (Wiencke 1989, 496 n. 4; Shaw 1987) where a sophisticated architecture is observed, the majority of the civilian structures are simple dwellings, like House A at Ayios Dhimitrios. In most cases, the foundations are so shallow that the lowest layer of stones is used as a doorstep. The resistance of a structure with such shallow foundations, bearing mud brick walls, must be very weak, even to an earthquake of small intensity.

The Possible Role of Earthquakes in the Destruction of Early Bronze Age Settlements

In Aegean prehistoric scholarship, destructions and changes of archaeological assemblages on a site are usually explained through migration or invasion theories. These historical models view material culture as inextricably linked to the ideological, ethnic, and social identity and structure of a population group, so that changes or innovations observed, for example, in pottery are projected onto other aspects of a culture. Such theoretical approaches of explanation of cultural change are rooted in the fundamental problem concerning the first arrival of the Greeks and the stages of their spreading over the Greek mainland (for the earliest relevant theories see Haley and Blegen (1928); an enlightening discussion of various explanatory models concerning changes in Aegean prehistory is included in McNeal, 1972 and Pullen (1985, 66-69). Caskey's suggestions on the destruction of the 'House of the Tiles' at Lerna towards the end of the EH II period constitute an authentic product of the migration-invasion approach. Systematic excavations conducted in the 1950's by Caskey at Lerna in Argolid had as a goal to provide the necessary stratigraphic basis for a precise definition of the three Bronze Age phases of southern Greece following the tripartite scheme that Blegen had initiated in the Aegean chronology (Blegen 1921; Caskey 1960, 285). The entire sequence of the layers at Lerna was divided by Caskey into seven groups (Lerna I–VII). Lerna III belongs to EH II and Lerna IV to EH III period, while only traces of EH I have been noticed at the site (Wienke 1989, 496, n. 1). The end of the EH II period at Lerna was marked by a fire which destroyed the monumental building known as the 'House of the Tiles'. According to Caskey, 'the burning of the House of the Tiles marked the end of the period II, and marked it very clearly indeed, both historically and archaeologically. This was the end of an era at Lerna' (Caskey 1960, 293). Correlating the evidence furnished at Lerna and other Early Bronze Age sites in southern Greece, Caskey pointed out that destruction levels have been observed not only at Lerna but also at Tiryns, Asine in the Argolid, Zygouries and perhaps Corinth in the Peloponnese and Ayios Kosmas in Attica (Caskey 1960, 301); yet he was cautious in drawing general conclusions on a probable common cause of the destruction, as most of the sites were only partially excavated. Regarding the evidence from Lerna itself, the difference in character observed between Lerna III and IV and the respectful treatment offered by the successors to the ruins of the House of the Tiles were interpreted by Caskey as indications that Lerna III ended under the force of invaders bearing features of the Lerna IV material culture, which was consequently defined as EH III. The origin of these people and the pattern of their spread into Greece have been the subject of further research (Caskey, 1960; 1965; 1971). Archaeological investigations and comparative studies of various categories of finds carried out during the past

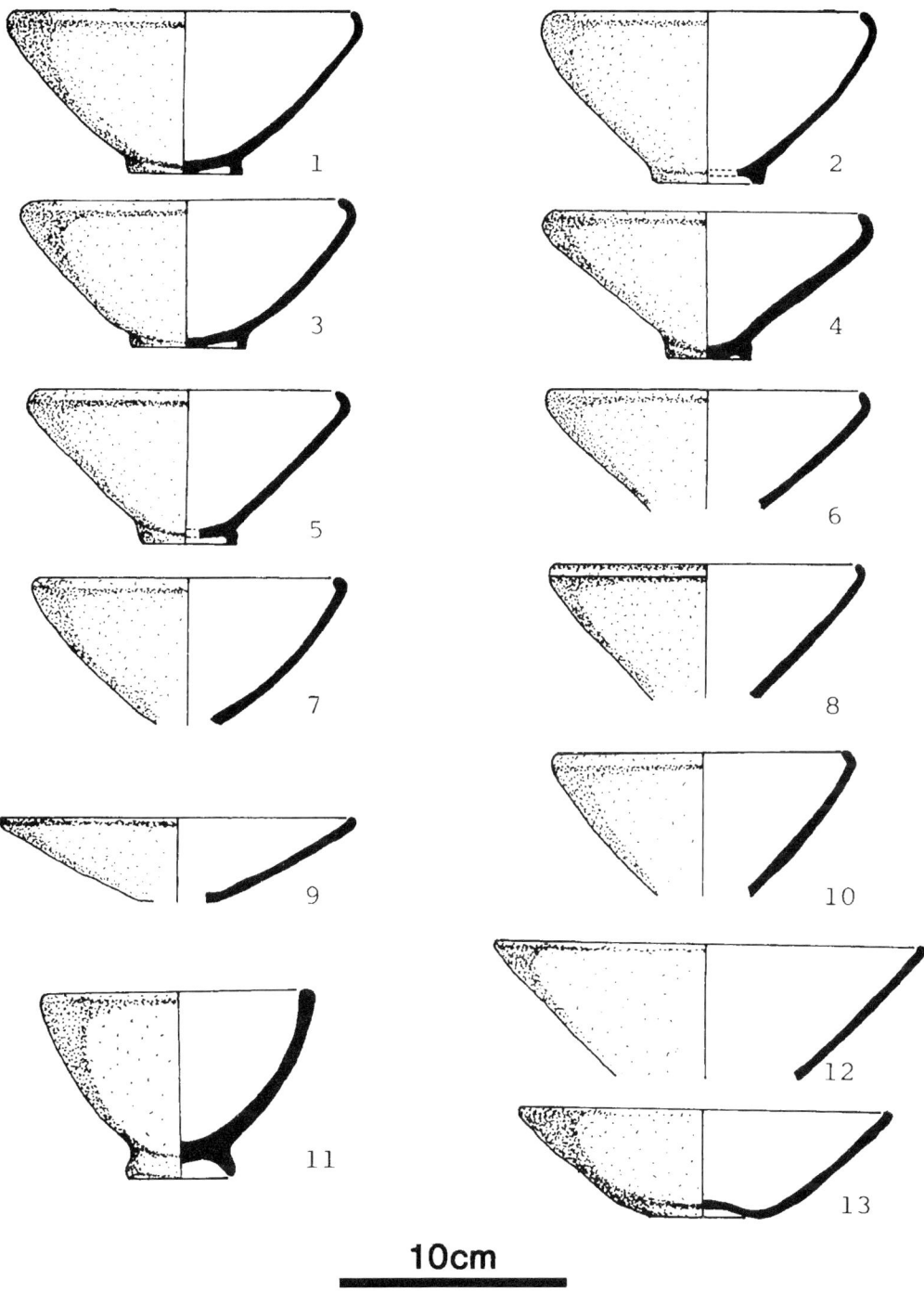

Figure 9. Pottery from Room III at Ayios Dhimitrios. Saucers.

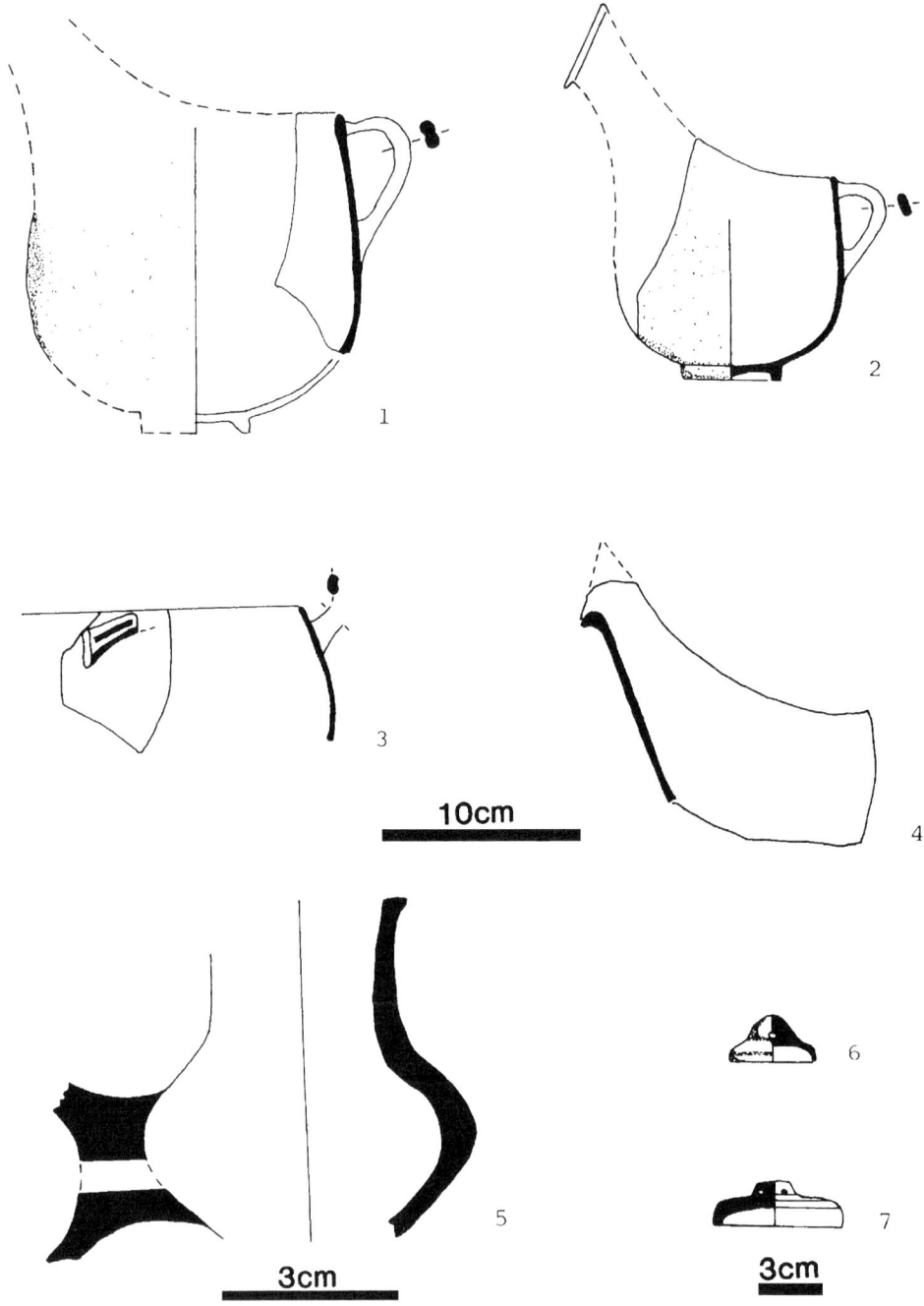

Figure 10. Pottery from Room III at Ayios Dhimitrios. Sauceboats (1–4), Lids (6–7), Kernos fragment (5).

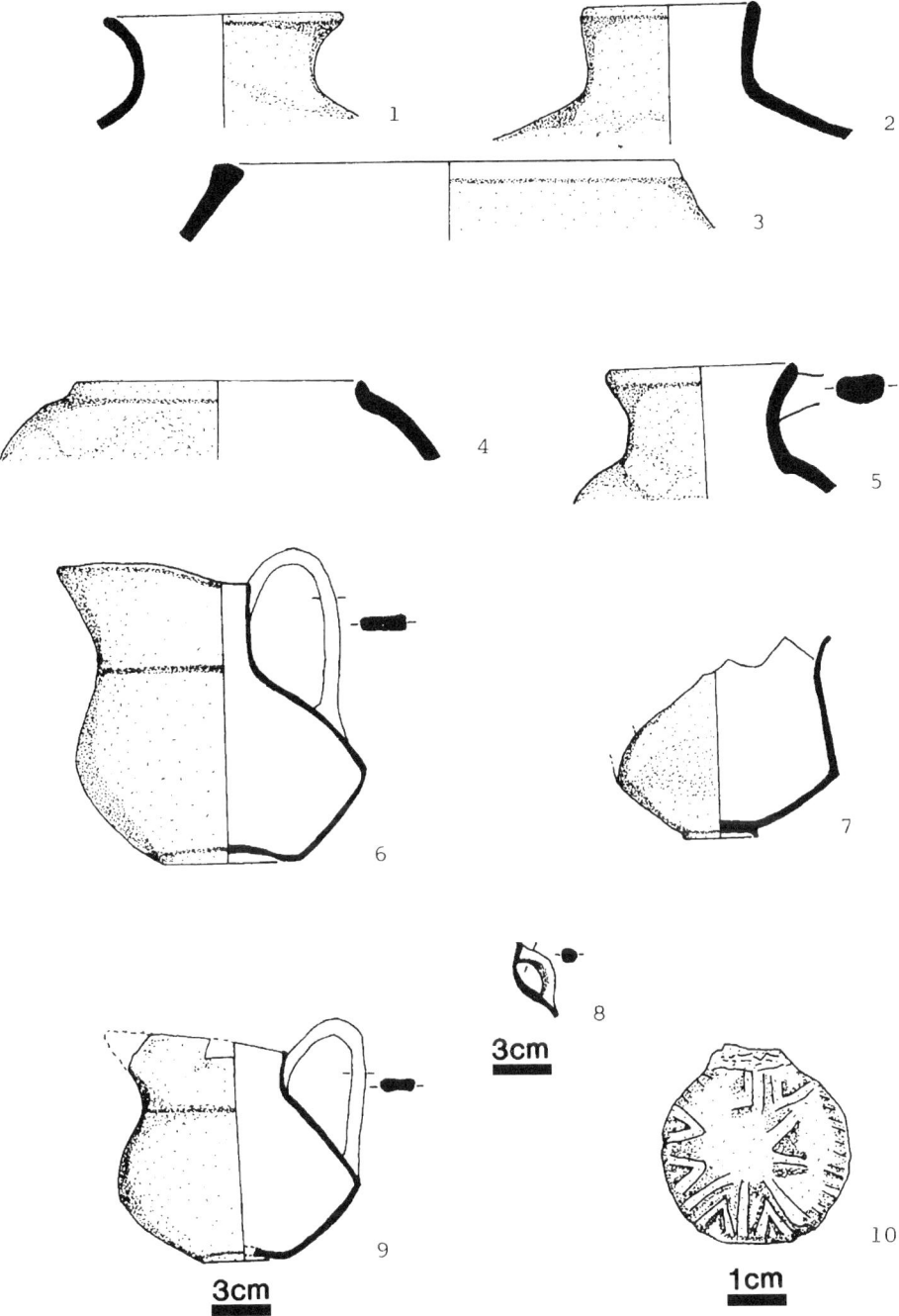

Figure 11. Pottery from Room III at Ayios Dhimitrios. Jars (1–4), Jug (5), Askoid Jugs (6–9), Clay seal impression (10).

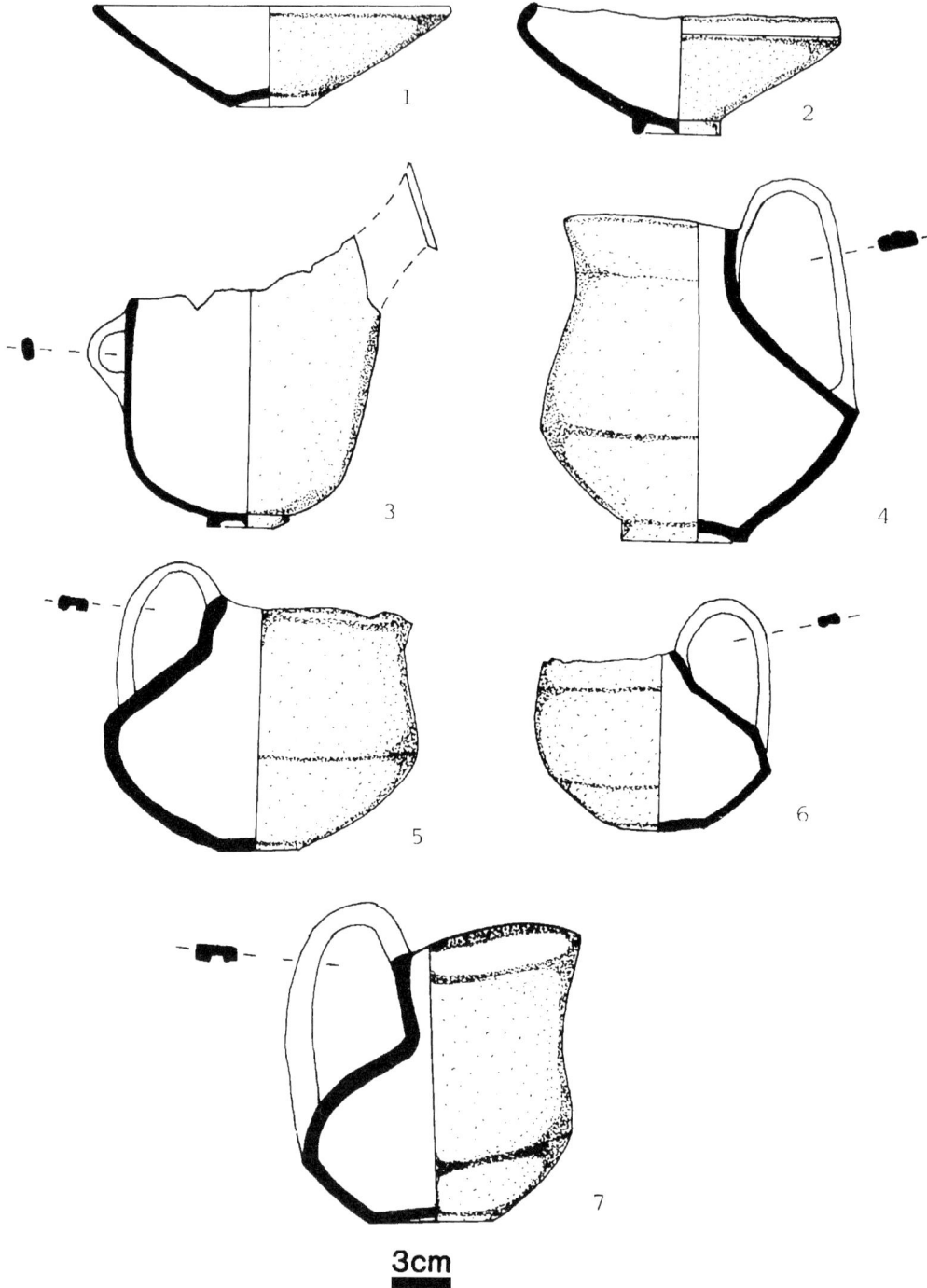

3cm

Figure 12. Saucers (1–2 from Voidokoilia), Sauceboat (3 from Voidokoilia), Askoid jugs (4 from Voidokoilia, 7 from Ithaka), Askoi (5 from Tiryns, 6 from Lerna).

two decades seem, however, to support a local evolution of EH III wares rather than their introduction from elsewhere. A few influences from Asia Minor cannot invoke a large-scale migration of new people (Rutter, 1979; 1983; French 1968, 166; Pullen 1985, 70–79). The lack of profound stylistic or technological differences in the flaked-stone industries of Lerna III and IV also argues against an invasion/newcomers theory. According to Runnels (1985, 390) who studied the material:

> 'The differences in the lithic industries between Lerna III and IV are not as profound as those detected in the architecture and other artifacts. The similarity in the technology of blade production and in tool types in all three settlements is too great to result from the mixing only of artifacts between the levels, and thus we may postulate a more or less continuous Bronze Age tradition of lithic technology at Lerna.'

The same author, however, proposes two hypotheses in order to explain the continuous tradition of lithic technology: either the tradition was transmitted by the survivors of the catastrophe to the new inhabitants or the newcomers belong to a widely spread technological tradition of the Aegean world (Runnels 1985, 390–391).

Recent excavations at Kolona on Aigina and Tiryns in the Argolid, only 5 km from Lerna, present a different scenario from that of Lerna. The third city (Stadt III) at Kolona, with the monumental 'Weisses Haus' resembling the House of the Tiles at Lerna, ended without any signs of violent destruction to support an invasion theory, according to the excavators (Walter & Felten 1981, 22; Felten 1986, 26). At Tiryns, after the destruction which demolished even the colossal Circular Building (Kilian 1986, 65) an intermediate phase has been noticed which was named by the excavators as 'Übergangsphase'. The pottery assemblage from this phase included ceramic types of both EH II and EH III (Weisshaar, 1981; 1982; 1983). Although the applicability of the Tirynthian sequence to other Peloponnesian sites has been questioned (Rutter, 1983), Caskey's invasion theory appears to be further weakened. Consequently, seismic destruction may be proposed as an alternative explanation to the observed gaps in the occupation of EH cultures and sites. Interestingly, the same scenario has recently been proposed for various Mycenaean sites (Kilian; Demakopoulou; Dakoronia; Sampson; Åström; Papadopoulos; Zangger; Maroukian and others, this volume).

The identification of geological records of possible earthquakes in southern Greece during the Early Bronze Age, and their study in comparison with the archaeological data, could perhaps explain the lack of destruction levels at the end of the EH II period at Boeotian sites like Eutresis (Caskey 1971, 779). More importantly, this would 'offer' future prehistoric research a complementary working model regarding the explanation of cultural change.

Acknowledgements
I should like to express my thanks to G. Korres for providing me the photograph of Fig. 4 and allowing me to study the material from his excavations, and to Mr A. Mastorakis for the inking of the pottery drawings. I owe much to fruitful conversations with colleague A. Dousougli and the comments of the anonymous reviewers of this paper.

References
Ashmole, B. & Yalouris, N. (1967). *Olympia: The Sculptures of the Temple of Zeus*. Phaidon Press.
Attas, M. (1982). Regional Ceramic Trade in Early Bronze Age Greece: Evidence from Neutron Activation Analysis of Early Helladic Pottery from Argolis and Korinthia. Unpublished PhD Dissertation, McGill University.

Blegen, C. W. (1921). *Korakou: A Prehistoric Settlement near Corinth*. Boston and New York: American School of Classical Studies at Athens.

Caskey, J. L. (1954). Excavations at Lerna, 1952–1953. *Hesperia* **23**, 3–30.

Caskey, J. L. (1956). Excavations at Lerna, 1955. *Hesperia* **25**, 147–173.

Caskey, J. L. (1960). The Early Helladic Period in the Argolid. *Hesperia* **29**, 285–303.

Caskey, J. L. (1965). Houses of the Fourth Settlement at Lerna. In *Kharisterion eis A. K. Orlandon* III, 144–152. Athens.

Caskey, J. L. (1971). Greece, Crete, and the Aegean Islands in the Early Bronze Age. In (I. E. S Edwards, C. J. Gadd & N. G. L. Hammond, Eds) *The Cambridge Ancient History, vol. I, part 2: Early History of the Middle East* (3rd Ed.), 771–809. Cambridge; Cambridge University Press.

Dinsmoor, W. B. (1975). *The Architecture of Ancient Greece* (3rd Ed.). New York; W. W. Norton.

Felten, F. (1986). Early Urban History and Architecture of Ancient Aigina. In (R. Hägg & D. Konsola, Eds) *Early Helladic Architecture and Urbanization*. Studies in Mediterranean Archaeology 76, 21–28. Göteborg.

French, D. F. (1968). Anatolia and the Aegean in the Third Millennium B. C. Unpublished DPhil thesis. Cambridge University.

Galanopoulos, A. (1940). Die Seismizität von Elis. *Gerlands Beitrage zur Geophysik* **55**, 92–107.

Galanopoulos, A. (1947). The Seismicity of Messenia. *Annales Géologiques des Pays Helléniques* **1**, 38–59. (In Greek)

Gardiner, E. N. (1925). *Olympia: Its History and Remains*. Oxford.

Haley, J. B. & Blegen, C. W. (1928). The coming of the Greeks. *Am. J. Archaeology* **32**, 141–154.

Heurtley, W. A. (1935). Excavations in Ithaca, II. *Annual of the British School at Athens* **35**, 1–44.

Kilian, K. (1986). The Circular Building at Tiryns. In (R. Hägg & D. Konsola, Eds) *Early Helladic Architecture and Urbanization*. Studies in Mediterranean Archaeology 76, 65–71. Göteborg.

Korres, G. (1977). Work, Research and Excavations at Pylia. *Praktika Archaeologikis Etaireias*, 229–295. (In Greek).

Korres, G. (1978). Research and Excavations at Pylia. *Praktika Archaeologikis Etaireias*, 323–360. (In Greek).

Korres, G. (1979). Excavations at Voidokilia. *Praktika Archaeologikis Etaireias*, 138–155. (In Greek).

Korres, G. (1980a). Excavations at Pylia. *Praktika Archaeologikis Etaireias*, 120–187. (In Greek).

Korres, G. (1980b). The Prehistory of Messinian Voidokilia according to the research of the years 1956, 1968, 1975–1979. *Epistimoniki Epetiris tis Panteiou Anotatis Scholis Politikon Epistimon*, 311–343. (In Greek).

Korres, G. (1981). Excavation at Voidokilia. *Praktika Archaeologikis Etaireias*, 194–240. (In Greek).

Korres, G. (1982). Excavation at Voidokilia. *Praktika Archaeologikis Etaireias*, 191–231. (In Greek)

McDonald, W. A. & Hope-Simpson, R. (1969). Further Explorations in southwestern Peloponnese (1964–1968). *Am. J. Archaeology* **73**, 123–177.

McNeal, R. (1972). The Greeks in History and Prehistory. *Antiquity* **46**, 19–28.

Müller, K. (1938). *Tiryns. Die Ergebnisse der Ausgrabungen des Instituts. Vol. IV: Die Urfirniskeramik*. München.

Pullen, D. J. (1985). Social Organization in Early Bronze Age Greece: A Multi-Dimensional Approach. PhD Dissertation. Indiana University. University Microfilms International. Ann Arbor.

Runnels, C. (1985). The Bronze Age Flaked-Stone Industries from Lerna: A Preliminary Report. *Hesperia* **54**, 357–391.

Rutter, J. B. (1979). *Ceramic Change in the Aegean Early Bronze Age*. Institute of Archaeology, Occasional Paper 5. Los Angeles; University of California at Los Angeles.

Rutter, J. B. (1983). Fine Gray-Burnished Pottery of the Early Helladic III Period: The Ancestry of Gray Minyan. *Hesperia* **52**, 327–355.

Rutter, J. B. (1985). An Exercise in Form vs. Function: The Significance of the Duck Vase. *Temple University Aegean Symposium* **10**, 16–41.

Rutter, J. B. (1993). Early Helladic Pottery: Inferences about Exchange and Production from Style and Clay Composition. In (C. W. Zerner & P.C. Zerner, Eds), *Wace and Blegen: Pottery as evidence for trade in the Aegean Bronze Age: 1939–1989,* 19–37. Amsterdam; J. C. Gieben.

Shaw, J. W. (1987). The Early Helladic II Corridor House: Development and Form. *Am. J. Archaeology* **91**, 59–79.

Walter, H. & Felten, F. (1981). *Alt-Ägina III, 1. Das vorgeschichtliche Stadt*. Mainz am Rhein.

Weisshaar, H. J. (1981). Ausgrabungen in Tiryns, 1978, 1979: Bericht zur frühhelladischen Keramik. *Arch. Anzeiger*, 220–256.

Weisshaar, H. J. (1982). Ausgrabungen in Tiryns, 1980: Bericht zur frühhelladischen Keramik. *Arch. Anzeiger*, 440–466.

Weisshaar, H. J. (1983). Ausgrabungen in Tiryns, 1981: Bericht zur frühhelladischen Keramik. *Arch. Anzeiger*, 329–358.

Wiencke, M. H. (1987). Lerna III Pottery: Chronological Development and Context. *Am. J. Archaeology* **91**, 273–274 (abstract).

Wiencke, M. H. (1989). Change in Early Helladic II. *Am. J. Archaeology* **93**, 495–509.

Zachos, K. (1986). Ayios Dhimitrios: An Early Helladic Settlement in Ancient Triphylia. In (R. Hägg & D. Konsola, Eds) *Early Helladic Architecture and Urbanization*. Studies in Mediterranean Archaeology 76, 29–36. Göteborg.

Zachos, K. (1987). Ayios Dhimitrios, A Prehistoric Settlement in the Southwestern Peloponnese: The Neolithic and Early Helladic Periods. Unpublished PhD Dissertation. Boston University.

SCIENTIFIC APPROACHES

Geomorphologic–seismotectonic Observations in Relation to the Catastrophes at Mycenae

Hampik Maroukian[a], Kaiti Gaki-Papanastassiou[a] & Dimitri Papanastassiou[b]

[a] Department of Geography–Climatology, Geological Section, University of Athens,
Panepistimioupolis, 157 84 Athens, Greece
[b] Seismological Institute, National Observatory of Athens,
P.O. Box 20048, 118 10 Athens, Greece

Abstract

A detailed morphotectonic investigation of the area of Mycenae (N-E Peloponnese) showed the presence of faults surrounding and intersecting not only the limestone hill on which the Acropolis of Mycenae was constructed but the surrounding area as well.

Along the N-E base of Mount Sara (S-E of Mycenae) and E of the Acropolis, a normal fault was located having an observable length of at least 2 km and a maximum vertical displacement of 3 m. Due to this fault, the main channel of the Havos stream was cut off and consequently deposited sediments upstream of the fault line. In these sediments potsherds of Mycenaean to Roman age were found.

This occurrence allows us to conclude that the catastrophes of the Acropolis of Mycenae and the surrounding area in the period of the 13–12th centuries BC should be attributed to the seismic activity triggered by the reactivation of this fault during Mycenaean times.

Introduction

Greece has the highest seismicity of all European countries and one of the highest in the world. Considering that there have been organized settlements in the Greek realm during the last 5,000 years, it is very probable that seismic events have been imprinted on ancient structures and are related to cultural declines or have influenced their evolution.

Mycenae is an important site, for which there is archaeological evidence of successive catastrophes in the period from the 13th to 12th centuries BC. In this paper the area of Mycenae is studied from a geomorphological and seismotectonic point of view, aiming to correlate these catastrophes with earthquakes.

The hill of Mycenae has an elevation of 280 m. It is located in the northeastern edge of the Argive plain between Mounts Charvati (805 m) in the N and Sara (660 m) in the SE. It is separated from Sara by a deep gorge which is traversed by the Havos stream (Fig. 1). The hillsides are surrounded by walls which turn the hill to an acropolis with an almost triangular shape and an area of 30,000 m².

Mycenae commands the plain and the main roads of the area. The surrounding mountains provide safety and easy defence against enemy attacks. Due to this advantageous position, the city of Mycenae became the regulator of commerce in southeastern Greece that assured wealth and high cultural development.

Mounts Sara, Profitis Ilias, Charvati and the hill of Mycenae are composed of Mesozoic massive limestones. East of them, there are flysch formations of Maastrichtian age. Around these mountain masses and at lower elevations, Plio-Pleistocene deposits are observed composed of marls and conglomerates as well as recent alluvial deposits (Tataris and Kallergis, 1965; Dufaure, 1977; Gaki-Papanastassiou, 1991).

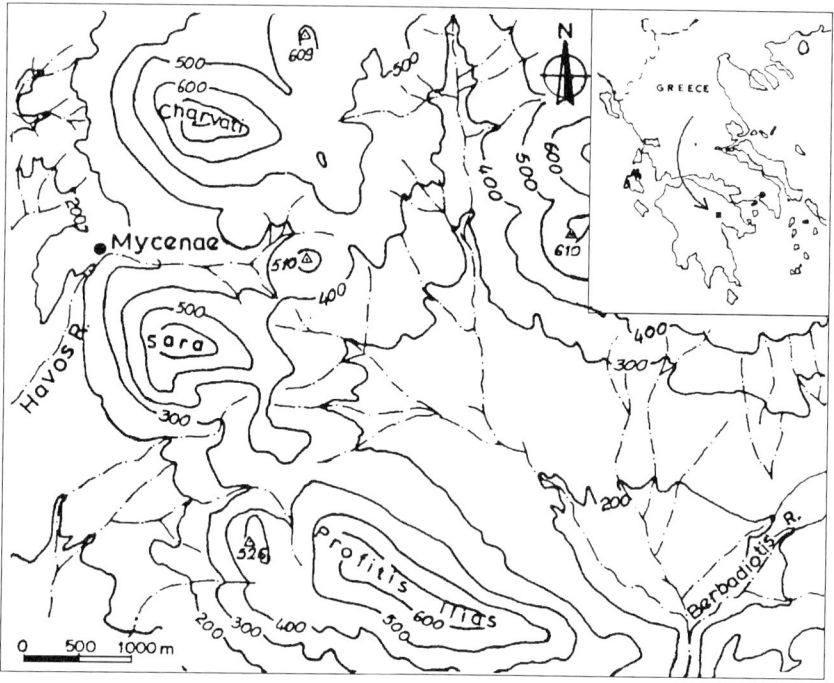

Figure 1. Topographic map of Mycenae and the adjacent area.

Through field work and the use of airphoto interpretation, detailed geological mapping was done at a scale of 1:5000 (Fig. 2).

Archaeological Evidence of Seismic Catastrophes

Mycenae, since the famous excavations by H. Schlieman in 1876, constitutes an important target for extensive and detailed excavations due to its great historical and cultural significance. The results of these recent excavations have given evidence of catastrophic events at the Acropolis and the surrounding area which were recently attributed to earthquakes.

In the 'Citadel House' of the Acropolis, two human skeletons were discovered, evidently not buried but killed and covered by the fallen debris (Ålin, 1962). Evidence of catastrophes in other places inside the Acropolis, such as the 'pithos room', the E wing of the great palace, the abandoned altar of the religious centre and the partially reconstructed Ramp House placed a general destruction of the entire palace at the end of the LH IIIB period (Taylour, 1964; Mylonas, 1966).

At the excavations of the Panagia houses further evidence was discovered, like a skeleton covered with fallen stones in House I, the buckled and shifted forward wall in House II, and the repaired and strengthened walls of House III. These catastrophes are attributed to an earthquake which happened in the middle of LH IIIB (Mylonas-Shear, 1987; French, this volume).

Catastrophes are also noticeable elsewhere in the area. In the West House, the House of the Oil Merchant, the House of Shields and the House of Sphinxes indications of destruction were found which occurred suddenly. In the House of the Lead, G. Mylonas found piles of stone and disintegrated mud bricks and over the threshold of a doorway a skeleton of a woman lying supine covered with stones. The skull of the woman had been crushed by fallen stones, evidence that the house was destroyed violently. In a building to the N of the Citadel, in the area of Plakes, several skeletons were found buried beneath the debris of a fallen structure (Mylonas, 1966).

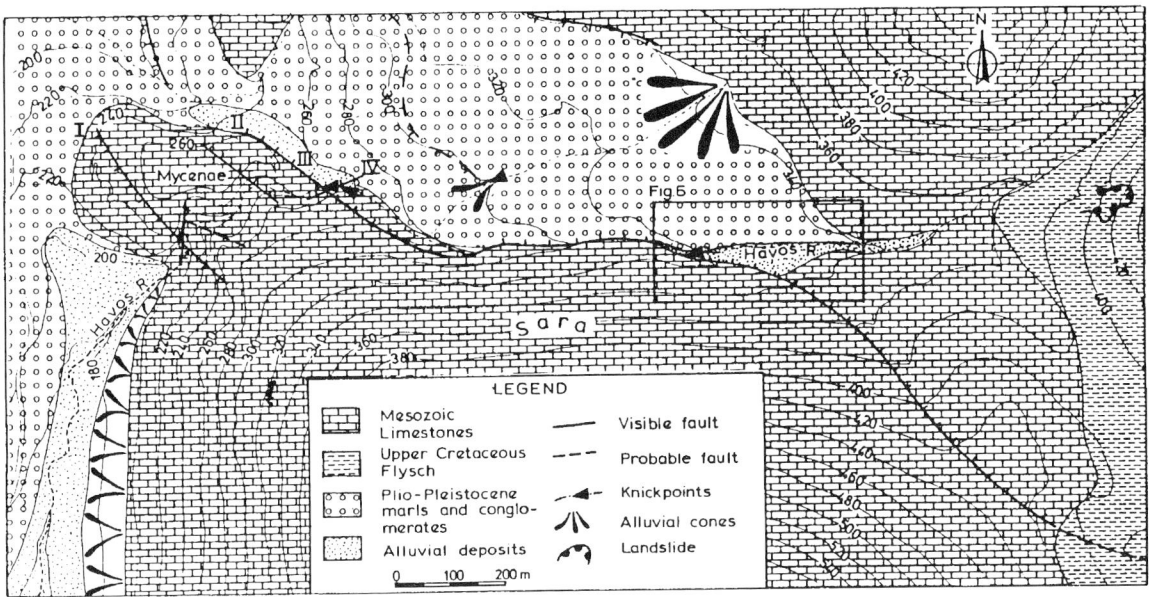

Figure 2. Geological map of the area of Mycenae.

French (1963), Mylonas (1966), Mylonas-Shear (1987) correlated these catastrophes with an earthquake which occurred shortly before the middle of the LH IIIB period, although Mylonas (1983), attributes the catastrophes to an earthquake at the end of the LH IIIB period. In addition, Kilian (1985) presumed three different catastrophic events which he attributed to earthquakes during the period LH IIIB1 till the end of LH IIIC.

Geomorphologic and Seismotectonic Observations

As previously mentioned, the hill of Mycenae is separated from the mountain mass of Sara by the gorge of the Havos stream (Fig. 2). This gorge has been cut through limestones. Its evolution was favoured by the presence of joints and a series of faults. In the area of the Acropolis of Mycenae a network of faults is observed having NE-SW and NW-SE directions which have played an important role in the shaping of the hill of Mycenae and the Havos gorge. The most significant faults, delineating the Acropolis of Mycenae, run NW-SE bounding the W and E side of the Acropolis. The most characteristic is located next to the Lions Gate (Site I, N130°, 61°W with a small left lateral component of movement). A normal fault is observed on the northern side of the Acropolis (Site II, N80°, 49°N) which continues on the eastern side (Site III, N132°, 46°E) (Fig. 3). It is worthwhile mentioning that the existing 'Cyclopean Walls' have been constructed on these fault scarps.

The flow of the Havos stream should have been affected by the activation of the fault at site III, blocking the stream and forming a knick-point at its extension at Site IV, in such a way that for a time before the Mycenaean period it flowed NE of the Acropolis. The presence of well-rounded pebbles and cobbles in the fluvio-torrential sediments in that area reiterates the position of the old flow of the Havos.

The diversion of the Havos stream from its old course to the modern one through the gorge should have occurred by headward erosion. The presence of remnants of an old wall at Site V leads us to the assumption that there had been a straightening of the channel towards the Havos gorge in order to cultivate a more extensive area of the old channel.

This fault extends further E of the Acropolis of Mycenae cutting through limestones (Fig. 4). At a distance of about 400 m E of the Acropolis it has a direction of N90° in its first 500 m and N120° for another km with

Figure 3. View of the eastern 'Cyclopean Walls' con-   Figure 4. Part of the principal fault observed E of Mycenae.
structed on the fault scarp.

a dip of 42°N and a small right lateral component of movement. Then it extends towards the adjacent drainage basin of the Berbadiotis river where it is lost. Where the fault exits the limestone terrain and enters the flysch formations and Quaternary deposits, the surficial evidence of the fault is impossible to trace.

The observed maximum throw at the fault scarp is 3 m forming a continuous fault scarp. The upper part of the scarp is intensely eroded and has a maximum value of 1.5 m, while the lower part is still fresh (Fig. 5). In some places, remnants of fault breccia are still seen on the fault scarp.

Fault scarp of similar appearance have been observed in other parts of Greece. These faults are presumed to have been reactivated in the last several thousand years (Armijo *et al.*, 1991, 1992; Roberts & Jackson, 1990; Stewart & Hancock, 1991). What is beyond any doubt however, and permits us to determine accurately the time of this reactivation, is the following geomorphic event. N of the fault, in the upper part of the Havos stream and at Site VI the channel cuts across the fault (Fig. 6). At this point and S of the fault an old inactive channel of the Havos stream is observed which extends to the E as far as the fault. Here, the fault plane shows signs of erosion by the old flow of the river through it. Today's flow of the Havos further N of the fault and its confluence with it further W could be attributed to the last reactivation of the fault. The observed uplifting of the southern block of the fault formed a barrier, blocking locally the natural flow of the Havos. In the newly formed depression the river deposited its sediments, while at the same time the blocked channel shifted to the

Figure 5. Close-up of the principal fault showing the intensely eroded upper part and the fresh lower part.

N until it found a natural exit over the fault, further W (Site VI).

The provenance of the deposits of the Havos stream is primarily from the erosion of the flysch formations together with some limestones located in the upper part of its drainage basin. Therefore, the observed deposits are composed mainly of fine particles including some isolated coarser limestone cobbles. These deposits attain at some points in the depression a thickness of up to 2.5 m. It is significant that we found potsherds from bottom to top, which were dated by archaeologists of the Argolid Ephorate, to be Mycenaean to Roman in age respectively. These observations allow us to conclude that the last reactivation of the observed fault should have occurred during Mycenaean times.

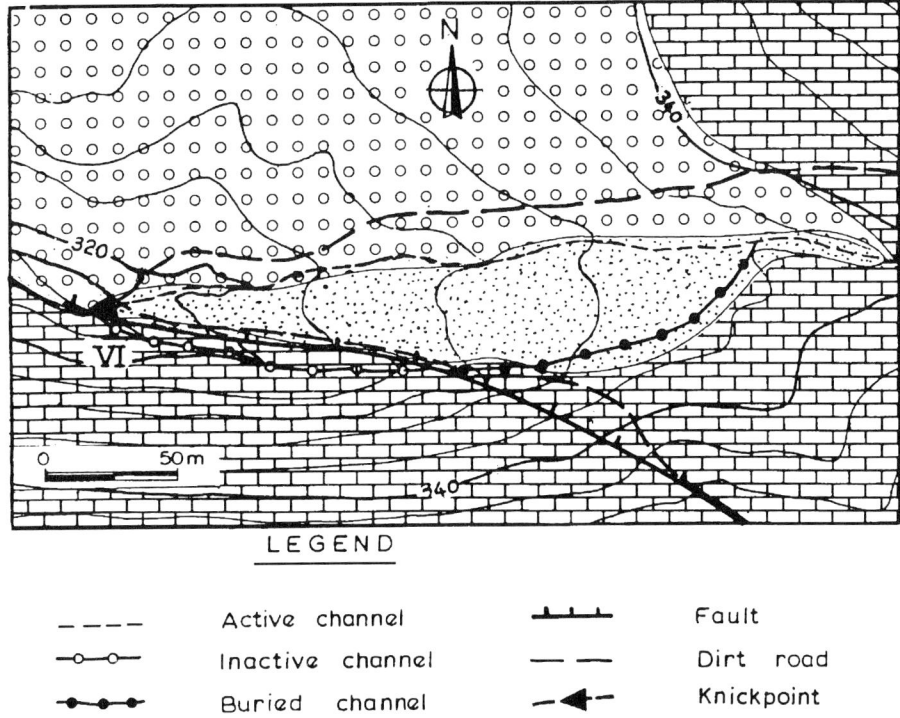

LEGEND

– – – –	Active channel	┴┴┴	Fault
–o—o–	Inactive channel	— —	Dirt road
•–•–•	Buried channel	–◄–	Knickpoint

Figure 6. Close-up of the area where the Havos stream was set off by the reactivation of the fault during Mycenaean times.

Discussion & Conclusions

The geomorphological and palaeoseismological study of the Mycenae area in conjunction with archaeological evidence has allowed us to correlate the observed catastrophes with earthquakes which occurred in this area during Mycenaean times.

Confirmation of this assumption constitutes the observed continuous fault scarp which has an observable length of 2 km. If we include that part of the fault which extends in easily erodible flysch and is impossible to see since there is no surficial evidence, then its total length should be 4–5 km.

An earthquake, that would have ruptured the total length of the fault, would not have been able to form the observed fresh scarp of 1.5 m in just one event. To corroborate this assertion we give the relation of the scale of the length of the observed surface rupture of normal faults and the resultant throw of recent earthquakes in Central Greece: on February 24, 1981, the Alkyonides earthquake (Eastern Gulf of Korinth), 15 km/80 cm (Jackson *et al.*, 1982); September 23, 1988 the Kalamata earthquake (SW Peloponnese), 6 km/18 cm (Lyon-Caen *et al.*, 1988). Thus we believe that the fresh, lower scarp of 1.5 m corresponds to more than one seismic event.

Through personal observations made after the Kalamata earthquake it is remarkable to note that at Eleohori village, N of Kalamata, there are sections of Mycenaean walls built on the ruptured fault, exactly like the walls of Mycenae. These walls experienced slight or no damage during this earthquake at Kalamata. This observation concurs with archaeological evidence for the area around Mycenae, where no extensive damage is reported for important Mycenaean structures like the Cyclopean Walls or the tholos tombs. On the contrary, the evidence from excavations of the houses shows that there are differences in the type of damage ranging in extent from slight to total destruction.

All this evidence allows us to suppose that the maximum size of the earthquakes which occurred in the Mycenae area should have been at least as strong as the Kalamata earthquake.

Beyond the seismotectonic observations of the fault and their relationships previously mentioned, another significant evidence which reinforces our assumptions is the geomorphological observation of the blocking of the Havos stream due to the reactivations of the fault. The presence of Mycenaean potsherds in the blocked sediments gives us a more precise dating of the reactivations of the fault.

It is believed that excavation of a trench in the Havos deposits in the area of its blocked and buried channel, studying the deposits not only vertically but also horizontally and dating the archaeological potsherds found in them, could lead to a more precise dating and a more thorough understanding of the occurrence of these seismic events.

References

Ålin, P. (1962). *Das Ende der Mykenischen Fundstatten auf dem Griechischen Festland.* Studies in Mediterranean Archaeology 1. Lund.

Armijo, R., Lyon-Caen, H. & Papanastassiou, D. (1991). A possible normal-fault rupture for the 464 BC Sparta Earthquake. *Nature* **351**, 137–39.

Armijo, R., Lyon-Caen, H. & Papanastassiou, D. (1992). East-west extension and Holocene normal fault scarps in the Hellenic arc. *Geology* **20**, 491–524.

Dufaure, J. J. (1977). Néotectonique et morphogenèse dans une péninsule mediterranéene: le Peloponnèse. *Rev. Geogr. Phys. Geol. Dyn.* **19**, 27–58.

French, E. (1963). Pottery Groups from Mycenae: a summary. *Annual of the British School of Archaeology at Athens* **58**, 44–52.

Gaki-Papanastassiou, K. (1991). The geomorphological evolution in and around the Argive plain during the Quaternary. PhD Thesis. University of Athens. (In Greek).

Jackson, J. A., Gagnepain, J., Houseman, G., King, G. C. P., Papadimitriou, P., Soufleris, C. & Virieux, J. (1982). Seismicity, normal faulting and the geomorphological development of the Gulf of Corinth (Greece): the Corinth earthquakes of February and March 1981. *Earth and Planetary Science Letters* **57**, 377–397.

Kilian, K. (1985). La caduta dei Palazzi Micenei continentali: aspetti archaeologici. In (D. Musti, Ed.) *Le origini dei Greci. Dori e mondo Egeo*, 73–95. Bari; Laterza and Figli..

Lyon-Caen, H., Armijo, R., Drakopoulos, J., Baskoutas, J., Delibassis, N., Gaulon, R., Kouskouna, V., Latoussakis, J., Makropoulos, K., Papadimitriou, P., Papanastassiou, D. & Pedotti, G. (1988). The 1986 Kalamata (South Peloponnesus) earthquake: Detailed study of a normal fault, evidences for east-west extension in the Hellenic arc. *J. Geophys. Res.* **93**, 14967–15000.

Mylonas, G. (1966). *Mycenae and the Mycenaean Age.* Princeton; Princeton University Press.

Mylonas, G. (1983). *Golden Mycenae.* Athens; Ekdotiki Athenon. (In Greek).

Mylonas-Shear, I. (1987). *The Panagia Houses at Mycenae.* University Museum, Monograph 68. Philadelphia; University Museum of Pensylvania.

Roberts, S. C. & Jackson, J. A. (1990). Active normal faulting in central Greece: an overview. In (A. M. Roberts, G. Yielding & B. Freeman, Eds) *Geometry of Normal faults*. Geol. Soc. Lond. Spec. Publ. **56**, 125–142.

Stewart, I. J. & Hancock, P. L. (1991). Scales of structural heterogeneity within neotectonic normal fault zones in the Aegean region. *J. Structural Geology* **13**, 191–204.

Tataris, A. & Kallergis, G. (1965). The geological structure of the mountain mass of Trapezona-Arachnaio and of the area Nafplio-Ligourio, NE Peloponnesus. *Geological & Geophysical Research*, IX/6, 195–220. Athens: IGME. (In Greek).

Taylour, W. D. (1964). *The Mycenaeans.* London; Thames & Hudson.

The Disappearance of the Ancient Towns of Dioscuria and Sebastopolis in Colchis on the Black Sea: A Problem in Engineering Geology and Palaeoseismology

Andrei Nikonov

Joint Institute of Physics of the Earth, Academy of Sciences of Russia,
Moscow 123810, Russia

Abstract

Three hypotheses regarding the disappearance and (partial) subsidence into Sukhumi Bay of the ancient Greek town of Dioscuria, subsequently Sebastopolis in Roman times, are proposed. (1) Drastic changes in the mouth-stream of the River Gumista and sea-shore line, accompanied by changes in topography, as well as the courses and locations of alluvial and marine accumulations, have taken place during the last 2500 years; they are responsible for the burial of the settlement. (2) The town area and most of its buildings have been abraded by wave action and submerged under water due to a secular gradual rise of sea level and/or slow subsidence of Sukhumi Bay bottom. (3) The ancient towns have undergone (catastrophic) disturbances and submergence as a result of land deformation due to landslides and strong earthquakes.

From an analysis of the available archaeological, engineering-geological and palaeo-geographical data the author concludes that Sebastopolis and probably Dioscuria, lying beneath present-day Sukhumi, were destroyed by very strong earthquakes which were accompanied by local subsidence of the bay bottom and a longer term secular rise of the sea level.

Introduction

The eastern coast of the Black Sea, known as Colchis, is well known as the destination of the Argonauts who are thought to have sailed there sometime in the 14–12th centuries BC. Indeed, it is from the myth of the Argonauts that we first learn, albeit in a limited way, about seismic activity in the area (Nikonov, 1983).

No significant earthquakes stronger than intensity V–VI have occurred within the area of study during the 19–20th centuries, thereby precluding any reliable assessment of large earthquakes in the region using traditional methods of seismology. The difficulties are associated, first, with the low seismic activity of the region during the period of instrumental observations (20th century) and, second, the absence of written records of past destructive earthquakes there. In view of this, seismologists have drawn the conclusion that the coast is subject to a small or moderate earthquake hazard. This is reflected in the official seismic zoning maps for the USSR (Fig. 1; Bune & Gorshkov, 1980). The author has made an attempt to use the archaeological data to assess past earthquakes but with totally different results (Nikonov, 1989). He also discovered traces of apparently the same destructive earthquakes producing tremors of intensity about IX on extant architectural monuments in Sukhumi (Fig. 2), where ancient Dioscuria and Sebastopolis were situated.

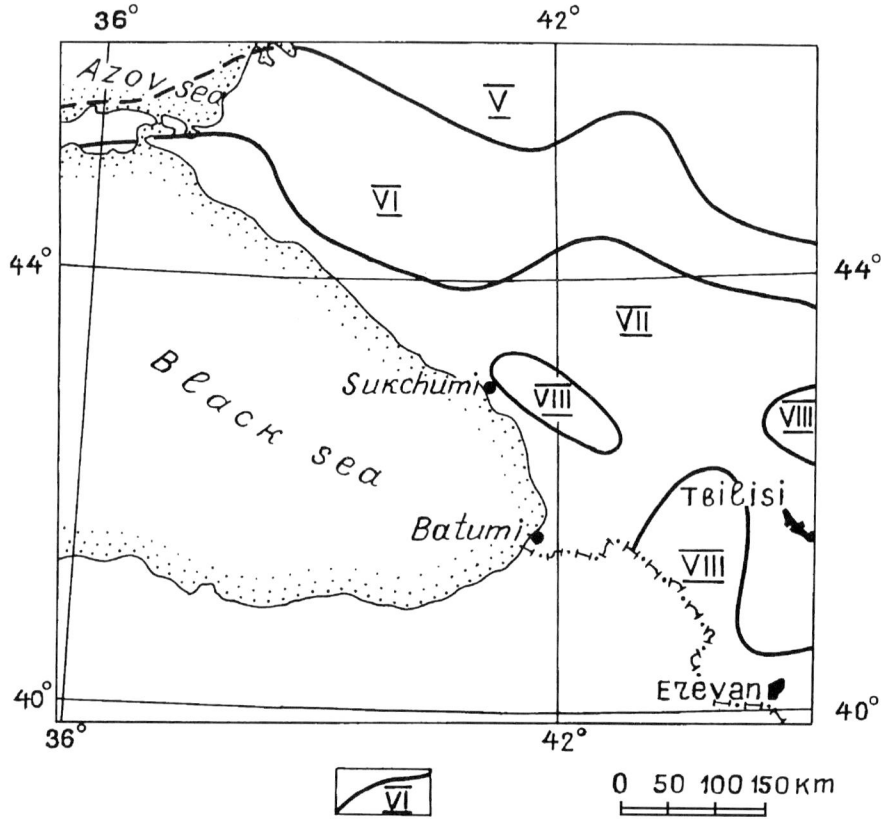

Figure 1. Part of the official seismic zoning map for the western part of the Caucasus, and location of the town of Sukhumi. Heavy lines denote areas of different seismic intensity (in the MSK-64 scale) (after Bune & Gorshkov, 1980).

Some Features of Seismic Destructions on Medieval Remains

Medieval structures occur near the present city, beyond the walls of the Roman Sebastopolis; these include the 'Bagrat Castle' and the Beslet Bridge of the late 11th or 12th century, and the early 18th century Turkish fortress Sukhum Kale. There are also remains of earlier Byzantine structures (contemporary with Emperor Justinian or later). Archaeological excavation within the NE corner of the Turkish fortress contains stoutly built early Byzantine structures whose foundations, dating to the 5–6th centuries AD, are broken with large cracks involving vertical and horizontal displacements of blocks and deformation (Figs 2A, 3, 4). The cracks and deformations are surely associated with seismic shaking. Most of the cracks traverse not only walls of the first construction period but also walls and outhouses associated with the initial building, reconstruction and reinforcing work. A few shorter cracks also penetrate the wall of the Turkish fortress. This damage resulting from repeated shakings was probably caused by large earthquakes occurring in the region during the 7th, 11th and 18th centuries. Since the damage to the building foundations was evidently serious, and in view of the evidence for large-scale subsequent fortifications and constructions, one can conclude that there were tremors of intensity about IX in the area.

The Destruction of Dioscuria

We have no written evidence of the disappearance of Dioscuria which is now situated on the bottom and shore of Sukhumi Bay (Fig. 2A). There is, however, an indirect indication in the Abkhazian legends referring to a great earthquake striking the city of the new-comers, the city being engulfed by the sea. Pliny wrote of Dioscuria of the mid-1st century AD that 'this city is now devastated', while Strabo speaks about it as 'a rich and flourishing city' at the beginning of the 1st century AD. It seems reasonable to propose that the city and environs were destroyed by a devastating earthquake in the first or second quarter of the first century AD and furthermore that, since no remains of the city have been found, the ruined city sank to the bay bottom. This hypothesis, among others, would explain the disappearance of Dioscuria in terms of a sharp change in the environment of the mouth of the Goumista River (Soloviev, 1947) and as a result of landslides (Razumov & Khazin, 1978). The discovery of remains of old masonry at the bottom of Sukhumi Bay in the 1980s (Figs 2A, B; Balabanov & Gaprindashvili, 1987) has been of crucial importance in locating Dioscuria and determining the causes of its destruction. A linear formation consisting of heaps of stone slabs was found at 6–10 m depth, some 0.4–0.6 km from the present-day shoreline, first through depth measurements and later by special diving studies. It is mostly 2–4 m in width, sometimes as wide as 15 or 40 m, extending from W-SW to E-NE for 0.6–0.7 km (see Figs 2A, B). The structure consisted of slabs of varying dimensions (1.0 x 0.5 x 0.2 m to 10.0 x 6.0 x 1.0 m) made of gravel-pebble-boulder filler with limestone mortar. Some boulders had diameters of 0.2

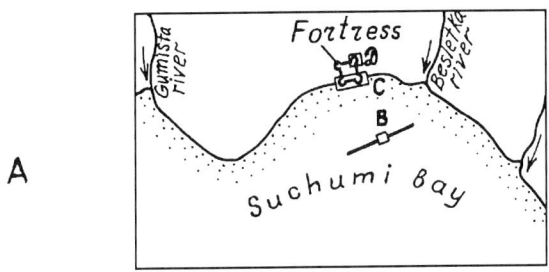

A

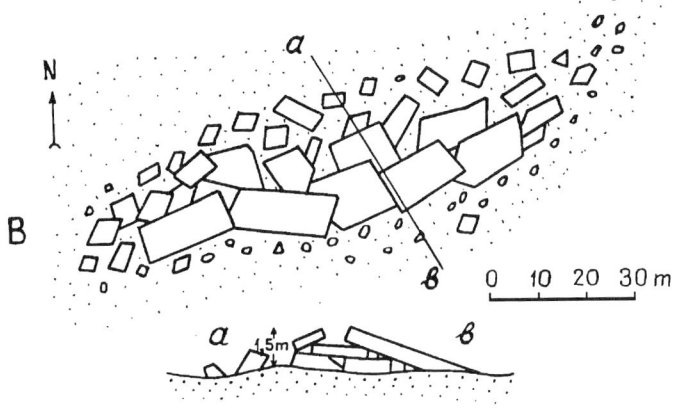

B

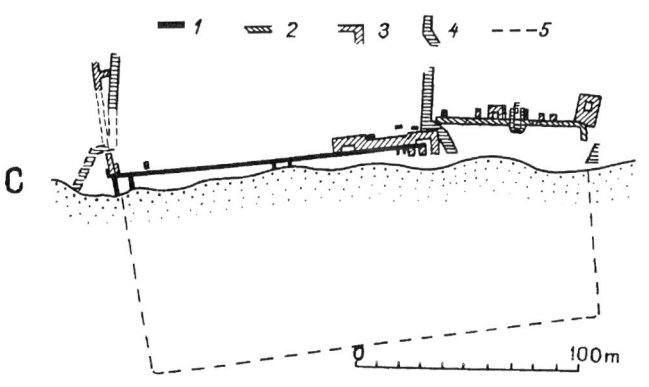

C

Figure 2. Location of discovered ruins of Dioscuria and Sebastopolis within Sukhumi Bay. **A** general situation; **B** a defensive wall of Dioscuria on the bay bottom; **C** walls of Sebastopolis; (**1** walls of the 1st century AD; **2** walls of the 1–2nd century AD; **3** walls of the 4th century AD; **4** walls of the Turkish period (18th century); **5** probable position of the Sebastopolis walls, under present sea-level.

and 0.35 m. No traces of mortar have been found between slabs, the construction being very likely mortarless. (We note at once that the walls of Sebastopolis were built of dry masonry, but not as a solid mass, with rows of bricks whose probable function was reinforcement against earthquake loads). There is no doubt that the man-made structure on the bottom along the shore is a large wall intended as the outer defence and probably consisting of curtain walls and towers. Balabanov & Gaprindashvili (1987) were able to date this wall to early antiquity and considered it to be part of Greek Dioscuria since marine deposits dated to 3610 ± 155 BP by radiocarbon, i.e. 1500–1700 BC, were found to be overlain by a heap of slabs forming a wall. Some shells were sampled in the depth range 0.7–2.2 m from a borehole 300 m SE of the end of the heap, where the bottom is as deep as 15.5 m. Clearly, the city as well as the surrounding settlements were built at the time (6–4th century BC) when the modern bay bottom was land.

Three possible scenarios for the destruction and subsidence of the Dioscuria walls at a depth of 6–10 m can be proposed: (1) the walls were destroyed by sea-surf erosion due to gradual sea-level rise, (2) a landslide and (3) an earthquake-associated subsidence. Balabanov & Gaprindashvili's (1987) preference for the hypothesis of sea-surf erosion is unacceptable for the following reasons:

- The wall is higher near the shore, at shallower depths where wave action is stronger (1.4–1.5 m) than away from it to the SW (0.7–1.1 m).
- The depth distribution within Sukhumi Bay has not appreciably changed for the last 80 or even 150 years.
- Gaps in continuous wall remains as long as 30 m do not in any way correlate with the bay depth and the extent of possible wave action.
- The wall was destroyed by blocks being pushed off or around rather than due to deterioration of the mortar and freeing of the filler. This must have taken place during abrasion and does not occur now even as the later wall of Sebastopolis is being undermined in the surf area. Rounding has affected small fragments only (pieces detached from blocks) that lie near the wall, not the slabs and blocks in the remains of the wall itself. This seems improbable if one accepts the hypothesis of gradual destruction of the wall by waves from an initial height of 6–8 m down to the present 1–1.5 m height. Rather, it seems that the wall had not been long in the surf area and rapidly sank beyond the surface wave layer and the associated shore area.
- The bottom sediments around the wall remains at depths of 6–10 m are mostly mud sands. The remains are totally overlain by bottom sediments at about 7 m depth near the NE end of the linear formation. This indicates a quiet depositional environment outside the surf zone, a natural occurrence at such depths.

The hypothesis of Dioscuria being submerged at the bottom of Sukhumi Bay by a landslide runs into difficulties. The modern shore shows no morphological signs of landslide; the shore has certainly been altered by human activity, but the bay bottom is flat and does not have any ruggedness except the wall ridge. Radiometrically controlled borehole data in the bay area do not provide evidence of any deformation or thickening in Holocene marine sediments, as would be expected in the case of a landslide displacement in the wall remains despite their appreciable length (700 m). We can, therefore, conclude that there are no indications of a landslide at the necessary scale to explain the observed destruction and subsidence.

The width of the tumble reaches 40 m near the N-E end of the wall with particularly large slab dimensions (as large as 10–12 x 6–8 x 0.3–0.4 m), the slabs being in positions that suggest a rapid tumbling from S to N. It is significant that slabs have tumbled down or dip steeply near the inner (shorewards) wall plane. The face of the outer wall edge has been lost, and all overlying slabs displaced tile-like southwards for 3–6 m. Fragments of many slabs have been moved from the inner face of the wall northwards for 5–15 m, that is by a distance roughly equal to the height of a corner tower. In the writer's opinion, these findings are more easily explained in terms of a seismic shock (or shocks) directed from S to N than in any other way. Support for this interpretation comes from underwater investigations that established sliding of the marine sedimentary cover and rock-sliding for bedrock in the upper part of the adjacent continental slope W of Sukhumi Bay (Ivanov et al., 1988).

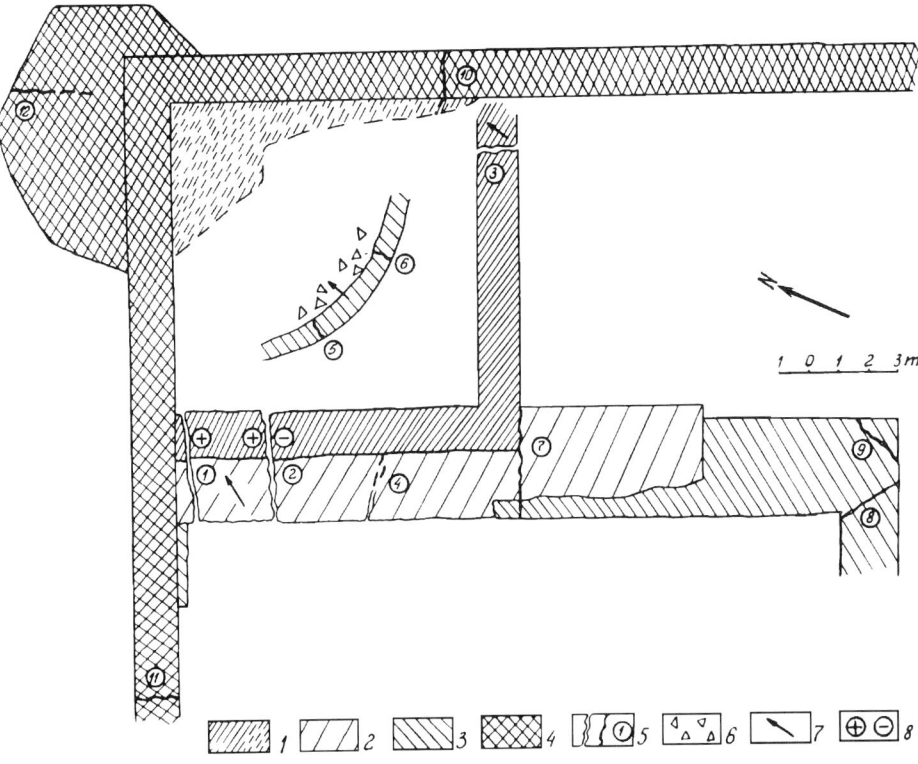

Figure 3. Traces of earthquake-induced failure in the Middle Ages structures of Sebastopolis (from an excavation at the NE corner of the Turkish fortress). **1–3** wall foundations of Byzantine structures of three successive periods; **4** wall of the 18th century Turkish fortress; **5** seismic cracks and fractures, numbered; **6** fallen wall; **7** direction of tilting in the foundation of the wall (shear); **8** uplifted and subsided wall blocks.

Overall, the most likely hypothesis is that Dioscuria was destroyed by a catastrophic earthquake (intensity IX) in the early half of the first century AD and that the subsidence of Sukhumi Bay by several metres is a consequence of that event.

Sebastopolis and the Causes of its Demise

Sebastopolis was founded on a new site (Fig. 2) not earlier than AD 20, since it was named in honour of Augustus (Sebastos in Greek). It was first mentioned in AD 75. The walls of ancient Sebastopolis close to the sea shore under the modern quay have been partly excavated. The walls were built of cobble stone (boulders and coarse granite pebbles) with whitish limestone mortar mixed with gravel. Two to four horizontal rows of bricks were used to strengthen the structure (Fig. 5) as an earthquake-resistant technique.

The remains of defence walls and towers belonging to three construction periods within the 1st–4th centuries AD have been discovered (Figs 2C, 6, 7). According to Voronov (1980), the oldest complex is situated in the eastern part as an extant wall with two towers protruding from the wall northwards (away from the sea). The wall is the northern extant segment of a major fortification whose greater part was situated in what is now the bay. Built against the northern face of the wall are five massive buttresses made of cobble stone with limestone

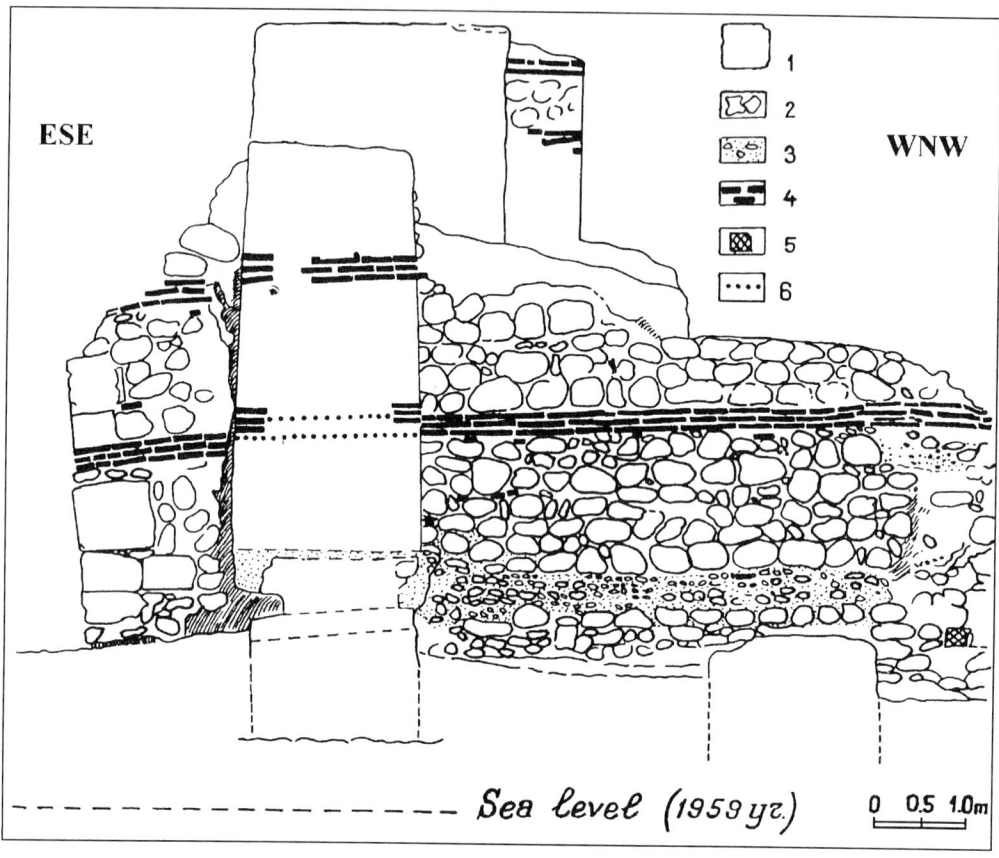

Figure 4. Part of Sebastopolis wall of the second period (after Trapsh, 1969). Symbol explanations: **1** stone blocks; **2** pebbles; **3** gravel with sand; **4** (baked?) bricks; **5** internal cross-holes; **6** inferred line of rows of bricks. The traces of disturbances (on the left) are clearly visible.

mortar. The buttresses were built later than the wall to strengthen against an incipient N-W tilt which Trapsch (1969) explains was caused by a sea transgression beginning at that time. This view may be challenged because (1) when the structure was in use, the wall was at the rear end and relatively distant from the sea, (2) a structure that is undermined by sea usually acquires a seaward tilt rather than one in the opposite direction, and (3) early Byzantine walls excavated within the Turkish fortress, i.e. far from the sea, also have a tilt away from the sea and bear traces of earthquake-induced failure. It should be noted that the buttresses themselves are also tilted to the N-W (Soloviev, 1947), that is the wall continued to experience a tilt away from the sea or received another impulse of deformation. Thus the wall tilt was due either to landsliding in the back of a sliding mass or to a non-uniform subsidence of the terrain following an earthquake.

The wall functioned until the 5th century, and its buttresses were apparently built during the earlier half of its period of use. The continuing subsidence of the bay bottom (or sliding of sedimentary layers seawards) was undermining the southern parts of the fortress, and the northern wall was tilting in spite of the reinforcement. This made it necessary to build a new fortress close by. The extant wall of the second construction period (Figs 4–6) was closer to the sea and continued along the shore with towers jutting out seawards. It was more solidly built; the foundations were broader and thicker, and the layer under the wall was strengthened by driving vertical piles into it 1.5–2.0 m long and by adding some lime (the cobblestone filler in the wall has more lime

Figure 5(a). Seismic crack across a Byzantine wall, point 1 on Figure 3, view from W (photo by A. Nikonov).

Figure 5(b). Seismic crack across a Byzantine wall with a horizontal displacement (western block moved northwards) (photo by A. Nikonov).

mortar; see Figs 5–7). The wall was built according to an old technique of reinforcement against non-uniform sagging and earthquakes; a frame of wood beams was arranged horizontally at a spacing of 2.5 m along and across the wall. Clearly, the builders had to erect a more stable and long-living fortress than the preceding one.

The wall foundation directly overlies the 1st century BC–1st century AD layer. The wall at the top bears evident traces of failure and deformations which are more likely to have been caused by strong seismic action. These include, for example, a 5–6° tilt of the edge block in a main cross wall strengthened against earthquake shaking, the tilt being to the SW rather than towards the sea (to the SE). Two blocks of masonry with rows of bricks inside are fractured by a vertical crack opened 5–15 cm, the SW block being displaced downwards relative to the longitudinal wall segment by 20–25 cm (see Fig. 5). Small cross cracks, 0.2–1.0 cm wide, traverse the main wall perpendicular to the sea; they could not have been formed by abrasion. These deformations in the seaside wall of the second construction period may also be attributed to earthquakes in the Middle Ages, although this is less likely, because by that time the base of the Sebastopolis walls had been buried in a compacted soil. It is the earthquake damage to the first fortress which logically explains the construction of a new smaller fortress.

Occupying one-third of the area of the previous one on whose ruins it was partly built, this fortress was also constructed of granite boulders with limestone mortar using square bricks and hewn limestone blocks at the corners. It dates to the late 4th century AD. What now stands on land is only the northern part of that construction complex. The cross walls are now under water (Shervashidze, 1967). Some remains of this third Sebastopolis fortress perpendicular to the shoreline and 1.8 m thick have remained under water as extended segments, some of which are upright, others are tilted somewhat to the W-SW. The fragmentary preservation along the strike and its tilt across the surf line may have been a result of earthquake during the Middle Ages.

To summarize, although archaeological exploration has included little systematic archaeoseismic research, and despite limited investigation of identified remains from the Sebastopolis fortifications, there are indications of failure in the upper parts of the fortifications and damage to their lower parts that can be dated numismatically to AD 337–338 (Trapsh, 1969).

Figure 6. Part of the Sebastopolis wall of the second period, (off the present-day town embankment). Heaps on the right are due to explosions in the 1950s and following abrasion (photo by A. Nikonov).

Figure 7. Part of the Sebastopolis wall of the second period near the present-day shoreline (photo by A. Nikonov).

The most likely inference is that the destruction is related to a strong earthquake of intensity at least IX–X in the mid-4th century AD, as well as by later ones (possibly in the 7th, 11th and 18th centuries). Some of the deformation and subsidence of the bay bottom as deep as 4–6 m, as well as the building of new fortified complexes, can be associated with large earthquakes.

Ancient town	Date	Type of structure	Max. distance from beach (m)	Max. depth (m)	Remains
Dioscuria	VI–I century BC	external defensive wall	400–600	6–10	no walls were found
Sebastopolis	I–IV century AD	fortress walls	0–100	4–6	parts of the walls are preserved
Sebastopolis	V–XI century AD	walls	–	–	all remains on land

Table 1. Position of Sebastopolis and Dioscuria remains on the Sukhumi Bay bottom and on land.

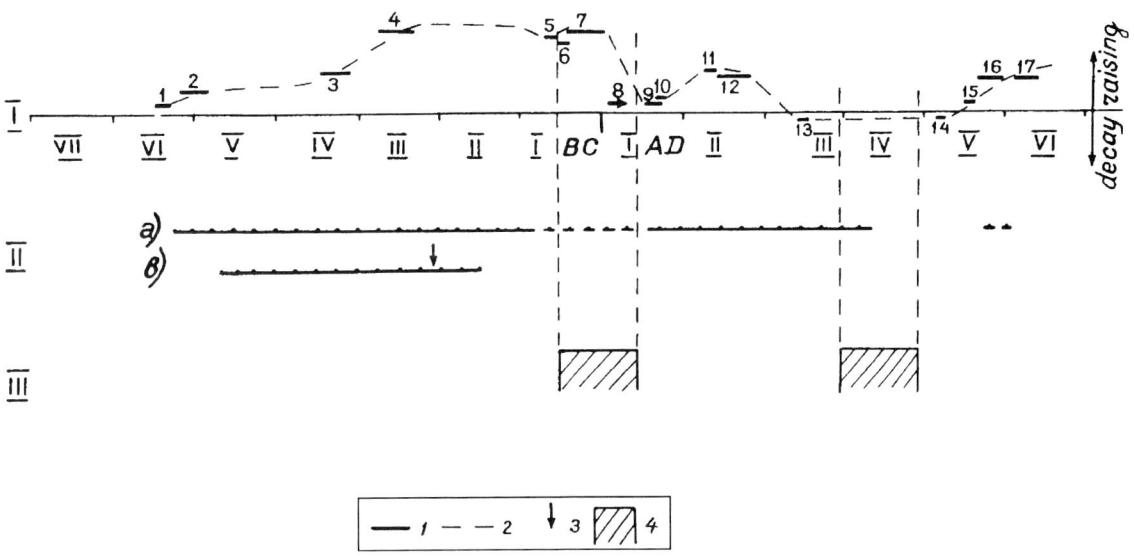

Figure 8. Data on the comparative development of Dioscuria and Sebastopolis.
I based on written sources: 1 Arrian; 2 Pomponius Mela; 3 pseudo-Skylax; 4 Timosthenes; 5 information about Mithridates; 6 Aristarchous Colchideus; 7 Strabo; 8 after Sebastopolis was named in honour of Augustus; 9 Pliny; 10 city's name during Vespasianus' reign; 11 Flavius Arrianus; 12 Ptolemeus; 13 not mentioned in an invasion of the Scythians; 14 Zosimus makes no mention; 15 Priscus Paneus; 16 Justinian's time; 17 Procopius Caesareus.
II based on archaeological data: **a** the city itself; **b** settlements on the hills. Dashed lines denote uncertain traces.
III probable interval involving earthquake signs from archaeoseismological data. Notations: 1time of fixed information; **2** likely curve of comparative development (rise-floruit-decline); **3** stone fall; **4** likely periods of destructive earthquakes.

Summary

The proposed urban development on the coast of Sukhumi Bay from the 6th century BC to the 6th century AD is shown schematically in Fig. 8. The upper portion illustrates the comparative prosperity and decay of the city inferred from literary sources. The archaeological record provides the middle part of curve II indicating the lifetime of the city (a) and its surrounding settlements (b). Shown separately (III) are the periods for which there are vestiges of earthquake damage in the old fortifications.

A satisfactory consistency emerges from the independent lines of evidence. The periods of decay in the 1st and 4th centuries AD based on historical and archaeological evidence are roughly contemporaneous and they correlate with the indications of major seismic activity. More precisely, the most likely dates of the seismic destruction of Dioscuria is the early 1st century AD and rapid decline of Sebastopolis in the late 330s AD. The former destruction event can be confidently attributed to seismic activity alone, while the latter may have been accompanied by an important subsidence. Sediment sliding on to the bay bottom, the eustatic rise in the Black Sea level and abrasion played a subordinate part in destroying remains of the cities and submerging them underwater.

The eastern coast of the Black Sea where catastrophic earthquakes are not known either from written records or instrumental observations has been investigated by the archaeoseismic method. An earlier summary of archaeological data from Colchis as a whole by the author (Nikonov, 1989) and the examination of archaeoseismicity in the area of Sukhumi city itself have led to the identification of catastrophic earthquakes with intensities around IX in the 4th, 7th, 11th and 18th centuries. A special examination of materials relating to the remains of fortifications of Greek Dioscuria and Roman Sebastopolis lying beneath modern Sukhumi and on the bottom of the adjacent bay reveals serious earthquakes during the early 1st century and mid-4th century AD which first caused the destruction of Dioscuria and afterwards a rapid decline of Sebastopolis.

The overall conclusion is that the Colchis area near Sukhumi, in contrast to the accepted notion (Bune & Goreshkov, 1980), is subject to destructive intensity IX earthquakes recurring every 300–400, possibly 700 years.

References

Balabanov I. & Gaprindashvili, M. (1987). On the question of localisation of ancient Greek towns Pitiunt and Dioscuria. *Trans. Acad. Sci. Georgian Rep., Ser. Hist., Arch., Ethn. Art Hist.* **2**, 151–159. (In Russian).

Bune V. & Gorshkov, G., Eds (1980). *Seismic zoning of the USSR territory.* Moscow; Nauka. (In Russian).

Ivanov, M. *et al.* (1988). Processes of sedimentogenesis and recent deposits composition on the continental margin of the Caucasus within the Colchis lowland. In *Geology of oceans and seas*, Abstracts of the VIII all — Union Conference of Marine Geology I. Moscow. (In Russian).

Nikonov, A. (1983). Earthquakes in legends and stories. *Priroda* (Nature) **11**, 66–75. (In Russian).

Nikonov, A. (1988). On the methodology of archaeoseismic research on historical monuments. In (Marinos, P. & Koukis, G., Eds) *The Engineering Geology of ancient works, monuments and historical sites* **3**, 1315–1320. Balkema; Rotterdam.

Nikonov, A. (1989). Unknown catastrophic earthquakes on the Eastern Black Coast: an experience in archaeoseismic reconstructions. *Proc. XXI General Assembly Europ. Seism. Comm.* (August 1988), 101–111. Sofia.

Razumov, G. & Khazin, M. (1978). *Submerged towns.* Moscow; Nauka. (In Russian).

Shervashidze, L. (1967). *Story of a town swallowed by waves: Sukhumi.* (In Russian).

Soloviev, L. (1947). Dioscuria — Sebastopolis —Tshum. *Trans. Abkhazian State Museum, Sukhumi* **1**, 99–147. (In Russian).

Trapsh, M. (1969). *Ancient Sukhumi.* Sukhumi. (In Russian).

Voronov, Yu. (1980). *Dioscuriada — Sebastopolis — Tshum.* Moscow; Nauka. (In Russian).

An Earthquake Engineering Approach
to the Collapse of the Mycenaean Palace Civilization
of the Greek Mainland

Gerasimos A. Papadopoulos

Hellenic Air Force Academy, Dekelia, Attika, Greece, &
Department of Seismotectonics, Earthquake Planning & Protection Organisation,
226 Mesoghion, 155 61 Holargos, Athens, Greece

Abstract

Present century data on Greek seismic intensities and their frequency distribution have been utilized to approach, in probabilistic terms, the validity of the archaeological suggestion that two main earthquake phases may have contributed drastically to the collapse of the Mycenaean palace civilization of the Greek Mainland. Our analysis indicates that the probability of observing at least one destructive shock at one or more sites, at time intervals of thirty years or more, is very high. This result supports independently the archaeological suggestion.

Introduction

During the 1st International Congress on the Thera Volcano held in Greece (September 1969), Pomerance (1971), discussing a paper presented by Galanopoulos (1971), stated that:

'The key and dominating factor in any criticism of the papers given at the International Scientific Congress on Thera is the unexplained failure by almost all the archaeologists, and geologists who chose to discuss the archaeological material, to reckon with the geopolitical, historical, geological and economic consequences of an area-wide disaster, on the Mainland of Greece and on its inhabitants, the Mycenaean Greeks ... How, therefore, can an archaeologically knowledgeable geologist avoid the problem and not mention once in his paper the Mycenaeans and the seismic disaster possibilities on the Peloponnese?'

From that text it is obvious that the possibility of an extensive seismic destruction of the Mycenaean palace civilization of the Greek Mainland has been under discussion for many years. Recently, Kilian (1981–82; 1984, and papers cited therein) suggested that two main cycles of earthquake destruction are recognised in the archaeological record of the LH IIIB phase of the Late Mycenaean palace civilization. Although the length of the time interval covered by each of the two phases is not known, it is likely to be of the order of some decades.

Such a suggestion puts a very clear archaeological problem: what has been the contribution of strong earthquake events in the collapse of the Mycenaean palace civilization? An equally important seismological question is: what is the probability of observing one or more destructive shocks in Mycenaean regions at time intervals of the order of some decades?

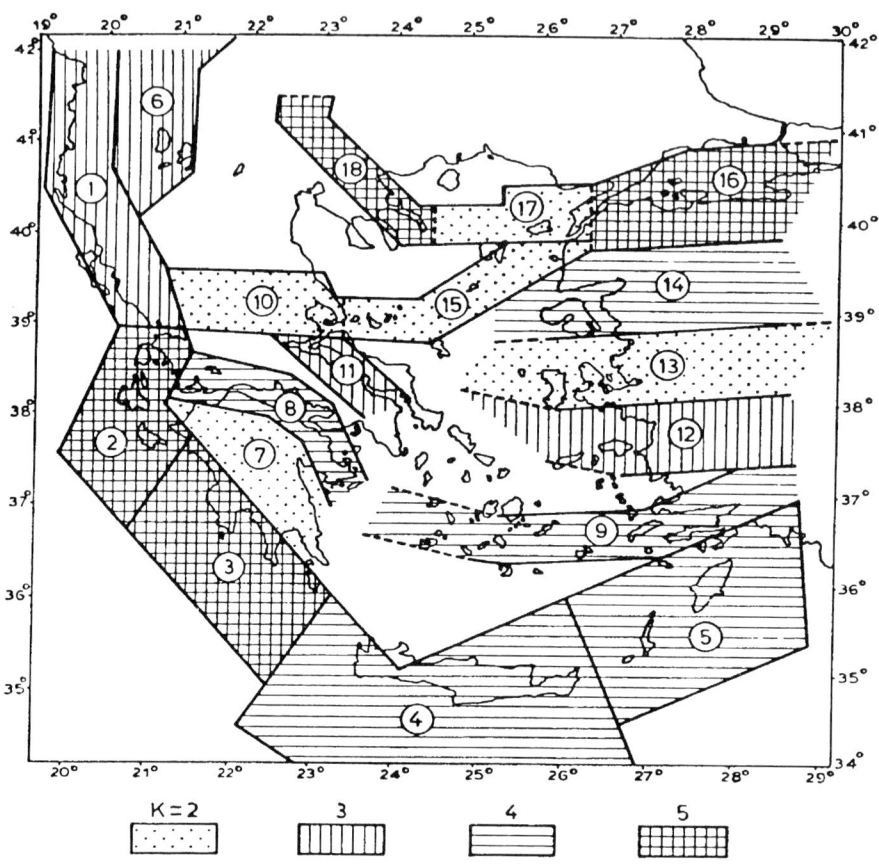

Figure 1. The relative hazard level in the several seismotectonic segments of the Aegean area (after Papadopoulos & Kijko, 1991). Low, intermediate, high and very high hazard corresponds to K = 2, 3, 4 and 5, respectively.

This paper deals with only the seismological problem, although it has been inspired by the archaeological question. Archaeologists should finally decide whether or not the present results are useful and of interest to their research problems.

The data used

Fig. 1 shows the main seismotectonic segments of the Aegean and surrounding regions, as well as their relative hazard level as determined by Papadopoulos and Kijko (1991). The Mycenaean centres of interest might be affected by the seismogenic sources located at several segments as follows: Tiryns, Mycenae, Midea, Profitis Ilias and Korakou by segment 7 and the eastern side of segment 8 (hereafter designated 8E); Pylos by segments 3 and 7; Thebes by segments 8E and 11; Kastanas by segment 18. Therefore, the present analysis has been based on seismological data available for these segments. Segment 8E covers the side located to the W of the meridian of 22° E.

The first reliable seismographic instrument in Greece was installed in 1910, and so it is only since 1911 that systematic earthquake recording has been possible. It seems that since that time the completeness magnitude threshold is about $M_s = 5.2$. However, earthquake magnitude does not measure adequately the destruction caused by the seismic events. It is better described by the seismic intensity, I, which practically takes only integer values ranging from 1 to an upper limit depending on the macroseismic scale used; for instance, up to 12 in the modified Mercalli-Sieberg (MM) scale. It is evident that for the purpose of our study seismic intensity is the most appropriate measure of the earthquake size.

All earthquakes of magnitude equal to or larger than 5.2 occurring in segments 3, 7, 8E, 11 and 18 during the interval 1911–1985 have been selected from the catalogue of Comninakis & Papazachos (1986). Next, the frequency-intensity diagram (Fig. 2) has been examined. Visual inspection of Fig. 2 shows that the reporting completeness is safe for $I > 6$ (MM).

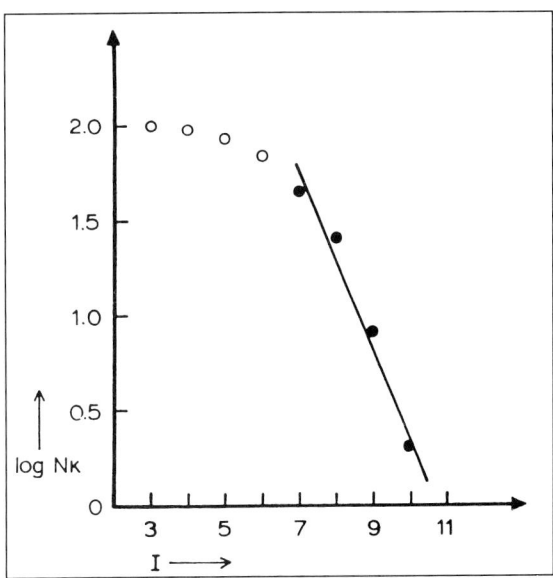

Figure 2. The intensity-frequency diagram for the segments 3, 7, 8E, 11 and 18. Straight line with parameters $a = 3.09$ and $b = 0.46$ has been determined only from complete data ($I > 6$).

Statistical Models and Results

Standard statistical models of the earthquake occurrence process have been applied in order to obtain probabilities of observing a certain number of destructive earthquakes ($I > 6$) in the segments in question. The frequency-intensity relationship

$$\log N_k = a_k - bI \tag{1}$$

has been determined by regression analysis for $I > 6$ so that the parameters a_k and b are equal to 4.97 and 0.46 respectively, where N_k is the cumulative number of earthquakes of intensity equal to or larger than a certain value I ($k = 75$ years). For $k = 1$ we get

$$\log N = a - bI \tag{2}$$

where

$$a = a_k - \log k \tag{3}$$

that is, $a = 3.09$. From (2) we get

$$T_I = 10^{bI} / 10^a \tag{4}$$

where T_I is the mean return period of earthquakes of intensity equal to or larger than a certain value, I. Putting $a = 3.09$ and $b = 0.46$ we get $T_7 = 1.35$, $T_8 = 3.89$, $T_9 = 11.2$ and $T_{10} = 32.3$ years. These values of T_I, however, describe return periods of shocks occurring somewhere in the five segments considered. A specific, reliable analysis for each one of the segments is hard to do because of the low number of events in each one of them. For this reason the problem has been approached by another independent examination.

The backbone of this problem is the assumption that the probability model, which describes adequately the time distribution of mainshocks, is the random or Poisson model (Schenková & Kárník, 1971; Dionysiou & Papadopoulos, 1991). According to this model, the probability of observing **x** events in a time interval **t** is

$$P(x) = \exp(-rt)\,(rt)^x / x!$$ (5)

$x = 0, 1, 2,\ldots,$

where $r > 0$, the mean rate of earthquake occurrence is the only parameter of the distribution. It is evident that the probability of observing at least one event is $P = 1-P(0)$.

The mean rates of earthquakes of $l > 6$ in segments 3, 7, 8E, 11 and 18 are $r_3 = 0.1067$, $r_7 = 0.0533$, $r_{8E} = 0.2133$, $r_{11} = 0.1600$ and $r_{18} = 0.1600$, respectively. For $t = 30$ years we get $P_3 = 0.959$, $P_7 = 0.798$, $P_{8E} = 0.998$, $P_{11} = 0.982$ and $P_{18} = 0.992$. Similarly, for $t = 100$ years we get $P_3 = P_{11} = P_{18} = 0.999$, $P_{8E} = 1$ and $P_7 = 0.995$.

Provided that earthquakes occur in different segments independently of each other, the probability of observing at least one destructive earthquake ($I > 6$) in more than one segment, **S**, in the same time interval is

$$P_i = P\,(S_1 \cap S_2 \cap S_3 \cap \ldots \cap S_i)$$ (6)

where $i = 1, 2, 3, 4, 5$ is the number of segments involved. Considering all the possible segment combinations, we find that P_i ranges between 0.744 and 0.990 for $t = 30$ years and between 0.992 and 0.999 for $t = 100$ years.

Conclusion

Analysis of seismic intensity data, existing since the beginning of the present century, indicates that the probability of observing at least one destructive ($I > 6$) earthquake, in one or more Greek mainland Mycenaean regions, in time intervals of thirty years or more, is very high. This result implies that from a seismological point of view the archaeological suggestion for two phases of destruction of several Mycenaean palace sites on the Greek mainland is reasonable provided that each one of these phases lasted for about thirty years or more.

References

Comninakis, P. E. & Papazachos, B. C. (1986). *A Catalogue of Earthquakes in Greece and the Surrounding Area for the Period* 1901–1985. University Thessaloniki Geophys. Lab. Publ. **1**.

Dionysiou, D. & Papadopoulos, G. A. (1991). Poissonian and Negative Binomial Modelling of Earthquake Time Series in the Aegean Area. *Physics of the Earth and Planet Interior* **71**, 154–165.

Galanopoulos, A. G. (1971). The Eastern Mediterranean Trilogy in the Bonze Age. In (A. Kaloyeropoulou, Ed.) *Acta 1st Int. Scient. Congr. on the Volcano of Thera* (Greece, 1969), 184–197. Athens; Archaeological Service of Greece, TAP Service.

Kilian, K. (1981–82). Historic Evolution of Peloponnese towards the end of the Mycenaean Age. *Peloponnisiaka* **8** (Proc. 2nd Int. Congr. on Peloponnese Studies (Patras 1980), 155–159. Athens. (In Greek with English abstract).

Kilian, K. (1984). About the collapse of the Mycenaean palaces of the Greek mainland. Paper presented to the *Orchomenos Congress.* (In Greek).

Papadopoulos, G. A. & Kijko, A. (1991). Maximum likelihood estimation of earthquake hazard parameters in the Aegean area from mixed data. *Tectonophysics* **185**, 277–294.

Pomerance, L. (1971). (Discussion on the paper of Galanopoulos, 1971). In (A. Kaloyeropoulou, Ed.), *Acta*

1st Int. Scient. Congr. on the Volcano of Thera (Greece, 1969), 203–207. Athens; Archaeological Service of Greece, TAP service.

Schenková, Z. & Kárník, V. (1971). Statistical and other characteristics of earthquakes in the Aegean region. *Geophys. Sbornik — Travaux Inst. Geophys. Acad. Tchécosl. Sci.* **351**, 149–166.

The Harbour of Aigeira
(North Peloponnese, Greece):
an Uplifted Ancient Harbour

Sofia Papageorgiou [a] & Stathis Stiros [b]

[a] Ephoreia of Marine Archaeology,
   30, Kalisperi St., 117 42 Athens, Greece
[b] Institute of Geology and Mineral Exploration (IGME),
   70, Mesoghion Street, 115 27 Athens, Greece

Abstract

The small cove of Mavra Litharia, between Akrata and Derveni, is identified with the harbour of the Hellenistic Aigeira and was perhaps the only ancient natural harbour along the N coast of Peloponnese. Exposed vermetids and pottery fragments cemented in marine conglomerates indicate that the site experienced about 2 m uplift since the Hellenistic period. Marine biological data and AMS radiocarbon dating suggests that 1 m uplift at least is episodic, probably seismic, dating from the Middle Byzantine period. Mavra Litharia is another case of an uplifted ancient harbour along the Greek coast.

Introduction

Uplifted ancient harbours in the Aegean have been reported from Crete (Spratt, 1865; Pirazzoli, this vol.; Pirazzoli et al., 1982; 1992) and Corinth (Wiseman, 1978; Stiros, 1988; Stiros & Papageorgiou, 1989; Pirazzoli et al., in press). Our research, based on archaeological, geomorphological, marine biological data as well as on AMS ^{14}C dating of marine fossils, revealed that an uplifted ancient harbour exists in the N Peloponnese, and that its uplift is most likely associated with an earthquake.

The modern cove of Mavra Litharia, near Derveni, Corinthia, where this ancient harbour has been identified (Fig. 1), is one of the rare sites along the N coast of Peloponnese providing a certain natural shelter for boats in case of bad weather. Hard limestones, cropping out in this site, form a small promontory. This type of morphology is an exception to the rather linear, fault-controlled and sandy coast of the N Peloponnese.

Ancient Aigeira and its Harbour

The ancient town of Aigeira, existed in Mycenaean times (known as Hyperisie in Homer: B, 573; o, 254); flourished in the Hellenistic period and especially during the wars between the Achaean and Aetolian Leagues, at about the end of the 3rd century BC (Pausanias VII, 26.; Polybius IV, 57). Important remains of large public buildings (a theatre, walls, temples, etc.) of Hellenistic Aigeira as well as finds of the Mycenaean and Roman periods have been brought to light during three major excavation campaigns (1916, 1925, 1971–1989) on a steep hill near modern Akrata (Verdelis, 1958; Alzinger, 1974; Alzinger, 1976 also for previous bibliography). Pausanias (VII, 26, 1) reports that Aigeira had a harbour which has been identified with Mavra Litharia, the

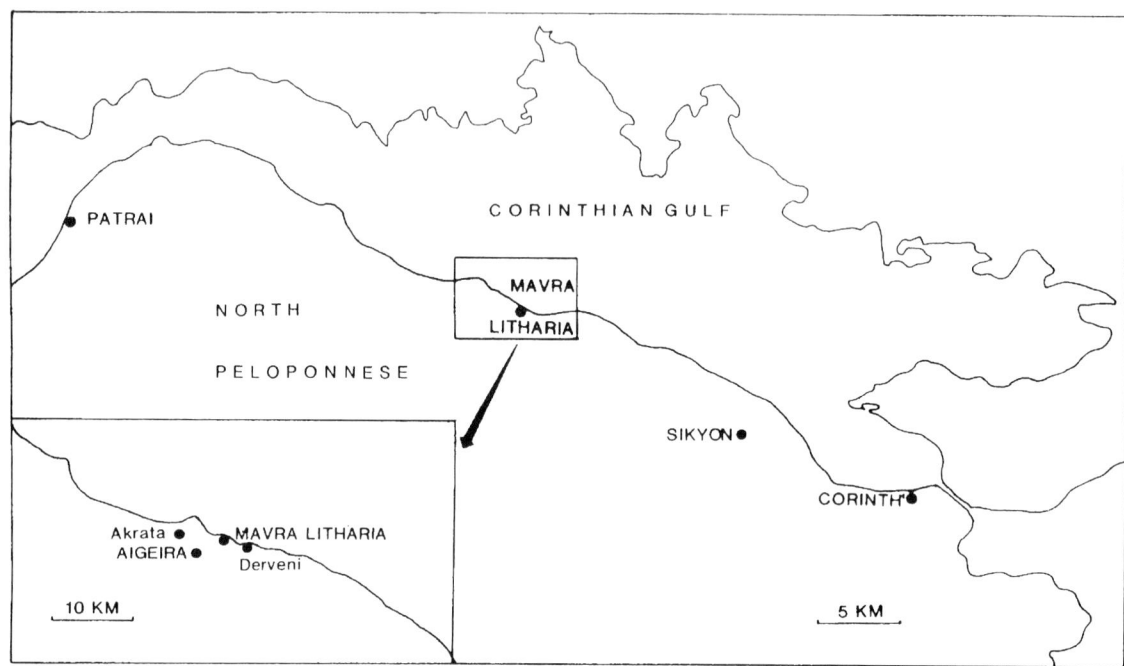

Figure 1. Location map.

small cove at the foot of the hill where ancient Aigeira is situated. The site was first mentioned in the 19th century by Leake (1836), who reported the existence of some ancient remains at this cove. Since then, no mention of the site have been made, and only recently Mavra Litharia was recognized as the site of the harbour of ancient Aigeira (Papachatzis, 1980; Stiros & Papageorgiou, 1989).

It seems that during antiquity, Mavra Litharia remained a small harbour serving local needs of the nearby Hellenistic and Roman town of Aigeira, while at the same time large artificial harbours were constructed close to the major N Peloponnesian cities (Patrai, Corinth, Sikyon). Today, the area has been drastically altered by ekistic development, which probably has destroyed most remains of the ancient harbour; some rectangular blocks and numerous pottery fragments of undetermined (Hellenistic?) age, rounded by the sea, are the only remains of the Aigeira harbour.

Evidence of an Episodic Uplift

The N Peloponnesian coast is an area of Quaternary uplift, as stratigraphic and geomorphological data reveal (Dufaure & Zamanis, 1980; Keraudren & Sorel, 1987). Stiros (1988), based on geodetic data, and Flemming & Woodworth (1988), based on tide-gauge data, concluded that uplift continued during the last 50 years, but there is additional evidence of uplift in the historical period: at the site of the ancient harbour numerous pottery fragments, most of them cemented into marine conglomerates, are exposed up to height of 2 m above present sea-level (Fig. 2); such conglomerates are formed at, or below, sea level. Obviously, in the case of Mavra Litharia, these conglomerates were originally formed at the floor of the harbour during its period of use (Hellenistic? times). Hence, at least 2 m relative land uplift postdating this period is inferred.

Evidence of uplift is provided also by remains of vermetid shells (*Dendropoma petraeum*, among others) which are observed up to a height of 1 m above present sea-level. This species is usually an accurate and precise indicator of sea-level change, for the upper limit of such living vermetids coincides with lower limit of the active mid-littoral zone. Consequently, the upper limit of such fossil vermetids indicates a former sea-level, 1 m higher than the present one. Furthermore, the preservation of vermetids at this height is indicative of a very rapid, probably episodic uplift (Stiros *et al.*, 1992; Pirazzoli, this volume).

Dating of the Uplift

A lower bound for the uplift of the harbour can be given by the pottery fragments that are cemented in the conglomerates: it is very likely that the uplift took place during or just after the period of use of the harbour. Although the pottery is difficult to date, for it is badly preserved, probably the period of use of the harbour coincides with the period of wealth of Aigeira during Hellenistic and Roman times. If this uplift took place during the period of use of the harbour, it was perhaps a reason for its abandonment.

A more accurate date is given by a radiocarbon date obtained with the AMS technique: a sample of a fossil *Dendropoma*, collected in living position from the height of 1 m above sea-level gave a calibrated age of about AD 1000–1200. This date probably corresponds to the time of the episodic uplift of the area (Papageorgiou *et al.*, 1994).

Figure 2. Pottery fragments (marked by arrows) cemented in the harbour remains of the cove at Mavra Litharia.

Correlation with known Seismic Events

The area of the Gulf of Corinth is one of the most seismically active parts of Greece and even the world, and consequently a seismic shock at that period is quite possible. Unfortunately, the historical seismic record for this period is very poor (Papazachos & Papazachou, 1989), and no evidence of great earthquakes exists. However, there is some archaeological evidence that perhaps can prove that great earthquakes did occur in the area during historical times (Papageorgiou *et al.*, 1994), but such events are too early to be correlated with the uplift discussed here.

References

Alzinger, W. (1974). Die Ausgrabungen in Aigeira. *Archaeologika Analekta Athenon* **7**, 157–162.

Alzinger, W. (1976). Aigeira 1975. *Archaeologika Analekta Athenon* **9**, 162–165.

Dufaure, J. - J. & Zamanis, A. (1980). Styles néotectoniques et étagements de niveaux marins quaternaires sur un segment de l'arc insulaire, le Péloponnèse. *Actes du Colloque 'Niveaux marins et tectonique quaternaires dans l'aire Méditerranéenne'*, 77–107. Paris; CNRS et Univ. Paris I.

Flemming, N. C. & Woodworth, Ph. (1988). Monthly mean sea levels in Greece during 1969–1983 compared to relative vertical land movements measured over different time scales. *Tectonophysics* **148**, 59–72.

Keraudren, B. & Sorel, D. (1987). The terraces of Corinth (Greece): a detailed record of eustatic sea-level variations during the last 500,000 years. *Marine Geology* **77**, 99–108.

Leake, W. M. (1836). *Travels in Morea*, vol. 3. London.

Papachatzis, N. (1980). *Pausanias' description of Greece* **4**. Athens; Ekdotiki Athenon. (In Greek).

Papageorgiou, S., Arnold, M. & Stiros, S. (1994). Co-seismic uplift of the harbour of ancient Aigeira (Central Greece). *Int. J. Naut. Archaeol.* **22**, 275–281.

Papazachos, V. & Papazachou, K. (1989). *Earthquakes of Greece*. Thessaloniki; Zitis Ed. (In Greek).

Pirazzoli, P.A. (this volume). Uplift of ancient Greek coastal sites: studies, methods and results.

Pirazzoli, P.A., Thommeret, J., Thommeret, Y., Laborel J. & Montaggioni, L. (1982). Crustal block movements from Holocene shorelines: Crete and Antikythira. *Tectonophysics* **86**, 27–43.

Pirazzoli, P.A., Ausseil-Badie, J., Giresse, P., Hadjidaki, E. & Arnold, M. (1992). Historical environmental changes at Phalasarna harbor, west Crete. *Geoarchaeology* **7**, 371–392.

Pirazzoli, P., Stiros, S., Arnold, M., Laborel, J., Laborel-Deguen, F. & Papageorgiou, S. (1994). Episodic uplift deduced from Holocene shorelines in the Perachora Peninsula (Corinth area, Greece). *Tectonophysics* **229**, 201–209.

Spratt, T. S. (1865). *Travels and Researches in Crete*. 2 vols. London; J. van Voorst.

Stiros, S. (1988). Model for the North Peloponnesian (Central Greece) uplift. *Journal of Geodynamics* **9**, 199–214.

Stiros, S. & Papageorgiou, S. (1989). Late Holocene sea level changes and some implications on the Neotectonics of Central Greece. *Bull. Geol. Soc. Greece* **22** (1), 259–269. (In Greek).

Stiros, S., Arnold, M., Pirazzoli, P.A., Laborel, J., Laborel, F. & Papageorgiou, S. (1992). Historical coseismic uplift in Euboea island (Greece). *Earth Planet. Sci. Lett.* **108**, 109–117.

Verdelis, N. (1958). *Bulletin de Correspondance Hellénique*, Chronique des fouilles en 1957, 726.

Wiseman, J. (1978). *The land of the ancient Corinthians*. Studies in Mediterranean Archaeology 50. Göteborg.

Seismicity and Seismic Hazard Assessment at the Site of the Temple of Epicourios Apollo (Vassai)

Dimitris Papanastassiou[a], George Drakatos[a], George Stavrakakis[a], John Drakopoulos[a] , J. Latoussakis[a] & Kostas Papandonopoulos[b]

[a] National Observatory of Athens, Seismological Institute,
P.O. Box 20048, Athens 118 10, Greece
[b] Ministry of Culture, Committee for the Preservation
of the Temple of Apollo Epicourios, Athens, Greece

Abstract

In this paper, we examine the seismicity and assess the seismic hazard at the region of the Temple of Apollo Epicourios, S-W Peloponnese, Greece.

A portable network of six seismographs was employed for eight weeks. Over three hundred shocks were located, which were recorded by at least three stations. A reliable velocity model was determined for the region, and the magnitude of each earthquake was estimated from the maximum trace amplitude as well as from the signal duration. Hazard analysis has been carried out, using the maximum magnitude method and the modified Cornell's method.

Due to the great importance of the structure, we also investigated the influence of the foundation soil on these ground movements. The foundation of the Temple is not the same everywhere and there is a high azimuthal variation of the relative ground movements, which represents different oscillations of neighbouring ground particles.

The results show that this situation, as well as a possible settling of the different foundation soils, act at the Temple in a more severe manner than the absolute increase of the seismic acceleration.

Introduction

The Temple of Apollo Epicourios stands as one of the most remarkable and best preserved monuments of classical architecture in the Peloponnese. The Temple is near the site of the ancient Arcadian town of Phigalia, 14 km S-W from the village of Andritsaina. It lies on a natural plateau (Vassai) of Mt. Kotilion, at an altitude of 1130 m above sea level. The building material of the Temple still *in situ* has deteriorated extensively which has reduced the static efficiency of most of the blocks and the structure as a whole. As the Temple is located in an active seismotectonic segment of the southwestern Peloponnese, the frequent seismic activity could be one of the most important environmental factors of deterioration.

The present study was carried out in order: (1) to examine the seismicity and the existence of probable active seismic sources in the investigated area, (2) to estimate the influence of the different foundation conditions of the ground movements and (3) to assess the seismic hazard of the region.

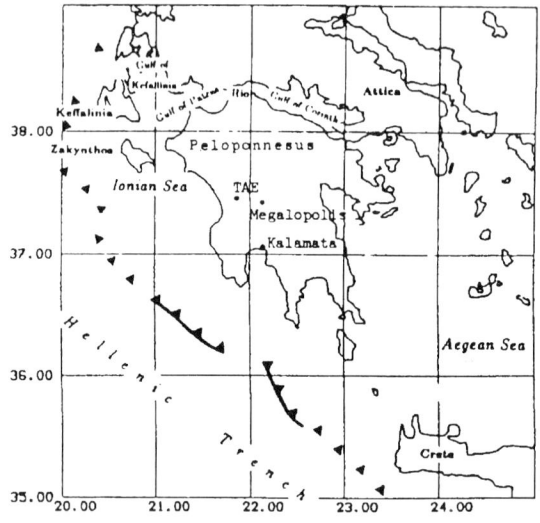

Figure 1. Map of the western Hellenic arc. TAE is the site of the temple.

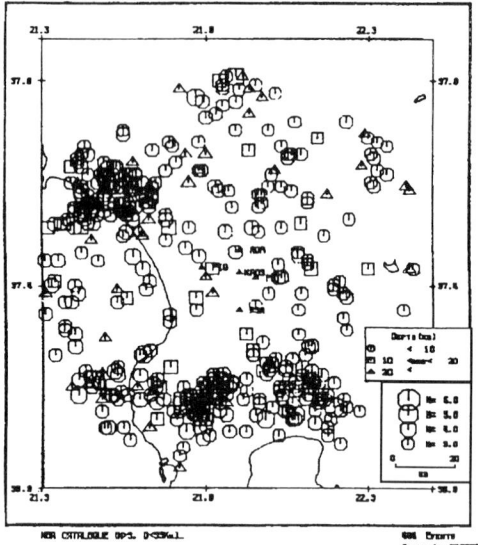

Figure 2. Seismicity of the southwestern Peloponnese.

Recent Seismic Activity of the Region

The site of the Temple and the surrounding areas are characterized by a high seismicity, caused by the seismic sources of: (1) the fractured zones of the Ionian Sea, (2) the Corinthian graben, (3) the depression basin of Megalopolis and (4) Kalamata-Messini, Kyparissia-Filiatra and Pyrgos-Olympia seismic areas (Fig. 1).

In Fig. 2, the seismicity of the region is shown for the last ten years, according to the data of the Seismological Institute of Athens. During the present century two large earthquakes occurred in the Megalopolis basin (Ambraseys, 1967). Their parameters (Makropoulos *et al.*, 1989) are shown in Table 1.

TABLE 1			
Date	**Coordinates**	**Depth**	**Magnitude**
1965 Apr 5	37.8 °N - 22.0 °E	15 km	6.0
1966 Sept 1	37.5 °N - 22.2 °E	34 km	5.4

These earthquakes caused accumulated damage at the Temple, and so there is no chance of estimating them separately. Thus, declination of the columns as well as displacements of the drums and the capitals are observed. A percentage of the vertical movements is caused by subsidence (Adronopoulos *et al.*, 1976). As the foundation of the Temple is based on different soil types (bedrock, debris), severe earthquakes such as those of 1965 and 1966 might have caused differential subsidence at the site of the Temple.

On September 13th, 1986 a destructive earthquake of $M_s = 6.4$ occurred in the Kalamata area about 65 km S-SE of the Temple. This earthquake did not cause any damage at the Temple.

Recording and Analysis of local Earthquakes

A portable network of six seismographs was employed for eight weeks in order to check the present possible process going on in the vicinity of the faults of the area surrounding the Temple. Our intention has been to locate as many events as possible in order to detect microseismic activity and to associate the source regions with surface fault traces.

This network provided a good coverage of the area. Over three hundred shocks were located using the HYPO71 computer program (Lee & Lahr, 1975) on the basis of having at least three readings of P — arrivals and one S — arrival (Fig. 3).

No detailed information on the velocity structure of the area is available. Thus, in order to find a reliable velocity model we selected 95 well recorded shocks (with more than five P and two S arrivals) that would be a representative sample of all shocks. At first, we located these events in a half-space with a P velocity ranging from 4.0 km/sec to 7.0 km/sec with a step of 0.25 km/sec, the V_p/V_s ratio being kept constant and equal to 1.73. Looking at the mean RMS by depth range, the minimum occurs at a P velocity less than 5.0 km/sec for earthquakes shallower than 5.0 km. For earthquakes with depths between 5.0 km and 10 km the minimum occurs at a P velocity between 5.5 km/sec and 6.0 km/sec and for earthquakes deeper than 10 km at a P velocity close to 6.0 km/sec. Thus, there is an apparent strong velocity gradient in the upper 10 km of the crust. We studied the influence of the V_p/V_s ratio also and we found that the minimum RMS at any P velocity was for a V_p/V_s ratio of 1.82.

We then tried to find a layered velocity structure that would account for the features described above. Because of the apparent strong velocity gradient in the upper 10 km of the crust and in order to avoid large velocity contrasts between layers for which we did not find evidence thereby creating problems, we used a multi-layer velocity structure instead of a simple one. The final velocity structure (Table 2) yields at all depths a smaller mean RMS than any of the half-space models. The obtained standard errors in the epicentral and hypocentral locations given by the HYPO71 (Lee & Lahr, 1975) computer program are smaller than 3 km.

The magnitude of each earthquake was determined from the maximum trace amplitude as well as from the signal duration of the event at each station. The conversion of the used instruments into an equivalent Wood-

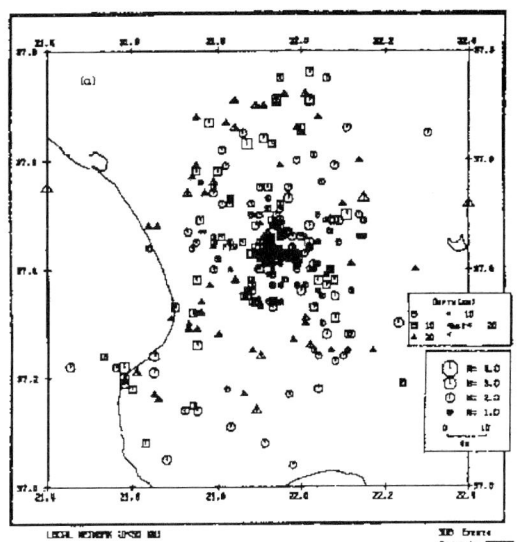

Figure 3. Map of the recorded earthquakes.

TABLE 2	
Velocity (km/sec)	Depth (km)
	0.0
4.90	
	5.0
5.70	
	10.0
5.85	
	15.0
5.95	
	25.0
6.25	
	30.0
6.50	
	40.0
8.05	

Anderson seismograph has been done with the appropriate calibration of the instruments and the use of special tables. So, measuring the maximum trace amplitude of each shock at each station, the local magnitude (M_L) is given by the formula:

$$M_L = \log(A) + C_1\log(D) + C_2 \tag{1}$$

where D is the epicentral distance in km, A is the maximum trace amplitude in mm and C_1, C_2 are constants for each station.

The duration magnitude of the shocks were determined from the duration of the signals, using the formula:

$$M_D = a + b\log(Dur) + cD \tag{2}$$

where Dur is the duration signal in seconds, D is the epicentral distance in km and a, b, c are constants for each station.

According to these formulae, the network recorded earthquakes with magnitude $M = 0.6$.

Influence of the Foundation Soil on the Ground Movement

The foundation of the Temple is not the same everywhere. The northern part of the Temple is founded on the bedrock, while the southern part lies on an artificial step of debris.

In order to investigate the behaviour of the different soils on the ground movement, we examined the recordings of two similar seismographs which were located at these different soils. In Fig. 4, the azimuthal plot of the relative increase or attenuation of the ground motion is shown, according to the function:

$$[(SA-NA)/SA] \times 100 \tag{3}$$

where SA and NA are the maximum amplitudes recorded on the artificial step and on the bedrock respectively. A relative increase of the order of 25% is observed at the southern instrument, which is compatible with the soft foundation soil at this site. The main feature observed in this plot is the high azimuthal variation of the relative ground movement, which represents different oscillations of neighbouring ground particles. This situation, as well as a possible settling of the different foundation soils, acts on the Temple in a more severe manner than the absolute increase of the seismic acceleration.

Seismic Hazard Assessment

The Temple of Epicourios Apollo is located in a seismotectonic segment of the southwestern Peloponnese of high seismic hazard (Papadopoulos & Kijko, 1991). Due to the great importance of the structure, hazard analysis has been carried out using the most well-known and acceptable methods:

(a) *Maximum Magnitude Method*

In seismic hazard analysis the spatial migration of seismicity along an active fault during a given exposure time is of great importance. Once the epicentres have been associated to the various seismic sources within the region, the development of earthquake recurrence relationships is required for each individual source. These are obtained (Gutenberg & Richter, 1944) by fitting a regression line of the form:

$$\log N(M) = a - bM \tag{4}$$

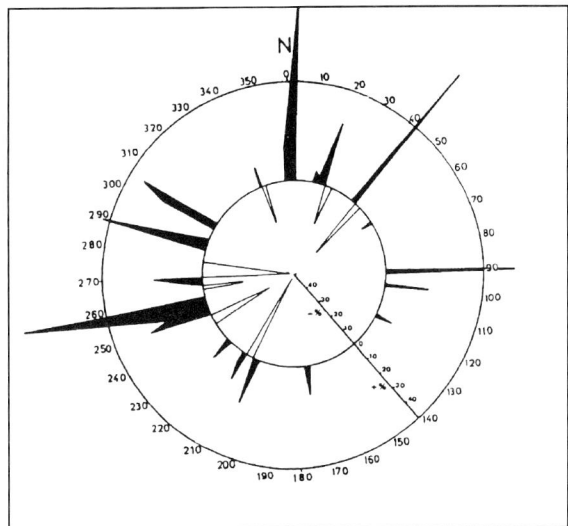

Figure 4. Azimuthal variation of the ground motion for the two different foundation soils.

▬ Increase of the ground motion (+ %).

▭ Attenuation of the ground motion (- %).

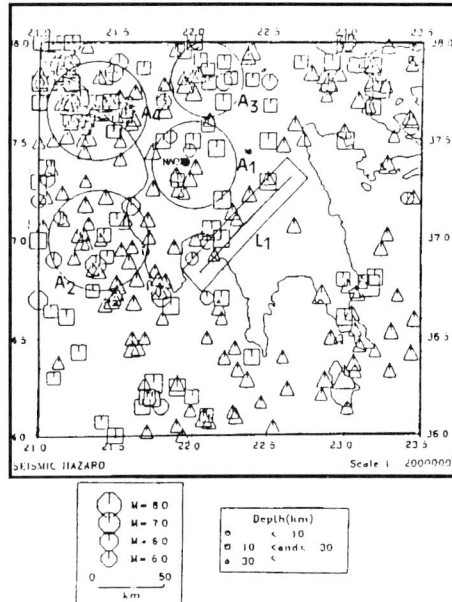

Figure 5. The seismicity of Peloponnese, 1900–1985. (Makropoulos et al., 1986).

to the magnitude distribution of each seismic source where **N(M)** is the cumulative number of earthquakes of magnitude greater than **M** and **a, b** are regression coefficients.

Coefficient **a** is correlated with the seismicity of the region, with the source area and to the time. Coefficient **b** is a measure of the source's seismic severity. The likely maximum magnitude is defined by the formula:

$$Mm = (a+blogt)/b \tag{5}$$

where **t** is the examined time period.

b) *Modified Cornell's Method*

Three different types of seismic sources have been proposed in order to estimate regional seismic hazard:

(1) *Point Source Model* makes the basic assumption that future seismic events in the region will occur in the same location as past ones. This is unrealistic in the sense that the possible spatial migration of the seismicity in the exposure time considered will be ignored.

(2) *Line Source Model* is used when earthquake epicentres lie along a line which can be assumed as an earthquake fault.

(3) *The Area Source Model* is used when earthquake epicentres are scattered over a region. An analysis based on this model corresponds to the assumption that the spatial migration of seismicity will be equal in all directions.

The basic assumptions (Cornell, 1968; Cornell & Vanmarcke, 1969; Stavrakakis, 1985) of the models are: (i) earthquakes are spatially and temporally independent, (ii) the probability that two seismic events will take place at the same location and at the same time approaches zero and (iii) the Poisson parameter **l** (mean rate of occurrence) is a constant variable.

The probability of having **N** seismic events of magnitude greater than **m** in the next **t** years is given by the formula:

$$PN(M > m,t) = \frac{\exp[-N(m)\ t]\ [N(m)}{t]^N\ N!} \tag{6}$$

Results

A. *Seismicity of the Region*

In total, 308 shocks were located. The earthquakes are spread over a wide area and no individual fault can be clearly seen. A cluster near the site of the Temple is attributed to the centre of the installed network. An examination of the depths shows that the majority of the events is located in the upper part of the crust, which means that the crust of the area suffered brittle deformation. This conclusion is also supported by the complex seismotectonic regime of the region.

During our investigation no large or moderate magnitude earthquake occurred which would have determined their focal mechanisms. But some information about the seismotectonic regime of the region was extracted from the focal mechanisms of the large earthquakes which occurred in the region on April 5, 1965, on September 1, 1966 (Drakopoulos & Delibasis, 1982) and on September 13, 1986 (Lyon-Caen *et al.*, 1988). These mechanisms suggest normal faulting in an almost N-S direction.

B. *Seismic Hazard Assessment*

In Table 3 the maximum magnitudes are shown for the region of Epicourios Apollo determined by the maximum magnitude method.

TABLE 3		
Time Period (years)	Earthquake Magnitude Prob. 63% to occur	Earthquake Magnitude Prob. 90% not to exceed
1	5.1	6.3
25	6.8	8.1
50	7.2	8.4
100	7.6	8.8
200	8.0	9.2

In Fig. 5, the distribution of epicentres is shown for earthquakes with magnitude M > 5.0 for 1901–1987 (Makropoulos *et al.*, 1989). As shown, the site of the Temple is surrounded by four areal seismic sources A1, A2, A3 and A4 and by the linear source L1.

Following the modified Cornell's Method (Stavrakakis, 1985), the maximum values of the expected accelerations are calculated for different time periods (Fig. 6a–d). At the site of the Temple, the maximum values of acceleration are also calculated for different time periods, which, with 90% probability, are not expected to be exceeded (Table 4).

TABLE 4	
Time Period (years)	Acceleration (gals) Prob. 90% not to exceed
50	240
100	310
200	370

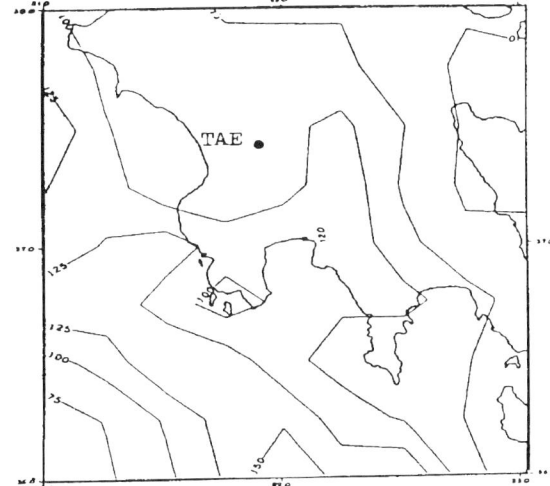

Figure 6a. Expected maximum acceleration 25 years mode.

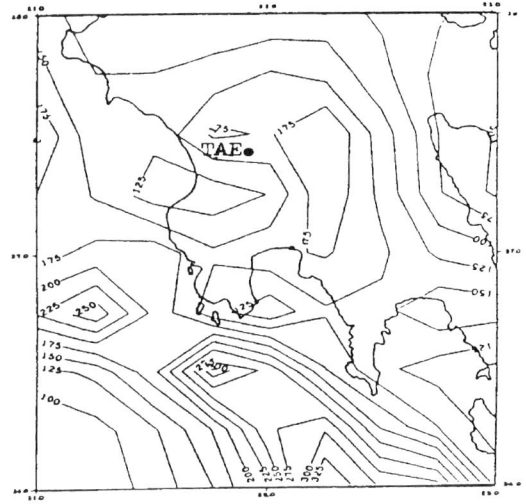

Figure 6b. Expected maximum acceleration 50 years mode.

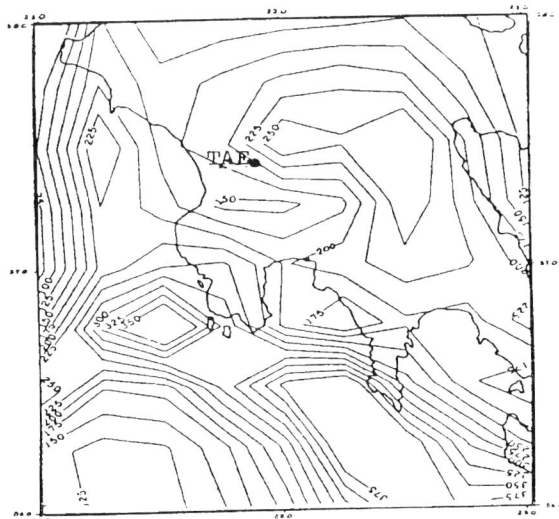

Figure 6c. Expected maximum acceleration 100 years mode.

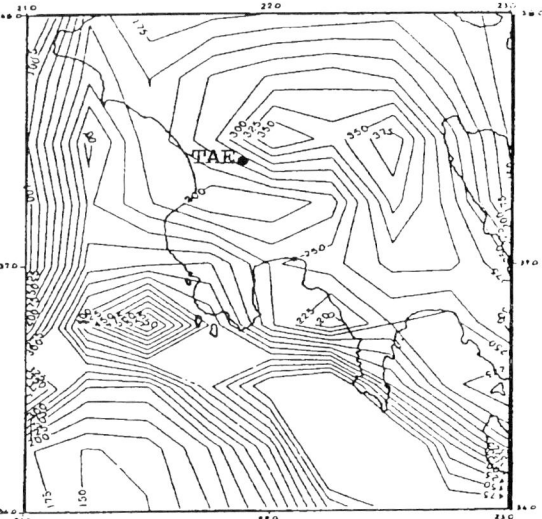

Figure 6d. Expected maximum acceleration 200 years mode.

Discussion and Conclusions

The present study was carried out in order to examine the seismicity and to assess the seismic hazard at the site of the Temple of Apollo Epicourios (Vassai).

The seismicity results show that the majority of the events are located at the upper part of the crust, to a depth ranging from 10 km to 15 km. This higher seismicity can be caused by the large fracturing of the region. The same conclusion was made by Leydecker *et al.* (1978) and Hatzfeld *et al.* (1990), who also examined the seismicity of the western Peloponnese.

The focal mechanisms of large earthquakes, which occurred in the past, show that the region is under extension with an E-W direction. This is also the tectonic regime which caused the Megalopolis depression. The results of seismic hazard assessment are compatible with the results of other researchers (Drakopoulos, 1980), as well as with the map of seismic hazard of Greece proposed by the Greek Seismological Institutions (Universities of Athens and Thessaloniki, Seismological Institute and ITSAK) (OASP, 1990).

The foundation of the Temple is not the same everywhere and there is a high azimuthal variation of the relative ground movements, which represents different oscillations of neighbouring ground particles. The results show that this situation, as well as a possible settling of the different foundation soils, act at the Temple in a more severe manner than the absolute increase of acceleration.

References

Ambraseys, N. N. (1967). The Earthquake of 1965–66 in the Peloponnesus, Greece. A field report. *Bull. Seism. Soc. Am.* **57** No. 5, 1025–1046.

Andronopoulos, B., Koukis, G. & Tzitziras, A. (1976). *Engineering Geology Study in the Area of the Temple of Apollo Epikourios (Bassai-Phigalia)*. Athens: Engineering Geology Investigation, I.G.M.E., n. 3. (In Greek).

Cornell, C. A. (1968). Engineering Seismic Risk Analysis. *Bull. Seism. Soc. Am.* **58**, 1583–1601.

Cornell, C. A. & Vanmarcke, E. H. (1969). The major influences on Seismic Risk. *45th World Conf. on Earthquake Engineering*. Chile.

Drakopoulos, J. (1980). *Seismic Hazard evaluation in the site of the Temple of Epikourios Apollo. Report submitted to the Ministry of Culture, 1980*. Publ. National Observatory of Athens. (In Greek).

Drakopoulos, J. & Delibasis, N. (1982). *The focal mechanism of earthquakes in the major area of Greece for the period 1947–1981*. Univ. of Athens, Seism. Lab. Publ. No 2.

Gutenberg, B. & Richter, C. (1944). Frequency of Earthquakes in California. *Bull. Seism. Soc. Am.* **34**, 185–188.

Hatzfeld, D., Pedotti, G., Hatzidimitriou, P. & Makropoulos, K. (1990). The strain pattern in the western Hellenic arc deduced from a microearthquake survey. *Geophys. J. Int.* **101**, 181–202.

Lee, W. H. K. & Lahr, J. C. (1975). *HYPO 71 (revised) a computer program for determined hypocenters, magnitude and first motion pattern of local earthquakes*. US Geol. Survey, Open File Report, 75–311.

Leydecker, G., Berckhemer, H. & Delibasis, N. (1978). A study of seismicity in the Peloponnese Region by precise hypocenter determinations. In (H. Closs, D. Roeder & K. Schmidt, Eds) *Alps, Appenines, Hellenides*. Stuttgart; Verlagsbuchhandlung, 406–410.

Lyon-Caen, H., Armijo, R., Drakopoulos, J., Baskoutas, J., Delibassis, N., Gaulon, R., Kouskouna, V., Latoussakis, J., Makropoulos, K., Papadimitriou, P., Papanastassiou, D. & Pedotti, G. (1988). The 1986 Kalamata (South Peloponnesus) earthquake: Detailed study of a normal fault, evidences for east-west extension in the Hellenic arc, *J. Geophys. Res.* **93**, 14,967–15,000.

Makropoulos, K., Drakopoulos, J. & Latoussakis, J. (1989). A revised and extended earthquake catalogue for Greece since 1900. *Geophys. J. Int.* **99**, 305–306.

OASP. (1990). *Seismic Hazard of Greece. Final Report*. Athens.

Papadopoulos, G. & Kijko, A. (1991). Maximum likelihood estimation of earthquake hazard parameters in the Aegean area from mixed data. *Tectonophysics* **185**, 277–294.

Stavrakakis, G. N. (1985). Contribution of Bayesian statistics to the seismic hazard evaluation in and around of the Crete island and simulation of strong ground motion. PhD. Thesis, University of Athens.

Numerical Simulation of the Seismic Response of Megalithic Monuments: Preliminary Investigations Related to the Apollo Temple at Vassai

Dimitri Papastamatiou & Ioannis Psycharis

Earthquake Engineering Laboratory,
National Technical University of Athens
157 00 Polytechnioupoli, Zografou, Greece

Abstract

We numerically analysed sections of the Apollo Temple at Vassai under strong earthquake ground motions. The site is exposed to large subduction earthquakes and to smaller local extension events in the W Peloponnese, Greece. We report on the initial phase of assessing the vulnerability of the Temple. In this phase the only link with the seismotectonic environment is the selection of representative recorded accelerograms.

The analysis confirmed the highly non-linear nature of the response of friction-cohesion ancient structures. Intact sections of the Temple showed substantial resistance to strong ground motions due to their capacity to absorb energy with large deformations that do not impair the stability of the structure. However, imperfections typical of the present condition of the monument, i.e. deterioration of the building stones and of the foundation material, substantially reduce the stability threshold.

Powerful numerical tools are available to assist rational schemes for the protection of ancient structures and to numerically test archaeological hypotheses.

Introduction

Ancient structures have survived in a frequently adverse cultural and natural environment. In any preserved form such structures offer the challenge to decipher this past environment and for this to be handed over to future generations. This effort has many different aspects and can involve many different disciplines. For the civil engineer the challenge is to understand the mechanical behaviour of the materials, the construction methods and the construction techniques. With this understanding he can document the history of an ancient structure and can take effective measures for its preservation. Moreover, the history of a particular structure provides evidence for the changes in its environment.

In this presentation we are concerned with transient changes of the environment, namely earthquakes. The structural response to such events will depend on the stability of the foundations and on the structure itself. Among the variety of ancient constructions we restrict ourselves to free-standing structures made of large stones and relying for their stability on the interface resistance of the building stones. This type of construction has been replaced by monolithic structures of concrete, steel and other modern materials. This evolution in building techniques has affected not only the techniques themselves but also the methods of structural analysis. The present limitations of computational techniques for the analysis of friction-cohesion structures are surprising. Such techniques, however, have been developed for the stability of fractured rock masses, where friction-cohesion is the only available mechanism.

We employed computational techniques developed for the stability of rock masses, namely the computer programme UDEC authored by Dr. P.A. Cundall of Minnesota University, to analyse the seismic response of elements of classical temples in Greece. Our report is based on a preliminary assessment of available numerical codes for the seismic analysis of the Temple of Apollo at Vassai, Central Peloponnese, Greece (Papastamatiou *et al.*, 1990). Although we make an effort in our presentation to keep the subject matter in focus, our results merely illustrate the potential of available numerical techniques.

The Temple and its Seismotectonic Environment

The Temple of Apollo at Vassai (C.P.T.A.E., 1986) was built in a remote part on the western mountain range of the Peloponnese (Fig. 1a). The monument was first described by Pausanias in AD 174. It then disappeared from historical accounts for seventeen centuries and was rediscovered, in 1765, by the architect traveller Joachim Bocher. Today the Temple is preserved quite well, after a restoration effort in the beginning of this century and despite the advanced deterioration of the building material (Theoulakis *et al.*, 1988; Beloyiannis *et al.*, 1988) and the foundation (Andronopoulos *et al.*, 1988). The deterioration of the building stones is accelerated by the adverse weather conditions (the structure is built at a height of approximately 1000 m above sea level). The slow erosion of the foundation materials has resulted in substantial leaning of some of the columns.

The ancient site is located in a tectonically active area of Greece (Fig. 1a). Our present understanding of this activity is dominated by two mechanisms: the subduction of the African Plate under the W Peloponnese and the extension of the Peloponnese crust. The former mechanism gives rise to infrequent large earthquakes when the subducting crust fails in compression, whereas the latter mechanism releases smaller earthquakes when the overriding plate fails in extension along normal faults. The subduction is taken up by substantial creep motion; only a small amount of the plate convergence is released by earthquakes. The large epicentral area produced by such an event in 1886 is shown on Fig. 1a (Galanopoulos, 1941) and appears to have been influenced by the excitation of intense movement in surface sedimentary formations. The extension mechanism is manifested mostly by earthquakes (Ambraseys & Jackson, 1990). These earthquakes show a relatively small epicentral area like the one produced by the 1986 Kalamata earthquake (Fig. 1a); as illustrated by this recent earthquake, the destruction potential in this small area is high.

The seismotectonic environment of the ancient site was represented with two registrations of earthquake motions (Fig. 1b): the motion recorded in Kalamata in 1986 and the motion recorded in Lima, Peru in 1974. Resort to the Peruvian subduction registration was deemed necessary because records from Greek subduction earthquakes do not exist. Fig. 1b also includes the El Centro 1940 accelerogram that has acquired a reference status in earthquake engineering. In the structural analysis the time characteristics of the three records were invariant, whereas the strength of ground shaking was increased by uniform scaling of the acceleration. This parametric scheme was selected to check the vulnerability of the structure. The actual risk (exposure of the structure to earthquakes) is related to the natural hazard at the site (exposure of the site to earthquakes) that is largely unknown due to limitations of the historical and the tectonic record. Historical accounts of earthquakes in the area have been recorded with completeness for the last two centuries only. Tectonic studies of the earthquake release along the convergence of the African and Aegean Plates or of the deformation history of surfacing normal faults in the area have not yet been brought to a conclusive state.

Numerical Analysis of Structural Elements of the Temple

The program UDEC (Cundall, 1971; Cundall & Hart, 1983) was developed over the last twenty years and has been extensively applied in problems involving fractured rock masses. The program models arbitrary geometries in two (UDEC) or three (3DEC) dimensions of discrete element assemblies with specified interface

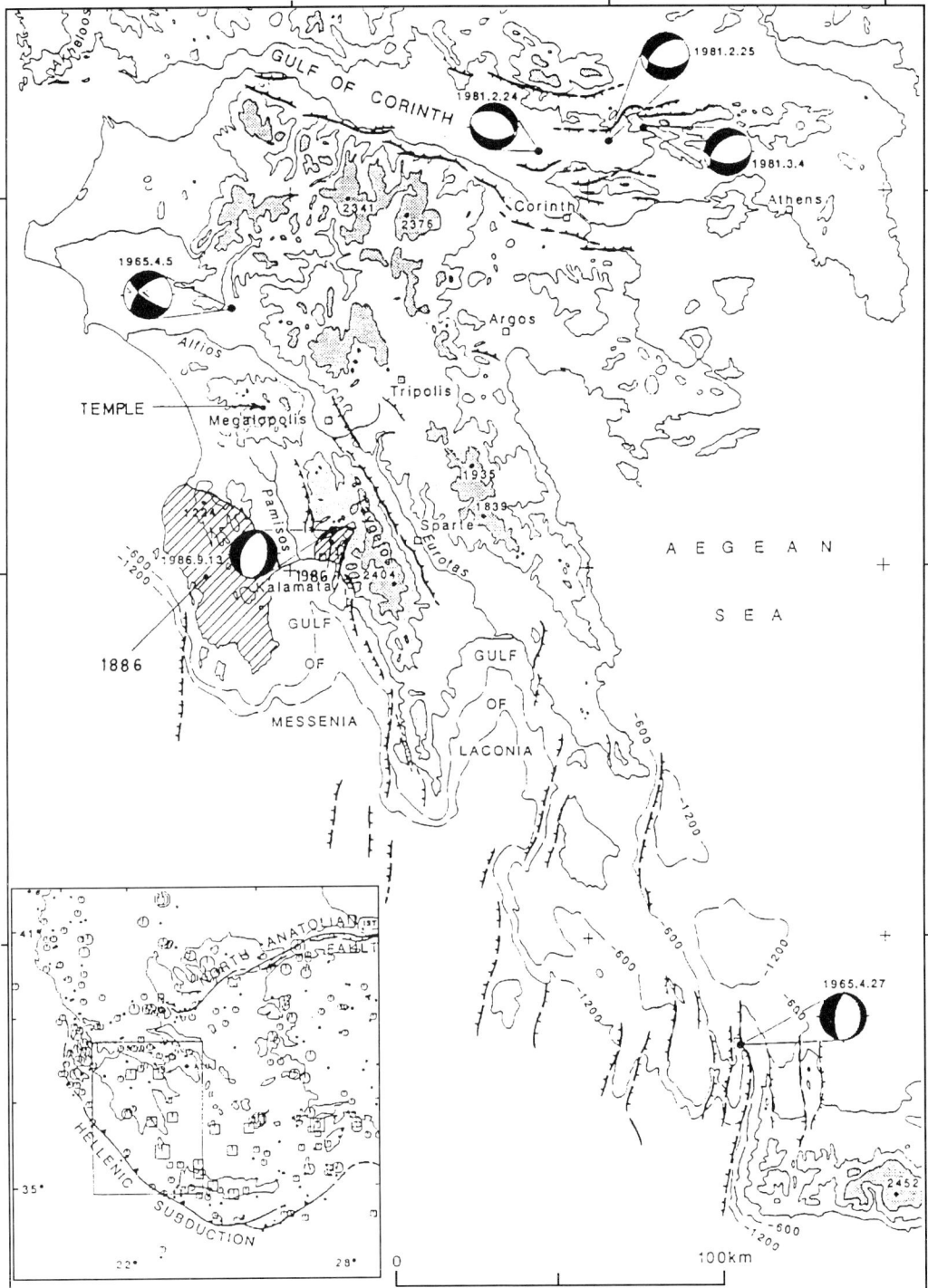

Figure 1a. Location of the Apollo Temple at Vassai and the seismotectonic environment (Lyon-Caean *et al.*, 1988). Shading indicates the epicentral areas of a small earthquake in 1986 and a large event in 1886.

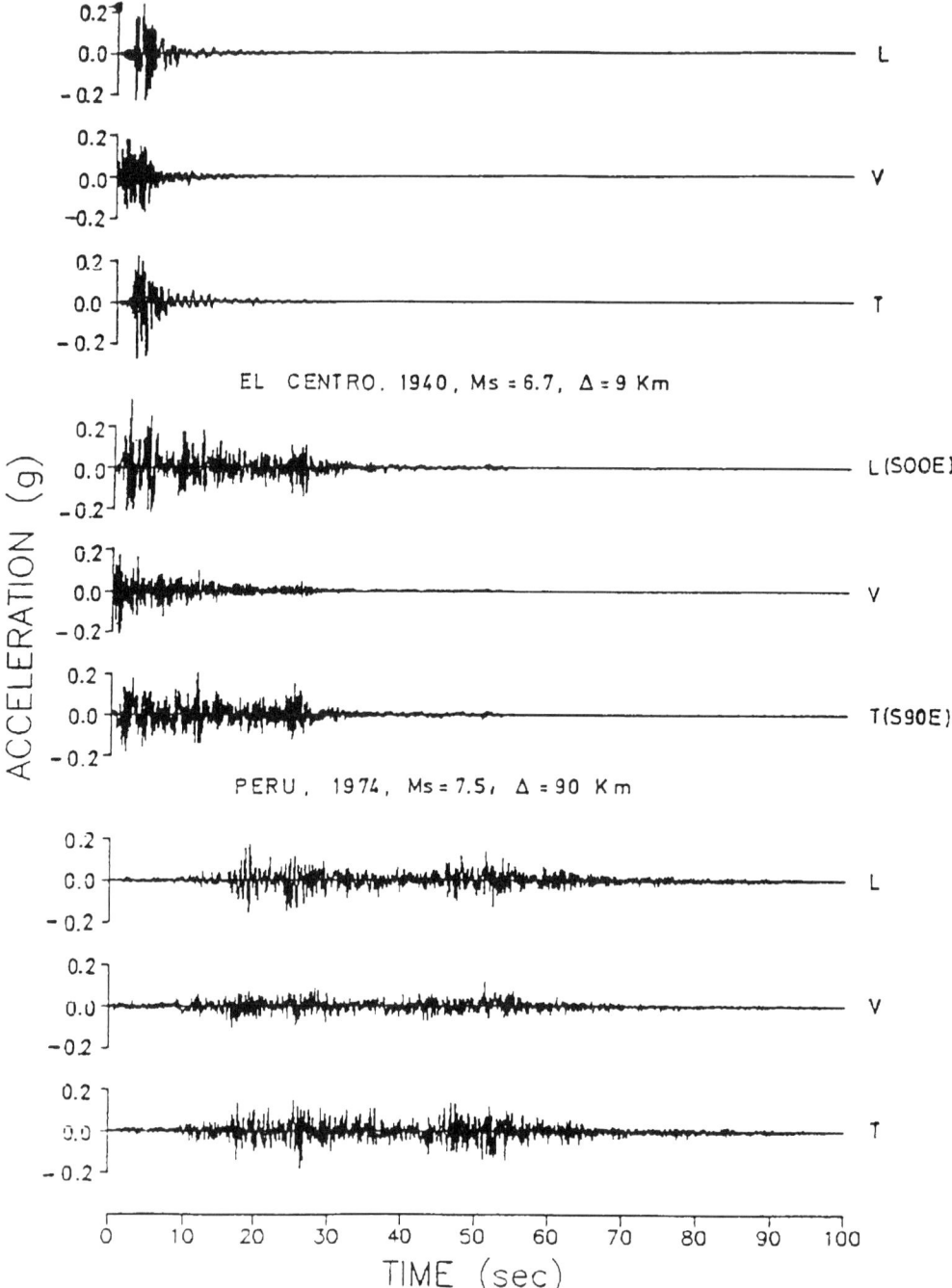

Figure 1b. The set of 3-component accelerograms representative of the Apollo Temple site exposure to earthquakes. All registrations are plotted on the same acceleration–time scale.

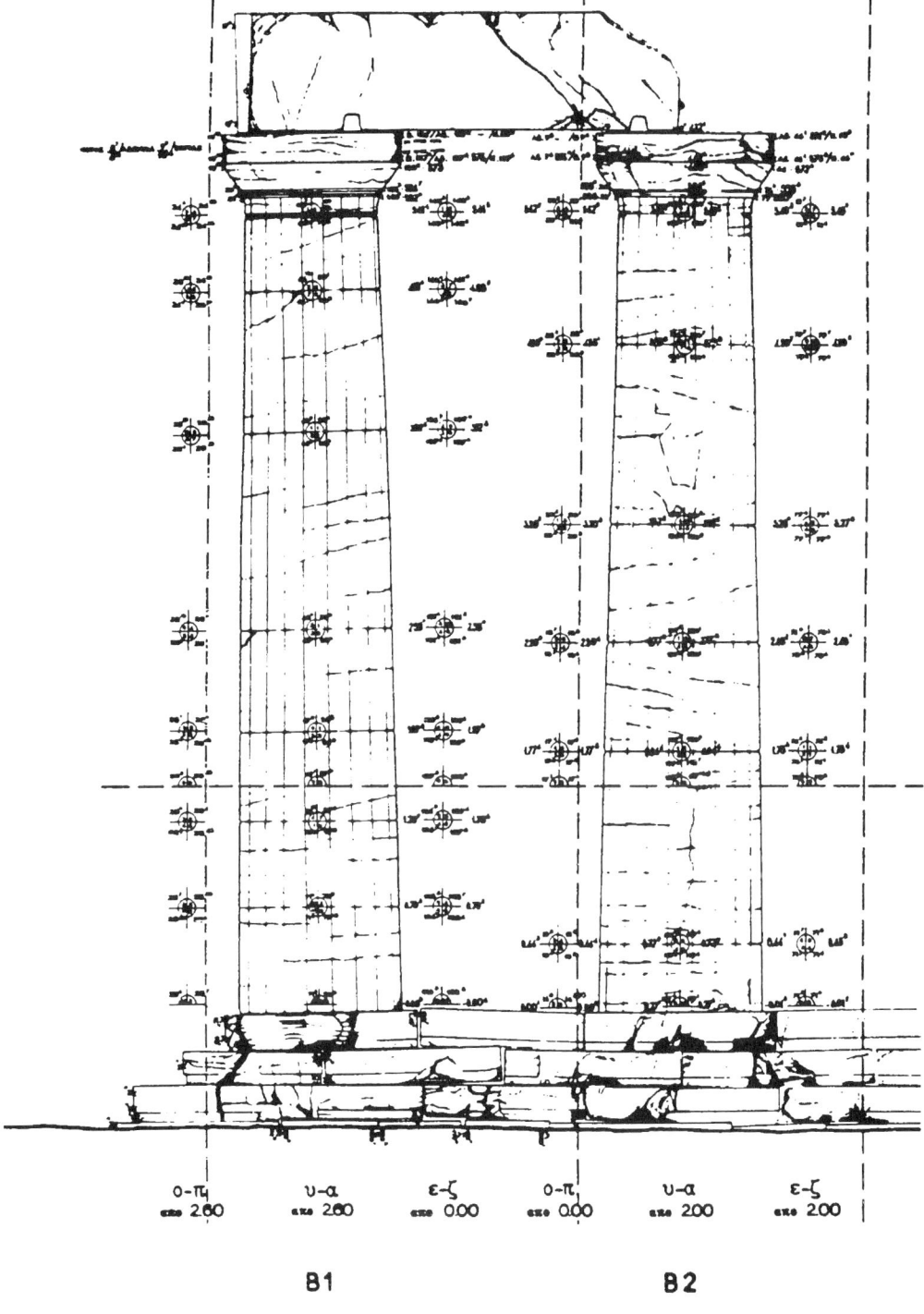

Figure 2. Detailed drawing (Archive, C.P.T.A.E.) of the part of the Apollo Temple that was modelled numerically.

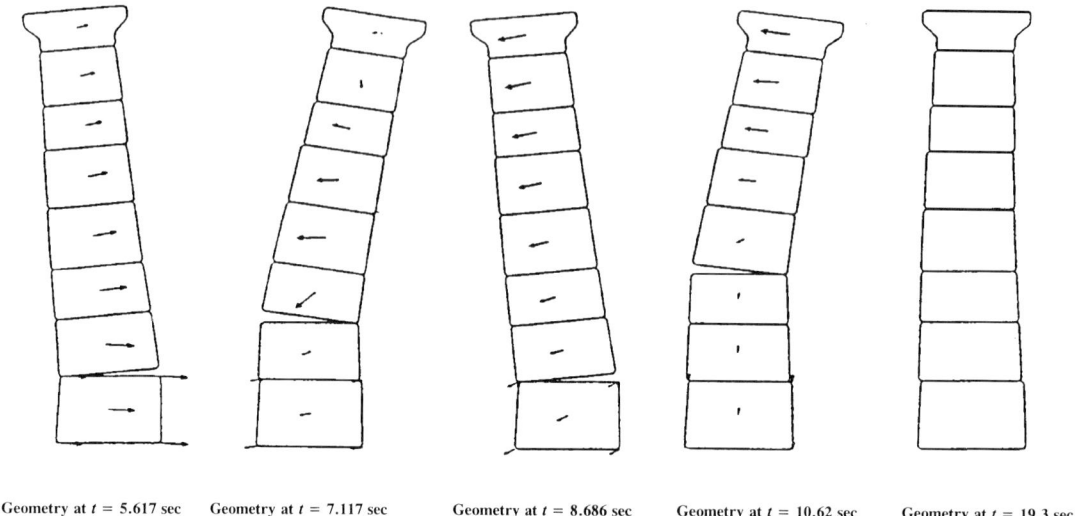

Geometry at $t = 5.617$ sec   Geometry at $t = 7.117$ sec   Geometry at $t = 8.686$ sec   Geometry at $t = 10.62$ sec   Geometry at $t = 19.3$ sec

a.

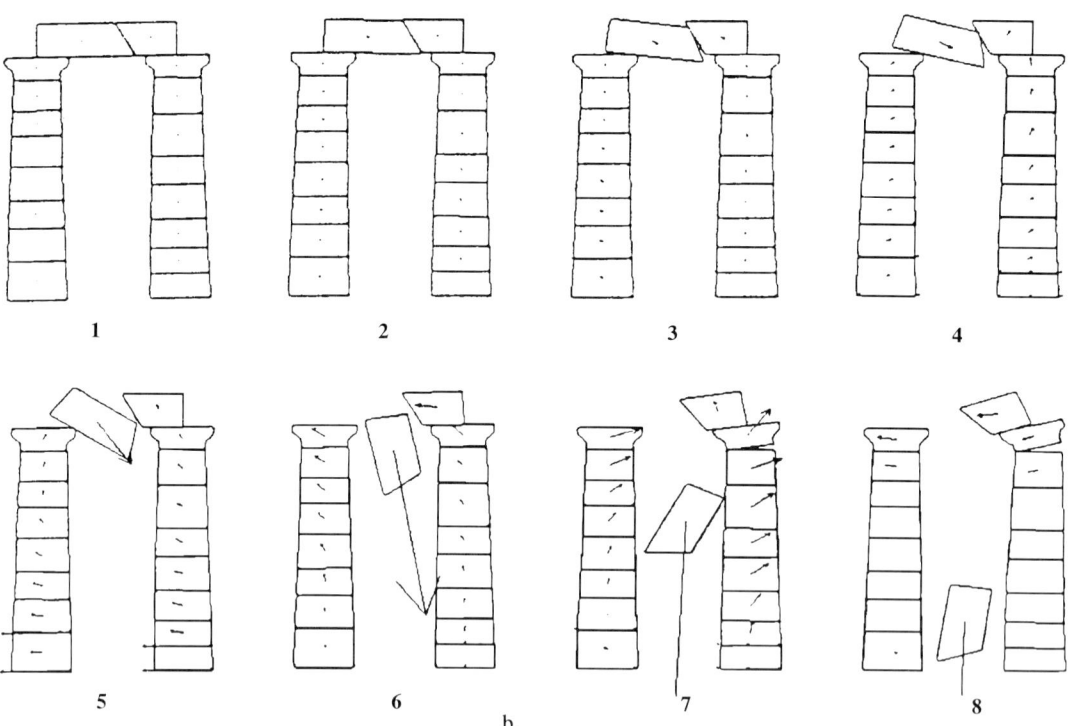

b.

Figure 3. Snapshots from the numerical analysis of:
  (a) A single column subjected to 5 times the Kalamata registration.
  (b) A two-column/beam system subjected to the Kalamata record. In this case the unscaled accelerogram was sufficient
    to fail the already faulted beam.

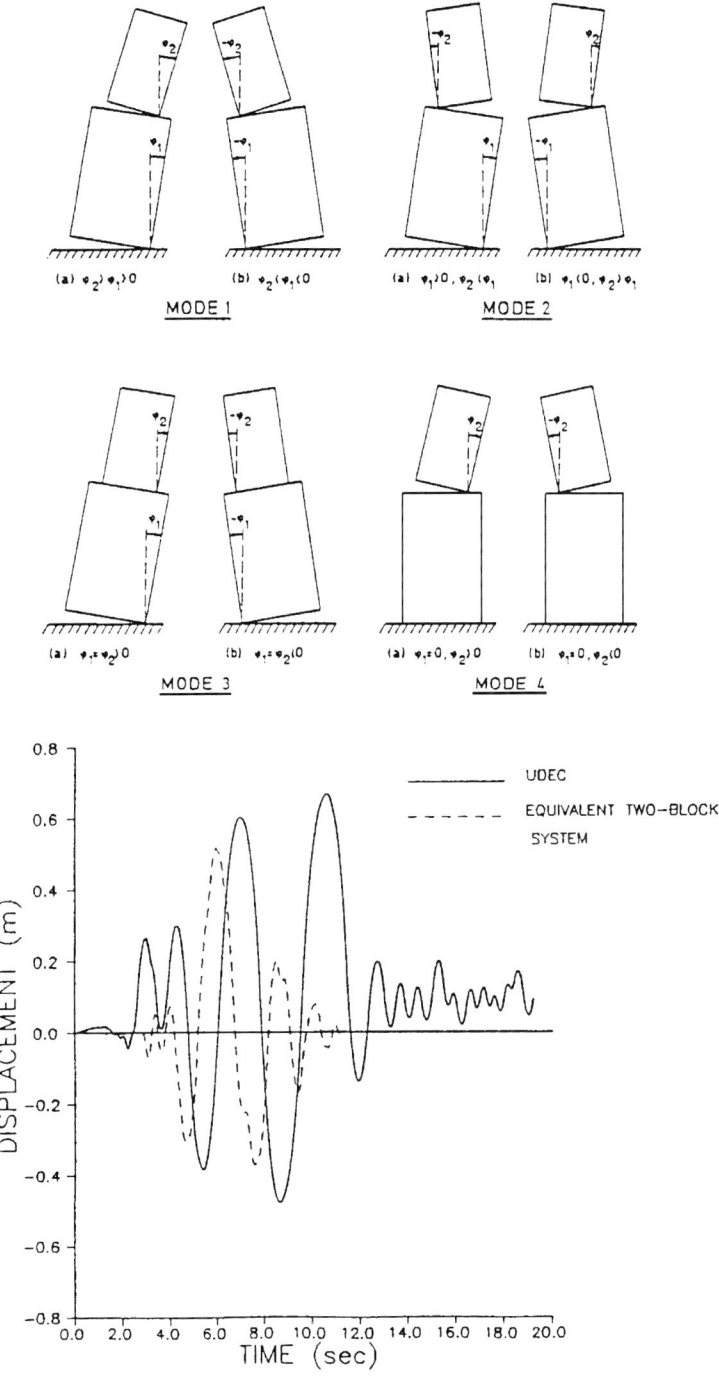

Figure 4. Vibration 'models' of a two-block rocking system and comparison of its analytical response with the UDEC numerical analysis. The time-history shows the top displacement for ground excitation 5-times the Kalamata registration.

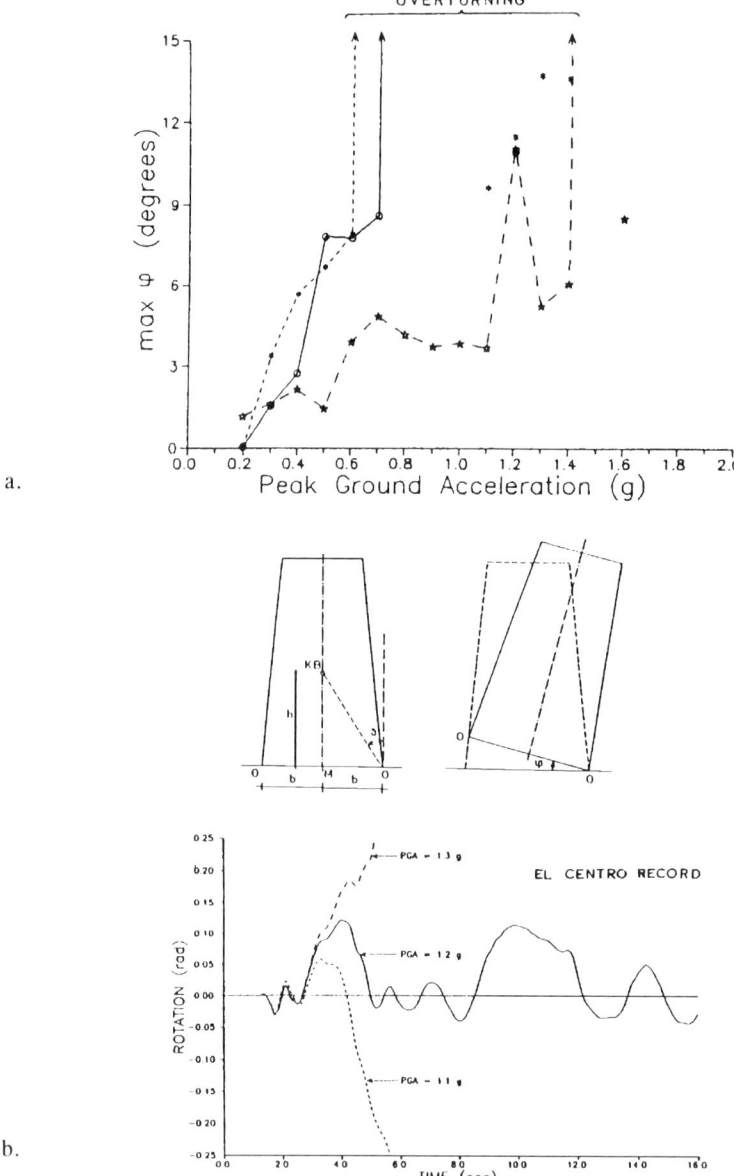

Figure 5. Maximum rotation of the monotholithic typical column subjected to the three earthquake records of Figure 1b after scaling w.r.t. the peak acceleration. The strongly non-linear nature of this response is illustrated with the time history of the rotation of the column subjected to three different scalings of the El Centro ground motion; the column did not fall at the intermediate scaling value of 1.2g.

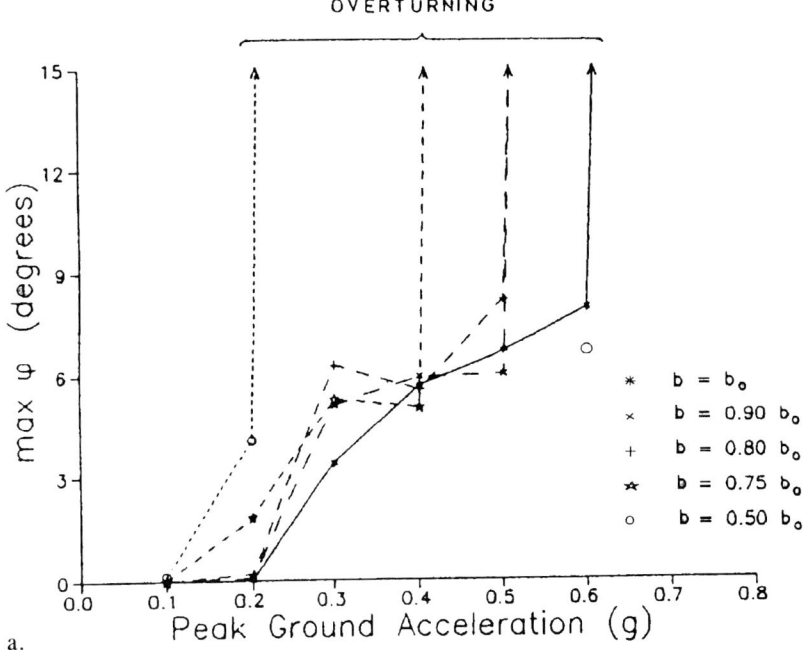

a.

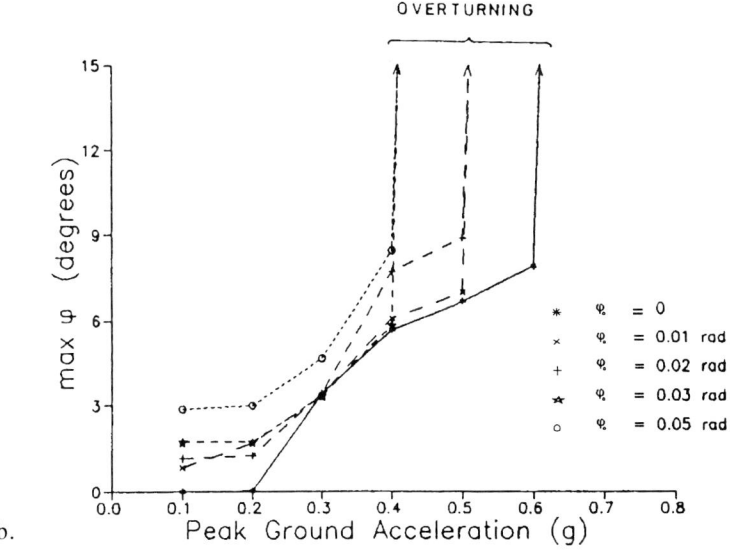

b.

Figure 6. Response of the monolithic column to the scaled Kalamata record:
(a) With reduced base of the column,
(b) With initial tilt of the column.

properties. It then keeps track, in real time during ground shaking, of the position of each block ensuring compatibility of the interacting neighbouring blocks. The motion of individual blocks is general: full sliding and rotational components. The program is written in Lagrangean formulation and can follow large displacements leading to collapse mechanisms.

Detailed drawings of the monument are available to specify the geometry of the numerical model (Fig. 2, C.P.T.A.E., 1986). Material properties of the building stone are being assessed in the laboratory; in the numerical analysis general properties were assumed from the literature.

A limited number of runs were conducted to demonstrate the capabilities of the 2-D program. Two geometries were considered: a free standing column and a two column-beam system. The analysis was carried out for the scaled combination of the Kalamata horizontal (pga = 0.24 g & 0.27 g) and vertical (pga = 0.22 g) components (pga represents percentage of the value of the gravity acceleration g).

The results of the free column analysis are shown on Fig. 3a for five times the Kalamata record at various times. The column sections were modelled accurately. As indicated by the velocity vectors, the bottom section was modelled as an elastic block, whereas the remaining sections were taken as rigid blocks. For the large deformations inflicted by the strong ground shaking this assumption does not alter the results substantially. Rocking occurred at the second and third sections, whereas the snapshot at rest (19.3 sec) shows that the bottom sections of the column have moved out. This deformation is hard to explain with another mechanism and when found in the field provides evidence of strong earthquake motion in the past. Such deformation exists on sections of the Apollo Temple.

The results of the two column-beam system are shown on Fig. 3b for the unscaled Kalamata record. In this case an imperfection was introduced to the beam that led to an early collapse mechanism. This example demonstrates the large deformation capability of the program. Note the falling part of the beam hitting the right column, as indicated by the velocity vectors.

Theoretical Predictions

For simplified geometries of the free standing column, theoretical predictions are possible (Psycharis & Jennings, 1983; Psycharis, 1990). We employed such predictions to gain an understanding of the deformation mechanism and to perform some parametric studies.

Fig. 3 suggests that a two-block model would suffice to describe the response of the column. The possible vibrations of a two-block rocking model are shown on Fig. 4 where also the theoretical prediction is compared with the numerical results. The comparison is surprisingly good, particularly if one takes into account that the theoretical model takes only rotations and horizontal ground motion.

The simple monolithic rigid block (Fig. 5) offers itself to useful parametric studies. A limited set of such studies is illustrated on Figs 5 and 6. Fig. 5 shows the instability threshold of a perfect column subjected to an horizontal component of the ground motions shown on Fig. 1b. The results are plotted with respect to the scaled peak ground acceleration and show the same instability level, at around 0.6 g, for the Kalamata and the El Centro records but a higher level (around 1.4 g) for the Lima record. This high value may indicate that peak ground acceleration is not representative of the damageability of the record. It is worth noticing that the column does not fall for pga's over the stability threshold. This is further illustrated on Fig. 5 for the scaled El Centro record: at 1.1g the column falls on one side, at 1.2 g the column does not fall whereas at 1.3 g the column falls on the other side.

Fig. 6 shows the response of imperfect columns. The imperfections are evident on the drawing of Fig. 2: reduced width of the base and initial tilt of the column. These types of imperfection are the two main problems of the monument in its present condition, namely deterioration of the building stones and of the foundation material. Reduction of the base to half the width (Fig. 6a) brings the stability threshold down to 0.2 g whereas an initial tilt (Fig. 6b) of 0.05 rads (about 3°) reduces the stability threshold to 0.4 g.

Discussion

The numerical analysis of perfect sections of the existing monument showed substantial resistance to strong ground motions. This resistance is achieved with internal dissipation of energy through large deformations of the building blocks. For a perfect section such deformations can occur without impairing its stability. For imperfect sections, however, the stability threshold is substantially lowered. Two such imperfections are typical deterioration effects for the Temple of Apollo: deterioration of the building stones and of the foundation material. Even in an intact part of the monument such imperfections may occur during shaking. The analysis presented here is very preliminary and any conclusions are deemed to be tentative. A valid conclusion, however, is that powerful numerical tools are available for the dynamic analysis of deformations induced on friction-cohesion structures. These tools can have a two-fold application: in the field of the restoration of ancient monuments and in the field of experimental archaeology.

For the restoration of monuments it is important to understand the dynamic response of the structure in seismic areas. This is essential for sensible protective measures as well as for testing such measures. Moreover, a numerical analysis is the only feasible approach: the analysis of the simple rigid block has demonstrated that scaling laws, a prerequisite of shaking table testing, do not apply to friction-cohesion structures, let alone the interaction with their foundations. However, confidence in the proper use of the numerical tools can be gained through numerical simulations of shaking table models.

In experimental archaeology, hypotheses on seismic damage can be numerically tested. Such documentation of the past of ancient structures would help to reconstruct the history of their environments e.g., the recent tectonic record. For example, the 1930 Salmas earthquake in N.W. Iran was caused by strike-slip on a fault (Berberian & Tchalenko, 1976). The fault crosses a cemetery, where the fault slip was of the order of 4 m, and induced a deformation field in the cemetery tombstones; this field has been partially recorded and constitutes a unique case, even in modern instrumentation terms, of recordings within $70 \times 40\,m^2$ across the fault.

Acknowledgements

We are grateful to the Committee for the Preservation of the Temple of Apollo Epikourios for financial support and encouragement. Our thanks are cordially extended to Mr K. Papantonopoulos for his help in formulating the problem and keeping the ancient structure in focus. The UDEC runs were performed by Itasca Inc., Minneapolis.

References

Ambraseys, N. N. & Jackson, J. A. (1990). Seismicity and associated strain of Central Greece between 1890 and 1988. *Geophys. J. Int.* **101**, 663–708.

Andronopoulos, B., Tzitziras, A. & Koukis, G. (1988). Engineering geological investigations in the area of Apollo Epicurios Temple at Phigalia (Peloponnese, Greece). In (G. Marinos & G. Koukis, Eds) *Proc. Intern. Symp. Eng. Geol. of Ancient Works, Monuments and Historical Sites*, 479–486. Rotterdam; Balkema.

Beloyiannis, N., Theoulakis, P. & Haralambidis, L. (1988). Causes and mechanism of stone alteration at the Temple of Apollo Epicurios at Bassai, Greece. In (G. Marinos & G. Koukis, Eds) *Proc. Intern. Symp. Eng. Geol. of Ancient Works, Monuments and Historical Sites,* 763–769. Rotterdam; Balkema.

Berberian, M. & Tchalenko, J. S., (1976). Field study and documentation of the 1930 Salmas (Shapur-Azarbaidjan) earthquake: In Contribution to the Seismotectonics of Iran, Geol. Survey of Iran, Rpt No. 39, Part II: 271–342.

C.P.T.A.E.(1986). *The temple of Apollo Epicourios at Vassae. Committee for the Preservation of the Temple of Apollo Epicourios.* Athens; Ministry of Culture.

Cundall, P. A. (1971). A Computer Model for simulating progressive large-scale movements in blocky rock systems. *Proc. Symp. of the Internat. Soc. of Rock Mechanics* (Nancy, France) **1**, paper II–8.

Cundall, P. A. & Hart, R. D. (1983). *Development of Generalised 2-D and 3-D Distinct Element Programs for Modeling Jointed Rock.* Technical Report prepared by Itasca Consulting Group Inc. for the U.S. Army Engineers.

Galanopoulos, A. G. (1941). Das riesenbeben der Messenischen Kuste vom 27 August 1886. *Prakt. Akadem. Athenon* **16**, 127–134.

Lyon-Caen, H., Armijo, R., Drakopoulos, J., Baskoutas, J., Delibassis, N., Gaulon, R., Kouskouna, V., Latoussakis, J., Makropoulos, K., Papadimitriou, P., Papanastassiou, D. & Pedotti, G. (1988). The 1986 Kalamata (S Peloponesse) earthquake: Detailed study of a normal fault and tectonic implications. *J. Geophys. Res.* **93**, 14967–15000.

Papastamatiou, D., Psycharis, I. & Elias, D. (1990). *An approach to the earthquake problem of the Temple of Apollo in S. Peloponnese, Greece.* Report to the Greek Ministry of Culture. (In Greek).

Psycharis, I. N. (1990). Dynamic behaviour of rocking two-block assemblies. *Earthquake Eng. Struct. Dyn.* **19**, 555–575.

Psycharis, I. N. & Jenning, P. C. (1983). Rocking of slender rigid bodies allowed to uplift. *Earthquake Eng. Struct. Dyn.* **11**, 57–76.

Theoulakis, P., Kouzeli, K. & Kilicoglou B. (1988). Provenance of the building material of the Temple of Apollo Epicurios at Bassai, Greece. In (G. Marinos & Koukis, Eds) *Proc. Intern. Symp. Eng. Geol. of Ancient Works; Monuments and Historical Sites*, 661–669. Rotterdam: Balkema.

Uplift of Ancient Greek Coastal Sites: Study Methods and Results

Paolo Antonio Pirazzoli

CNRS, Laboratoire de Géographie Physique,
1 Place Aristide Briand, 92190 Meudon-Bellevue, France

Abstract

Marks of coastal uplift can be recognized from various kinds of indicators (geomorphological, marine, archaeological). Certain indicators, or a cluster of converging evidence, may even suggest that uplift movements occurred in some cases very rapidly, or even suddenly at the time of a great earthquake. Examples of inferred seismic uplift which took place during historical times are briefly reported from Euboea Island, western Crete and Seleucia (Seleukeia) Pieria.

Introduction

Most archaeological remains give no evidence on how far from sea level they were constructed. In only a few cases is it possible to specify whether ancient sites have subsided or have uplifted since the time they were inhabited. An uplifted site on dry land is usually hard to distinguish from a site which was constructed at a higher elevation or further inland. In certain cases, however, the occurrence of elevated marine marks on the remains, or elevation inconsistencies in artifacts which had clearly been intended for use close to sea level, may reveal that a change in the relative sea level did happen. In other cases an uplift movement may be suggested by nearby geomorphological or bioconstructed features (elevated notches, benches, beachrocks, beach deposits, marine incrustations, *Lithophaga* holes, etc.), which may sometimes provide a way to obtain radiometric estimations of the emersion date.

In this paper, after a brief presentation of the most significant geomorphological, archaeological and marine biological indicators of rapid vertical movements in coastal areas, a few case studies of uplifted sites will be reviewed.

Geomorphological indicators

An uplift movement affecting a coastal region will generally leave many elevated depositional and erosional marks. Depositional indicators will include elements such as elevated beach deposits (sometimes in the form of beachrocks), littoral bars, lagoon or estuary floors and emerged marine deposits. Such elevated depositional units can be useful for estimating the amount of vertical displacement, but usually provide little information on the rate of the tectonic deformation.

Erosional marks of former sea levels will appear clearly on recently uplifted limestone coasts, especially where the tidal range is small and the site sheltered. They will include notches, benches, pools, sea-caves and other typical inter-tidal features. Elevated tidal notches will provide the most precise indications, their retreat point corresponding closely to a former mean sea level position. In addition, the shape of representative notch

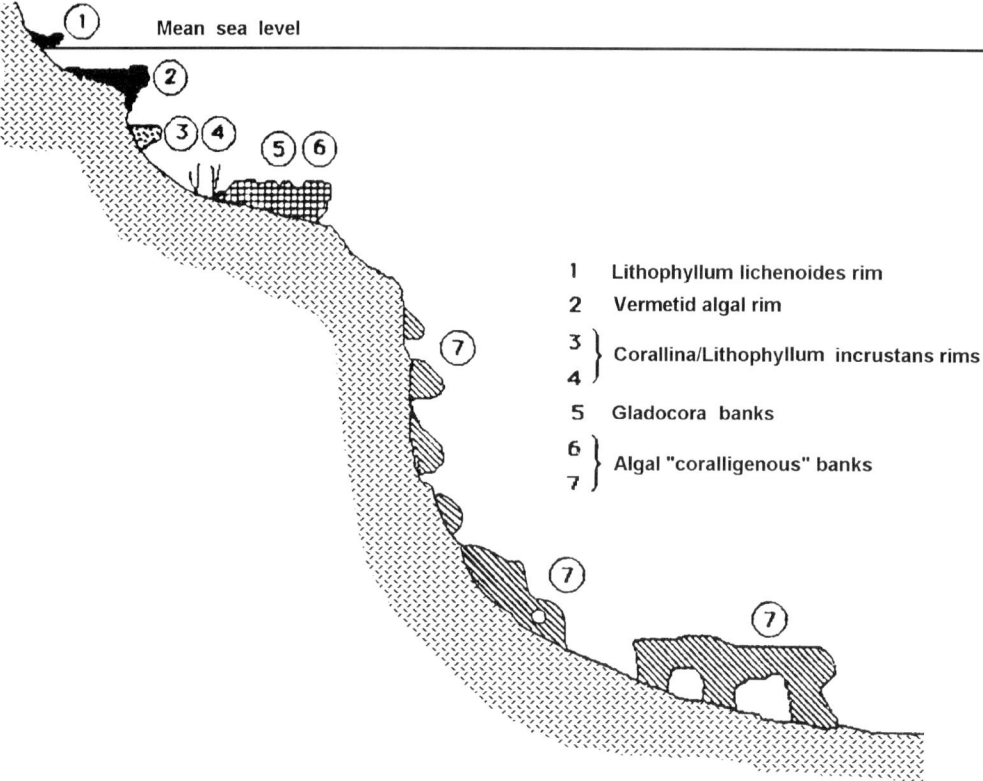

Figure 1. Zonation of some forms of Mediterranean biogenic constructions (from Laborel 1987, Fig. 1).

profiles may provide qualitative indications on the approximate duration of the period of relative sea-level stability preceding the uplift, and even on the speed of the relative sea-level change (Pirazzoli, 1986a).

Archaeological Indicators

Among archaeological remains, the most useful are obviously those implying specific activities closely related to the sea (sailing, fishing, boatbuilding, salt production, shell gathering, etc.). Two main categories can be distinguished: (1) those which must have been located near a shoreline and, according to their use, must have remained emerged or submerged, and (2) those belonging to structures partly underwater and depending for their use on tidal fluctuations and marine conditions.

Very precise indications are often provided by remains of the second category, which enable margins of uncertainty in relative sea-level change to be estimated, e.g. from slipways, certain harbour constructions, and especially fish tanks (Pirazzoli, 1976; 1988). Archaeological remains can provide not only very precise dates of the time they were in use, but also in some cases bear evidence of the occurrence of catastrophic events (Stiros, 1988; Di Vita, 1990).

Marine Biological Indicators

On rocky coasts, uplift movements will leave many kinds of marine biogenic constructions exposed, some of which are clearly related to former sea-level positions (Fig. 1). In the Mediterranean, where the tidal range is generally of decimetric order, the rim constructed by *Lithophyllum lichenoides*, frequently found in the surf zone slightly above sea level, is the highest biogenic building. Just below this level, near the uppermost limit of the sub-littoral zone, the vermetid *Dendropoma petraeum* and/or the coralline alga *Neogoniolithon notarisi* develop in marine incrustations, which may form a continuous rim projecting at sea level from cliffs, or a veneer capping the outer part of erosional benches, or even in pools and micro-atoll shapes. Less frequent than the preceding bioconstructions, biogenic rims built by *Corallina* or by *Lithophyllum incrustans* are less precise sea-level indicators, since they can be found from just below sea level down to several metres deep. Biogenic rims are often hard and resistant to erosion. Once uplifted, they may be preserved for a relatively long time.

In the northern Aegean Sea, where cold winter winds and currents limit the development of reef builders, biogenic constructions are usually absent. Here traces of erosion left by biodestructors, e.g. the upper limit of *Lithophaga* perforations, can provide very reliable sea-level information (Fig. 2). Fossil biogenic remains are often reliable material for radiocarbon dating. With the accelerator mass spectrometry (AMS) technique, even very small samples can be used to obtain radiometric dates.

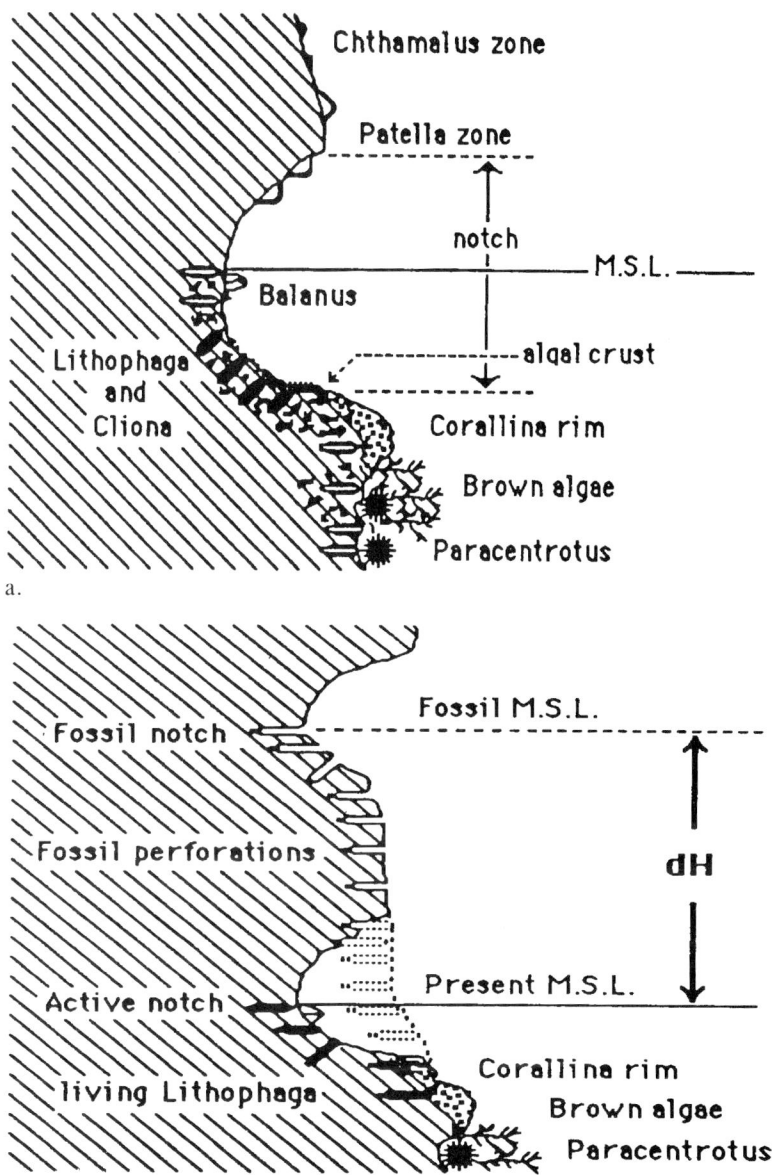

Figure 2(a). Typical profile of biological zonation on hard limestone coasts. (b). Measurement of the difference in level dH between the present sea level and a former elevated sea level using *Lithophaga* burrows (from Stiros *et al.*, 1992, Fig. 4).

Evidence of Rapid Uplift

Sudden vertical movements occurring at the time of a great earthquake (co-seismic) may be different from, or even opposite to, gradual movements occurring slightly before (pre-seismic) or after (post-seismic) the earthquake, or during the period between two major earthquakes (inter-seismic).

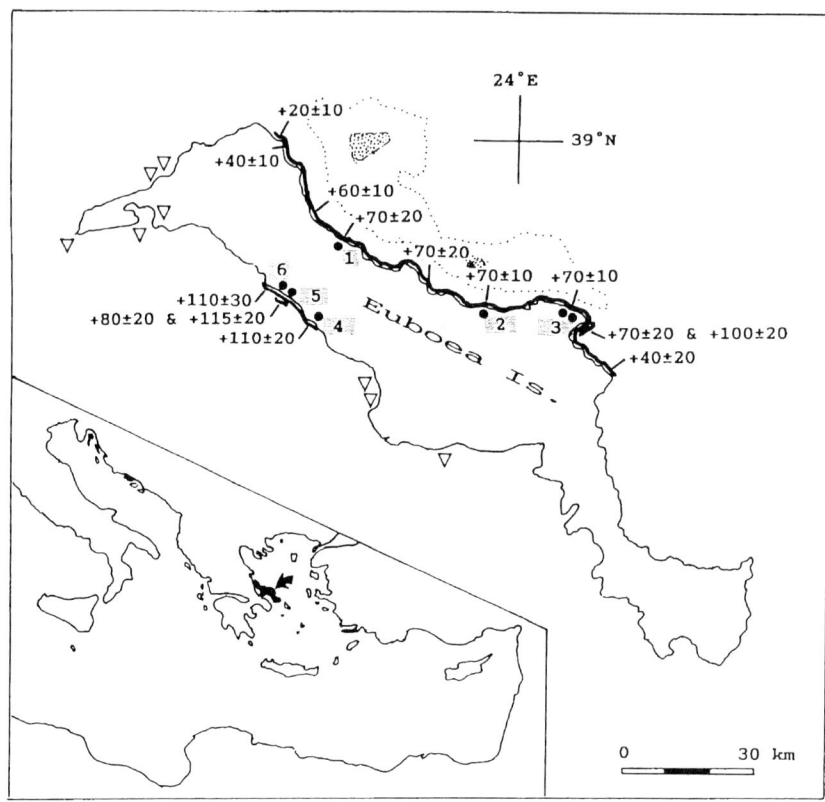

Figure 3. Location of late Holocene crustal displacements observed in Euboea Island. Heavy line: occurrence of a single elevated shoreline; double heavy line: two superimposed elevated notches; the amount of present-day emergence is indicated in centimetres; filled circles: locations of dated samples (8 samples from 6 locations); open triangles: locations of submerged archaeological remains. A submerged escarpment existing N-E of the island is indicated by the –400 m bathymetry (dotted line) and two zones deeper than –1000 m (dotted areas). (From Stiros *et al.*, 1992).

The fact that a certain vertical displacement took place in a very short period of time is not always easy to demonstrate. Geomorphological indicators alone (stepped erosional benches or depositional platforms) may lead to ambiguous interpretations, since the effects of an instantaneous movement cannot always be distinguished from the effects of events lasting for decades or even for a few centuries. To be fully convincing, the interpretation of a movement as co-seismic should therefore include clear evidence (biological, stratigraphical, archaeological, historical, etc.), or at least a cluster of converging indications, suggesting that the displacement could have taken place only in a very brief space of time.

For example, preservation of *Lithophaga* shells inside fossil burrows is generally indicative of a very rapid change in sea level, since in the case of a slow uplift (of the order of mm/yr or even of cm/yr) these fragile remains would have been altered and destroyed within a few years by mid-littoral bioerosion, which is generally considered as being about 1 mm/yr at least (Torunski, 1979). Among the published evidence of very rapid, probably sudden uplift movements, the most convincing is probably that reported from western Crete, where very fragile *Bryozoan* skeletons were found in an almost perfect state of preservation in raised sea caves (Thommeret *et al.*, 1981, Fig. 8).

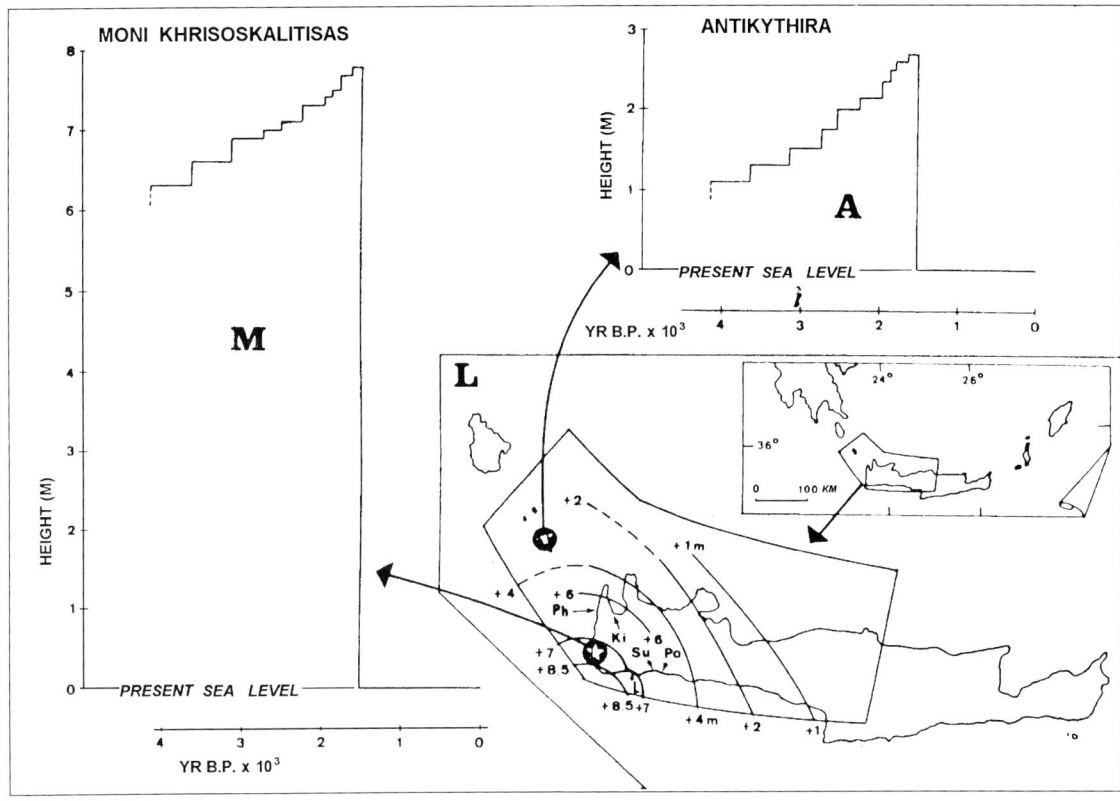

Figure 4. Tentative boundaries of the lithosphere block about 200 km long which was uplifted and tilted in the Hellenic
Arc in AD 365, with elevation contours of the upheaval measured in metres; Ki = Kisamos, Ph = Phalasarna, L =
Lissos, Su = Suia, Po = Poecilassus. M = late Holocene relative sea-level variations at Moni Khrisoskalitisas (south-
western Crete). A: relative sea-level variations in Antikythira island. (From Pirazzoli, 1986b).

Case Studies

Three examples of co-seismic displacements having uplifted coastal areas are briefly reported in Euboea Island,
western Crete, and the Seleucia (Seleukeia) Pieria area.

Euboea

On the northeastern coast of Euboea Island, late Holocene uplift is indicated by a nearly continuous exposed
notch and by perforations of *Lithophaga*, which testify to an almost uniform relative sea-level drop of about
0.7 m along a distance of almost 70 km. On the side of the Gulf of Euboea, uplift was about 1 m over a distance
of *c*. 20 km. In at least two places, remnants of a second, probably slightly older notch a few decimetres higher
are preserved (Fig. 3). The shape of the notch profiles suggests that emergence occurred in two steps, and each
time was relatively rapid. Further evidence is given by the occasional occurrence of *Lithophaga* shells, still
in growth position, preserved inside their burrow in spite of the very close proximity of a regular wave-action
zone.

AMS radiocarbon dating of eight samples of *Lithophaga* shell fragments collected on the Euboea coasts has enabled Stiros *et al*. (1992) to ascribe the elevated marks to two upward co-seismic movements, which occurred during the periods 1050–900 BC and 510–380 BC respectively. The submergence date of various archaeological remains which can be observed in various parts of the island (Fig. 3), as much as 2 m deep, is not known.

Western Crete and Antikythira

The sequence of vertical movements which have taken place in the western part of Crete and in Antikythira over the last few thousand years are known in detail, owing to a series of emerged, superimposed shorelines, some of them intersecting archaeological sites, which have been identified and dated (Thommeret *et al*., 1981; Pirazzoli *et al*., 1981, 1982). They correspond to the most spectacular tectonic movements which have occurred in the Mediterranean during historical times: a series of small, probably sudden subsidence movements, between about 4000 and 1700 years ago, followed by a strong uplift movement, accompanied by northeastward tilting, which had an almost rigid effect on a huge lithospheric block about 200 km long (Fig. 4). The largest vertical displacement (about 9 m) has been measured near the S-W corner of Crete, suggesting that the epicentre of the corresponding earthquake was located near the Hellenic Trench, off this corner. According to the most recent data available, this earthquake occurred on 21 July AD 365 (Pirazzoli *et al*., 1992).

Elevated shorelines in Crete and Antikythira are easily recognizable from a great variety of geomorphological and biological evidence, supported by several dozen consistent radiocarbon dates (Laborel *et al*., 1979; Thommeret *et al*., 1981; Pirazzoli *et al*., 1981, 1982; Kelletat & Zimmermann, 1991). The sites of several ancient Cretan harbours mentioned by historical sources (Poecilassus, Suia, Lissos, Phalasarna, Kisamos) can be seen today on completely dry land (Fig. 4), where traces of raised shorelines are often marked on structures cut by man into the rock. In Antikythira, a slipway cut into the limestone ends abruptly at about 1.5 m above sea level (Flemming & Pirazzoli, 1981). At Phalasarna, where the harbour cited by Strabo, Dionysius Calliphontis, Ptolemy and the Stadiasmus had in fact been destroyed and abandoned in the first century BC (Hadjidaki, 1988; Frost, 1989), Pirazzoli *et al*. (1992) have recognized not only traces of co-seismic displacements, but also deposits left by two tsunami waves, probably corresponding to events which occurred in AD 66 and AD 365 respectively.

Seleucia Pieria

Geomorphological surveys in the area of the ancient harbour of Antioch in Turkey have revealed the existence of elevated marine notches and biogenic rims formed by vermetids, oysters and calcareous algae, giving evidence of two rapid land uplift movements, probably of co-seismic origin. The first uplift, which took place *c*. 2500 years ago, caused a vertical displacement of about 1.7 m. The second uplift, which can be ascribed to the great earthquake of May AD 526, was accompanied by a 0.7 to 0.8 m upheaval (Pirazzoli *et al*., 1991). The latter movement caused a rapid silting of the Seleucia Pieria closed harbour basin and entrances, thus preventing its further use (Erol & Pirazzoli, 1992).

Conclusions

Palaeoseismicity is a recent, but rapidly developing field for research. Early pioneer studies on vertical seismic displacements, generally isolated, have been reported from Japan (Sugimura & Naruse, 1954, 1955; Yoshikawa, 1970; Yonekura, 1972), the Lebanon (Fevret & Sanlaville, 1965), New Zealand (Wellman, 1967), Alaska (Plafker & Rubin, 1967), Chile (Kaizuka *et al*., 1973) and from a few other areas.

In seismic regions with a long history, like the Mediterranean, a critical approach to historical records of earthquakes has been proposed by Ambraseys (1971). Today, the number of scholars working on palaeoseimicity is large enough to justify the recent creation of an international project of the Inter-Union Commission on the Lithosphere devoted to the study of great Holocene earthquakes.

In tectonically active coastal areas, marks left by ancient shorelines can provide very useful data concerning the approximate age, distribution and succession of vertical displacements and the limits between lithospheric blocks of different tectonic behaviour. They can also lead to an estimation of the recurrence interval of major earthquakes. The eastern Mediterranean, where several crustal plates come into contact with each other, implying strong seismic and tectonic activity, is an especially favourable area for paleoseismic studies. The fact that the tidal range is generally very small, increases accuracy when determining former sea-level positions and hence vertical co-seismic displacements. The great number of classical sites which have been affected by great earthquakes during their long history can only increase the possibilities of accurate correlations.

Only a few case studies of uplifted sites have been mentioned above; a few other sites are being studied. The scientific potential is enormous however, especially in Greece, and most of the work remains to be done.

Acknowledgements

Parts of the research results summarized here have been funded by the Commission of European Communities 'EPOCH' Programme (contract No. CP90–0015) and by the 'Coopération Scientifique et Technique Franco-Hellènique'. This is also a contribution to the Working Group 'Palaeoseismicity of the Late Holocene' of the Inter-Union Commission on the Lithosphere, to the IGCP Project No. 274 ('Coastal evolution in the Quaternary') and to the INQUA Neotectonic Commission. Ms M. Delahaye has kindly revised the English.

References

Ambraseys, N. N. (1971). Value of historical records of earthquakes. *Nature* **232**, 375–379.

Di Vita, A. (1990). Sismi, urbanistica e cronologia assoluta: terremoti e urbanistica nelle città di Tripolitania fra il I secolo A.C. e il IV D.C. In: *L'Afrique dans l'Occident Romain. Collect. Ecole Franç. Rome* **134**, 423–494.

Erol, O. & Pirazzoli, P. A. (1992). Seleucia Pieria: an ancient harbour submitted to two successive uplifts. *Int. J. Naut. Archaeology* **21**(4), 317–327.

Fevret, M. & Sanlaville, P. (1965). Contribution à l'étude du littoral libanais. *Méditerranée* **6**, 113–134.

Flemming, N. C. & Pirazzoli, P. A. (1981). Archéologie des côtes de la Crète. In: *Hist. Archéol.*, Dossiers 50, 66–81.

Frost, F. J. (1989). The last days of Phalasarna. *Ancient Historical Bull.* **3**, 15–18.

Hadjidaki, E. (1988). Preliminary report of excavations at the harbor of Phalasarna in west Crete. *Am. J. Archaeology* **92**, 463–479.

Kaizuka, S., Matsuda, T., Nogami, M. & Yonekura, N. (1973). Quaternary tectonic and recent seismic crustal movements in the Arauco Peninsula and its environs, central Chile. *Geogr. Rep. Tokyo Metrop. Univ.* 8, 1–49.

Kelletat, D. & Zimmermann, L. (1991). Verbreitung und Formtypen rezenter und subrezenter organischer Gesteinsbildungen an den Küsten Kretas. *Essener Geogr. Arb.* **23**, 168.

Laborel, J., Pirazzoli, P., Thommeret, J. & Thommeret, Y. (1979). Holocene raised shorelines in western Crete. In *Proceedings International Symposium on Coastal Evolution in the Quaternary*, 475–501. Sao Paulo.

Laborel, J. (1987). Marine biogenic constructions in the Mediterranean. *Sci. Rep. Port-Cros Natl. Park, Fr.* 13, 97–126.

Pirazzoli, P. A. (1976). Sea level variations in the northwest Mediterranean during Roman times. *Science* **194**, 519–521.

Pirazzoli, P. A. (1986a). Marine notches. In (O. van de Plassche, Ed.) *Sea-Level Research: A Manual for the Collection and Evaluation of Data,* 361–400. Norwich; GeoBooks.

Pirazzoli, P. A. (1986b). The early Byzantine tectonic paroxysm. *Z. Geomorphol., Suppl.* **62**, 31–49.

Pirazzoli, P. A. (1988). Sea-level changes and crustal movements in the Hellenic arc (Greece). The contribution of archaeological and historical data. BAR Int. Ser., **404**: 157–184.

Pirazzoli, P.A., Thommeret, J., Thommeret, Y., Laborel, J. & Montaggioni, L. F. (1981). Les rivages émergés d'Antikythira (Cerigotto): corrélations avec la Crète occidentale et implications cinématiques et géodynamiques. In: *Actes du Colloque 'Niveaux Marins et Tectonique Quaternaire dans l'Aire Méditerranéenne'.* CNRS et Univ. Paris I, 49–65.

Pirazzoli, P.A., Thommeret, J., Thommeret, Y., Laborel, J. & Montaggioni, L. F. (1982). Crustal block movements from Holocene shorelines: Crete and Antikythira (Greece). *Tectonophysics* **86**, 27–43.

Pirazzoli, P.A., Laborel, J., Saliège, J. F., Erol, O., Kayan, I. & Person, A. (1991). Holocene raised shorelines on the Hatay coasts (Turkey): palaeoecological and tectonic implications. *Marine Geology* **96**, 295–311.

Pirazzoli, P.A., Ausseil-Badie, J., Giresse, P., Hadjidaki, E. & Arnold, M. (1992). Historical environmental changes at Phalasarna harbor, west Crete. *Geoarchaeology* **7**, 371–392.

Plafker, G. & Rubin, M. (1967). Vertical tectonic displacements in south-central Alaska during and prior to the great 1964 Earthquake. *J. Geosci. Osaka City Univ.* **10**, 53–66.

Stiros, S. (1988). Archaeology — A tool to study active tectonics. *Eos,* December 13, 1638–1639.

Stiros, S. C., Arnold, M., Pirazzoli, P.A., Laborel, J., Laborel, F. & Papageorgiou, S. (1992). Historical coseismic uplift in Euboea Island (Greece). *Earth Planet. Sci. Lett.* **108**, 109–117.

Sugimura, A. & Naruse, Y. (1954, 1955). Changes in sea level, seismic upheavals, and coastal terraces in the southern Kantô region, Japan (I) (II). *Japanese J. Geol. Geogr.* **24**, 101–113; **26**, 165–176.

Thommeret, Y., Thommeret, J., Laborel, J., Montaggioni L. F. & Pirazzoli, P. A. (1981). Late Holocene shoreline changes and seismo-tectonic displacements in western Crete. *Z. Geomorphol.,* Suppl. 40, 127–149.

Torunski, H., 1979. Biological erosion and its significance for the morphogenesis of limestone coasts and for nearshore sedimentation (Northern Adriatic). *Senckenbergiana Marit.* **11**, 193–265.

Wellman, H. W. (1967). Tilted marine beach ridges at Cape Turakirae, New Zealand. *J. Geosci. Osaka City Univ.* **10**, 123–129.

Yonekura, N. (1972). A review on seismic crustal deformations in and near Japan. *Bull. Dep. Geogr. Univ. Tokyo* **4**, 17–50.

Yoshikawa, T. (1970). On the relations between Quaternary tectonic movement and seismic crustal deformation in Japan. *Bull. Dep. Geogr. Univ. Tokyo* **2**, 1–24.

Prehistoric Earthquakes and their Consequences, as Preserved in Holocene Sediments from Volos and Argos, Greece

Eberhard Zangger

Department of Earth Sciences, Cambridge University,
Downing Street, Cambridge CB2 3EQ, U.K.

Examination of Holocene deposits in auger cores and construction trenches provides clues for tectonic movements in prehistory (Zangger, 1991). One auger core traverse between Neolithic Dimini and the present coast of **Volos** in Central Greece revealed, firstly, that the sea used to extend *c.* 2.5 km farther inland extending almost to the site of ancient Dimini. Secondly, the Holocene stratigraphy indicated a subsidence of the central plain of 3.1 m due to block tectonic movements. The Gulf of Volos has been notorious for earthquakes at least during the last few centuries (Schneider 1968, 72; Papazachos *et al.,* 1983). Most of these are attributable to offsets along a major E-W striking normal fault stretching from Volos to Velestinon. Another normal fault, however, runs parallel to the first one on the southern side of the Gulf of Volos from Pevkakia-Magoula to Paliouri (Ferrière, 1982); this fault was crossed by the auger core traverse shown in Fig. 1. The displacement of Holocene deposits occurred in two steps: the first one resulted in 1.7 m subsidence before 3000 BP; the second movement of 1.4 m must have occurred *c.* 1000 years ago (Fig. 2). The core stratigraphy provides no hints that would indicate whether these displacements happened suddenly, in which case they would have been accompanied by earthquakes, or whether they took place in the form of slow creep which is also known from Greece (Billiris *et al.*, 1991). Since Volos, however, constitutes one of the most earthquake-prone regions in Europe, these offsets as recorded in the Holocene sediments were most likely accompanied by strong earthquakes in prehistoric and historic times.

In the **Argive Plain** in southern Greece, earthquake damage has been recognized in archaeological excavations at Mycenae, Tiryns and Midea, but no quakes are reported in historic records. Once again, auger cores from the coastal plain provide evidence for active tectonic movement in the form of uplift of the Arcadian mountains on the western side of the Argolid. The main fault extends N-S from Argos to Lerna; its offshore continuation has been detected during a marine shallow-seismic survey of the Gulf of Argos (van Andel *et al.*, 1990). The fault displaced the Pleistocene red beds at the bottom of the stratigraphy as well as a superimposed Early Bronze Age alluvium (Fig. 3). Movement rates amounted to 2.5 m in 5000 years averaging 0.5 m per 1000 years (Finke 1988, 103). This observation was confirmed by a pipeline construction trench, 1.5 km long and 6 m deep. In this exposure, the displacement of the Early Bronze Age alluvium, sandwiched between two layers of lacustrine deposits from ancient Lake Lerna, turned out to be more complex than recognizable in auger cores. The offset, though very pronounced in the schematic core cross sections, is hardly discernible by just looking at an outcrop without using instruments. The steep angle of the faults in Figs 1–4 results from 40–50x vertical exaggeration.

Finally, on the opposite side of the Argive Plain, around Tiryns, an unusual ephemeral flood was found in the Holocene stratigraphy which accumulated up to 5 m of alluvium, especially E of Tiryns. This flood would

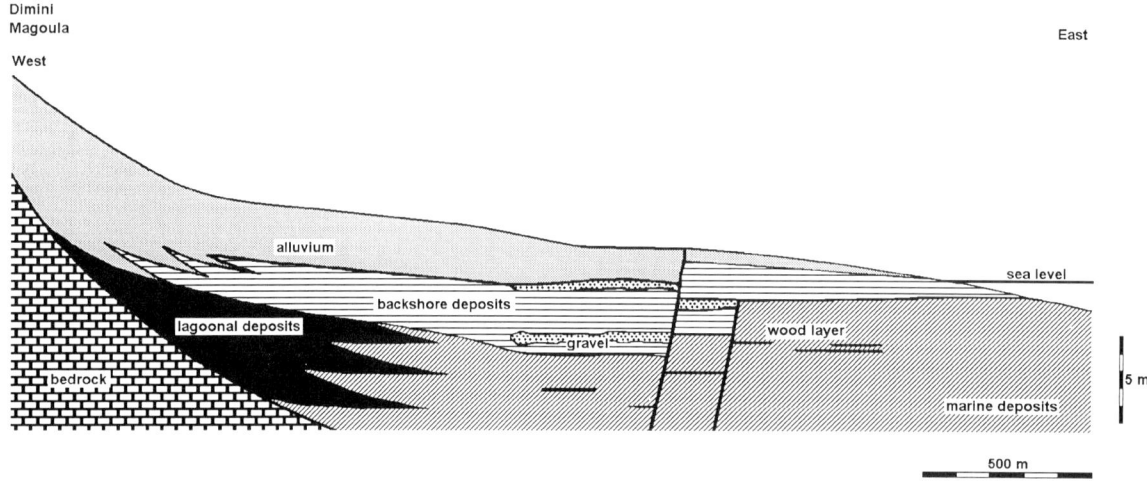

Figure 1. Auger core section across the floodplain of Volos. The bottom layer consists of fine-grained reduced marine deposits extending to the base of Dimini, where they develop a lagoonal character (clay-rich, grey color, abundant organic material). The marine mud is covered by silty backshore deposits and floodplain alluvium laid down by ephemeral stream floods. A normal fault can be seen in the profile, displacing the deposits, including a gravel layer and a wood layer.

have occurred 'simultaneously', that is given an error margin of *c.* 30 years for LH III pottery dating, with an earthquake around 1200 BC, as detected in archaeological excavations. But there are no indications for considerable tectonic displacement on this side of the Argive Plain. An Eu-Tyrrhenian beach-conglomerate including shells of *Strombus bubonius,* and thus dating to the last interglacial sea level maximum at *c.* 115,000 BP, is exposed on the northern side of Nauplion at 2 m above present sea level, precisely at the elevation where it must have been deposited. Similar results were obtained from power holes drilled on the eastern side of the Argive Plain. Thus, this area seems to have been tectonically stable at least for the last 100,000 years. Nevertheless, the Bronze Age sites could, of course, have been damaged during an earthquake which accompanied movement along the fault on the western side of the plain. Even in that case one would still need to determine how the earthquake could have caused an ephemeral flood. It may have triggered a landslide, rendering loose material for further downstream transport by a perennial river. On the other hand, the Mycenaean dam E of Tiryns, built in its present form after the flash flood, may have had a predecessor that collapsed during the earthquake at 1200 BC.

References

Billiris, H., Paradissis, D., Veis, G., England, P., Featherstone, W., Parsons, B., Cross, P., Rands, P., Rayson, M., Sellers, P., Ashkenazi, V., Davison, M., Jackson, J. & Ambraseys, N. (1991). Geodetic determination of tectonic deformation in central Greece from 1900 to 1988. *Nature* **350**, 124–129.

Ferrière, J. (1982). Paléogéographies et tectoniques superposées dans les Hellénides internes: les massifs de l' Othrys et du Pelion (Grèce continentale). *Soc. Géol. du Nord*, Publication 8.

Finke, E. (1988). *Landscape Evolution of the Argive Plain (Greece): Paleoecology, Holocene Depositional History and Coastline Changes.* PhD dissertation, Stanford University. Michigan; University Microfilm International, Ann Arbor.

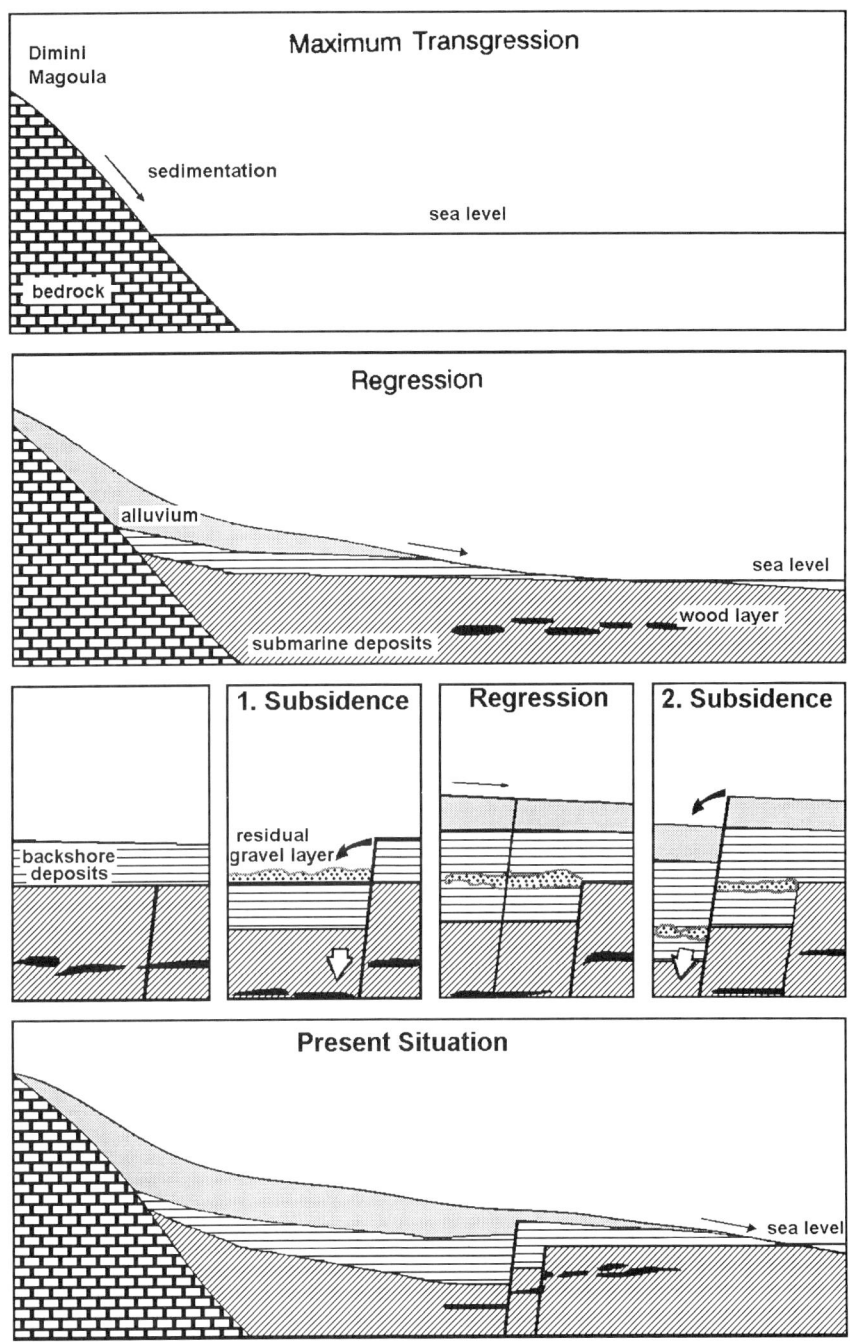

Figure 2. Depositional history of Dimini Bay. During the maximum transgression in the Neolithic, the sea stretched landward to Dimini. Soil erosion and redeposition caused a swift regression. When the first subsidence took place, the marine mud was already covered by back-shore deposits. The regression continued after the faulting. During the second subsidence a residual gravel layer originating from the first off-set and the floodplain alluvium was displaced (after Finke, 1984).

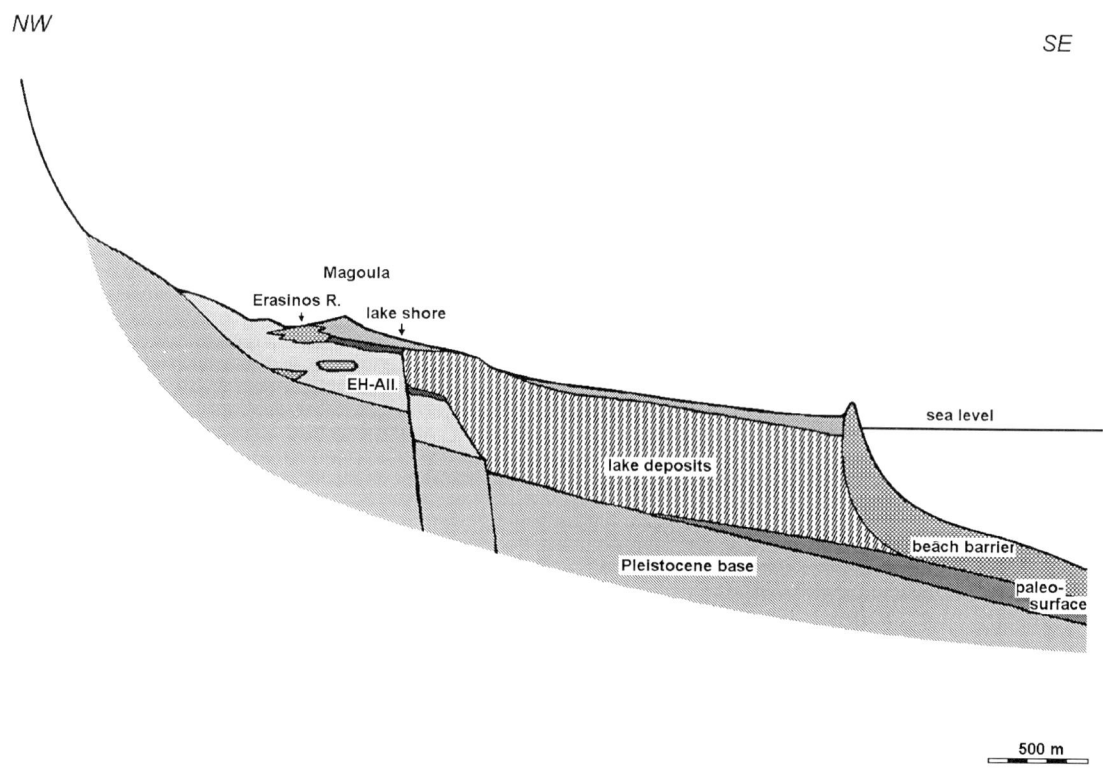

Figure 3. Section through Holocene and Pleistocene sediments between Magoula and the sea in the Argive plain. A
Pleistocene paleosol occurs at the bottom of all cores and at the surface west of the section. On the seaward side of the
profile a paleo-surface (A horizon) is preserved on top of the Pleistocene base. The existence of Lake Lerna is
represented by thick and extensive lacustrine deposits. The lake was separated from the open sea by a beach barrier.
Only limited alluviations occurring in the Early Bronze Age were found in this traverse (EH–All.). Paleo-A-horizon
(dark layer on top of EH–All.) indicates landscape stability.

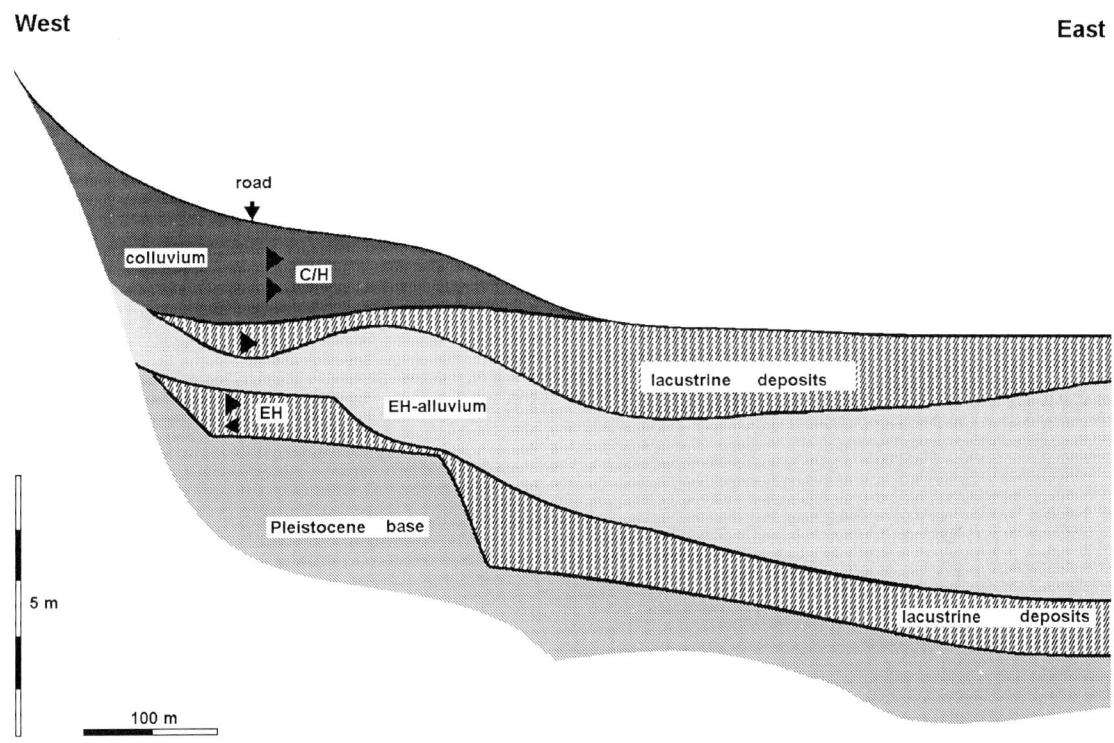

West **East**

colluvium

road

C/H

EH

EH-alluvium

lacustrine deposits

Pleistocene base

lacustrine deposits

5 m

100 m

Figure 4. An exceptionally large trench (1.5 km long, 6 m deep) provided the opportunity to verify the auger core data in the Argive plain. At the base is a Pleistocene paleosol covered by dark gray lacustrine deposits belonging to the Lernaean Lake and containing Early Helladic I sherds. Subsequently, alluvium dated by the presence of many Early Helladic II sherds filled the lake. It is covered in turn with another lacustrine layer indicating a second lake stage. The final layer is a colluvial deposit containing many dispersed Classical and Hellenistic sherds. A Classical house (C/H) was found in this colluvium about 1 m under the main road to Argos. The complex stratigraphy in this trench is assumed to represent an uplift of the mountain ranges in the west relative to the coastal plain. It should be noted, however, that the vertical scale is *c.* 40x exaggerated; the displacement of the Pleistocene base is, in reality, much shallower.

Papazachos, B. C., Panagiotopoulos, D. G., Tsapanos, T. M., Mountrakis, D. M. & Dimopoulos, G. Ch. (1983). A study of the 1980 summer seismic sequence in the Magnesia region of Central Greece. *Geophys. J. Royal Astron. Soc.* **75**, 155–168.

Schneider, H. E. (1968). Zur quartärgeologischen Entwicklungsgeschichte Thessaliens (Griechenland). *Beiträge zur ur- und frühgeschichtlichen Archäologie des Mittelmeerraumes* **6**, 1–127.

van Andel, Tj. H., Zangger, E. & Perissoratis, C. (1990). Late Quaternary History of the Gulf of Argos, Greece: Soil Horizons and Transgressive/Regressive Cycles. *Quaternary Research* **34**, 317–329.

Zangger, E. (1991). Prehistoric Coastal Environments in Greece: The Vanished Landscapes of Dimini Bay and Lake Lerna. *J. Field Archaeology* **18** (1), 1–15.

APPENDIX

Thoughts on the Perception of the Earthquake
in Greek Antiquity

Lazaros C. Polimenakos

19, Esperou Str., GR 175 61 Palaeo Phalero, Greece

'Φύσις κρύπτεσθαι φιλεί'
Heraclitus

This paper attempts to bring together many of the facts associated with the perception of the earthquake as a natural phenomenon in both the classical and preclassical eras as echoed in Greek mythology. The information presented here is not new. The purpose is to identify and emphasise those elements that are related to the generation and occurrence of earthquakes in an attempt to understand their impact on ancient Greek society as well as society's attitude towards them.

Pre-Homeric times[1]

During this period the entity of Poseidon is dominant in the consideration of physical phenomena. In spite of the common view that he is only associated with the sea, he actually appears to play a much wider role during pre-Homeric times. Until the establishment of the olympian religion, Poseidon together with his brother deities, Zeus and Hades, are in authority over the world.[2]

The older and basic quality of Poseidon as master of the earth and husband of Γαία (not exactly the Earth since this is referred to as 'χθών') is expressed by the terms 'γαιάƒοχος' (earth-shaker) and 'γαιήοχος' (earth-holder: one who embraces the earth). This comes from the reference to Poseidon in Minoan-Mycenaean scripts as well as Hesiodic and especially Homeric texts. In the linear B tablets Poseidon appears as 'Εννοσίδας (Ενοσίγαιος)' and 'γαιάƒοχος', both meaning he who shake/move the earth).[3] A related tradition mentions that the area of Delphi was initially owned partially by Poseidon and Gaea, supporting the etymology of Poseidon's name as being 'πόσις' (spouse) of the 'δα' (earth), hence husband-master of Gaea (**EM**: Poseidon). Throughout *The Iliad* and *The Odyssey* as well as Hesiod's works, Poseidon is continuously referred to as 'χθών, ενοσίγαιος' and 'γαιήοχος'; there are only a few instances where Poseidon is attributed bynames associated with the sea '(κυανοχαίτης and ταράσσων πόντον he who shakes the sea)'.[4] Moreover, reference

---

[1] Pre-homeric time is defined in the present work as the time preceding the events described by Homer in *The Iliad*. Homeric and post-homeric times are defined accordingly.

[2] Homer, *The Iliad* **15**, 184–205. Pauly-Wyssowa *Real Enzyklopedie* (**RE**) and *Hellenic Mythology* (**EM**), *The Gods* (Ed. Athinon): Poseidon.

[3] See **RE**, Erdbebenforschung; also the information from the tablets of Pylos: N.Masouridis, *Linear B* (Ekd. Filon 1989) 131; Ventris & Chadwick, *Documents in Mycenaean Greek* (1956); and M. Gerard-Rousseau, Les mentions religieuses, *Incun. Graeca* **XXIX** 1968.

[4] See Homer, *The Iliad*, ch. 7, 8, 13, 14, 15, 20, 21, esp. 13:10–135; 15:184–205 and 20:54–70. *The Odyssey* ch. 1, 5, 6, 9, 13. Hesiod, *Works and Days*, *Theogony*, *Heoiai*, *Shield of Heracles*, *Epic Circle*, *Homeric Hymns* (Loeb Classical Library); also, in **RE**: Poseidon, 15).

is made to earthquakes characterised by a motion of the sea, implying the existence of seismic sea waves felt in the sea as well as on the coast. Consider, for example, the following: 'πάντες δ' εσσείοντο πόδες πολυπίδακος Ἰδις και κορυφαί, Τρώων δε πόλις και νήες Αχαίων' ... there were shaken all the foothills of Ida which has many springs, the city of Trojans and the Achaean ships (*Iliad* **20**, 59-60; also *Iliad* **14**, 392; **21**, 387 and *Odyssey* **5**, 366).

A very revealing reference to the nature of Poseidon appears in the Orfic Hymns. Poseidon, the child of Rea and Kronos, is called: Ποσειδάον γαιήοχε, κυανοχαίτα, ἱππιε ... αλίδουπε, βαρύκτυπος, εννοσίγαιε ... ειναλίοις ροίζοισι τινάσσων αλμυρόν ύδωρ, έδρανα γης σώζοις ... Poseidon, you who hold the earth, dark-haired, horse like ... who shake the sea, who heavy shatter, who shake the earth ... and with sea whistles the salt water high throw, saves the earth's foundations).[5] From the following references to Rea and Kronos, it appears that they express Earth and Time respectively: '... (Ρέα), Κρόνου σύλλεκτρε μάκαιρα ...μήτηρ μεν τε θεών δε θνητών ανθρώπων, εκ σου γάρ γαία και ουρανός ευρύς ύπερθεν και πόντος, πνοαί τε' ... (Rea) happy wife of Kronos ... mother of the gods and the mortal human beings; from you comes the earth and the broad sky and the sea as well as wind (Orfic Hymn n.14 to Rea); '... κόλποισιν αφράστοις δεξαμένη γενεήν επί πάν προχέει τροχάουσαν' ... since in you accepted, you give birth, transform, while in a rapid moving state);[6] '... αιώνος Κρόνε παγγενέτωρ, ... -γέννα, φυής μείωσι, Ρέας πόσι' ... Kronos, father and generator of time, you are the cause of birth — the beginning — and death of nature, husband of Rea ... (Orfic Hymn n. 13 to Kronos)[7].

Poseidon is worshipped both on land and coastal areas. The site names Αιγαί and Ελίκη, which refer to more than one place in Greece, represent Poseidon's places of residence according to Homeric texts.[8] Most probably these two sites were affected by large earthquakes. The bynames 'ασφάλειος' (protector of buildings), 'ελελίχθων' (unifier of the earth's interior), 'σεισίχθων, εννοσίγαιος' (shaker of the earth's interior) are characteristic of the attitude of the people living in those areas, against the earthquake[9]. Places bearing names related to Poseidon (sons, daughters, beloved persons etc.) as well as worship venues [10] might well indicate areas of high seismicity during antiquity. These characters are thought to resemble one or more of the several attributes of Poseidon's nature, originating from an effort to interpret phenomena of the natural environment in a broad or local scale; the latter appears to be associated with tales of 'cruel' sons of Poseidon

---

[5] Orfic Hymn n.17 to Poseidon; see I Passas, *The Orfics* (Athens 1981); also **RE**: Poseidon, 14 and 15-21.

[6] Orfic Abstracts, *Francixus Patricius Discussion Peripatetica* 3, 5, 326, XXXIV.

[7] This aspect, apart from the clarity in expression and its poetic sense, is of interest today since there are strong indications that phenomena occurring either at the surface of the earth or beneath it (earthquakes, volcanoes, atmospheric disturbances) are due to processes taking place in the interior of the earth. However, these processes seem to be determined from the 'position' of the Earth in planetary space and especially its movement which, on the other hand, represents a change in the state of the earth with respect to time (see also Lambeck & Hopgood, *Geoph. Journal Royal Astron. Soc.* (London), 1982). This is taken further by the fact that in Hesiod's 'Θεογονία' Poseidon holds the Titans imprisoned in the Tartara: this can mean that Poseidon guarantees the order of the natural world (**EM**: Poseidon), thereby being master of the evolution of natural processes. See also **RE**, Poseidon: 14 and 21.

[8] See Homeric Hymns, hymn n.22 to Poseidon; *Homer Epigrammata*, VI, and in various passages in *The Iliad* and *The Odyssey*, Loeb Classical Library.

[9] See **RE** and **EM**: Poseidon.

[10] In the following, I would like to quote names associated with Poseidon (**RE**: Poseidon, 10-13, 17, 30):

a. Worship venues (adjective): Arkadia, Athens, Sparta, Gythio, Thera, Helike (γαιήοχος), Lesbos, Efessos, Delfi (σεισίχθων), Athens, Kilikia, Tenos, Rhodes, Syros, Thera, Arkadia, Ephessus Megalopolis, Kyzikos (ασφάλειος).

b. Sons-daughters: Avderos, Athos, Almops, Astakos, Asopos, Delfos, Dyrrachios, Helieus, Thassos, Thesseus, Ialyssos, Kamiros, Kenchrias, Leches, Lindos, Megareus, Myton, Nauplios, Parnassos, Polyphemos, Selinous Televoas, Hyperenor, Phaeax, Pthios, Phoenix, Chios, Astypalaia, Kalaureia, Lamia, Rode, Torone.

c. Beloved persons of Poseidon, from: Thraki, Pleuron, Troezen, Rhodes, Boeotia, Eleusis, Argos.

d. Quarrels with other deities (place): Athena (Athens, Troezen, Thebes), Hera (Argos), Apollo (Delfi), Zeus (Aegina), Dionysos (Naxos), Helios (Akrokorinthos).

(e.g. Sarpedon, Skyron Prokroustis) (see also **EM**: Poseidon). From this discussion, it is suggested that Poseidon was not simply master of Gaea-earth and earthquakes: he incorporates the result of a transformation of the state of the earth with respect to time; he presumably expresses the driving force of all processes which occur either in the interior of the earth or at its surface: earthquakes, volcanoes, atmospheric disturbances and possible climatological alterations among them. On the other hand, the ability of Poseidon to disturb the sea can either reflect an atmospheric disturbance (gale) or even the effect of seismic sea waves (tsunamis) which usually accompany large earthquakes in the Aegean and Ionian Seas.

However, the respect with which Poseidon was held declined gradually. His worship retreats in a local and regional sense: he quarrels with other deities over the patronage of areas traditionally associated with him. These areas should have been, or were located near to, areas of high seismicity. The following comment comes from **EM** (Poseidon): 'The confinement of Poseidon to the sea comes in the end of the evolution of his nature and restricts his reputation of the pre-olympian religion, ..., where his worship appears to compete ... the worship of Zeus ... The above is clearly evident ... in the distribution of the authority over the world into provinces ... and in local, rural and worship traditions showing Poseidon as losing his authority over beloved or disputed places, after arguing with other deities ...', as in the case of the quarrel with Athena for the guardianship of Athens.[11]

Post-Homeric times

The main source of information is Ionia whose philosophers must have given thought to the nature of earthquakes. For many of them, υγρόν (liquid) or υδατώδες ον (watered being) were their main cause. The motion of a liquid layer, on which the ground lies, is responsible for the occurrence of earthquakes, according to Thales: '... εφ᾽ ύδατος κείσθαι (την γην) ...' (the earth) resting on the water (Thales, in Hermann Diels, *Die Fragmente der Vorsokratiker* **77**, 36).

Epicouros suggests that '...υπό πάχους αέρος του υποκειμένου υδατώδους όντος ανακρουομένην αυτήν (την γην) και οίον υποτυπτομένην κινείσθαι; ενδέχεσθαι δε και σηραγγώδη τοις ανωτέρω μέρεσι καθεστώσαν υπό του διασπειρομένου πνεύματος εις τας αντραειδείς κοιλότητας εμπίπτοντας σαλεύεσθαι ... ' it is possible that the earth is being shaken by the dense air, which underlay a watered being, and while she is being shattered by it in her interiors, she moves. It is then possible that the earth, the upper part of which is full of pores, is being shaken by the incoming spirit (Hermann Usener, *Epicurea*, 350).

The Stoics refer to a 'being with the properties of water' which, being in motion and exhaling, causes earthquakes: '... σεισμός εστί το εν γη υγρόν εις αέρα διακρινόμενον και εκπίπτον ...; το ύδωρ ... συνεχές ταυτώ (e.g. the earth) παντελώς υπάρχειν αυτό ...' the earthquake is the liquid analysed in the earth and transforms into another state of lower quality. The water ... is continuous within the earth and exists everywhere therein (Chryssippos in: Ioannis ab Arnim, *Stoicorum Veterum Fragmenta* VII).

Demokritos informs us that the earth is 'πλήρης ύδατος' (full of water) and she '... τούτου κινείσθαι ...' gets in motion because of it. That this water is regarded as being transformable (Demokritos, in H. Diels *op. cit.*) suggests that rather than being the liquid we know as water is instead some different liquid material inside the earth, possessing all of the properties mentioned.[12] This information, however abstract, provides us with the image of a medium on which the earth lies and which brings the earth under motion, causing earthquakes. Moreover, following Epicouros, this motion is induced by a motion of 'πνεύμα' (spirit) through a porous body beneath the earth (the ground).

---

[11] See **RE**: Poseidon, 28, 29; D. Kyskyras, The contribution of mythology and archaeology in seismology, *Bull. Geol. Soc. Greece* **XVIII** (1986) 5–15, in greek; E. Simon, *Die Goetter der Griechen* (Hirmer 1969) 70.

[12] We could consider them, especially Epicouros, as the first to introduce the concept of the asthenosphere, a body in the state of a dense liquid of very high temperature on which the lithosphere lies.

The predecessors of Aristotle, Anaximandros, Anaximenis, Anaxagoras and his pupil, Archelaos, think of the 'πνεύμα' as being the cause, either in a cold or warm state. It enters subterranean cavities and during its effort to exit causes earthquakes. On the other hand, Antiphon refers to a subsurface fire as being responsible for the generation of earthquakes: ' (το πύρ) καίον γαρ την γήν και συντήκον γρυπάνιον ποιεί ... σείεσθαι την γην παλλομένην' [(the fire) burns the earth and melting it forms a swell ... shaking the (trembling) earth]. In general, Aristotle's predecessors consider as a generating cause the energy produced by physico-chemical processes regarding the 'υδατώδες'. Seneca refers to two anonymous thinkers who expand on the idea of the subsurface fire introducing the 'πνεύμα' which, here, originates from the high temperature of subterranean waters; then, as it exhales, causes the earthquakes as well as volcanic eruptions (see Seneca, *Natur. Question.* VI; **RE**: Erdbebenforschung and; H.Diels, *op. cit.*, the related lemmata).

Aristotle states that ' ... (ο σεισμός) μεν γαρ εν τη γη την αρχήν έχει' ... (the quake) has its origin inside the earth (*Meteor.* 2, 8, 368b). This consists of an original reference to the fact that an earthquake occurs following processes taking place in the interior of the earth. Aristotle refutes some older ideas as being false because, according to them, the earth should continuously shake after an earthquake; however, 'η αιτία' (the cause) of earthquakes is 'εκ φύσεως περατή' (bounded by nature).

What causes earthquakes? 'Ουκ αν ουν ύδωρ, ουδέ γη αίτιον είη, αλλά πνεύμα της κινήσεως, όταν έσω τύχη ρύεν το έξω αναθυμιώμενον' ... Neither water nor the earth is the cause of the motion, but the spirit, when it happens to infloat, that which is outwards exhaled *(Meteor.* 2nd, 8: 365 b21–366 a5); ' ... η ορμή του πνεύματος ... ανάλωσε την ύλη ... εξ'ης εποίησε τον ... άνεμον, ον καλούμεν σεισμόν ...' the onrush of spirit ... consumed the matter ... out of which it created the wind which we call (an) earthquake' (*Meteor.* B, 8th: 368 a6–a11).[13] Aristotle considers the kind and magnitude of the earthquake as being related to the state of the causative force and that of the subsurface: 'Αίτιον δε του μεν μεγέθους, το πλήθος του πνεύματος, και των τόπων τα σχήματα δι' ών α ρυή;' ... 'For the cause of the magnitude (is) the magnitude of spirit and the shape of the places through which it is flowing' (a.a., 368 a2–6). He also mentions that the greater the energy accumulated and the looser the structural bounds within an area, the greater will be the magnitude of a forthcoming earthquake (*Meteor.* B, 8th, 365 b2–b15 and 366 a31–b7). He also discriminates between earthquake types (*On the Cosmos*).

For Aristotle, earthquakes do not occur wherever and whenever: 'κατά μέρος δε γίνονται οι σεισμοί της γης ...' the earthquakes occur in certain areas' (*Meteor.* 2, 8, 368b). The seismogenic area is not unlimited and the subsurface is not continuous: 'Ετι δε περί τόπους τοιούτους οι ισχυρότατοι γίνονται των σεισμών, όπου η θάλασσα ρώδης, ή η χώρα σομφή και ύπαντρος' ... 'Now, in those places the severest earthquakes occur, where the sea is 'in motion' or the land is porous and cavernous' (a.a. 366 a24–26). Consequently, certain regions are quoted throughout Aristotles' work as being 'seismogenic'. As for the time of occurrence of earthquakes, he states that the seasons showing higher seismicity are spring and autumn while, within a day, such a seismicity should be observed during the first morning hours and noon, when the 'πνεύμα' relaxes, being accumulated in the subsurface: 'και έαρος δε και μετοπώρου μάλιστα ...; αι γαρ ώραι αύται πνευματωδέσταται; ... ' and in spring and autumn the most ... for these seasons are the most spirited' (a.a. 366 a31–b7).[14]

Thus, it is the Aristotelic view that gives us for the first time a discrimination of meanings (causes and effects). In stressing the terrestrial nature of the earthquake, he appears to have a better understanding than

---

[13] The common view is that Aristotle considers the 'άνεμος' (wind) as entering subterranean cavities and in its effort to exhale involving an intake of energy, it causes earthquakes. See also the english translation in the familiar text (Loeb Classical Library, 365 b28–366 a2) where the 'πνεύμα' is translated as wind. Being aware of the difficulties in the translation of the terms, Aristotle also makes use of his probable experience of conditions associated with earthquakes; I would therefore cautiously suggest that 'πνεύμα' expresses accumulating potential energy in a geologically and structurally inhomogeneous area where geological formations are likely to break, causing an earthquake to occur.

[14] This statement together with the belief that great quakes are more likely to occur during dry and warm times, as in the summer, still survive in parts of rural Greece.

any of his predecessors of how earthquakes occur. On the other hand, unlike his predecessors and successors, his position is privileged because a large part of his works survives.

Unlike Aristotle, Pythagoras envisaged earthquakes as part of unified natural process. Mythological facts are associated with his own numerical consideration of the universe. He therefore associates the property of Poseidon as a seismogenic force with the numeral eight which in Pythagorean notation represents stability, small sensibility to changes, the power of Poseidon, and the basis of universal harmony (see Timaeus Lokris, Moderatus Pythagorius in: Mullachius, *Fragmenta Philosophorum Graecorum*, v.11). Another mention probably locates the earthquake as a result of internal terrestrial processes: 'και τον σεισμόν εγενεαλογεί ούδεν άλλον είναι η συνοδόν των τεθνεώτων' ... 'and the earthquake he categorized as being nothing else but an escort of the dead' (Pythagoras, in H. Diels, *op. cit.*). This incorporation of the entity of Poseidon in the Pythagorean perception of the universal making, its advancement and integration into an unified framework is very important: it seems that Pythagorean thought attempts to re-establish a disturbed continuation between mythology and natural thinking of historical times.

The ultimate reference to a person related to the study of earthquakes in Greek antiquity comes from Strabo. He refers to Poseidonios from Apameia, Syria, who he holds in particular esteem. To Poseidonios is attributed the most systematic study and interpretation of earthquakes among other natural phenomena, based on the work of Aristotle, whose concepts he is thought of as expanding and integrating: he attributes significant changes in the ground's state to earthquakes and attempts an evaluation of the earthquake generation depth; he takes account of the mythological aspects — worship of Poseidon even in remote inland areas — in the study of seismicity for each area. Above all he observes that the cause of earthquakes lies not in the faults but in the exhaled 'πνεύμα' through the faults (see **RE**: *Erdbebenforschung* (*Poseidonios*) and Strabo, *The Geography of Greece*, v. 1,3,5,6, Loeb Classical Library).

Epilogue

In Greek antiquity, the earthquake was perceived as a terrestrial phenomenon. Irrespective of the source of the seimogenic cause, whether intra — or extra — terrestrial, it occurs following internal earth processes. It depends on the quality as well as the quantity of the generating cause and the internal structure of the earth which explains why earthquakes occur in certain areas and at certain times.

A unified and integrated perception of natural processes (and earthquakes, as part of it) appears to have existed at the time of the events quoted in Homer's works. These processes echo the activity of a unique generating cause, which is expressed in the entity of Poseidon as 'master of natural processes'. The extent of the worship of Poseidon should be related to the relatively intense geophysical processes within the greater helladic area; this activity seems to decrease at the time of the establishment of the olympian religion system and is expressed in the demise of his worship.

In the philosophical investigations during post-Homeric times, a basic natural element (αήρ, γη, ύδωρ, πυρ), as perceived by certain philosophers, is attributable in each case to earth (the ground), motion and earthquakes. There is a tendency towards establishing the 'πνεύμα' as the main cause of earthquakes, although it is not possible to push this hypothesis too far. Finally, it is most important when studying ancient references to earthquakes to be cautious of the possible perception of ancient people regarding geophysical processes, such as volcanism and seismicity as well as seismic sea waves, especially in an area like Greece and its neighbouring regions. Terms such as υγρόν, υδατώδες, ον, πνεύμα, αναθυμιάσις etc. should be considered in close comparison to what they intended to describe, particularly since invaluable accompanying or interpretative information is most likely lost for ever. One also has to bear in mind that natural phenomena were perceived in antiquity as expressions of a unique generating process.

INDEXES

Earthquake Catalogue

Main earthquakes (certain and possible) reported or discussed in this book

dating	site/area affected	reference
c. 3200BC (EH II) ??	Messenia, Peloponnese	Zachos
c. 2500BC (EH II)	Thebes, central Greece	Sampson
c. 2000BC	Sodom and Gomorrah, Israel	Nur & Ron
c. 1650BC	Knossos·	Sampson, Stiros & Jones
c. 1450BC (LM IB)	Crete	Vallianou
c. 1300BC (LM IIIB)	Crete	Vallianou
c. 1300BC	Troy	Stiros
c. 1250BC (LH IIIB1)	Tiryns	Kilian
c. 1250BC (LH IIIB1)	Thebes, cental Greece	Sampson
c. 1250BC (LH IIIB)	Mycenae	French, Maroukian *et al.*
c. 1200BC (LH IIIB2)	Tiryns	Kilian
c. 1200BC (LH IIIB2)	Midea, Peloponnese	Åström & Demakopoulou
c. 1150BC (LH IIIC)	Kynos, central Greece	Dakoronia
c. 1100BC (LH IIIC late)	Kynos, central Greece	Dakoronia
c. 1000BC	Jericho, Israel	Nur & Ron
c. 1000BC	Euboea	Pirazzoli
c. 500BC	Seleucia Pieria, S. Turkey	Pirazzoli
464BC	Sparta, Greece	Stiros
c. 450BC	Atalandi, central Greece	Stiros
426BC	Locris, central Greece	Ambraseys, Korres
c. 400BC	Euboea	Pirazzoli
before 100BC	Messenia, Peloponnese	Spondylis
c. 90BC	Pella, Macedonia	Stiros
31BC	Qumran, Israel	Nur & Ron
31–30BC	Gortyn, Crete	Di Vita
c. AD 20	Dioscuria, Sukhumi, Black Sea	Nikonov
AD66	Crete	Pirazzoli
AD100	Gortyn, Crete	Di Vita
c. AD175	Olympia, Peloponnese	Zachos
c. AD260	Achinos, central Greece	Papaconstantinou
c. AD300	Stobi, Skopje	Gebhard
c. AD330	Sebastoupolis, Sukhumi, Black Sea	Nikonov
AD363	Scitopolis/Bet Shean/Masada (?), Israel	Nur & Ron
AD365	Crete	Pirazzoli
c. AD365	Kourion, Cyprus	Stiros, Stiros & Jones
c. AD365	Corinth, Peloponnese	Rothaus
c. AD375 (false entry)	Corinth, Peloponnese,	Rothaus
c. AD400	Kenchreai, Corinth, Peloponnese	Rothaus

c. AD500	Olympia, Peloponnese	Stiros, Zachos
AD526	Seleucia Pieria, SW Turkey	Pirazzoli
c. AD560	Gortyn, Crete	Di Vita
c. AD620	Gortyn, Crete	Di Vita
c. AD670	Gortyn, Crete	Di Vita
AD749	Scitopolis/ Bet Shean/ Masada, Israel	Nur & Ron
c. AD1000	Aigeira, Peloponnese, Greece	Papageorgiou & Stiros
before the 13th *c.* AD	Athens	Korres
??	Athens	Stiros
??	Rome	Stiros
AD1296	Pergamon, Turkey	Rheidt
1688	Smyrna, Asia Minor	Stiros
1705	Athens	Ambraseys, Korres
1739	Fuyun, China	Stiros
1785	Chalkis	Ambraseys
1889	Athens	Ambraseys
1894	Athens	Ambraseys, Dakoronia
1930	Salmas, Iran	Papastamatiou & Psycharis
1965/66	Megalopolis, Peloponnese	Papanastasiou *et al.*
1970	Gediz, Turkey	Rheidt
1981	Athens	Ambraseys, Korres
1986	Kalamata, Peloponnese	Maroukian *et al.*, Stiros

Subject Index